CHINA'S AMERIC

China's American Daughter:
Ida Pruitt (1888–1985)

Marjorie King

The Chinese University Press

China's American Daughter: Ida Pruitt (1888–1985)
   By Marjorie King

© **The Chinese University of Hong Kong**, 2006

ISBN 962–996–221–7

THE CHINESE UNIVERSITY PRESS
The Chinese University of Hong Kong
SHA TIN, N.T., HONG KONG
Fax: +852 2603 6692
      +852 2603 7355
E-mail: cup@cuhk.edu.hk
Web-site: www.chineseupress.com

Printed in Hong Kong

Dedicated to my family

Contents

Photographs follow page xxiv

Preface

B rown bag lunch in one hand, cane in the other, Ida Pruitt tottered into the seminar room where other students and I were practicing our conversational Mandarin. A thick, "earthy" Shandong accent remained in her speech, although she had left the small village of her birth at age twelve, more than seventy-five years before. I was in awe of this frail little lady whose books on Chinese women I so admired and whose work with the Chinese Industrial Cooperatives I had researched for my master's thesis.[1]

During the course of several years, I joined the coterie of students around the small table in her apartment's breakfast nook, framed by bay windows full of potted African violets. Over home-cooked Chinese dinners and Sunday morning waffles, I learned that many a China watcher had interviewed her here and not a few Chinese dignitaries had sat around the same table, on pilgrimage to one of America's earliest and most steadfast "old friends of the Chinese people." The trite phrase took on a new note of sincerity when applied to a woman who remembered the Boxer Rebellion of 1900 and whose professional reputation had suffered during America's decade of Communist witch-hunting because she had extended her friendship beyond the Nationalist Chinese to their enemies, the Communists.

Although most of us were sixty years younger, none of us thought of calling her by the respectful term "Madame Pruitt" used by the Chinese visitors, or "Teacher Pruitt" used by the staff and patients at the Peking Union Medical College (PUMC) hospital, where she headed the Social Service Department for eighteen years. To us, she was always "Ida," said with as much respect and affection as students in the late 1960s and early 1970s could bestow on anyone over thirty! We were all captivated by her stories of China—the traditional village of her childhood, Beijing before modern city planners got to it, and revolutionaries whom she hid in her Beijing home. But I was most drawn to the spark of curiosity in Ida's eye and her genuine concern for us all—the students, the community of Powelton Village in West Philadelphia, and the little girl from neighboring Mantua whom she tutored.

As an aspiring historian, I yearned to know more about this

independent American woman writer and activist, who, many people remarked, looked and acted remarkably Chinese. Living in China between 1888 and 1938, she had observed and sometimes participated in the Chinese people's struggle to create a modern society, against which the forces of colonialism and domestic reaction raged. What kind of life did she live as an American and as a woman during the tumultuous decades before the Communists came to power? How did she feel about the revolution? What might Americans learn about China from her first-hand experience? Living at the turn of the twentieth century, did Ida experience anything like the internal struggles my friends and I, as women of intellect, passions, and political commitments, were confronting at century's end?

Other historians of modern China dissuaded me from making Ida the subject of my doctoral dissertation, explaining: "Ida was a friend of famous people, not famous herself." Although I remained in contact with Ida, I gave up the idea of writing about her for four years—precious years in the life of an elderly woman, years I might have spent interviewing Ida before her memory faded. Only after studying women's history was I able to challenge the conventional paradigm of "important" historical figures. Gradually, I began to rethink the advice given me by senior historians.

One day, while visiting Ida, I asked what was in the stacks of boxes in her bedroom. "Oh, those are family papers. Would you like to see them?" Over forty-five boxes of genealogical charts, personal and professional letters, drafts of unpublished manuscripts, diaries, photographs, records of dreams and psychoanalysis, and travelogues lay before me, a veritable treasure trove of documents detailing the lives of Ida, her parents, her ancestors, and many players in modern Chinese history.[2]

After finally regaining my composure, I asked if I might use these materials to write her story. "Well, certainly dear, if you think it might hold any interest or value," she replied in a self-deprecating tone. By age ninety, she may have forgotten just why she, and her foremothers before her, had chronicled their lives and saved all of their published documents and personal papers. Clearly, the women of Ida's family had carefully preserved the records of their lives, aware at some level of consciousness of their place in history. This biography relies to an extent on their personal papers. Ida's story is told from her point of view against the backdrop of her maternal ancestors. The accounts were often written many years after the fact. Wherever possible, additional perspectives are also included to support or challenge the record as she and her family members recollected it.

And so Ida Pruitt, the "friend of famous people," became the subject of my dissertation and this book. The intervening years between my discovery of Ida's boxes and writing this preface have been filled with sorting, identifying, and organizing the documents before beginning to read them and reconstructing her life. Like other biographers, I have struggled with the inevitable tendency to overidentify with my subject's issues and project mine onto her.

But a judicious amount of imaginative empathy with both the subject and audience is required of any writer attempting to bring life to her characters in a comprehensible way to readers of a new generation.[3] Although I have adhered strictly to the record of Ida Pruitt's life and the history of China and the United States, as documented by the sources, my selection and presentation of the material reflect the issues of my generation of American women and my personal interviews and informal conversations with Ida from 1978 until 1985. I will forever remain in Ida's debt for the privilege of reading her personal and professional papers and for granting me permission to write her story.

A great many people saw the importance of a biography of Ida's life and lent their full support in essential ways, for which I am deeply grateful. Foremost among them are Ida Pruitt's family, especially her nephews John, Dean and Jack Pruitt, who entrusted me with the papers of their aunt and grandparents. I greatly appreciate the interest and help of adopted daughters Tania Manooiloff Cosman Wahl and Guijing Ho and Tania's husband Theodore Wahl.

The Committee on Scholarly Communications with China, the National Endowment for the Humanities, and a St. John's University faculty development grant provided indispensable aid for travel as well as for my wonderful research assistants Todd Pavel, Brett Haberstick, Michelle Maack Friedricks, Stuart Shulte, and Mark Schlough.

I sincerely appreciate the assistance of Thomas Rosenbaum of the Rockefeller Archive Center and Laura O'Keefe of the Manuscript and Archives Division of the Research Libraries at the New York Public Library. Laura's help went far beyond that of an archivist. I also value the aid of the staff of the Rare Book and Manuscript Library of Columbia University and the Seeley G. Mudd Manuscript Library at Princeton University.

The administration and medical records department of the Peking

Union Medical College deserve special thanks for allowing a scholar to use their patient files and for accommodating my needs during a year's research. This unprecedented intrusion into the life of a busy hospital was facilitated by Dr. Li Weiye and Dr. Liu Xinru. Former PUMC social caseworkers, Yu Xiji and Zhu Xuance, former student Lin Qiwu, and former PUMC nurse, Liu Jinghe graciously discussed the PUMC with me for many hours.

Likewise, the staff and executive members of the International Committee for the Promotion of the Chinese Industrial Cooperatives offered invaluable assistance over many years' time. Vice-president Lu Wanru, Executive Secretary Guo Lina, Isabel Crook, Michael Crook and Pat Adler must be singled out for their steadfast support. Original Chinese Industrial Cooperatives leader Peter Townsend provided very valuable information. Israel Epstein, who was one of the original cooperative movement's activists, offered a careful reading and political insights.

Scholars who lent crucial support include my dissertation advisers Allen F. Davis, S.M. Chiu, Robert Schwoebel, and Waldo H. Heinrichs. John King Fairbank's enthusiastic encouragement and his critical reading of my dissertation were indispensable. The New York Humanities Council sponsored seminar on the Theory and Practice of Biography at New York University, led by Dr. Kenneth Silvermann, provided me with crucial insights. Mary Ellen Zuckerman, Allyn Rickett, Adele Rickett, Leslie A. Flemming, Glenn Shive, Stephen R. Mackinnon, Steven I. Levine, Constance J. Post, Richard Shaull, Yamaguchi Mamoru, Daniel W. Crofts, William W. Moss, Charles W. Hayford, A. Tom Grunfeld, Eric Hyer, Christina Gilmartin, Maxine Miska, Cherie Barkey, Nancy Johns, Margaret Randall, Ruth Gillman and Jane Madsen McCabe also read and offered thoughtful comments of the work in progress.

Many friends gave concrete help toward this project's completion. Among them are Katya Peterson, Pierre Landau, Matt and Mary Beth Tucker, Linda Haynes, Kari An Salyer, Shoshona Shea, Brenda Baker, Margaret Kearns, and Katie Reece. They and other dear friends lent their spiritual and emotional support, without which the project would surely have failed.

The love and faith of my husband, Jay Shumway, my sisters, Patty Leiendecker and Betsy Robb, brother-in-law Jeff Robb and niece Mackenzie, my son, Alex Berger, my "almost daughter" Nora Berger-Green, and my former husband/ongoing friend, Jeffrey Berger was more important than they will ever know. Words can never adequately express my gratitude toward my father and mother, George W. King and Rosemary Y. King, for their unflagging support. And finally, I am in the debt of my editors, Wendy Yau and Esther Tsang at the Chinese University Press, for their care, patience, and enthusiasm during many months of painstaking effort to bring this project to completion.

Introduction

*C*hina's American Daughter is the story of Ida Pruitt, an American woman who was born and lived in China from 1888 until 1938, then lived in the United States from 1939 until her death in 1985. She has been called "half Chinese" and "truly bicultural." She was "heart and soul with the Chinese common people," one of few Western residents of Beijing who even talked with the ordinary citizens.[1] Throughout her life, Ida struggled to define herself within both the American culture and the Chinese environment in which she was born and raised.

To be bicultural or multicultural in an era of global telecommunications and massive migrations is almost commonplace, yet among today's "global nomads" or "third-culture kids" the feeling of not fully belonging to any country remains.[2] In contrast, to be an American expatriate in the late nineteenth century, as the United States began to spread its young wings abroad, was an unusual phenomenon.[3] Ida felt that Americans saw her as a "freak." The children of missionaries ("mishkids") were the largest group of Americans living outside the United States. Most of these expatriate children returned to the United States for school or attended boarding school with other children of foreign nationals.[4]

Ida Pruitt and her brother, John, were among a very few children who were home-schooled and remained at their parents' mission post in a small village for most of their childhood. As she reached adolescence, both Chinese and American cultures' gender restrictions prevented her from playing outside so she was even more isolated from society than was her brother. As an American girl raised in rural China, her struggle to develop an identity was infinitely more challenging than for most young women.[5] The nature of her childhood relationships with her parents and her Chinese caregiver (or amah) sowed the seeds of her unusually strong identification with Chinese culture and with the growing nationalist movement.

From the time she first began to write about her life, Ida expressed vehement feelings about the attitudes of Westerners in China. Her reaction echoed that of the Chinese people, who resented the foreigners' attitude of moral superiority as much as their economic and military intrusion. Since the seventeenth century, when Jesuit missionaries first

served at the Ming dynasty court, Europeans and then Americans have
tried bringing spiritual salvation and material betterment to the Chinese
people. When the Chinese declined to convert to Christianity, democracy,
humanism, or the other imported ideologies, the well-intentioned but
arrogant Westerners responded with bewilderment, anger, and a sense of
betrayal.[6] Ida witnessed these reactions in her own parents and in the
Western missionary, business, and diplomatic communities. She
understood the Chinese reasons for rejecting the foreign belief systems
and resolved never to be personally offended by Chinese nationalistic
actions.

Ida's critique of foreign colonialists in China, including the American
reformers among whom she worked, and the alternative model for Sino-
American relations that she helped to shape are the two sub-texts of her
professional and political work, as well as her writing. Self-identified
with the Chinese culture, Ida held fast to her belief in the capacity of
Chinese women and men to transform their traditional civilization into a
modern nation independent of outside colonial powers. Her books and
stories were objectively anti-imperialist, although she never directly
addressed China's semi-colonial status in her writings. Instead, in her
writings and translations, she consciously attempted to preserve the best
of Chinese culture in some of its rich variety without resorting to
orientalist stereotypes and caricatures. As Ida recorded the stories of
individual Chinese women and men, she found her own voice and gave
expression to newly discovered aspects of herself.

Today, Ida Pruitt is known only for her two accounts of traditional
Chinese women, *A Daughter of Han: The Autobiography of a Chinese
Working Woman, Ning Lao T'ai-t'ai* (1946; reissued 1967) and *Old
Madam Yin: A Memoir of Peking, 1926–1938* (1979). Both received
critical acclaim at the time of their publication. Excerpts from the
former have been included in a number of anthologies. The book
continues to be used by both women's studies and Chinese studies
classes throughout the United States.[7] Few people, even among scholars
in Chinese and women's studies, are aware of Ida's other publications—
an autobiography of her childhood, short stories, professional social work
articles, and translations—or her considerable accomplishments as the
founder of medical social work in China and as an active leader of a
grassroots cooperative movement in China.

Ida's identification with the Chinese culture affected her personal life
as well as her work. The balance between public and private spheres,

never easy for modern women, was even more difficult for a woman negotiating two cultures' roles and expectations. Quite consciously, Ida established a home that straddled both cultures and created a supportive structure in which her adopted daughters grew up. Her closest friends— Chinese and Western—challenged social norms and accepted individual differences. However, she was unable to find a male companion who could fully understand and support her.

During her early adulthood, like many young women, Ida defined a primary part of her identity in terms of a personal relationship with a man. Despite her accomplishments and talents, she felt incomplete without a husband or close companion. Lois Rudnick has coined the phrase "male-identified women," to describe this sense of self that handicapped Mabel Dodge Luhan. Luhan devoted her life to preserving the spirit of the Pueblo Indian culture, much as Ida devoted hers to preserving the best of Chinese tradition. Luhan's belief that women's destinies depended on men for their realization kept her from developing "a clear and coherent direction for herself." Ida's sense of reality, like that of Mable Dodge Luhan, was vicarious, filtered through the lens of a man's love, unable to see herself independent from the relationship. Both women suffered from debilitating depressions but unlike Luhan, Ida sought psychotherapeutic help.[8] Eventually, Ida was able to establish a clearer sense of herself that enabled her to develop a rewarding personal life as well as accomplish her professional goals.

Over the course of Ida's life, the sheltered "mishkid" from the Chinese countryside became a strong, respected, and beloved woman in both China and America. Although she did not engage in feminism as an ideology or participate in feminist organizations, she came to appreciate the value of feminist ideas.[9] Her life process was a feminist one, "a personal rather than a collective attempt by women to mold their destinies in the world and achieve autonomy." This is to say that she broke away from family obligations and views that limited her early opportunities, created an independent identity and established intimacy within her personal relationships.[10] She encouraged the social workers to be strong women and recorded the lives of strong Chinese women, but did not primarily view life through the lens of gender.

Rather, Ida's perception was that of a woman uncomfortable with her colonial privilege. As a writer, social worker, and political activist who lived for fifty of her ninety-six years in China during a period of rising nationalism and revolution, Ida strongly identified with her Chinese neighbors, friends, patients, and colleagues. She consciously utilized her privileged place in the colonial power structure to benefit and empower the Chinese. Her writing defied orientalist stereotypes of the day.

Unconsciously, however, Ida retained remnants of the imperial worldview she had inherited and observed around her. She identified with Kim O'Hara, the protagonist in Rudyard Kipling's novel, *Kim,* who loved playing the "Great Game" of imperialism. British royalty fascinated her, especially the power held by English queens. Mary, Queen of Scots, particularly appealed to Ida. When Mary was executed for treason, she went "bravely and with honor—a victim perhaps of her own pride and recklessness, but ultimately a pawn in the power vortex of love, religion and politics."[11]

In much the same terms, Ida wrote about Chinese empress Alute, wife of the Tongzhi Emperor. Referring to the Empress Dowager's order for Alute to follow tradition by committing suicide after her husband's death, Ida described the girl's "integrity that had made her brave enough to struggle against the Old Empress," and the courage to die when she had to...."[12] Although Queen Mary and Empress Alute each died a martyr's death, Ida did not comment on that injustice. Bravery, honor, integrity, courage—these were the qualities that attracted Ida to the royal women of two historic empires, even though she believed in the equality of modern nation-states in the modern world.

All the values, experiences, and goals of Ida's life came together in the Chinese Industrial Cooperative movement, nicknamed the "Gung Ho Cooperatives." She played a leadership role in the Gung Ho movement for thirteen years and fervently advocated these grassroots, worker-owned enterprises as the way forward for China's future. "Indusco," the American support group for the cooperatives that she founded, became the precursor for the many international non-governmental organizations now working in China. Indusco's policy of working in an equal, non-partisan fashion with their Chinese colleagues bears Ida's mark.

As Ida engaged in her three careers, she played many roles, among them China hand, administrator, intellectual, teacher, salon hostess, outspoken advocate, and player in the anti-Japanese underground. She was a secular missionary helping save patients' livelihoods and Chinese national integrity, a pilgrim journeying toward her own truth and enlightenment and a catalyst for Chinese-initiated social work programs and cooperative business enterprises. Within and beyond these lay another role—mediator and bridge between Chinese and Western cultures.

As she constructed a mature identity in the margin between her two countries, the mediator role gave Ida a purpose in life, a method of interacting with the world, and a self-definition.[13] In turn, she made a unique contribution to the organizations and causes that she served.

List of Abbreviations

AACIC	Association for the Advancement of the Chinese Industrial Cooperatives
ABMAC	American Board of Medical Aid to China
ANZACs	Australian and New Zealand Army Corps
CAC	China Aid Council
CCP	Chinese Communist Party
CIC	Chinese Industrial Cooperatives
CNRRA	China National Relief and Rehabilitation Administration
CORSO	Council of Organisations for Relief Services Overseas
CWA	China Welfare Appeal
GMD	Guomindang (Nationalist Party)
ICCIC	International Committee of the Chinese Industrial Cooperatives
IMF	International Monetary Fund
Indusco	American Committee in Aid of the CIC
PLA	People's Liberation Army
PUMC	Peking Union Medical College
UCR	United China Relief
UNRRA	United Nations Relief and Rehabilitation Administration
USC	United Service to China

Chronology of Ida Pruitt

December 23, 1888	Born Penglai (called Dengzhou by missionaries), Shandong, China (Childhood home in Huang county or Huangxian)
c. 1891	Family traveled in the United States on furlough; Ashley born in Ohio
c. 1897	Began attending school in Yantai (known as Chefoo among missionaries) until 1906
1900	During the Boxer Rebellion the Pruitts took early furlough in the United States for one year
1901–1902	Attended school at British China Inland Mission School in Yantai but removed from school when John got pneumonia
1902	Missionaries built new training schools in Penglai; the Pruitts moved to Penglai
1906–1909	Traveled to the United States to attend Cox College, Georgia; studied literature
1909–1910	Graduate school at Teachers' College, Columbia University; studied 19th century literature and philanthropy
1910–1911	Taught at St. Christopher's Orphanage in Dobbs Ferry, New York
1912	John died of typhoid; Ida returned to China
1912–1918	Studied Chinese with her father's teacher; began working at Wai Ling School for Girls in Yantai
1918	Returned to the United States, settled in Philadelphia with friend Edna to care for her two brothers who were in school there; began social work
c. 1920	Spent six months at Massachusetts General Hospital studying social work under Ida Cannon
1921–1938	Head of Social Service Department at Peking Union Medical College

1938	While on way back to the United States to visit family, met Rewi Alley and remained in China till 1939 to help set up Chinese Industrial Cooperatives
1939	Returned to the United States; settled in New York to set up Indusco
1939–1951	Held positions as Executive Secretary, International Field Secretary, and China Representative of Indusco, Inc.
1951	Retired from Indusco; moved to Philadelphia to be closer to family
1951–1968	FBI file active; was approached twice by FBI for enlistment (9/2/54, 11/19/57), IP refused both times
1952–1954	Board of directors of China Welfare Appeal
1955	Moved to Powelton Village, Philadelphia, where she lived the remainder of her life
1959–1960	Traveled to China and England
Early 1960s	Chair of Powelton Village branch of the Women's International League for Peace and Freedom
1972	Traveled to China
1985	Died in Philadelphia

1. The Pruitts in Atlanta, Georgia, 1901: (from left) John, Anna, Ida, C.W., and Ashley in his father's arms.

2. Ida and her mother in the seat. C.W. on horse behind the seat. The Western woman wearing a hat standing beside C.W. Pruitt may be Anna Hartwell.

3. Penglai Baptist church

4. The Western-style building behind the wall is part of the Baptist mission.

5. Ida in her father's arms.
Huangxian, circa 1890.

6. Ida as a young woman

7. Ida as a young woman

8. Ida teaching at the Wai Ling Day School for Girls in Yantai, 1912–1918.

9. Ida and her father, C.W. Pruitt, 1917 or 1918.

10. Ida with Guijing (left) and Jing Feng, circa 1918.

11. New Year's Eve party, Ida on left.

12. Ida's home on Xiao Yang Yibin Hutong, Ida in center.

13. Ida and Jack MacIntosh on a hike in the Western Hills, circa 1930.

14. Courtyard of Ida's compound, Beijing, 1936: (left) Tania, Ida, Guijing.

15. Old Madam Yin in her garden, circa 1930.

16. Old Madam Ning enjoying a cigarette in Ida's courtyard, circa 1935.

17. Ida during her "Gung Ho" years. Note her insignia.

18. Hong Kong, 1939: (left) Israel Epstein, Ida, Frank Lew, Rewi's housemate, Edgar Snow.

19. Ida on board ship as she leaves for America, 1939.

20. Ida and Jim Bertram, 1939.

21. Ida and Rewi in 1972 at the Summer Palace.

22. Ida and Talitha Gerlach in Penglai, 1972.

23. Ida at an anti Vietnam War rally.

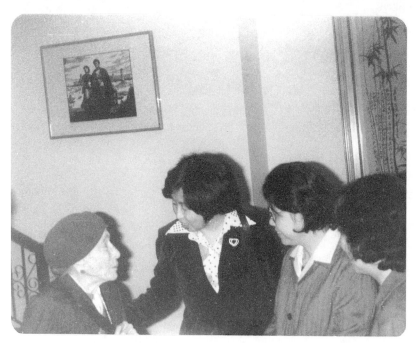

24. After President Carter's decision to normalize diplomatic relations with the People's Republic of China, in the liaison office of PRC, 15 December 1978.

25. In Ida's apartment in Philadelphia with Tania, around 1981–1982.

Prologue

C rowds bearing fruit, flowers, and candy cheered as the *City of Pekin*, the largest American ship afloat, sounded the gong and drew up the gangplank. Someone started to sing "Coronation," then "Blest Be the Tie that Binds," as others on board ship and on shore joined in. Then followed "America" as the ship sailed out of the San Francisco harbor, whereupon at least one of the passengers broke down in tears. Twenty-five-year-old Anna Seward was en route to a new life as a single woman missionary in China.

Long distance travel was not foreign to the young woman from Ohio. Four years earlier, Anna rode third-class across the United States for three weeks on the *Emigrant* train to Los Angeles, then to the town of Ojai, California, where she taught school to repay her father's debts. Indeed, her westward impulse was a trait handed down through the generations of women in Anna's family, who often repeated the story of seventy-three-year-old foremother Sarah Treat Fenn Fellows. In 1818, the family matriarch journeyed with her family from Connecticut to Ohio, seated on her "bobbed rocker" inside a covered wagon.

After the family homestead was build in Tallmadge, Ohio, Sarah parked her rocker in front of a big, bay window overlooking the village green, becoming the first of five generations of women to sit at the "grandmother's window."[1] Family stories boasted that up to four generations of women clustered around that window. Sarah's daughter, Urania Durand, and granddaughter, Miranda Ashley, saw their teaching and medical work in Tallmadge as part of the civilizing impulse of Christian women on the new frontier. Sarah's great-granddaughter, Uda, was inspired by the story of Ann Hasseltine Judson, who traveled to Burma as a missionary shortly before her own great-grandmother started for Ohio. Uda yearned to travel to the Northwest as a missionary to the Native American Indians.[2] Illness in the family kept her tied to the grandmother's window but she instilled her sense of mission and adventure in her daughter, Anna.

The bobbed rocking chair eventually made its way across the ocean to the small Chinese village where Anna made her own home, testament to the pioneering spirit of the women in her family. As a single woman, then as a wife and mother, Anna drew on the physical fortitude, educational and medical skills and religious convictions of her foremothers to bring "Christian civilization" to the Chinese.

Single American women began to travel overseas as missionaries soon after reading Ann Hasseltine Judson's letters in the missionary press in which she described her educational ministry to the women and children of Burma. By 1861, the year before Anna Seward's birth, at least half of all foreign mission board workers were women and the first national, inter-denominational women's missionary organization was formed.[3] The Women's Union Missionary Society of America for Heathen Lands, and the denominational women's mission boards, which soon followed, were financed by "second gifts," the donations of churchwomen above and beyond their family donations to the general mission boards.[4]

On Valentine's Day, 1886, the Women's Foreign Missionary Society of the Presbyterian Church contacted Anna Seward in California, inviting her to be their representative in China. Anna "wrastled" with the decision for several months:

> I have a deep desire to make my life count for more than it can here, where I am surrounded by people as good as I. I crave the chance to "come out strong."... But oh, I don't want to leave America....
>
> Once I turned the matter down with a peremptory "No." Then came the distressing realization that there is something that I am unwilling to do for my Lord, there is one part of my heart that is still supreme. I must be *willing* to go....

By May, Anna had a change of heart. "I now *want* to go to China."[5]

The *City of Pekin* sailed across the Pacific and stopped for several weeks in Yokohama, Japan, before continuing to Shanghai. Stepping off the ship for the first time, Anna experienced the extreme mood swings typical of many travelers: "I am now in picturebook land.... It was quite a wrench to leave ... the pleasant companions whom we shall never see again. The past looks pleasant in contrast with the unknown future."[6]

Anna stopped for a few days in Shanghai, where she was repulsed by deformed beggars and swinging buckets of manure. Soon, she was on the road again. This time, she traveled by steamer several days up the coast of China to Yantai (traditionally known as "Chefoo"), a seaport in the Shandong peninsula, which boasted a population of 29,000. Like other Chinese cities, Yantai was surrounded with a wall, the gates of which were closed nightly. City streets were narrow enough for pedestrians to touch the shops on either side. The American Presbyterian Church and the China Inland Mission had established hospitals and schools as well as churches since the 1860s, resulting in a church membership of about three thousand by the time Anna Seward arrived.[7]

But Yantai was only a rest stop for Anna. From there began the most arduous leg of her journey, a two-day ride by mule-drawn cart (*shenze*) to her final destination, Penglai city, noted in Chinese mythology as the home of the Eight Immortals.

As was customary for single women missionaries, Anna Seward lived with a married missionary couple while beginning the formidable task of Chinese language study. According to a family story, one morning Anna answered the door to find a Chinese scholar. His long, blue gown, short, sleeveless black jacket, even his shaven head, covered with a round, melon-section skullcap from which hung the customary queue were Chinese. "But the eyes were blue, more blue than any eyes she had ever seen." He was Cicero Washington Pruitt, the widower from the Baptist Mission. In three months, despite Anna's hesitation, they were married after C.W. reassured her that she would learn to love him.[8]

C.W. Pruitt had been in China for five years before meeting Anna Seward. His route to China was as direct as hers was twisted; his impulses were as simple as hers were complex. Whereas Anna's life showed no China-direction until she was twenty-four years old, C.W. planned to preach the Gospel in China since a conversion experience at age thirteen.[9]

C.W.'s childhood in the north Georgian mountains centered on a yearly revivalist camp meeting, the "root experience of backwoods southern religionists."[10] His eclectic education at Furham University nine years after his conversion experience was specifically designed for the life of an evangelist in China. In anticipation of learning written Chinese for future biblical translation, he specialized in Greek. Pruitt was following the basic evangelical belief in the transformational power of the written word.[11]

Before C.W. departed for China in 1881, the secretary of the Southern Baptist Mission Board gave him money enough for two, hoping in vain that the lonely young man might "persuade some young woman" to accompany him. Within a year after his arrival in China, C.W. had convinced Ida Tiffany of the Presbyterian Mission to marry him, but she died only a few years later from typhoid.[12] His marriage to Anna Seward in 1887 earned Pruitt the reputation in some quarters of "a praying missionary who preyed chiefly upon the Presbyterian Mission."[13]

1

At Home in China

The spirit niche, where the tablet to Heaven and Earth normally resided, stood empty. Dressed in a Chinese jacket and skullcap in front of the vacant niche, C.W. Pruitt proudly held his chubby-cheeked infant daughter, Ida. The photograph, probably taken by his wife, Anna, captured the missionary's serenity, determination, compassion and sense of humor, qualities developed during a decade of evangelizing the "heathen" in north China.

Something of the little girl's spirit was caught in the photograph, as well. As her father's gaze turned away from the camera and his wife, Ida stared directly at the machine held by her mother, a portent of the many future confrontations between the daughter and mother. Her eyebrows were furrowed, as if she were made uncomfortable by the desecrated spirit niche behind her.[1]

Although less than two years old in 1890, Ida already had experienced a moment of separateness from the world around her. Her first memory was of the rough handle of a mule litter, the "wheelbarrow-like" conveyance in which the women of north China commonly rode. "This is not me," she exclaimed.[2]

As she wrote her childhood autobiography, many decades after first sensing "the other" as distinct from herself, Ida perceived a major theme of her life to be the quest to understand herself and the other "in ever widening circles—of experience, of thought, and of understanding." Eventually, the circle widened to encompass the two major cultural traditions in which she was raised—Chinese and American—from which she selected and combined the habits and thoughts, which defined her.[3]

The Family Home in Song Family Village

In telling her own story, and in keeping with Chinese literary convention, Ida began with the house in which she was raised: "A house is an outermost covering, more permanent than the clothes we wear and more permanent to the Chinese families of that time, who lived for generations in one house, than the flesh and bones of their bodies."[4]

The Pruitt family home and the Southern Baptist Mission station occupied a traditional Chinese family compound in Song Family Village, Huang county (Huangxian, in modern Longkou), near the northern coast of Shandong province. Bought from the principal family of Huangxian, the compound consisted of seven courtyards and eleven one-story houses within those courtyards. Altogether, the site stretched the length of a city block—plenty of room for a church, school, and clinic, as well as the Pruitt family home, garden, and barnyard animals.

Possession of the property was unusually peaceful and happy, compared with the hostility, which greeted most missionary homebuyers. By the late nineteenth century, Protestant missionaries had established about 500 mission stations in 350 different cities and towns. Protestant and Catholic missionaries combined totaled about 2,000. Yet fewer than 60,000 Chinese had converted to Christianity—30 converts per missionary.[5] Like most Chinese, the villagers of Huangxian feared the "foreign-devils" and resisted their encroachment into village neighborhoods. But the aristocratic Ding family was desperate for ready cash to support the patriarch's opium addiction. The Pruitts' representative was well aware of the family's predicament and understood the family's reticence to sell to foreigners. After a spate of visits between both families' representatives, during which the decision was justified by rumors of a ghost on the property, the Ding's settled for the very low price of $1,660.31, less than two years' worth of missionary expenses.[6]

The Ding family ghost never materialized for Ida, but the compound's spirit possessed the little girl for her entire life. Early memories of the compound's geometric layout, paper lattice windows, high outer walls, potted trees and flowers in the courtyards, and sloping tiled roofs conveyed an overall pattern of dignity, formality, and privacy, a pattern which satisfied, comforted, and embodied China to Ida.

Growing up in the halls and courtyards of the haunted house of Song Family Village, Ida felt herself to be a part of Chinese life stretching back thousands of years:

Stepping through the gate, over the threshold, into the Eastern Watchman's Walk, was always an adventure. I would hold my breath as I looked up and down its empty sweep. This was the only part of the compound untouched by our alien life. Men of the past still lived there where they had practiced archery and held meets with their friends.... In that instant of crossing the threshold the walk was mine and theirs....[7]

Turning toward the second gate of the compound, famous among the villagers for its heavy, wide spreading tiled roof and beautifully carved crossbeams, Ida recalled observing the entrance ritual of Chinese scholars as they mounted the steps toward the hall of the ancestors. The hall's open rafters, polished beams, brick floor, and latticed windows and doors became etched in the girl's memory. Although the hall had been transformed into a Baptist church by wooden benches and curtains, in her mind it became an ancestral hall again. The preaching platform turned into the ancestral shrine. The table holding the Bible gave way to the mat where Ding family members kowtowed to their ancestors. Patterns of people standing and kneeling replaced the rows of pews. Try as she might, Ida's imagination failed to turn the shrill sounds of translated Christian hymns into deep chest tones of Buddhist chants. However, the Hall's Chinese spirits lived on in the churchgoers' scents of garlic, chives, and onions and in their indigo blue, cotton clothing.[8]

Ida's autobiographical reflections of her childhood in Song Family Village, written after a long life as mediator between her two cultural traditions, utilize the descriptions of her home in the Chinese compound to convey her sense of identification with the Chinese culture against the onslaught of the Western religion and other forces for change. Her essay reconstructs her childhood to connote a visceral reaction to the architectural modifications of the ancestral hall. In her retelling, Ida experienced the excavation of a deep baptismal pit as a wound to her own flesh that broke the harmony of the court. The traditional Southern Baptist immersion of new church members seemed grotesque and indecent to her. From a word or a glance of the onlookers, she intuited their disapproval, as well.[9]

Villagers' reactions to other Western innovations were more blatant. They stopped and stared at the "fast-moving, glittering, bell-ringing" Crescent brand bicycles. Donkeys balked and deposited their riders in the dust as the mechanical steeds approached. Ida refused to ride her new bicycle out of sympathy with the traditional agrarian way of life where the only sounds were human voices, cloth-soled shoes cart wheels, and horse hooves.[10]

Ida's early, gut-level preference for Chinese culture extended to north China peasant food. Festival treats such as moon cakes and bamboo-wrapped, glutinous rice stuffed with dates, held a much more vivid and affectionate place in her memory than her mother's makeshift American holiday dinners. Her descriptions of meat-filled dumplings—seasoned with anise, black and green pepper, garlic, ginger, and soy sauce—stimulate the reader's appetite. The chopping sounds as housewives prepared the meal's meat and vegetables became symbolic of "all that is most dear in the home" in one of Ida's essays published in the *Atlantic Monthly*.[11]

Anna Pruitt's letters home and interviews by her grandchildren fifty years later both describe her early revulsion against the tastes, smells, and spaces of China, which contrasted sharply with her daughter's sinicized sensibilities. To Anna, the Chinese material culture, far from representing a different but equally beautiful civilization, was concrete evidence of "heathen" China's need of Christianity.[12] Her children's preferences hurt Anna like a betrayal. C.W. merely observed wryly that the Pruitts were "not yet heathen enough" to eat such things.[13]

Anna eagerly took up housekeeping in the renovated Chinese compound as an "object lesson" about Christianity for the village women. From the earliest American missionary society, the American Board of Commissioners of Foreign Missions to the twentieth century inter-denominational literature, women's essential role was defined as transmitter of the "decencies of civilized life" to the pagan by establishing a "home with the open door" in the midst of "heathenism."[14]

American food was central to Anna's image of her home. She bought a cow to provide milk for her children, made jelly from seaweed, and imported dried chipped beef and Libby's corned beef as an alternate to chicken, lamb, and fish. She would not serve pork, the "meat of the people." "It wasn't supposed to be good for us," Ida remarked sardonically.[15]

Holiday meals played an especially important role in Anna's efforts to create an American home. Like other missionary women, Anna went to great lengths and used ingenious substitutes to reproduce traditional American Thanksgiving and Christmas dinners. A typical menu included goose, cranberry sauce made of thorn apples, sweet potatoes, cabbage, bean soup, pickled peaches, Indian pudding, fruit, nuts, and candy.

Pumpkin and mince pie were other favorites. However, nothing tasted as good to Anna as did the American originals.[16]

As a child, Ida could not understand her mother's tastes in food or her insistence on importing American dishes. Her mother's air of superiority over the Chinese sparked in Ida a fierce loyalty to the culture of her playmates and neighbors. The emotional and spiritual significance of Anna's American meals were lost on Ida and her brothers. Reflecting back, she understood that American food and furniture were important to reinforce the missionary women's identities in an alien culture that they considered inferior to their own.[17]

Anna was intent on establishing a "tasteful, civilized, cultivated home" for her children, for fear they would "lose everything by living as they must in the midst of heathenism." But the American supplies failed to console the homesick woman, who prayed for "more grace in our hearts—more love for the dirty, greedy, selfish, prejudiced people for whom we work."[18] She had to force herself to open her home to the "wretched" Chinese people for whom she had relinquished her life in America.[19]

C.W.'s feelings about their Chinese compound-turned-home and mission station were similar to his daughter's. Son of a poor widower from the mountains of north Georgia where houses consisted of one-room log cabins and had neither indoor plumbing nor outhouses, C.W. was not a product of the same industrializing, modernizing America as was his northern wife. Long after the Pruitt family moved to a Western-style house in another mission station, he called the "beautiful Chinese house" in Song Family Village his real home.[20]

The different backgrounds and temperaments of Anna and C.W. created tensions that took a toll on their daughter. Ida remembered her parents' resentments and arguments far more vividly than any of their positive interactions. On one occasion, she was playing in the garden near a rosebush. Her parents failed to notice her as their discussion heated up:

> Of course if you think that is the right way to do it, do so by all means.
> But Anna—I came to consult you. I want your opinion.
> But my opinion is not worth anything. I do not know Chinese as you do.
> I wish you would … listen to me. If I did not value your opinion I would not ask you.
> You value my opinion? I suppose that is why you let …
> Do we have to go all over that again? His voice rose.
> There you are, losing your temper, and you a missionary.

Yes, and who is driving me to it? Who could live with such a woman?
Then why did you marry me? I am sure that I did not ask you.

Ida looked up from her play to see her mother concentrating on her
knitting. Anna's controlled remoteness probably maddened her husband.
He could not let his anger out on her school, which he believed in, or do
her physical harm. But Anna's photographs sunning on their glass plates
were vulnerable.

> He leapt upon them. He crushed them under his feet. He stamped hard for
> his soft-soled Chinese shoes gave him little assistance. Without a word,
> Mother went into the house, got a broom and dustpan, and swept up the
> debris, then went back to the house in the Women's Court ... where she
> usually stayed.
> I was sick under the rosebush.[21]

Reflecting on this argument many years later, Ida understood the
basis of her mother's unhappiness—an unresolved love affair. Anna
showed her daughter a packet of letters tied together with a blue ribbon,
and idealized the man who wrote them, Mr. Combs. They had been
engaged but parted in a quarrel, she for China, and he for Cuba. Just
before the birth of her third child, Anna received a letter from him, asking
for forgiveness and proposing marriage.

To Ida, Mr. Combs came to occupy a shadowy place just lower than
God, Grandma Seward and Queen Victoria.

Ida believed her mother, "living with a man she did not love, in a
country forever alien," was basically an unhappy person, who in turn, was
responsible for her husband and daughter's unhappiness. She absolved
her father of any part in the marital strife.

Ida's account of her parents' marriage and family contrasted
markedly with their own portrayal of life together in China. As young
marrieds, Anna and C.W. wrote weekly letters to Anna's family in Ohio.
Anna described herself as a "poor, lovelorn creature" when her new
husband of three years traveled throughout the province to evangelize the
population. C.W. wrote that he missed the "light of our household" in her
own, infrequent absences. To an extent, these early expressions of
affection can be viewed as standard rhetoric of romance intended to
comfort Anna's distant mother. However, many genuine signs of the
Pruitt's intellectual and emotional companionship shone through the
letters, as well.[22] The contrast between Ida's portrayal of her parents'
marriage and their own representations is stark.

Memories of other family dynamics also differed markedly. Anna reported Ida's birthday celebrations as special family events to which missionary friends were invited or which Chinese schoolgirls made over. On Ida's seventh birthday, she exclaimed, "O mamma, you don't know how happy I am." This was the year she was allowed to have her own room and Big Ida's washbasin. (Big Ida was C.W.'s first wife, Ida Tiffany. Naming a child after a deceased spouse was a Southern tradition. One can only speculate that a second wife from the North, such as Anna, might resent the first wife's namesake.)[23] Yet since her birthday fell just two days before Christmas, Ida always felt her family neglected it.[24]

Even into her own old age, Ida doubted her mother's love, believing that Anna loved her three sons and the Chinese schoolboys more than she loved Ida. She struggled between feelings of hostility and respect toward her mother, certain that Anna agreed with the Chinese and American societal preference for sons.[25]

Ida's resentment is ironic because the missionaries crusaded against the traditional Chinese preference toward sons, and Anna dearly wanted another daughter. Writing to her closest American friend who had just given birth to a girl, Anna exclaimed there is "nothing in the world as sweet as a girl baby." When Robert, their third son, was born, Anna wrote, "We didn't get our first choice in the matter of sex, but we did get our second."[26]

Obviously, Ida's sense of being slighted did not always reflect the literal truth of her family experiences. Rather, her feelings were rooted in some subtler family dynamic than an uncelebrated birthday or her mother's alleged male preference. She explored these selective memories in diaries written during psychoanalysis many years later and in published and private essays. Family letters also describe the interactions of the Pruitt family and shed light on Ida's deep resentments.

Anna and C.W. always numbered their children six: Ida (b. 1888), John (b. 1890), Ashley (b. 1892), Virginia (b. 1896), Robert (b. 1897), and Dudley "Mac" (b. circa 1902). Virginia lived for less than two months after her birth. Ashley died before his sixth birthday.

Three-year-old Ida was called "Papa's girl." According to Anna, Ida still held a special place in his heart when she went off to boarding school at age nine. C.W. traveled a day's journey by bicycle to meet Ida at the inn halfway between Song Family Village and the China Inland Mission School in the coastal city of Yantai. In his memoirs, C.W. recalled Ida's happy, appreciative smile.[27]

John was "Mama's boy." Ida tried but couldn't cry when her mother left for a few days, but John, at age six, cried over a story and climbed into his mother's lap.[28]

Ida remembered that her father wound the clock and preached on Sundays, read his English and Chinese books, and talked graciously to all callers. "He comforted a little girl when he happened to see that she was unhappy, and sometimes took her for a walk in the fields." "Mother ... was the one who told us what we wanted to know and what to do. It was Mother to whom we went for what we wanted even though now I know we would more likely have got it from Father."[29]

Anna struggled to "share her best with the Chinese" in compliance with missionary ideals of Christian motherhood.[30] Three-year-old John and five-year-old Ida played daily with the neighbor boy, although the boy's family publicly opposed the foreigners. When somewhat older, the children played with Chinese Christian children. Anna and C.W. prayed for the Chinese playmates that their children "might be kept from evil in China." When Ida and John played with each other, they often lapsed into Chinese, although their mother encouraged English-speaking.[31]

Anna disagreed with local childrearing customs. The Chinese had a different sense of playthings and appropriate conversation around children. Anna's strongest complaint was that the Chinese spoiled their children, referring to one trouble-making student as a "pampered, mother-spoiled wine bibber." She was also uncomfortable with the custom of breast-feeding on demand. Anna believed that Chinese parents' failure to discipline their children led to neglect and even death. Chinese Christians' childcare customs were no different than their heathen neighbors'. Anna was especially disheartened that one of the leading church members, Mr. Fan, neglected his diseased and disfigured five-year-old boy.

Ida was raised by her Chinese amah as much as by her American mother. Jiang Dasao or "Dada," as her young American charges pronounced her name, was nurse (amah) to Ida, John, and Ashley. Dada's entire family worked for the Pruitts. Her husband was the cook, her son the "boy," and her married daughter the substitute baby-sitter. For years, the Jiang family lived in rooms off the farm courtyard of the Pruitt compound before renting a house in the nearby village.[32]

Ida considered Dada's influence more significant in her life than her parents' in some ways, and recognized many of her own thoughts and attitudes as Dada's. Dada stayed with the children all day in all parts of the compound. She awakened them in the morning and saw that their faces were washed. She played games with them and took them on daily walks. The children knew Dada was on their side, such as the time she secretly gave each child a forbidden peach during diarrhea season. "We loved Dada" was Ida's simple evaluation of their amah; she never said the same of her own mother.

Outside her home, she was exposed exclusively to the Chinese ways of child rearing for five years until another missionary family moved to the district. Ida viewed Chinese attitudes toward sexuality, childbirth, and childrearing more favorably than did her mother. Chinese children, hearing the common term for childbirth, "to pick up" a baby, pictured "their mothers picking up babies by the side of the road as they picked up dried grass, twigs, and leaves for burning in their cook stoves." Chinese Christian women wondered how missionary women could "pick up" white babies in Huangxian. A white baby did not look quite right. "Well, anyway, he is reincarnated from a Chinese," Ida imagined them saying. With all the teeming Chinese souls waiting for rebirth, how could the little white baby have any other kind of previous life?[33]

The birth of Robert illuminated contrasts between American and Chinese customs of sexuality, childbirth, and child rearing, and underscored the tension between mother and daughter. Anna mentioned none of her pregnancies in letters home until after the successful births. Seven-year-old Ida was sent away for three weeks before Virginia's birth but two years later remained at home for Robert's birth. Anna thought it strange that the nine-year-old girl was not surprised by the appearance of a new baby, underestimating her daughter's powers of observation: "No one tried to keep any pregnancy secret and mother, like the Chinese women, went on with her usual occupations.... I had seen her body grow larger and heavier day by day."[34]

As a child, Ida sat with Chinese women as they talked about boy babies' "birdies." "All the little boys had them. I saw the little boys all summer running around in their little red aprons or with nothing on at all.... A little boy wearing the split trousers of childhood might squat and show that he was a boy."[35]

In contrast, Anna was embarrassed by "these unpleasant objects" when she saw a naked boatman. When churchwomen made Ida a traditional boy doll complete with a beautifully stitched and shaped "birdie," Anna made them rip out the genitals. The Chinese women failed to understand why Americans insisted on neutered dolls. Ida wondered why a doll should not have what all boys had, and never warmed to the castrated doll.[36]

C.W. viewed sexuality, pregnancy, and childbirth no more openly than did his wife. His Georgian tradition allowed pregnant women outdoors only after dark. The Pruitts' sexual reticence carried over to daily interactions with their children. C.W. romped on the floor with his small children and shared his bed with Ashley, but Ida best remembered him withdrawing into his study or into his own mind. Cool and intellectual, Anna never cuddled or kissed the children, expressing her affection instead through reading aloud, cooking, and sewing. Anna tired of breast-feeding, blaming it and possibly the nursing first baby for her ills. She substituted Millins food and condensed milk for John and Ashley with "splendid" results. Ida noted Chinese mothers' custom of wrapping their babies in a "second womb," their overlapping coats, until the babies were old enough to push themselves out.[37] The contrast between her own aloof mother and the physical nurturance of Chinese mothers was not lost on the sensitive little girl.

Three months after Robert's birth, the tragedy of losing a child struck the Pruitts for the second time. They had accepted two-month-old Virginia's death as God's will and an opportunity to share the Christian message with Chinese families grieving their own children's deaths. Five-year-old Ashley, the family favorite, died quite unexpectedly of typhoid. C.W. sobbed with grief for the little boy whom he had dressed in the morning and put to bed with him at night. Anna suffered a lengthy psychological depression and religious crisis. Both seemed to treasure baby Robert all the more after Ashley's death. "We all give ourselves to enjoying and loving him more than we ever felt that we had time for before with the others," reflected Anna. Baby received whiskery kisses from his father and slept with him after weaning. "Sometimes we can hardly do our work for playing with ... the precious little fellow."[38]

Anna's Victorian views toward sexuality, her non-demonstrative manner toward her first three babies, and her serious depression after Ashley's death left their mark on her daughter. Ida felt her mother did not love her. In need of more nurturing than her parents were able to give, she soaked up the Chinese openness, warmth, and affection toward small children, and directed her own love toward the Chinese people and culture.

Christian Motherhood

If Anna Pruitt noticed her daughter's feelings of estrangement from her, she did not mention her concerns in letters to family and friends in America. Instead, she described her daily life, the family's health, and her evangelizing efforts, seemingly unaware that even her religious devotion drove her daughter toward the eclectic Chinese way.

Teaching the next generation about the love of God was the sum and substance of missionary women's work and the ultimate hope of missions. Whether through schools and work among "heathen" women, or through their own home life, missionary women were seen to have a special ability and responsibility to teach Christianity to the children. Conversely, when the children of missionaries rejected their parents' religious vocation and experienced any problems, missionary women received much of the blame. Missionary women's reputation depended to a great extent on their children's religious convictions and behavior.[39]

Anna knew that her long, weekly letters to her parents in Ohio were shared among family friends and relatives, as well as the members of the Congregational Church facing her family's homestead across the Tallmadge village green. The proud mother's reports of her daughter's religious devotion reflected well on her missionary work as well as motherhood. Anna gladly described for her American audience Ida's request for her own Bible and her desire to read the testament at prayer time. Ida also organized a pretend church service and delivered the sermon to her attentive parishioner, John.[40]

When Ida was eight, she gave her parents reason to believe she had "experienced a work of grace in her heart and been born again," in her mother's words. For months, Anna realized Ida was not really happy. One evening she burst into tears, saying, "I can't be *an-wen* (at peace)." She cried for a long time in her father's arms, and confided, "I feel as though I would die tonight and go to hell." Anna interpreted Ida's outburst as the child's awareness of her own sinful nature. Two weeks later, Anna wrote,

> After her father had talked with her very tenderly of the Savior, she became suddenly light-hearted and has been so ever since. [written two weeks later] ... When I can have the assurance that each of my children is a child of God there will be nothing left for me to fear. Even sickness and death have lost their terror.[41]

No doubt, Anna's religious aspirations for her children were genuine at a certain level. Her American Midwestern Protestant community, particularly her own parents' lives, revolved around their church and a system of beliefs that she never questioned. Yet Ida judged her mother's religion as more social than deeply personal. Anna saw the world in practical terms and was well aware of American public opinion. Her children's spirituality reflected on her as much as on themselves. Thus, Ida's religious bent was to a certain extent a product of her mother's wishful thinking. After Ida had begun boarding school and was developing, in her words, a "high immunity to anything said in any pulpit," Anna still believed "Ida has a much more religious turn of mind than I had at her age."[42]

Ironically, C.W., the Southern Baptist who experienced a conversion at age twelve, expressed a less fundamentalist religious desire for his children than did his Congregationalist wife. Much later in life, he explained his evolving theology:

> The idea of the deity has grown in my mind until now…. I realize that he fills all space and maintains relations with all creatures and loves all intelligent beings as children with capacity for unlimited development. This is the idea of God I should love dearly to pass on to all my children.[43] [underlining his]

As a child, Ida's religious feelings involved not so much beliefs as questions about life and death, heaven and hell, as well as reactions against the Christian intrusion in the Chinese culture she loved. When Virginia died, Ida was sad because her little sister made her feel less lonely. The death of brother Ashley, Ida's playmate for six years, took a much larger toll on her.[44]

Ida used the mixed imagery of the Baptist Heaven and her Chinese environment to understand her siblings' deaths:

> … the thunder was the sound of the carts in Heaven rumbling along the streets paved with gold, the way our carts rumbled on the mill stones on the street outside our Great Front Gate; … the lightening was when the doors of Heaven opened a bit and let the light through.
> That was where Ashley and Virginia were now.[45]

The images of heaven came from the illustrated hymnals and Sunday School literature, not from her parents, who taught goodness on earth and a very indefinite Heaven. In fact, Reverend Pruitt's sermons never spoke of hell-fire and brimstone for the damned or pearly gates for the saved, like those of many other missionaries. He always spoke of the love of God and Jesus and the brotherhood of all mankind. This bored the little girl, but she grew to respect him for it. C.W.'s position was a Southern Baptist Armenian theology, which "avoided extreme positions, focusing on the proclamation of the gospel to all men and the obligation of men everywhere to believe."[46]

As Ida became aware of the differences between the Chinese and the Christian missionary cultures, she resented Christianity's intrusion in the Chinese culture.

Experiences among the villagers led Ida to challenge Christianity. One day when walking with her mother, Ida, using her mother's best manner, said to an unhappy-looking woman, "You must not be unhappy, there's a Heaven to go to and God is ..." The woman interrupted, "Why have another world? There's enough trouble in this one. When I reincarnate I want to come back as a ... donkey or pig. It is too difficult to be a human being."[47]

On another occasion, Ida was surprised to see the handsome new Chinese schoolteacher, a Presbyterian, walk out of communion. Ida researched the Baptist position on baptism by immersion, the criterion for receiving communion in the Southern Baptist Church. Using the concordance, nowhere in the Bible did she find a command to dip people under water. This was Ida's first exposure to the exclusivity of Christian sects and it shocked her inclusive Chinese mind.[48]

So began the questioning process whereby Ida ultimately rejected all organized religion. More than a rebellion against her parents was involved. The brunt of her anger targeted Christianity for destroying Chinese patterns, and she rejected the foreign religion's exclusive dogma, which could not fit itself into the Chinese Way. The missionary strategy of building a Christian American home, marriage, and family in a totally alien civilization converted some Chinese to Christianity but ultimately Anna's own daughter chose Chinese spiritual values over those of her mother.

As an intellectually-inclined woman, Anna was pleased that her daughter was a reader, frequently bragging to Grandma Seward about her "bookworm's" love of histories, Shakespeare, Grimms' fairy tales, Greek myths and children's classics. Ida was better informed than her mother about the news of the 1898 Spanish-American War.[49]

However, Anna was insensitive to the reasons behind Ida's avid reading: sex role stereotyping and feelings of isolation. The growing girl was not allowed to play with the schoolboys, whom John had taught to play football, or help groom the mules which occupied innumerable hours of her brother's childhood. Ida was expected to engage in ladylike activities such as lace making, or listen to the women's conversations. But Ida was "bored with their endless talk of babies and sickness and the goodness of God." She seldom had Chinese girls to play with as they were busy caring for younger siblings. Ida was alone for much of the time.

Ida escaped from loneliness into other times and places. She was especially fond of biographies of Mary, Queen of Scots. She sympathized with the values by which Mary ruled, the tragedies of her love life and the dignity with which she faced her execution. The organ packing case in the back courtyard became her refuge.[50]

Concerned with their children's schooling and proud of their "bookworm" daughter, the Pruitts planned an academic curriculum of exclusively Western literary and scientific subjects. The Chinese language was used for conversation, not a subject for study on its own merits. C.W. studied classical Chinese in order to translate portions of the Bible into the language of China's ruling scholar-gentry class. Anna studied the common "women's language" to teach the gospel, not to learn from the Chinese women. They encouraged their ten-year-old daughter to teach English in the girls' school run by Christians of Huangxian. Several times weekly, she taught English to the wife of her father's Chinese teacher. Neither parent ever suggested that Ida sit in on the Chinese language classes at the boys' school.[51] Ida never learned the written Chinese language, although she formally studied it many years later in Beijing.

Ida did not consciously hate her mother. "I accepted [Mother and Father] as they were and did not think too much about them." Instead, Ida resented her mother's failure to adapt to China. Anna could never look Chinese; her large nose betrayed her. Anna criticized the "seamy" side of the native brethren who lacked the "high standard of moral living" which she considered normative among Westerners. Her friendships with Chinese women were patronizing efforts at religious conversion, in Ida's view. Such expressions of moral self-righteousness, which painted the entire populace of Christian nations as pure and which defined the Chinese culture as immoral, were communicated in many ways, direct and subtle, to the Chinese population as well as to her sinified daughter.

Anna saw very little of beauty around her. Even the smell of indigo dye, which to Ida was a fragrance associated with Song Family Village and the common people, was a "stench" to Anna. Like many other missionaries who found the Chinese odors their greatest challenge, Anna was overpowered by the smell of the neighboring dye shop invading the air of her American home.[52]

In contrast, C.W. seemed virtually to have become Chinese. Ida admired her father's adaptation to Chinese ways in order to help build genuine friendships between the Chinese and Westerners. His blue eyes did not seem to give him away, as Anna's nose did. In a sign of respect for the people Anna labeled "seamy," C.W. always stayed indoors during the grave-sweeping festival to avoid embarrassing his Chinese Christian friends who still participated in this form of ancestor worship after conversion to Christianity. He understood the importance of maintaining the surface harmony of events. To Ida, her father, walking through the Chinese wheat fields, had the face of a prophet. He was gentle, yet courageous. Behind a serious demeanor, he had a twinkle in his eye.[53]

Left unspoken was a more fundamental aspect of Ida's love for her sinified father. Like the Chinese amah, C.W. Pruitt warmly empathized with his daughter. He intervened on Ida's behalf. He took time for the troubled child. His own difficulties with his complex and insensitive wife, which drove him into his study and away from the family, probably endeared him to his daughter. The more Anna struggled to maintain an American home and family life, the more her husband and daughter were attracted by the human sensibility of Chinese culture.

2

"The Home with the Open Door": Anna's Story

D ecades before Mary Schauffler Platt entitled her missionary tract *The Home with the Open Door*, missionary women such as Anna Seward Pruitt committed their homes to the cause of evangelism. The door to Anna's Christian home in China swung open in two directions. When she was not inviting Chinese women inside, she left the security of her home to minister to Chinese bodies, minds, and souls. During her early years, as her Chinese language skills became proficient, Anna, as other missionary women, began to visit her neighbors and friends. Her family doctoring and teaching evolved into a medical clinic and boys' school.[1]

As a young mother, Anna Seward Pruitt began calling on neighbor women every afternoon. With baby Ida at her breast, Anna generally was well received and felt encouraged by the women's apparent interest in the gospel.[2] Within two years, strange Chinese women no longer took flight, but invited Anna into their homes. Such visits were not easy. Anna met with hostility, laughter, interruptions, and a completely alien view of the soul from her own Christian concept. In moments of candor, she admitted her preference for staying home with her own children.[3]

When doors of the gentry class were eventually opened to the foreigners, these visitations were strained. Chinese women returned Anna's visits, their initial timidity eventually overcome by their curiosity about the foreigners' household belongings. Anna followed the technique developed by earlier women missionaries of using the Chinese interest in the "big-nosed" ones' strange ways and possessions to overcome bizarre rumors about the missionaries. Favorite curios at the Pruitt compound included the stereoscope, bicycles, organ, sewing machine and water pump.[4] Ida remembered that her mother received these one-time visitors graciously. After showing them around the house, she tried to tell them something about the gospel.[5] Very occasionally, women came for spiritual direction or for asylum from the world, such as the case of the woman who stayed with the Pruitts awhile after her second suicide attempt.[6]

Anna was overwhelmed by the requirements of entertaining aristocratic Chinese ladies. Rules of etiquette and propriety were strict. Elaborate Chinese foods were necessary. Most difficult of all for Anna, whose entire life was devoted to good works, was the gentry ideal of leisure. "I tell them the Lord is not pleased with idleness."[7]

In addition to the one-time visitors, both Anna and C.W. developed a group of Chinese friends and acquaintances from among the Chinese converts. These friendships were the "real heart of successful women's work."[8] However, Anna's occasional references to her Chinese women friends in letters home failed to convey the Chinese women as unique personalities. Hers was a rather patronizing, instrumental attitude toward the Chinese women.[9]

Ida found some of her mother's one-time visitors "very beautiful and stylish-looking," dressed in the outdoor costume appropriate for visiting, but considered her mother's friends boring and ugly.[10] In physical appearance and personality, Anna's Chinese Christian friends all deviated from Chinese social convention. Ida conceded that perhaps the women were seeking God, as were many of the church members. But perhaps they also found a social life in this new club that they were denied elsewhere. For one reason or another, these Chinese Christian converts were outcastes in the broader society, not typical of Chinese womanhood.[11]

The peasants who called on her father, on the other hand, seemed to represent the finest qualities of the Chinese culture. In Ida's retelling, they possessed a dignity and integrity common to all the Chinese people who figured in Ida's own later writings and speeches. C.W. developed a close personal friendship with his Chinese language teacher that lasted fifty years, a relationship based on mutual respect of each man's culture.[12]

Anna's medical clinic evolved from nursing her own children's frequent illnesses. She could not deny care to the Chinese neighbor children that she gave her family. Thus, an ever-wider circle of Chinese were scrubbed, doctored, and comforted.

Anna took on her task as an intellectual challenge. *The Complete Family Doctor* was a constant household reference book. Ida and John remembered the book for its transparencies of the human anatomy ...

minus all the female and male genital organs. Anna experimented with home remedies, made her own cough syrup and distilled the family's water. In later years, she established a community apothecary, compounded many of her own medicines and received wholesale rates on other drugs. Periodically, she organized "vaccinating bees" of calf lymph. For slight "bilious attacks" she administered salts, calomel, and quinine. Exhausted by the demand for her medical advice, she began holding clinic hours. Midwifery services, of course, observed no schedule.[13]

Missionary educators initially limited instruction to literacy and the moral education of housewives. Later courses of study trained Chinese women to be doctors, teachers, and Bible women. Although missionary educators believed all of these professions worked to the glory of God, their conservative colleagues remained unconvinced.

Anna and C.W. Pruitt's sympathies initially lay with the evangelical Gospel Mission, which opposed schools. In 1893, after visiting the Southern Baptist mission in Canton, they realized that their extreme views were driving Chinese Christian children into Presbyterian schools. After Gospel Mission founder, T.P. Crawford, forced his wife's boys' boarding school in Penglai (which missionaries called Dengzhou) to close, the Pruitts opened one in Huangxian to fill the gap.[14]

In 1897, although controversy over female literacy in romanized Chinese still raged among missionaries, Anna began to teach English to the village schoolgirls every afternoon. Nine-year-old Ida actually led the classes, as the girls preferred her as their teacher. The purpose of English instruction was to prepare the girls as wives for students attending Anna's boys' boarding school, many of whom sought jobs in the modern treaty port of Tianjin.[15]

Women missionaries soon discovered the difficulties of establishing Western-style marriage among their Chinese Christian students. Marriage between two Christian converts didn't end polygamy, female subordination, bound feet, and other forms of mistreatment. Missionaries disagreed as to the proper course of action against polygamous marriage among the native brethren. In 1907, a resolution of the China Centenary Missionary Conference to accept secondary wives into church membership was so controversial that it was referred back into committee. The Pruitt's mission station forced a young wife to divorce her husband when he took a concubine. Ida never forgot or forgave the missionaries for this action, which caused the first wife's social ostracism and left her in dire economic straits.

Other missionary demands of Chinese converts were equally
disturbing to Ida as she grew to understand how they divided families and
destroyed ancient customs. Ancestor reverence presented one of the most
serious dilemmas for missionaries and potential converts. The central
ritual of ancestor reverence involved bowing to the family ancestral
tablets during weddings and other important ceremonial occasions.
Missionaries prohibited such bowing by Chinese Christian converts,
viewing the ceremony as the worship of idols or "graven images." Eldest
sons of gentry families, who were expected to conduct these family
rituals, were particularly reticent to convert.

Likewise, Christian girls engaged to non-Christian boys were forced
to chose between their new religion and their familial duties. If they
refused to bow to their husband's ancestors, they faced rejection by
parents, in-laws, and other relatives. At times, their lives were threatened.

In later years as a social worker and political activist, Ida was
haunted by her parents' actions and the good intentions of other
Westerners, who all too often failed to see the long-term implication of
their reform efforts. Her opposition to their charity projects and U.S.
government policies alienated Ida from her countrymen and women.

Behind the Closed Door

Anna Seward Pruitt, like most missionary women, constantly moved back
and forth between her various roles. Through her home, school, and clinic,
she at once evangelized and mothered her family, the schoolboys, and the
larger Chinese Christian community. The efforts to juggle all of her roles
and to conform to the missionary expectations took their toll on Anna, as
she repeatedly suffered from physical exhaustion, illness, and the guilt
associated with unfulfilled expectations.

Many times, Anna did not know which of many tasks to tackle
first — which of her roles to play. However, she felt her mothering role
underlay all others. She seemed proud that her motherly touch with the
Chinese students was well regarded among students' families.[16] Anna
obviously thrived on her teaching and administrative work in the boys'
school, as she expanded the curriculum and her own involvement in the
program over the years. Yet, in letters to her mother, she felt the need to
balance each account of the school with a story of caring for her own
children and home. "You may criticize me and say I leave no time for the
children, but … they are in the program all the time and are never long

out of my sight or hearing."[17] Her children seemed to sense their mother's tension between them and the schoolboys and played on her feelings of guilt. "Mother always loved the schoolboys best," became an axiom between Ida and John.

Anna's conflicting duties to family and mission were sometimes resolved in favor of home life, and other times in favor of evangelizing and schoolwork. Writing to her mother and to her good friend, Hattie Wright, Anna emphasized her own home. "I don't think there is another life that would afford me quite so much mental satisfaction as housekeeping .... I have too much of other kinds (of work) to do."[18] Yet, judging from the amount of time and attention she devoted to developing the boys' school, as well as her extensive publications on behalf of missions, Anna's intellectual bent and administrative aptitude would have been frustrated tremendously by a life devoted exclusively to housekeeping and childcare. In fact, she never considered decreasing her schoolwork. The poverty and distress around her, as well as the mission's expectations, made Anna feel lazy for devoting any time, effort, or money to herself.[19]

For missionary women such as Anna Seward Pruitt, then, "women's work for women" meant the constant juggling of family and missionary roles and the subordination of personal needs and desires to religious duties. Sacrifice of self for others, an ideal of both nineteenth century American womanhood and of Christianity, found its highest expression in Christian women on the mission field. If many missionary women fell short of the ideal by devoting most of their time and energy to their own families, many others, Anna among them, conscientiously tried to live up to the ideal of playing all of the familial and missionary roles well.

If anything, Anna excelled at the missionary roles over her familial roles, mothering her schoolboys like her own children. And, by fulfilling her Christian duty, this intelligent, capable, and ambitious woman was able to juggle a career, of sorts, with a family, as few women in America were able to do in her generation. Anna's long days of household and school management, evangelism, and mothering were tiring but personally fulfilling. Her schedule was full but not overwhelming. Her many accomplishments were a source of pride.

All too often, however, Anna's long days were followed by even longer nights spent nursing her own sick children or spelling another missionary mother. Illness was a constant part of life in the China missions. Anna spent months at a time too ill to care for herself or her children during the early years. C.W. took over her schoolwork and the childcare, aided by other missionaries and the Chinese servants. Every letter of Anna's to America was filled with stories of their miseries.

Christian missionaries understood that their lifetime commitment to foreign missions might well mean a short life of great personal suffering. Even harder to bear was the death of their small children, which occurred at a considerably higher rate than among children in America, especially before age two.[20] In one year alone, over twelve missionary children residing in Shandong province died.[21] The women tried to live by the Christian belief in an afterlife, cheering themselves up by imagining their little children happily at play in a better world. They felt they must show their faith in God's will by their own willingness to give up their children to death.

When John was seriously ill, Anna wrote, "If the dear Lord wants to take our baby home to Heaven I do not want to be unwilling." Yet she did not give up her child without a fight. She made the arduous journey by s*henze*, a mule-drawn litter, to Yantai, seeking medical care for him. When Ida was sick with typhoid or malaria the next year, Anna comforted herself that "only God knows where her dear beautiful soul can best live to His glory."[22]

After two-month-old Virginia died, Anna used her personal grief to the good of the missionary cause. "God helps me not to long to have my baby with me …. Thoughts of my baby in Heaven make me love Chinese children and mothers more and long to do them good."[23]

Anna initially responded in the same way to six-year-old Ashley's death two years later. "I shall rejoice abundantly if his homegoing [sic] may be used to point others to Heaven and make them seek the treasures…." As the months passed, however, Anna's acceptance of death took on a morbid tone. "Nothing on earth seems worth working for save the coming of Christ's Kingdom." She could not put her heart into her work on earth, which looked less attractive than Heaven to her. At age thirty-six, Anna counted more friends "on the other side" than on earth. "I've seen one whole generation pass away…. I myself am middle-aged and so happy to think that my days are gliding swiftly by. I do not crave long life."[24]

Anna was to live another fifty-one years. However, in the year that followed Ashley's death, she struggled against the "selfishness" of psychological depression that made her desire only to sit with her three remaining children. She complained that her brain was tired and her mind difficult to compose. She felt she could no longer bear the "sights and sounds of heathenism," the streets lined with manure heaps and compost piles, or the houses full of vermin. She yearned for the "health-giving properties" of clean, foreign houses, well-kept streets, and "honest white faced people." "Of course if [the Chinese] were as good and well off as we there would be no need of us here ...."[25]

Ashley's death intensified many of Anna's worst fears and prejudices about life in China. She had always been repulsed by the filth and stench around her, but now she feared germs as much as Satan, himself. She was loathe to let Chinese people into her home and sent her children to another part of the house when entertaining guests.[26]

Feelings of isolation from America and from others like themselves added to Anna's depression. After the Stephens family, their closest white neighbors, departed, Anna was as homesick as when she first arrived in China. Her loneliness continued to feed her depression over a year after Ashley's death. The courageous example of other missionaries whose losses were greater than her own lifted her spirit somewhat. However, the themes of loss, guilt, and loneliness persisted during the Boxer Uprising and a year's furlough in America.[27]

Anna's relationships with the Chinese seemed to grow more distant over time. During the first years of their lives in China, C.W. and Anna both studied Chinese customs and defended Chinese civilization for its learning, politeness, and patience against the Europeans, who seemed to respect only brute force. Anna was ashamed of America for passing the Geary Bill in 1893, which allowed the deportation of all unregistered Chinese from the United States.[28] But in the same year, Anna wrote of her own Chinese acquaintances as "exceedingly frail and faulty human beings."[29]

Her patience with the Chinese seemed to be overtaken by self-righteous judgments as the years passed, especially after Virginia and Ashley's deaths. In her letters, she accused the Chinese of meanness, lying, "fathomless lust and hate" and general immorality. She concluded generations were necessary "to give the rank and file of [Chinese] Christians the same high standard of moral living that obtain in the best of the nineteenth century occidentals."[30] Anna admitted that the church members were loving and appreciative, and that Chinese were generally kind and thoughtful. However their "seamy side" predominated in Anna's view despite her prayers for "a better appreciation of our own sins in order to feel the right degree of charity for others."[31] She blamed the

Chinese, as well as herself, for her children's deaths and could no more forgive them than forgive herself.

C.W. Pruitt's relationships with the Chinese were significantly different from his wife's. His life in some ways represented an alternative model of Sino-American interactions, a non-interventionist position of accepting differences without judgment. Ida picked up her father's basic attitude. If Anna Seward Pruitt's bonding with other missionary women paralleled her estrangement from the Chinese, C.W. Pruitt's close friendship with his Chinese teacher and his respectful relationships with the Chinese brethren no doubt reflected his generally non-judgmental attitudes toward Chinese. C.W. studied Chinese life and culture to gain the respect of the people. In his words, "It takes a lot of training to know how not to be offensive."[32]

C.W. did not necessarily like the qualities that his wife found distasteful. But he seemed to reverse Anna's emphasis, generalizing from the good attributes of individual church members, and dismissing their weaknesses as exceptions. "One only needs to live among the Christians of Shandong for ten years and learn from them their language and many other things to highly prize them." He found people in Huangxian to be hard and cold, but attributed those qualities to their mercantile absorption in finance and trade, not to their inherent "Chineseness." He was as disheartened as Anna by the "Rice Christians" whose major inspiration for conversion was self-interest. However he gently chided Ida for mimicking her mother's condemnation of one such woman. "You must not judge her. It is between God and her conscience."[33]

Anna and C.W.'s different attitudes toward the Chinese developed from their original motivations for becoming missionaries. To C.W., becoming a pastor on the mission field offered him a "wider life" unavailable to him in the North Georgia mountains. Behind his concern to guide the "heathen" toward Christ was a simple desire to study and understand life more profoundly than was possible as a Georgian farmer. "I want to know the Truth. I think I have found it." But his entire life was spent studying another people's understanding of the Truth; he developed a great appreciation of Chinese ways to Truth.[34]

In contrast, the goal of Anna and most missionaries' work was to save the Chinese souls, cure their ills, and otherwise improve their living conditions. She studied their language and customs to convert them to Christianity, cleanliness, and a better way of life, not to better understand either the Chinese or herself. Unfortunately, if the goals are to save, cleanse, and help, but not to understand or value people as they are, people might have to be sacrificed in order to be saved. Anna concluded that all the Chinese peoples' sorrows were due to sin, for which the Pure Gospel of Jesus was the only cure. "As they are now, every effort to ameliorate their condition only gives them more opportunity to serve their own lusts...."[35] The Chinese problem was sin; the solution was Christianity. To save Chinese souls from sin, missionaries would have to *impose* the Gospel.

From this justification for exercising moral force over an immoral people, it was but a short logical step to justifying the use of political and military force to "save" the Chinese. Anna and many other missionaries interpreted the political and military expansion of Western powers at the turn of the twentieth century as an expression of superior moral force. She hoped the Chinese defeat at the hands of Japan in 1895 would "turn [China] from her conceited trust in herself and her idols to humble faith in the one true god." She feared that if "the sleeping giant's" war spirit were aroused before her conversion to Christianity, "she could conquer the whole world and introduce the pigtail and shaven head into New York and London." The war with Japan was beneficial for the Chinese, in Anna's opinion.[36]

After Japan's victory over China in 1895, Anna viewed the Western powers' scramble for concessions with some ambivalence. Ultimately, she supported the maneuvers as a way to prevent further killings of Westerners and as a means to move China along the "road to an enlightened civilization." Europeans made a great mistake by treating China as a Christian country, in her opinion. "There is nothing in the Chinese government save age that deserves respect."[37]

Even after she admitted that the German soldiers stationed in north China were no better than Chinese soldiers, and that their treatment of the Chinese was "worse than dogs," Anna retained her trust in the Great Powers. She was especially proud of America's new imperialistic position. During the Spanish-American War of 1898, the Pruitts flaunted their stars and stripes with much pride. *Harpers Weekly* supplied much patriotic paraphernalia that extolled America's new imperial status.[38] Ida and John had U.S. gunboats and flags on their silverware and scarf pins. At a celebration in honor of several missionary birthdays and anniversaries, the group sang "America" and waved American flags.[39]

Anna's trust in military intervention by the Great Powers to further the Christian conversion of China reached its peak during the Boxer

Uprising of 1900. A populist movement against Westerners that originated in northwest Shandong province, the Boxers were supported by a hard-core conservative faction at the Qing court. Anti-Christian hostility and a severe economic crisis stimulated disorder, riots, and banditry throughout China in the 1890s, culminating in the killing of over 200 missionaries and possibly 30,000 Chinese Christians in 1900. In some provinces, up to one-third of the Christian converts were slaughtered for their beliefs. Many times as many victims suffered at the hands of the punitive Allied expedition.[40]

Anna blamed the Germans for provoking the violence against foreigners in Shandong. Although she considered the break-up of China inevitable, Anna welcomed "any nations ... heroic enough to ... [bring] order out of chaos." However, she felt the Boxers' persecution of Christians "may be needed to make the Christian Church in China pure and devoted and free from worldly greed."[41]

C.W. was much more inclined to lay blame for the Boxers' massacre on the secret imperial edict to attack Christians, as well as the widespread resentment against Roman Catholic missionaries. The Catholics were known for using their foreign privileges to help converts win legal suits.

Anna's eagerness for Western intervention against the Boxers was consistent with her general attitude that a superior Christian civilization had the right to save immoral pagan peoples from themselves. The salvation of Chinese souls might well require persecution and sacrifice by the converts, just as Anna and all the other missionary women were called upon to make the ultimate sacrifice, the deaths of their children.

C.W. shared his wife's theology and general trust in the civilized Christian powers. However, his emphasis was different. He did not challenge the "right" of the Powers or the missionaries to intervene on behalf of Christian civilization, but he challenged the "wisdom" of such forceful conversion. Likewise, the persecution and sacrifice of Chinese converts and his own children might be necessary for the Christianization of China, but he accepted such sacrifices with grief and humility, not Anna's resentment, guilt, and righteousness.

Anna's estrangement from the Chinese and her struggle against loneliness, bitterness, and depression were all kept behind the closed doors of the missionary compound. Outwardly, she seemed to have close Chinese women friends and generally congenial relations with her neighbors in Huangxian. These friendships were no doubt sincere, but were based on the Chinese acceptance of Christianity, rather than either the Chinese or the American woman's acceptance of each other. The relationships failed to stimulate the hope for mass conversion or genuine mutual understanding.

The mounting crisis of the Boxers during the spring and summer of 1900, while exposing deep Chinese anti-foreignism, especially hostility toward missionaries, also brought out the personal friendships between individual Chinese and missionaries. More than a year before the Uprising, Anna wrote, "We have this great security, the people, our neighbors, [who] are our friends and believe that we are willing to stand by them in trouble." As events intensified in June of 1900, Anna expressed sympathy with the Boxers against the involvement of Catholic missionaries in Chinese lawsuits. The Chinese in Huangxian talked freely with C.W. of their pride in the Boxers without realizing he was an obnoxious foreigner, too. Convinced that their neighbors and church members depended on them, the Pruitts resisted the urgent messages to flee to a friendly gunboat off the coast of Penglai. They preferred to trust in their neighbors and the "best elements" as a force for peace, and willingly shared the risks of their native Christian brethren.[42]

Ida and John were attending the China Inland Mission School in Yantai, two or three days' travel from Huangxian, when the Boxer Uprising began. John was quite stirred up by the situation and urged his parents to come to Yantai right away. Ida's concern for her parents' safety was offset by the excitement of visiting classmates' homes in the settlement, according to her mother. However, Ida's perception of that time was not nearly so happy. She remembered the dread that the students felt when, one by one, their classmates were called from the classroom to hear of their parents' deaths. Her own best friend, Bena, lost her parents this way. Ida comforted her friend in silent walks in the hills.[43]

Finally, in late June, Huangxian filled with "patriots" practicing semi-religious exercises. Even the City Council began drilling in preparation against the "foreign devils." The city was aflame with Boxer placards. Reports came in that the entire population on the far side of the Yellow River had stopped farming to engage in the trance-like movements. The Pruitts saw that the Boxers had become a well-organized, widespread machine. They realized their local reputations were small protection to them and a great liability to the native Christians. After struggling with the desire to protect their property, comfort their friends, and finish the school year, they decided to heed the U.S. Consul's order to leave the interior for Yantai.[44]

Anna and young Robert traveled to Yantai without incident. They later learned that their *shenze* carriers had considered dumping them in the river. However, having been paid before the trip, they decided they should uphold their end of the contract by safely delivering their passengers to their destination. C.W. traveled the distance separately by bicycle. A stone-throwing man chased him on foot but C.W. sped away and arrived safely.[45]

As long as they were stuck indefinitely in Yantai awaiting the outcome of the violence, the Pruitts decided to take their home furlough one year early. They traveled to Shanghai on an ordinary coastal steamer, to Vancouver, British Columbia by ocean liner, and finally by Canadian Pacific Railroad to Tallmadge, Ohio.[46] From her base at the "Grandmother's Window" of the old homestead, Anna and her family toured the country for a year speaking to friends and relative, churches, and missionary societies of America about her thirteen years' work for women on the China mission field.

3

Leaving Home: Ida's Journeys between China and America

S ailing into the San Francisco harbor in 1900, on furlough for the first time since she was three years old, Ida and John hugged the railing to see the "real America." Ida was disappointed that "Golden Gate" was not really golden, but just two bluffs on either side of the channel. She and John were amazed by the size of the horses loading on the docks. Most incredible of all to the children, still unconscious of their colonial position in China, were the white men pushing wheelbarrows! They had never seen laborers of their own race before.

"Now we were to see wonderful America. Now we were to have playmates." But the children's wish to make friends was not to be. No sooner had Ida and John settled into one place and met some American children than the family moved on to visit other relatives or speak about China at other churches. When Anna spoke with congregations about her mission work in China, she dressed Ida and John in their Chinese clothes. Standing on a platform, motionless while her mother stirred the hearts of churchgoers with stories about the heathen in China, Ida felt like Exhibit A. John was Exhibit B. She hated it.

While in Atlanta, Georgia, the children attended school for several months. Here was Ida's opportunity to find American playmates.

> "Do Chinese eat with chopsticks?" The question carried the implication of strange, barbarous ways. Before I could do more than say "Yes," would come the next question, "Is your mother Chinese? Is that why your eyes slant?" And before I could answer those who had the answers already in their own minds, they were away ... and I was again alone.[1]

The furlough that Anna cherished only deepened Ida's sense of isolation and widened the mother-daughter gap. After Ida returned to

China with her family, she and John entered the British China Inland
Mission School in Yantai, located on Shandong's Zhifu peninsula, for the
years 1901–1902. Then John came down with pneumonia and Anna
withdrew both children. For the next four years, between the ages fifteen
and eighteen, Ida lived in the interior of China with at most four
European families. Caught between the young children and the adults of
the mission, and increasingly aware of her separateness from both the
missionaries and the Chinese community, teenage Ida spent her days
reading and riding her donkey.[2]

After the Boxer Rebellion was quelled, missionaries began the
process of rebuilding and reconceptualizing their goals and purposes in
China.[3] American Protestant congregations contributed more generously
than ever to the foreign missions, moved by the stories of atrocities
committed against missionaries by the Boxers and inspired by the
upsurge in Chinese attendance at Christian churches after the Boxers
were subdued.[4] With the new financial base, missionaries began the
process of "institutionalization" in earnest, a liberal trend in Christianity
begun with the Social Gospel in the late nineteenth century.

Anna Seward Pruitt initially was not sure what to think of this
institutional work when in 1898 Mr. Cornwell of the Chefoo Presbyterian
Mission began consulting with the management of a Chinese silk factory
towards improved working and living conditions for the employees.[5] By
1902, however, Anna was delighted with the implications of "institutionalization" for their own Southern Baptist mission station. The mission
bought a stretch of land outside Huangxian on which they built a training
school for preachers, a hospital, a boys' college-preparatory school, and
western-style, two-story homes for all the missionaries. This complex
grew to become the North China Baptist Junior College.[6]

Even while the new buildings were rising in the outskirts of
Huangxian, the mission decided that the new training school for preachers
would be built in Penglai. C.W. Pruitt became a member of the theology
faculty. Although Ida had been born in Penglai, the move away from the
Chinese compound in Huangxian where she spent her childhood was "the
first time I ever remember being really unsure of my universe."[7] Ida's
heart sank at the sight of foreign houses sticking up "boldly and baldly
in … good wheat land … where the houses lay graciously low to the
ground and nestled among the trees." With the move away from the
Chinese compound in the Song Family Village, the missionaries' only
contact with the Chinese was through institutions—the school, clinic, and

pulpit. No longer were missionaries living among the people, relating their message through their own homes and lives.

Both Anna and C.W. Pruitt were in their element. Living in an American-style home by the sea, surrounded by a garden full of American vegetables and a thicket of trees, Anna hosted missionaries from all over China during the summer months. She taught high school subjects to John and Ida during the mornings. Afternoons were devoted to visiting Chinese homes with the Bible women or socializing with other missionary wives. In addition to his administrative duties, C.W. Pruitt taught theology to future Chinese pastors.

The father, who at one time was the only one able to comfort his lonely little daughter, completely faded out of his teenage daughter's life. Anna tried to bring Ida into the women missionaries' conversations. But to Ida, these talks were very dull. They stressed "one talent" and Christian resignation, while Ida yearned to develop many talents and to live abundantly. When Ida expressed her own thoughts, the missionaries stared blankly back at her. Ida began to think something was wrong with her. Looking back, she wondered why the missionaries didn't encourage their children to learn Chinese painting, calligraphy, and music. Instead, Ida's "talent" was limited to cutting out many-colored paper doll clothes.[8]

Ida's feelings of ever-greater distance between herself and the missionaries, who themselves were literally moving away from the Chinese people, were not compensated by the same feelings of closeness with her Chinese neighbors that she had experienced as a child in Huangxian. After the death of Ida's old amah, Dada, Ida shared the feelings of Dada's husband that life had lost its flavor.

Penglai, west of Yantai, was a conservative city steeped in the lore of the famous Eight Immortals who made their home in the Penglai Pavilion on a rocky promontory. The refraction of sun over Bohai Bay creates mirages best seen from Penglai, from which centuries of travelers reported sightings of gold and silver palaces.[9] Naval bases were built during the Yuan dynasty and expanded in the Ming dynasty to defend against foreign sea attacks. These proved useless against the British and other Europeans, however, who forced open the port after the Second Opium War in 1858. Residents still harbored ill feelings toward foreigners and refused to speak with them.

In such an environment, Ida's only opportunity to socialize with Chinese was through the mission. She enjoyed visiting with Lily, the milkman's daughter, and with Mei, the pastor's daughter. But both girls were eighteen years old and preoccupied with the arrangements for their marriages, while Ida was, in her words, "still almost a child" in these affairs.

Ida's world, then, was very circumscribed at a time when she yearned to expand her horizon. In conservative Penglai, women did not walk the streets without covering their faces with black gauze. Ida could not even wander along the beach for fear of her reputation. These were, to Ida, "four lost years."[10]

Riding her donkey, reading fairy tales, cutting out paper dolls, Ida waited to turn eighteen, waited for college in America, waited "for the wonderful things I knew were going to happen...." She pictured herself in the United States as a beautiful woman, dressed in lovely clothing, pursued by handsome men.

Plans were made for college. Anna assured both John and Ida that the ultimate decision was their own. They could attend Berkeley and live with "Big Ida's" sister or they could attend Cox College in College Park, Georgia, a suburb of Atlanta. A devout Baptist who recently lost his own daughter would pay for Ida's tuition at Cox College and the Woman's Missionary Society in Atlanta would watch out for her. Ida knew which college she was expected to choose. "Mother never owned—perhaps even to herself, that she made [our minds] up for us." Neither Ida nor John considered rebelling against their mother.[11]

Ida tried to make the best of her college years. By her junior year, she was the class president. Classmates remembered Ida's odd laughter and accent, her rhyming verse and her constant smile. She helped to found and became the editor-in-chief of a literary magazine called "The Den." The stated purpose of the magazine, probably penned by its editor-in-chief, was to encourage student's writing and other ambitions. "... Who knows but that there may be among us some embryo author who shall one day rival George Eliot or Elizabeth Barrett Browning...."[12] Clearly, as a frequent contributor of essays and poetry, she was one of those aspiring young writers.

On at least one occasion, she used the magazine as an outlet for her frustrations with Americans' preconceived notions about China. "The Life of a Chinese Girl" began with the idea Ida heard in all her father's sermons, which she hammered home in her own future work and writings: the universality of human nature behind its variations in outward appearance and environmentally determined development. "So when we come to consider a foreign nation let us always bear this in mind, and we will see that they are not so strange after all, and that perhaps it is we that are the most artificial." Very few Western writers of her era expressed this position or took issue with the imperialistic view of other races as subject and inferior to white Europeans and Americans.[13]

The essay approached the study of Chinese women very differently from missionary women's characterization of benighted female victims of paganism or the common belief that Asians value human life less than Westerners do. Ida described girls' free, happy play in the streets and the affection bestowed by their loving families. Then followed an analysis of the economic, social, and religious reasons behind families' preference for boys over girls. Poverty drove women to strangle baby girls whom they could not feed, yet mothers could not look on their beloved baby daughters for fear their "heart would relent." One woman who later converted to Christianity expressed remorse for her sins of so killing her six daughters "... and yet she did what she thought was best."

In keeping with a lifelong fascination with traditions and legends, Ida recounted several stories about footbinding. Even after admitting the cruelty of this "barbarous practice," she urged the reader against harshly judging the custom.[14]

In Ida's written memoirs of her years at college, Cox was nothing more than high school. Few of the girls responded to the urging of the editor of "The Den" to set their goals higher than the latest fashions and boys. Ida, too, liked boys and pretty clothes but she sensed that people disapproved of missionaries' having social lives. In fact, during the Pruitts' furlough of 1908, some of the church ladies complained to Anna that Ida was frivolous to enjoy parties and want new clothes like the other girls of her age. To Ida's surprise, her mother responded by giving her daughter a low-cut, lace dress and holding parties for the young people of the church.[15]

At Cox College, Ida had a "beau" whose parents never left the two young people unsupervised. A boy named Henry became a friend with whom she could talk freely. She also was matched with the most eligible bachelor of Baptist society, but the two had nothing to say over drinks at the town soda fountain.[16]

Ida found kindred spirits in two girls at Cox College. The three obtained special permission to take walks together in the woods while the other girls rocked on the front porch. Ida and her friends imagined that the woods were inhabited by the fairies of their childhood tales and shared a mystical experience that revealed a soon forgotten "great purpose."

Ida yearned for meaningful conversation. She confided in one of the women teachers whom she considered to be more genuine than the others. To illustrate her understanding of the concept of "truth" as she struggled to understand it, Ida drew a series of overlapping circles, no two of which could be identical. "No two people could think the same thoughts, have the same experiences, [or] feel the same things. Even among close people, areas exist which the other could not know." The teacher seemed to understand that Ida's areas of overlapping with anyone were very small segments of the circle of her life.

Ida spent her summers between college terms at the Seward family home in Tallmadge, Ohio. The community lived by a pattern very similar to that of the China mission stations. Social activities revolved around the church and local sports. She later reflected that the similarity between village life in Ohio and the China missions delayed her understanding of the very different pattern of modern urban American life from the traditional Chinese culture, and of her separateness from both patterns.[17]

When visiting her father's relatives in the mountains of north Georgia, Ida observed a social pattern even closer to the agricultural-handicraft society of the Chinese farmers. The Southern Baptists in north Georgia, like the Chinese converts in north China, entered and sat separately, men on the right, women on the left. Only the fire and brimstone preaching and the emotional conversion experiences of the congregation were uncomfortable to her.

One of the young Georgian farmers liked Ida. Cousin Minnie served as his spokesperson. "Ben says he doesn't suppose you would think about marrying a farmer and settling down here...." Ida recognized the approach as Chinese-style match-making. She liked these north Georgia people and their way of life and considered accepting the proposal. In the end, however, she declined, realizing that she sought broader horizons.[18]

Throughout her accounts of her college years, Ida's theme is the gap between herself and others, whose world was so much smaller and homogeneous than hers. The different patterns of thinking and communicating of her several cultures puzzled Ida to the depth of her being and caused her periods of great loneliness.

One of Ida's aunts from Ohio, aware of the stultifying, anti-intellectual environment of Cox, urged Ida to transfer to Wellesley for her final year of college. Ida decided to finish what she had started, even though she learned little. This "hang-on" quality about herself was both her nemesis and her strength in years to come.[19]

Smothered by southern, small town traditions, Ida eagerly began a year of graduate school at Columbia University Teacher's College in 1909, financed by funds set aside by her parents for this purpose. "I was happy. Ideas burst on me from every side.... Here was mental freedom." She saw girls working on their doctorates who were also popular with boys.

Buoyed by the prospect of being both smart and popular, Ida devoured New York's opportunities. As part of a class at the School of Philanthropy, now the New York School of Social Work, she toured a police court, Ellis Island, factories, and the Old Tombs prison. Ida became a counselor at a Fresh Air camp for slum kids in 1910 and was infected with head lice for the first time. She attended everything from opera, starring Enrico Caruso, to political meetings supporting the Wobblies.

Yet even at Columbia, amidst her new friends and stimulating environment, Ida did not feel at home. She identified more closely with characters in her "Nineteenth Century Literature" course than with twentieth century New Yorkers. Rudyard Kipling's *Kim,* in particular, gave her the comfort she missed elsewhere. Like Kimball O'Hara, she imagined walking the roads of Asia, visiting the crowded kitchens of her girlhood, and observing her father and old friends.[20] She came to identify with the young Irish orphan who avoided missionaries and other "white men of serious aspect" and embraced Hindi and Indian village culture as his own.[21]

One incident of the novel especially resonated with Ida during her American stay. During an illness, Kim felt his soul was "out of gear with its surroundings." He repeatedly questioned and struggled to find his identity, which was both that of a British agent in the "Great Game" of imperialism and a disciple of an elderly Tibetan monk.[22] Kim accompanied his Buddhist teacher on a pilgrimage seeking Enlightenment and Truth. The new ideas and ways of life in New York, so completely different from her own, left Ida rootless, spiritually malnourished, and emotionally unstable. She yearned to find a spiritual guide to accompany her on the search for her identity.

The Pruitts' savings lasted for only one year's study. In 1910, at age twenty-one, Ida didn't consider applying for a scholarship or seeking part-time employment in order to stay on, although she later wondered what kind of scholar she might have become if given the encouragement to continue graduate work.[23]

At the time she never considered herself capable of further academic work so she applied to teaching positions in the United States. Worried for fear of failing at a job, she grabbed the first offer—St. Christopher's Orphanage at Dobbs' Ferry, New York. During the year 1910–1911, she taught the third and fourth grades and was asked to remain for a second year.[24]

Ida recognized the orphanage position as another cul-de-sac in her life. Before she could submit her resignation, however, she received a telegram from Ohio. Her brother, John, had eaten ice cream and became ill. As Ida traveled from New York to Ohio, John died of typhoid at age twenty. His appointment to the new United States Foreign Service in Beijing came on the day of his funeral.

The loss of her closest brother, only fifteen months younger than herself, who had been Ida's playmate in childhood and companion on the American adventure, was very bitter for Ida. He died of typhoid in America, the wonderful land of their childhood dreams, after surviving dread diseases in the Chinese hinterland. Ida could not weep or cry out for John. The hurt went deep and lodged with the other hurts, to surface at unguarded moments for many years to come. Part of herself had died with him.

Ida knew then that she could not continue teaching at the orphanage. Neither could she aspire to the husband and house that was promoted in the *Saturday Evening Post*. She felt she must return to China in John's place to comfort her parents. In addition to the deaths of three children, their fifth child, Robert, had lost his eyesight from an archery accident two years beforehand. Anna suffered guilt the rest of her life. Ida always felt that her mother tried to make the other family members feel guilty, too. This inherited guilt may have added additional impetus to Ida's decision.[25]

Ida's father, mother, and little brothers, fourteen-year-old Robert and ten-year-old Dudley ("Mac"), met Ida's ship in Yantai. She settled down with her family in the Western-style house in Yantai where her family lived briefly.[26] The great historic changes taking place around her in early Republican China, the volatile politics of the warlord years begun by Yuan Shikai, barely touched the lives of most people in Yantai, which was living on the memories of its past. The first emperor of China, Shi Huangdi of the Qin dynasty (r. 246–209 B.C.), had performed rites at the Temple of the Sun God. The "Martial Emperor," Wudi of the Han dynasty (r. 140–86 B.C.), had passed through Yantai as he led China's imperial expansion. During the Yuan dynasty, grain from south China was transported to the north through Yantai. From the Tang dynasty, voyages to Korea and Japan were launched from Yantai and the coastal fortification system was built to defend against intruders.[27]

Ida felt she had returned to a life of understandable rules and a recognizable pattern. She studied Mandarin with her father's teacher, Mr. Sun. Along with the adult vocabulary Ida required in order to read and speak articulately in Chinese, Mr. Sun taught Ida to recognize the Chinese way of seeing things "as they are, not as we think they are, or as we would like to have them."

Ida's early adulthood in Yantai from 1912 to 1918, during which time she developed her adult identity, became a time for her to sort out her childhood worldview based on missionary tenets from the Chinese pattern of thinking. She had very little exposure to the modern American pattern even as early Republican China began learning it.

Although Ida felt at home in China, her family relations were strained almost to the breaking point. Before Ida had unpacked after the voyage from the United States in 1912, Anna began to interrogate her about her love life. From then on, Anna constantly urged Ida to marry. She introduced her daughter to missionary men, for whom Ida had no use, and discouraged Ida from meeting the more worldly-wise, attractive men of the international settlement. Years later Ida admitted to herself that she was also attracted to Chinese men. "All the first years of my life I had seen only Chinese. Father also wore Chinese clothes and walked like a Chinese walks. Why ... should [I] not ... respond to a Chinese?" Consciously, Ida and everyone else assumed that Chinese and Americans could not have romantic thoughts about each other. But unconsciously, her attraction to Chinese men continued as a deep love for traditional China and her people.

Anna dominated all conversations with her daughter. Gradually, Ida gave up talking, resigned that her mother simply considered her an "appendage who must act in the ways to give her the most satisfaction." Ida's self-doubt intensified. What was the matter with her? Why was she so very unhappy? She felt her mother as the "'Old Man of the Sea' on her shoulders, riding her and sucking life from her like a vampire."[28]

When her heart was crowded or her soul was troubled, Ida ran to the upstairs verandah and looked out at the rolling hills ten kilometers to the south. They seemed to cradle Penglai like a mother comforting her child. She would recite Psalm 121: "I will look unto the hills/ from whence

cometh my help." And then as a "victorious antiphony," Psalm 24 came
to her:

> Who is this king of Glory?
> The Lord strong and mighty,
> The Lord mighty in battle.

Ida took comfort from imagining the hills as a strong and nurturing
mother and from seeing the battles as those of the spirit and those for a
better world. She associated the Yantai hills with the promise of Psalm 24:
"Who shall ascend into the hill of the Lord? He that hath clean hands and
a pure heart...."

During the summer of 1915, to relieve the relentless pressure she felt
from her mother, Ida visited friends in Beidaihe, a summer resort by the
sea. One night Ida awoke, hyperventilating from anxiety. She chanted the
Psalms as the stars above comforted her instead of Penglai's hills.[29]

Her friends, the American consul Julean Arnold and his wife
Gertrude, invited Ida to live with them in Beijing. She visited them during
the following fall. Ironically, in light of her later appointment to the
Peking Union Medical College (PUMC) in 1921, Ida joined the Arnolds
for a dinner honoring Dr. Simon Flexner and William H. "Popsy" Welch,
who were then planning the PUMC. Julean Arnold urged Ida to stay in
Beijing to organize the new American School. The breathtaking grandeur
of the city tempted her, but Ida felt she must return to face her problems
in Yantai.

Ida probably never directly confronted her mother to resolve the
conflict between them. Confrontation was inimical to both the Chinese
and the missionary cultures. Although she began to associate with other
young Westerners, Ida continued to feel trapped inside a "magic circle"
of rigid expectations set by her mother and her mother's religion, a circle
that separated and isolated Ida. For years after leaving her family home in
Yantai, Ida struggled to break out of the "magic circle" in order to
achieve greater intimacy in her relationships but she continued to suffer
from a sense of loneliness and disconnection with most people.

Ida began a career in missionary education by conducting afternoon
arithmetic and singing classes for girls ages six through eight at the Wai
Ling Day School for Girls, which Anna had founded. By the time Ida left
Yantai six years later, she was the school's administrator, nurse, drama
director, and teacher of Chinese classics, Old Testament history, and
physical education. The "go through the readers as fast as possible"

approach to study developed into a regular curriculum under Ida's administration. Four full-time teachers, a part-time music instructor, and occasional lecturers upgraded the school's standards to approach those of a college preparatory school. Two or three girls did continue their studies in college, but most left school after age fifteen to marry.

A few former students, notably She Huizhen who later became part of Ida's social work staff in Beijing, believed that Wai Ling Day School for Girls helped to change the traditional Chinese culture, improved living standards, and relieved women's suffering. Ida's perspective was much less idealistic. She thought many parents viewed the school as a place to keep their growing girls safe until marriage age and raised the value of their daughters in the marriage market.

Whatever the significance of the mission school, Ida enjoyed teaching about King David of Judea one hour and emperors of the Ming dynasty the next. She shared her long walks in the hills, which she had so loved as a twelve-year-old girl at the China Inland Mission School, with her own young students.[30]

In recognition of Ida's work, the mission appointed her to a 1917 committee to study and draft China-wide curricula standards. Her appointment alarmed Ida, who envisioned herself becoming a "dried-up prune," an "old-maid" missionary administrator.[31] Within the year, she resigned from Wai Ling Day School for Girls and returned to the United States.

During her early years at Wai Ling School, Ida taught arithmetic, singing, and games to the young children. Day after day, a little girl about five years old, who lived across from the school, solemnly stared at the school children's games with her deep brown eyes set in a little round face. From school gossip, Ida learned that the girl was being raised by the "Madam" of a brothel. She was to be a servant until age fifteen, when she would be introduced to the trade of prostitution. As time went on, the girl's appearance confirmed gossip that she was beaten and abused. Stories told that the child was forced to sleep on the floor with the dogs or on the coffin prepared for the old grandfather.

The little girl's plight made Ida resolve to help her escape from her daily abuse and future life as a prostitute. Her sensitive face and beautiful eyes moved Ida to consider adopting the girl. Inquiries of the American consulate got Ida nothing except a proposition by the consul. She then determined to kidnap the girl. One day, Ida walked into the schoolyard, held out her hand to the girl, and said, "Come with me." Without the slightest hesitation, the child went with Ida. The Madam's two daughters and all of the other little servant girls trailed behind.

Snow lay on the ground. The girl was barefoot and wore only a thinly padded coat and pair of unlined cotton trousers, both crawling with lice. As Ida undressed her for a warm bath by her fireplace, she saw the little body was criss-crossed with scratches. One foot was swollen with chilblains.

The next day the Madam, Mrs. Zhang, and her tall son came to call. Ida was petrified that, by force of numbers, they could carry away the child while she stood by helplessly. After quickly calling a friend for help, Ida instinctively acted according to the patterns of the culture she shared with her guests, offering them tea and cookies. As she later explained her reasoning, "Face would keep them from leaving the house during the few minutes I was in the next room.... We must not let anyone lose face...." The surface, once broken, lessened the powers of bargaining and allowed for the use of force to carry away the girl. In retelling the story, Ida emphasized one of the principles she applied as a social worker and political activist later in life. "Whatever happened, we had to continue to live in the same world and must show the mutual respect of one human being to another.... Face was the outward evidence of the inner respect of one's self and of one's way of life. This must not be taken from anyone."

After nibbling at a cookie, the Madam rose. Turning to the child, she commanded, "Come. It is time to go home." The child shrank back and barely breathed, "No."

Just as Ida thought all was lost, her friend rushed in. As the Western man bantered with the Madam's son, Ida and the Madam began their business discussion—the bargaining forces now even. They talked sums of money not to buy the girl but to compensate Mrs. Zhang for the girl's expenses. The Madam never made any effort to get the child back or paid further attention to her. Public opinion among the Chinese in the school, church, and village was with Ida. She had assumed complete responsibility for the child and would give her a better chance in life.

Mei Yun, the name Ida gave to the little girl, in her later writings, called Ida "Gugu," or "Aunt," since unmarried, single women could not be called "Mother."[32] Ida's parents were "Grandfather" and "Grandmother" to Mei Yun, whose real name was Guijing. She lived in the girls' boarding school, which Ida administered, but she had the run of the Pruitt household. When "Gugu" left again for the United States, Guijing remained behind. In good Chinese fashion, she remained under the care of her "grandparents"—Anna and C.W. Many years later, she remembered the family as wonderfully protective of her and much closer to the Chinese people than were other missionaries.[33]

Before kidnapping Guijing, Ida weighed in the balance the troubles the girl would face from growing up as the child of a single woman from another culture as compared with the future she faced as a prostitute. Ida had a well-developed awareness of her own inner conflicts as a woman not firmly identified with either Chinese or American culture. She observed other bicultural people: Some handled the mixture of cultures graciously, others were crushed, but "all showed signs of the pain that came from conflict." Ida decided she could offer Guijing an incomparably better life than could a brothel-owner, but resolved to make that life as Chinese as possible.

Ida's six years in Yantai during her late twenties were enriched by little Guijing and her Chinese students. She also began to enjoy a social life she had lacked during her teenage years. Ida especially cared for "Jack of the gray eyes" despite his missionary background. Her social group, in which she soon took a leadership role, included young Westerners from the diplomatic and business communities as well as the missions. Ida pictured herself as a "thread weaving back and forth" between these communities.[34] Her self-image of bringing two worlds together, which she later expressed with words such as "bridge" and "mediator," served as the strong, guiding identity she required to successfully navigate adulthood.

Many years after leaving Yantai, Ida recorded her memories of the foreign community through short stories. Ida's essays focused on marriage, no doubt, as a means to cope with her mother's constant pressure on her to marry. The constant theme of her fictionalized essays was the triumph of duty, responsibility, and authority over feelings of the heart. A tragic tone pervaded all of the stories of expatriate Western marriages. The one exception was an account of Mrs. McMullen who, forced to support herself after her husband's illness, devoted her life to a school for ex-slave girls. Her happiness came from mothering Chinese girls caught between two ways of life, not from a relationship with a man. The parallel between Mrs. McMullen and Ida's own later life in Beijing (named Beiping in the Republican China) is striking. The reader is left to wonder if Mrs. McMullen was a role model for Ida or if Ida re-invented the older woman in her own image.

Ida's depiction of unhappy missionary marriages is in stark contrast to her short stories of Chinese couples. Although traditional Chinese marriages were arrangements by match-makers to suit family needs, and were often polygamous, Ida portrayed the couples as contented and sometimes quite loving. These stories of Chinese and American couples were an ironic reversal of the formulaic missionary literature in which miserable Chinese wives victimized by their pagan husbands were saved by Western Christian women.[35]

The group of friendships for which Ida had longed her entire life was short-lived. In 1914, the foreign community in Yantai was drawn into events begun in Europe. The young men soon departed to serve in the Great War. Several were killed. Among them was her special friend, Jack, who was gassed in Gallipoli. Ida attended a service for Jack in the chapel they had often attended together. "I let the gracious service sink into my soul as I watched the green leaves against the blue sky outside the diamond-shaped panes." As her group of friends fell apart, the conservative climate of both Chinese and Western communities in Yantai, as well as her own family environment, became more stultifying to the young woman. In the summer of 1918, Ida was twenty-nine years old. Restless to experience the modern world, Ida resigned from the Wai Ling Day School for Girls and booked passage for the United States.

Standing on deck with the ship's captain, the glory of the fading sunset around her, Ida felt that she must articulate a question which surely would cut her off forever from her home, family, and church. Afraid that she would drop into an everlasting void, yet intuitively aware that voicing her doubt was a necessary step toward her autonomous identity, Ida spit out her words: "I'm not sure that I believe in the existence of life after death." "Many people feel that way," responded the young officer.

Suddenly Ida found herself "on ground more solid than ever … a great wide plain on which strode strong, vigorous people."[36] They rushed forcefully forward, heads lifted, singing, whistling, and humming. By 1918, when Ida returned to the United States, America had joined the Allies' fight for democracy. Their idealism infected Ida. She found herself drawn to the American cause and wanted to do her part in the struggle.

Neither Ida nor her traveling companion, Edna, knew anyone in America except Ida's family. Anna had left Yantai a year or so beforehand to settle Robert and Mac in Philadelphia. Robert attended the School for the Blind in Overbrook before transferring to the University of Pennsylvania. Mac attended West Philadelphia High School. Hoping to soon return to China, Anna was eager for Ida to begin caring for her two brothers. Thus, Ida and her friend found themselves boarding in a semi-detached, Victorian row house in West Philadelphia with Ida's brothers. Her rebellion against her mother would have to wait. (One way Ida later rebelled against her mother was by smoking. "I knew mother would never approve. So it was with defiance to her controls and ... standards that I lit that first cigarette.")[37]

Together, Ida and Edna searched for employment. Determined not to fall into the same rut from which she had just emerged, Ida refused to consider teaching, one of few available jobs for women. She and Edna applied for factory work. The manager took one look and dismissed them with the offhand comment, "too rough for ladies." Ida began to argue that America was a democratic country without any ladies, but Edna pulled her away.

Through her mother's missionary connections, Ida eventually was hired as a "cub" social worker with the Philadelphia Society of Organizing Charity. It seems that wartime demand for social workers to work with American troops overseas had left a dearth of workers at home. During her year or so as a case worker in Philadelphia, Ida was called upon to do things she never knew existed, so different had been her life from the usual American pattern. Casework was difficult for her. She felt social workers were intrusive and was barely able to live on her salary.

Ida's continuing sense of disconnection from modern American culture was heightened in Philadelphia. She understood her separateness not only as differences in cultures but in economic and historic periods. She felt "cabined" by the organization of American social life into age, same sex, or "young marrieds" groups. "Perhaps the machine made our houses physically more comfortable but it made human relations more difficult and the real comfort of life is in harmonious and pleasant human relations."

Within the year, life as a social worker in a modern American city proved to be no more stimulating for Ida than mission teaching in China. Her social life among other single career women was far less emotionally fulfilling than even the "dull" missionary community in Yantai. Following an especially frustrating encounter with an Italian case in south Philadelphia, Ida resigned from the Family Society. She realized that social work among Italians required studying their language and literature to understand their minds, values, and social patterns. If she were to put so much effort into studying another people, that people would be the Chinese. Ida began searching for a job to take her back to China.[38]

4

From "Women's Work for Women" to Social Work: The Social Service Department at Peking Union Medical College

"**H**ave you heard? The Rockefeller Foundation is looking for a social worker for their new hospital in Peking [Beijing]. They can't decide whether to get someone who knows social work and teach her Chinese or someone who knows Chinese and teach her social work.... You know both. Why don't you apply?" Ida remembers first hearing about the position of medical social worker at the Peking Union Medical College Hospital (PUMC) in this way from her supervisor at the Philadelphia Society of Organizing Charity, Betsey Libby, in the spring of 1919.[1] Edith Shatto King of the National Social Workers' Exchange notified the Rockefeller Foundation of Ida Pruitt as a candidate for their position, but because of Ida's lack of both formal social work training and experience in medical social work, she was not the Foundation's first choice as administrator of social services in the hospital.[2]

By December, when the Rockefeller Foundation remained no closer to finding an experienced social work administrator willing to take on the job in Beijing, Ida again inquired about the position. Letters of recommendations written on her behalf praised her "remarkable grasp of casework problems."[3] Her supervisor at the Philadelphia Society of Organizing Charity believed that Ida's frankness in facing her own family problems (caring for two younger brothers, one of whom was blind, and a Chinese woman friend) gave her casework a distinctive quality. Somehow she was able to help the families face their problems as frankly as she confronted her own. Miss Libby also noted that, like many other caseworkers, Ida's interest lay in human problems, not organization. She was not "instinctively a systematic person."[4]

If, despite her lack of formal training, Ida was a "natural" for casework, her unique qualifications for the position in Beijing obviously were a knowledge of the Chinese people and language possible only by growing up among the Chinese.[5] Indeed, throughout her eighteen years at the PUMC, Ida was criticized for various failings as an administrator, but her critics always were forced to concede her unique ability to understand and relate effectively to the Chinese patients and their families.

On February 22, 1920, Dr. Franklin C. McLean, director of the PUMC, 1916–1920, wrote to Henry Houghton, director, 1921–1928, notifying him of Ida Pruitt's appointment as medical social worker. This was an appointment which particularly pleased McLean, but not because of Ida's unique familiarity with China and the Chinese. Rather, he noted her background as a missionary teacher and daughter of long-time Southern Baptist missionaries to China. This must have impressed the Rockefeller Foundation trustees, among whom several represented mission boards in the United States. Ida's appointment as medical social worker at the PUMC was approved.[6]

The Peking Union Medical College (Beijing Xiehe Yiyuan) was incorporated in July 1913, after a Rockefeller-funded commission first explored the possibility of creating a nondenominational, Christian university for medical research in China in 1906. This interest paralleled the increasing American awareness of China in the early twentieth century, as well as the Rockefeller Foundation's entry into medical education. John D. Rockefeller, Jr. was a devout Baptist. His personal religious convictions, as well as his interest in China, ensured the institution's ongoing Christian character.

Ida was the obvious choice for the position because of her grounding in the culture and language of China and her experience as a social worker. In the eyes of the Foundation and the China Medical Board, Ida's most significant qualification was her missionary background. They hoped her Southern Baptist credentials would provide the Foundation a means to bridge the distance between the religious and secular methods of trying to "save" China.

However, thirty-one-year old Ida was no longer a missionary and her self-identification with the Chinese separated her from American secular reformers. Her motivations for seeking the PUMC position were, first, a simple desire to find a way to support herself while living in the country and among the people she understood and loved, and, second, to "be somebody," to have a career and professional colleagues and friends. Through the years, she encountered some criticism from the PUMC administration for failing to meet their unarticulated expectations of her as a missionary.

The image of "bridge" suited Ida well, however. One of her major roles at the PUMC, as elsewhere, was that of mediator between the Chinese and American peoples and cultures, and ironically, between the Chinese patients and medical personnel.[7]

Ida was put on the Rockefeller payroll immediately after her hire in early 1920. Because of her inexperience in medical social work, she was sent to Massachusetts General Hospital to work for a year with Ida Cannon.[8] This internship, of sorts, had a formative influence on Ida's ideas about medical social work. Her own principles and methods of approaching medical social work, though interpreted and implemented differently in Beijing, echoed both Ida Cannon's work and the thoughts of Dr. Richard Cabot, who founded the field of medical social work at Massachusetts General Hospital in 1905.[9]

Ida Pruitt absorbed Cannon's ideas about the importance of social readjustment of the individual to society, the emphasis on individual character change over social factors in disease and health, the careful study of the subtle reaction of human nature to circumstances, and the preferred use of casework before all other methods of work. She also seemed to have learned the secret of Ida Cannon's interviewing technique—the use of indirection for maximum disclosure of unexpected sources of anxiety and difficulty. She later repeated to her students Cannon's principle of considering the patient's own plan for implementing the physician's instructions. Her ease at learning these principles and methods of social casework came, perhaps, because she was a "natural" as her supervisor in Philadelphia had put it.

She may have been a "natural" at indirection and gaining the patients' cooperation because of the early role model she had in her Chinese amah, "Dada." Her challenge to the technical orientation of modern Western medicine, which her missionary mother admired and studied in the Chinese interior, arose both from her childhood in a Chinese village and from her professional training with the pioneers in the modern American social work profession.

If Ida learned the principles and methods of hospital social work with ease, she lacked initiative in implementing the administrative ideas at Massachusetts General Hospital. Cannon questioned Ida's capacity for executive work, noting "readjustment was difficult for her." Cannon was concerned enough to recommend psychiatric treatment to help Ida overcome a "lack" in some unspecified "fundamental things." She voiced her reservations about Ida's appointment to the position in Beijing to Henry Houghton, the director, but he decided that Ida was still appropriate for the job. Cannon could only hope for the best, reporting shortly before Ida's departure for China that the psychiatrists seemed "distinctly helpful to her point of view."[10]

What were the "fundamental things" which Ida lacked? What was so wrong with her "point of view" that Cannon reconsidered her initial recommendation of Ida for the PUMC position? Basically, Ida's point of view was not that of an American woman who had grown to adulthood during the first generation of professional opportunities for women. She did not share the "new spirit" that accompanied the final drive for women's suffrage before its final passage in 1920.[11]

Ida was not an emancipated, career-oriented woman who had learned to take initiative. She had learned the Chinese students' passivity that left the burden of thinking on the teacher. The New Thought Movement of the 1919 May Fourth era had not affected Ida, who later described her lack of initiative: "I had been brought up in the old culture that had not yet made any changes. Everything had always been arranged for me...."[12] It never occurred to Ida to ask questions of Miss Cannon or the supervisors. "One does not question one's teacher or answer back."[13]

The "New American Women" who filled the ranks of the teaching and social work professions had learned to combine an assertiveness necessary in a career with traditional images of women as "tender mothers, angels of mercy, and keepers of the morals" in order to avoid threatening men.[14] In contrast, Ida's images of women consisted of her mother's dominant role in the family and in her school, and her Dada's role as a traditional Chinese woman. Each woman combined assertiveness with submissiveness, but in ways very different from American "angels of mercy." Their "points of view" certainly were different from those of American women. This must have led to dissonance between Ida and her social work teachers in Boston. In later years, Ida's style at the PUMC was more personal than professional. She involved herself in patient and employee lives in ways that modern Americans found intrusive and meddling. In short, she played the role of a Chinese grandmother in a family, which threatened her male colleagues in ways American women administrators could avoid.

Not only was Ida's style and viewpoint representative of a different culture, but it also was reminiscent of an earlier stage of social work in the United States. In 1890, charity work, predecessor of professional casework, involved a personal concern for an individual's spiritual and material elevation. Ida retained and thrived on this personal involvement with individual patients and their families. By the 1920s, social work in the United States called for efficient administration, according to a prominent social work educator. The "passion for professionalism" demanded specialization. This, in turn, demanded objective, scientific attitudes toward the problem and the client, "peculiarly suited to fluidity and the impersonality of an urban-industrial world." Ida belonged to a static, highly personal, pre-industrial world. Efficiency and managerial qualities were hardly her strong suit.[15]

Ida was aware how different her worldview was from that of Bostonians. "Those first six months were the grimmest months I ever spent. Never before or since have I been so lonely." No one realized that the American social work student was as disoriented as any other foreign student. No one considered including Ida in the international student orientations. The experience later made her sympathetic with the Western-born Chinese students in Beijing.[16]

Ida's loneliness was compounded by her association with young doctors at Massachusetts General Hospital, "very desirable young doctors ... the kind of men I wholly approved of...." But she was focused on training for her position at the PUMC and did not get involved with any of the men. Looking out over the Charles River at night, Ida perceived that the laborers and their girlfriends huddled on the benches had a fuller life than she had.[17]

At noon, Ida often sought out the Chinese collection at the Museum of Art. She always visited a standing Buddha, whose heavy lids were lowered as though he were looking into the far distance or within himself.

> The corners of his mouth curled upward and as I watched their upward curve the tendrils of my soul which had snarled and wrapped themselves into a tight knot would gradually uncurl. He seemed to be saying, "Eons have passed and eons will come. Why let the little things of life perturb you?" And I would leave in peace.[18]

Thus Ida negotiated the alien emotional terrain of the United States. She likened her struggle to building a bridge, "strand by strand across the Pacific to be able to walk in comfort in both [worlds]." After completing the social work program at Massachusetts General Hospital in April 1921, she once again departed for China. In a reference to the Chinese-style architecture of the PUMC, she asserted expansively, "I could go through the great, high vermillion gates waiting ajar for me under the roof of green glazed tiles." Her bridge felt solid. "I walked toward the great wide gate waiting for me—to pass through and enter a world as an independent human being and do the work I should do and enjoy being alive."[19]

Early Years of the Social Service Department

Ida had visited Beijing in 1915, just three years after the Chinese empire became a Republic. The capitol had already begun to modernize. By the time of her return six years later, telephone and motorized transportation, electric lights and trolleys, cinemas, newspapers, factories, and modern government bureaucracy imposed a Westernized urban overlay on the ancient city's pattern.[20]

More than in other Chinese cities, modern inventions and traditional patterns co-existed.[21] The PUMC actively promoted modern Western medical technology and social reforms. Ida's rural Chinese background and social work training both predisposed her to work within Chinese tradition on her patients' behalf. Her position as hospital social worker within the reformist institution became that of mediator between the modern West and traditional China.

Ida's arrival in Beijing, May 1921, marked the end of the Rockefeller Foundation's two-year study of hospital social service, their search for a social worker and the beginning of the Social Service Department of the PUMC. The only trained social workers in China at the time were a few secretaries in the Young Women's Christian Association (YWCA). Trained in organizational development, they practiced a very different kind of social work from the casework begun by Ida Pruitt at the PUMC.

The president of the Rockefeller Foundation, George E. Vincent, accompanied Ida on her round of home visits during his tour of the PUMC at the end of Ida's first year there. He later reported that Ida's friendly approach and her fluent Chinese evidently made a favorable impression on the patient, family, and the assemblage of neighbors who gathered to observe the foreigners. The scene he described was similar to the missionary home visitations that as a child Ida had made with her mother. Her qualifications and aptitude for the job, so obvious to Vincent, were a product of her missionary past, even while Ida rejected the goals of missionaries.

In this phase of development, social work leaders were unclear whether hospital social work principles and methods were transferable to China. Ida was confident that American social work methods would succeed in China. "We soon found that human needs and human nature are the same the world around. A Chinese may cut his coat on a different pattern from that of an American, but what he wears is a coat after all."[22] Ida's idealistic belief in the universality of human nature, based on her father's sermons, had not changed twenty years after she first proclaimed it in Cox College's student magazine. Ida's perspective about human nature and human needs was clearly reflected in her articles about social work in China. As in her other writings, she utilized simple examples from her casework to explain herself. In any country, she wrote, those without pain need a note or home visit to remind them to return to the hospital for a check-up. The social worker's job was gently to remind the patient of the check-up. Perhaps bus-fare to the clinic was needed. The social workers wrote letters to the patient's employer asking permission for the patient to attend the clinic, and performed other tasks particular to the situation.[23]

The same human emotions, in Ida's view, led to different points of resistance to the social worker because of different cultural patterns. For instance, there was less resistance in China than in the United States about disclosing personal family information. Resistance was considerably greater in China about financial matters; secrecy was a family's only protection from hordes of distant relatives and the "squeeze" of the tax collectors.[24]

Ida's sense of common humanity behind different cultural patterns between the Chinese and the American people, of which she first wrote in her college magazine, contrasted with most missionaries' and other Westerners' views, who historically have seen East-West differences as virtually immutable. For missionaries, the critical difference was that between Christian and pagan: the Saved and the Damned. Missionary women's belief in a universal womanhood simply assumed women's special, separate nature outside of history and culture. Ida rejected their analysis of women's special nature. The popular secular version of this view is the commonplace that Orientals are "inscrutable" and regard human life cheaply, and thus are hardly human, as we understand the word. The popular press, the visual media, and politicians have all helped perpetuate this idea that the East-West gap is between fundamentally different beings.[25]

The image of beings fundamentally different from Westerners led

American reformers, both religious and secular, to attempt to remold the Chinese into their own image. The nineteenth century image was of individual religious conversion to Christianity. The twentieth century image became societal conversion to democracy and material progress.[26] In contrast, Ida's assumption of the common humanity of Americans and Chinese was in accord with her goal at the Social Service Department of the PUMC. It was not one of individual religious conversion or social change but rather social harmony. She trusted that Chinese society has evolved methods satisfactory to itself to resolve life's major problems. The goal of her department was to "get the patient back into social life to the place for which he or she is best fitted." In the vast majority of cases, this meant his family, where everyone knew his lot, functions, place, and what would happen to him.[27]

Ida's goal of social harmony might be seen as traditional Chinese fatalism but was consistent with the modern American social work profession as taught by Dr. Richard Cabot, founder of medical social work, and her teacher, Ida Cannon. Arising from both her Chinese upbringing and her professional social work training, her goal was a far cry from her parents' goal of Christianizing China through conversion of individual Chinese, and from her PUMC colleagues' goal of reforming, modernizing, and Westernizing the Chinese. Ida had found a career compatible with her bicultural identity.

Social Casework at the PUMC

As it evolved, the work of the Social Service Department was divided into three main categories: regular clinic and ward visits, in which every patient was seen at least once; home visits; and record-keeping.[28] Routine ward cases included: cardiac, tubercular, carcinoma, orthopedic, unmarried mothers, syphilis, gastro-intestinal, and obstetrical and gynecological.[29] Clinics included: general medical, general surgical, cardiac, skin, syphilis, ear-nose-throat, and genitourinary, men's orthopedic tubercular bone, and tumor.[30]

Cases fell into four basic categories. First were those needing no outside resources. The social worker served to coordinate and communicate between relatives and other social resources, and to clarify the medical treatment to the patient and family. The majority of cases were of this category. Cases cared for wholly by the Social Service Department fell into the second category. Third were those referred to other agencies. In the last category were those cases dropped because the patient proved unable to perform the job found by the social worker, the family refused aid, or the patient was "character deficient, a drifter, or waster."[31] Ida clearly preferred the second type of case that the department handled from start to finish. By and large, it is this type from which she drew her stories about the department.

Although casework remained the primary technique used during Ida's administration of the department, her staff also engaged group work, reform, and research. Ida was instrumental in founding a number of social service agencies to provide support systems for her clients whose families were unable to perform this traditional function in Chinese society. Her department provided social workers to several social reform efforts and opened the 40,000 casework records to social researchers.[32] But the real "work from the heart" lay in the individual cases of Chinese patients and their families.

Ida was criticized for sloppy record keeping and insufficient attention to statistical research, to which she responded, "We have no statistical way of measuring the success of the adjustments to life made for the patients." She was content with the personal reports by former patients about their successful reintegration into society.[33] Individual re-adjustment to life in the transitional society of Beijing during the 1920s and 1930s remained the focus of both Ida's social work and her professional articles. Her later literary writing tapped into the same theme.

The interview method was key to understanding the patient and his situation due to space limitations. Interviews with patients were conducted while sitting in the hospital corridors. Ida believed that the public nature of such interviews ironically made the patients feel less self-conscious with the social worker. The systematic note taking and routine of the corridor-interview gave patients confidence that the procedure was part of the hospital pattern. If the patient seemed nervous about others hearing his story, and after his confidence was gained, a consulting room could be made available.

From her office, Ida could overhear much of her staff's interviews with patients. "When I hear the voice of the social worker more than that of the patient; it is not a good interview...."[34] According to one staff member, "Anyone who has worked with Miss Pruitt for some time will be familiar with one statement, 'Know your patients.'"[35] It seemed a difficult lesson. Ida repeatedly stressed the importance of recording the patient's beliefs about himself and the world, even if those beliefs appeared on the

surface to be far from reality.... Such beliefs would show the pattern of
the patients' fears and misconceptions, and therefore give the social
worker insights into the real situation.

Ida stressed as another fundamental principle that the patient's own
plans worked best. When the patient was told clearly about his physical
limitations and needs, as well as the community resources available to
him, he often was able to plan for his future.[36]

Initial home interviews of patients' families, neighbors, employers,
and co-workers, then follow-up home visits after the patients' release
from the hospital were essential parts of the casework method. Many a
medical prescription had to be altered after learning the patient's overall
life situation. Such was the case of the policeman advised by his doctor to
cut down on his workload due to heart problems. The caseworker
discovered that the man already had a light workload as a night desk clerk.
The man's heart trouble was only one of many family problems,
including malnutrition of all members and the death of the baby. His
problem was extreme poverty because the government owed him many
months' back pay. Hunger was a problem shared by at least seventeen per
cent of households who comprised Beijing's lowest income group.[37]

The Social Service Department tackled the problem of finding food,
shelter, and jobs for patients' family members.[38] "Often the rickshaw puller
gossiping outside the gate brought us more information than the social
worker talking inside." They were able to travel to parts of the city where
young, well-dressed women could not go. The task of pullers or "coolies"
generally was to convince the patient to return to the hospital for a check-
up.[39] Like the Social Service clients, rickshaw pullers lived a precarious
existence as members of the lower working class. They, too, lived in the
poor houses of Beijing's winding, warren-like alleys (*hutong*). Among their
peers, the "pullers" exchanged news and rumors. They were "perpetual
witnesses and occasional actors" in the history of Republican China.[40]

Ida came to depend on such sources of information concerning her
patients because her focus was on understanding the individual within the
social pattern of his life. She knew the limits of her own ability to
uncover the whole picture of a person's life. She recognized that even her
Chinese workers—urban, college-educated, and modern—needed to
listen to the patient and see his world before solving his problems.

This attitude presupposed a basic rationality on the part of the patient.
Ida insisted that the patients' wants and refusals were reasonable, if not
always readily apparent. One old lady from a wealthy warlord family

asked the Social Service Department to arrange the adoption of her fifteen-year-old grandson. Ida was accustomed to taking unwanted babies from poor families, but this was the only son of a wealthy and powerful family. Why should he be given up to an adopted family? During the course of conversation, the elderly woman's reasoning emerged. She had seen another amputee on the ward who was adopted by a hospital physician and sent to the Presbyterian Mission School. She would do anything, even give up the only family heir, to get the boy into a Western school.[41] When Ida explained that the Chinese woman could apply for her grandson's admission to the Presbyterian School as well as the doctor could, the old lady spoke no more of adoption and began recounting to Ida the lad's wedding preparations.

Looking back on her years at the PUMC, after meeting many thousands of patients and their families and solving their problems case by case, Ida found herself asking basic questions about all of the age old problems which the department handled: When does the comfort of the individual give way to the good of the family or society? When is the divide between the old and new crossed and the new set of values become dominant?[42]

The strain between the group and the individual was a tension between tradition and change, between the old order of the Chinese village of Ida's childhood and the new order of the Rockefeller medical research hospital. It is this friction of which Ida wrote in both her professional articles and her many short stories about the PUMC patients. She picked a few cases and reworked them in her stories about Old Beijing, cases she felt best exemplified the typical patient problems and departmental solutions.

Often, the department played a mediating role. One particular difficult case involved a typhoid patient who refused to continue treatment and insisted on returning home at great risk to his life. Ida discovered that his reason for leaving the hospital was worry about his wife's health. The wife was extremely upset, believing him to be with another woman rather than in the hospital. The old mother-in-law had tried to clear up the confusion by verifying her son-in-law's presence in the hospital. However, she had used his "milk name," while he had registered under a completely different "school name." Ida finally persuaded a delegation of village elders to make the journey into the city and verify the man's hospitalization. At that point, both husband and wife were able to calm down and recuperate.[43]

When necessary, the PUMC Social Service Department functioned to legitimate the new order against the old. To one young couple whose complex family problems had provoked epigastric pains in the wife, the Social Service Department "represented modern public opinion in showing them it was right to move out of the family home." Ironically, to further her modern goal, Ida styled herself as a traditional grandmother/mother-in-law by considering the needs of the entire family.[44]

Most patients' social needs required a combination of Rockefeller resources and familial support. Where the family had broken down, Ida stepped in with agency support services. The innumerable cases of malnourished infants were examples of cases needing immediate material aid and Western-style social service agencies. (Klim infant formula if no wet-nurse was available, foster care in either the Women's Hostel or the "Home-Finding Society," and other medical care.) If the mother or another nursing woman was able to care for the baby, Ida preferred to supplement the woman's meals to build up her milk supply rather than providing infant formula. Each foster family was closely monitored and studied to understand the problems that had led to the infant's malnutrition. Solutions adhered to traditional patterns as much as possible.[45]

A very large majority of PUMC patients had contracted tuberculosis, which complicated other medical and social problems. Much time was spent teaching patients and their families the use of sputum cups, separate eating bowls and chopsticks, and separate sleeping quarters. However, Ida recognized that tuberculosis, then the chief cause of death in the world, was a disease of poverty. All the sputum cups in the world were as useless as the missionary injunctions against paganism had been in nineteenth century medical work as long as the root causes of filth and poverty remained. "What could the hospital or the Public Health Department do for those … who never had enough to eat?"[46]

Traditional reasons for such financial duress included individual illness, natural disasters, crop failure, and the like. Ida's department could struggle against these hardships, providing temporary relief until better times returned and finding jobs for those permanently uprooted from the land. Family-based patterns for resolving problems remained useful.

However, Beijing was undergoing turbulent social upheaval that defied either traditional solutions or modern social work strategies. Within five years after the 1911 Republican Revolution, the Chinese government experienced a leadership vacuum that hundreds of contending local warlords failed to fill. Beijing's government leadership repeatedly changed hands. Government services and social order deteriorated. Public morale plummeted. Manchu noblemen and bannermen accustomed to "eating Yellow Grain," that is, receiving a stipend from the Emperor, became a drain on national coffers.

The 1917 Russian Revolution produced a flood of refugees from Siberia to Tianjin and then Beijing. British, Americans, Germans, and other foreign businesses introduced industrial factories, breaking up the old handicraft economy so crucial to the Chinese farmers' incomes. By the early 1930s Japan joined the ranks of foreign powers occupying ever-greater parts of north China. Farmers increasingly were unable to meet their expenses and were forced off their land and into the cities, joining the ranks of rickshaw pullers and factory workers who were paid less than living wages.

Warlord politics during the 1920s produced six major wars on the north China plain. Troops occupied peasant homes and requisitioned their food. Men were often conscripted into competing armies, while the women and children flooded into Beijing for safety. By 1926, 200,000 to 300,000 refugees vied for scarce city resources. On a single day, as many as 30,000 rushed through Beijing's Xizhi Gate, alone. Police reported finding a daily average of thirty-five bodies—residents and refugees who died of cold and hunger in spite of government soup kitchens that served 80,000 meals a day.[47]

The wars generally were fought along the railroad lines and so disrupted Beijing's system of communications and distribution of food and coal.[48] Hordes of unkempt soldiers, suffering from syphilis, tuberculosis, trachoma, and dysentery, overwhelmed hospital clinics.

As the multiple crises of twentieth century China played on each other and expanded exponentially, patients' financial duress was increasingly harder to resolve in traditional ways. Finding employment for members of the patients' families became increasingly difficult.[49] The husband of one twenty-seven-year-old woman who died of pneumonia might have been speaking for millions when he sobbed, angrily, "My wife died of poverty and worry and lack of food."[50]

Ida's individual, personalized study of each patient, his family, and community resources gave way to fund-raising, organizing, and staffing a millet gruel station for refugees.[51] But the demands of institutionalized work for the Chinese, which had so invigorated her mother, drained Ida. Ida's gift was finding help for her patients from within their own culture so as to minimize their dependence on foreign assistance and maximize their ability to help themselves in their own ways. By the 1930s, this approach to social service could no longer help a people caught in the middle of a century of revolution.

Ida left no record that she questioned her individualized, traditional approach. But the staggering workload of the department and her increasing dissatisfaction with the job she had loved spoke for her. Instead of complaining, Ida focused on preserving the lives of common Chinese people among whom she grew up, and who she had grown to know better through her social work. She began recording the stories of her patients. She gathered poems, temple inscriptions, lore about Beijing's buildings, historical notes about Chinese opera, and contemporary folk tales circulating in the city.

Ida recorded her patients' cases more as an outside observer than as an involved social worker. In professional journal articles, she attributed individual clients' actions to rational reasons or universal emotions that readers from other cultures could understand, a theme which she later elaborated in her fictional stories. Her perspective, though based on her identification with traditional Chinese popular culture, in some ways was consistent with twentieth century social workers' training.[52] By establishing and developing the Social Service Department, Ida consolidated her own identity. By writing about her cases, she tried to preserve the Chinese common people's identity.

In her professional articles, Ida occasionally adopted a literary style. "The Mother Has Wrapped Her Heart around the Child" is from *Hospital Social Service*, not a short story. In "The Flood," her theme was the close margin of life for the flood victims, who depended on one man's earnings to care for ten or more family members. "Sketches of Relief Work in Peiping, China" emphasized the heroic and courageous acts of the common people. Neither of these reports discussed social service work per se. Ida's professional articles about urban problems usually made a link with agrarian peasant life. Discussing Chinese students, she compared their insecure toehold in the modern age with peasants' sturdy grounding in the past. Peasants might be bewildered by the changes brought by the twentieth century but they were not lost as were the students.

Ida's favorable treatment of Chinese peasants developed out of her rural childhood environment and home life. Her earliest memories were of a loving Chinese mother figure and her sinified father. C.W. Pruitt plowed the north Georgian fields as a boy and lived as poorly and simply as the Chinese peasants to whom he devoted his life. In Ida's eyes, her father, and by association, the Chinese peasantry, were "as genuinely good as anyone I know."[53]

The positive, universalistic thrust of Ida's writing about Chinese people contrasted sharply with the negative, irrational portrayal of Chinese and other non-Christian peoples in the writings of her mother and several generations of missionary women. The missionary legacy, visible in best-selling books, films and public policy toward Asia, has lasted throughout the twentieth century and into the twenty-first.[54] Co-existing with this image of Chinese as other, as a minor theme, stands the image of our common humanity in Ida's work and writing.

5

Chief of Social Service, Departmental Dowager, and a Dangerous Woman

I da Pruitt headed the Social Service Department at the Peking Union Medical College (PUMC) from 1921 until 1939. In this position, she recruited and trained the first social caseworkers in China and established hospital social work as a permanent department in the PUMC.

Ida's staff during the early years consisted of two Chinese chosen for their familiarity with the traditional Chinese social structures and customs. Mr. Wang Zeming was a Manchu hired shortly before Ida's arrival. He had studied in the School of Mongolian and Tibetan Affairs and knew Beijing inside out, especially the customs of the north, including Mongolia and Tibet. The other staff member had been a teacher in the Chefoo Mission School where Ida had taught years before. She was "of the people," having grown up in a rural village, yet she knew something of the new through her association with the mission school. Ida valued her common sense and knowledge of the popular customs.[1] Subsequent staff members consisted predominantly of Yenching (Yanjing) University sociology majors due to the proximity of the university to the PUMC. Soon students from Shanghai College, Jinling College, Tsinghua (Qinghua) College, and Cheeloo (Qilu) University also participated in the work of the Social Service Department as unpaid apprentices supervised by a senior staff member. Cantonese, Fujianese, and most other dialects of China were represented on the staff at most times.[2] By 1938 Ida had expanded her department to a staff of ten men and twenty-four women, of whom two were Russian interpreters.[3]

Ida selected student social workers from sociology departments of major colleges and universities, assuming educated youth to have initiative and "elastic minds" for creating and executing plans.[4] However, college students generally were from wealthy homes and assumed their duty as students was to learn new Western social patterns. Ida, viewing Beijing as one large village with an overlapping of imperial and Manchu patterns, wanted students to understand the structure of traditional village China. Therefore, all but one of her students was selected from moderate-income families, that they might better understand the poor from the experience of their families and neighbors.

The qualities Ida sought in a social worker were difficult to find. Most sociology students were interested in "prestige and adequate salaries," and thus unwilling to gamble on an unknown field. "Public-spirited" students, on the other hand, turned to either religious organizations or teaching. Another vaguely stated feeling associated social work with almsgiving, and therefore a less than suitable profession for the college-educated.

Once chosen, student social workers were trained on the job, where "much of the teaching was incidental to the care of the patients."[5] By the early 1930s, an apprenticeship system of three years was developed, consisting of a caseload, conferences, and lectures. Ida, herself, lectured twice a week and conducted daily conferences with some staff. (She also lectured in "Casework Methods" at Yenching University until 1936.) Volunteer American social workers and two Chinese workers trained in American schools of social work made up the supervisors.[6] Until 1930, all trained workers were absorbed by the PUMC, as female workers stepped down to marry. Thereafter other hospitals and social agencies requested social workers and sometimes sent their own personnel to be trained in social work at the PUMC.[7] Others among Ida's students went on to practice social work throughout China as well as overseas. One of Ida's protégés pioneered social work courses at the University of Hong Kong. Her students became the "pillars of Hong Kong social agencies."[8]

Ida became known as the founder of social casework in China. She was credited with developing a highly efficient social service department at the PUMC that broke the ground for medical social service. Her department was praised in a report of the PUMC as conducting a "mission of friendship" to the Chinese public that attained "unbelievable follow-up results."[9]

However, the department and Ida remained at the center of controversy throughout her eighteen years at the PUMC. Ida's ongoing difficulties with hospital administration and some physicians involved many dynamics, including Ida's position in the hospital hierarchy, her gender, rivalry between nursing and social work, and her self-appointed roles as mediator and dowager at the hospital.

Ida's ongoing difficulties with hospital administration and physicians no doubt partially derived from her administrative status. Ida's position as medical social worker and later as chief of social service equaled that of a medical department head. She reported directly to the director of the hospital, an honor shared with only one other woman, the dean of the School of Nursing.[10] This high status as a woman administrator at the PUMC raised Ida's visibility within the institution, a situation that brought mixed blessings. At the PUMC, as in the United States, male medical and administrative personnel were not accustomed to staff women in positions of equality. The nurses at the PUMC, as in U.S. hospitals, were the doctors' assistants. They were instructed in "silent submission to discipline" under male physicians.[11] Only the social worker was in a "position of self-reliant judgment and planning in her own sphere." She was therefore the physicians' consultant and peer.[12]

Ida found herself and her department at odds with both the hospital administration and the public health workers. Her defense of high professional standards was in response to Director Roger Greene and his successor Henry Haughton's efforts to replace trained social workers with trained public health nurses or untrained Chinese staff. This was a common political issue in American hospitals at the time. Medical social workers were continually called upon by hospital administrators to justify the expense of their department, the only hospital department that did not bring in income on a "fee for service" basis.[13] In 1923 the PUMC administration distributed a hospital-wide questionnaire about the value of the Social Service Department for the various medical departments and clinics. In 1938, the administration finally succeeded in strengthening the role of the public health nurses and downplaying the role of the social caseworkers with the non-renewal of Ida's contract.[14]

When the PUMC administration questioned her about the intrusion of her workers into physicians' and nurses' areas, she reassured them to the contrary. In the questionnaires distributed to department heads during the 1923 reappraisal of the Social Service Department, most medical department heads called her work valuable, even indispensable. The head of neurology, Andrew Woods, wrote that Ida's work was "distinctly helpful, even signal" to the task of getting patient background. Woods observed the social workers as uncommonly willing to help the doctors. Their interpretations went beyond simple language translation to explaining the clinician's meaning to the patient and family. The social workers created in the patients a willingness to return for follow-up observations and treatment, which alone warranted the continuation of the Social Service Department, in Wood's view.[15]

Ida probably did not initially see her role as social worker among medical doctors in conflicting terms.[16] By the time the underlying conflicts between Ida and the medical administration surfaced during the 1923 reappraisal of the Social Service Department, her contact with patients had clarified to Ida her differences with the medical administration. This time, she didn't reject the PUMC, as she had the missionaries. She knew that many staff doctors valued her department's work. Further, she realized the social work profession was similarly attacked in the United States. Instead of leaving, Ida dug in to do her job properly.

Some staff members were also dissatisfied with their department chief. One criticized the quality of caseworker. He characterized Ida's methods of selection and training as *shou zhu dai tu* (waiting under the same tree where a rabbit once was found dead for more to come).[17]

Ida instinctively avoided angering her staff. She spent a great deal of energy trying to develop the potential of all staff members, even those with obvious limitations. Whether consciously or not, Ida was operating as the grandmother/mother-in-law of the departmental family, not the professional administrator. The dowager's familial role wasn't to "up build" the family by expelling unsatisfactory members, but to train each member to participate in the family as best he could.[18]

Like the dowager of a family, Ida took on ultimate responsibility for all departmental matters. At times, this role became overwhelming and she lost her temper with the staff. Her detailed, step-by-step instructions to the workers, necessary for the slower members, became irritating to others, who complained that she treated them like children.[19] Ida unconsciously followed the traditional Chinese pattern of mutual responsibility and obligations that she so admired. She placed herself in the role of strong female figure within the family, a role she later described in two books. Ida naturally took on the responsibilities and assumed her staff would dutifully oblige. Ironically, these Western-educated, urban students were following the modern, American pattern of more egalitarian relationships between professional colleagues. Ida was "undemocratic," "unfriendly," and "bossy," to one student, who later considered herself more American than Ida.[20]

If Ida embodied the more notorious qualities of the grandmother/

mother-in-law to her students, she also offered them the enveloping warmth, acceptance, and lifelong guidance promised by close familial relationships. Friends characterized Ida in similar terms.[21] Some staff valued this relationship with their boss. The student who later founded social work in Hong Kong remembered Ida as "a loving parent who saw you as a child, never mind you're already a professional expert. I learned so much from her through direct teaching, observation, and inspiration which enabled me to develop into an independent person in my later years."[22]

The major tension at the hospital for Ida was between the Western-oriented physicians and the Chinese patients. No doubt she was acutely aware of the patients' and staff's growing nationalistic feelings after the May Thirtieth Movement of 1925. This escalating series of demonstrations was provoked by British and Japanese killing of Chinese factory workers in Shanghai. By early June, student demonstrators in Beijing marched to the Legation Quarter, which was just across Chang'an Street from the PUMC. They mobilized townspeople at rickshaw stands, teahouses, and other public spaces. The massive assembly at Tiananmen Square on June 10 included contingents from all walks of life: workers, rickshaw pullers, servants, guards and peasants, as well as students and professionals.[23]

Sensitive about the Rockefeller hospital's presence in an increasingly anti-foreign environment, her concern focused on the Chinese doctors, who were almost as foreign to their patients as were the genuine "long-nosed" doctors. Almost inevitably they were from modern, urban, educated families in the coastal cities, while their patients were of the Beijing *hutong* (twisting alleyways) or the rural villages. Only five of the medical students accepted by the PUMC between 1931 and 1943 were not from missionary-sponsored colleges, a phenomenon that "de-nationalized" them, according to the nationalistic students from Chinese schools. Certainly, since tuition and expenses at the PUMC were ten times greater than at the next most expensive medical school in China, such future doctors were a highly specialized, Western-oriented elite with shallow roots in the Chinese soil.[24]

In case after case, Ida found the problem lay, on the one hand, in the physicians' lack of understanding of the patients' circumstances and mental pattern before prescribing medicine and treatments. On the other hand, the patient frequently failed to respond clearly to the physicians' questions out of fear, anxiety, or simply a language barrier.

Since English was designated as the hospital's official language, Ida's bilingual ability was one of her strongest qualifications for the position of social worker. More surprising, she also interpreted and mediated among the Chinese—between doctors and patients, and between patients and their families, employers, social agencies, and other community organizations.[25]

A simple but significant case typified Ida's role in the hospital. During rounds one morning, an old country woman, sitting cross-legged in the middle of the hospital bed, said flatly, "Doctor, I want to go home." "Yes, you are well. You may go home," said the professor of medicine, his face that of a calm, thoughtful scientist. "But doctor, I want to go home," the woman repeated, her face puckering. The professor had spoken perfect Mandarin, but his Hunanese intonation was unintelligible to the woman. The resident physician stepped forward, but his Anhui accent betrayed him. The intern tried, but his Sichuan tones mystified the woman. So Ida, the only foreigner in the group, communicated the message to the patient. "With the intonations of the country people, which these highly bred and highly educated men would have been unwilling to use, I said exactly the same words as they had used and the old woman settled back content."[26] The gulf was not only between Westerners and the Chinese, but as this story illustrates, between Chinese professionals and the country people.

Ida's critique of the modern health care system arose from both her professional training as a social worker and her childhood in a Chinese village.[27] Ida's rational support for the position of social work leaders, who emphasized "adapting" clients to the world from which they came, was built on an emotional foundation—her anger toward her mother and other missionary healers. They treated individual Chinese peasants' maladies, but the missionary movement to which they belonged disrupted the fabric of Chinese family and village life. The social work critique of modern medicine may well have given Ida a critical analysis of western medical care where previously she simply felt hostility.

Ida labored hard to teach the mediator role to her staff. The concept in her mind was a *shuohede*, one who "talked into harmony." Her literary and autobiographical writings praised this old Chinese pattern of settling arguments within families, between families, or between villages:

> Often, when I was a child, as we walked through the village, we would see a knot of men, sitting on their heels in a circle, discussing some problem. One man and then another would speak and the mediator, the *shuohede*

would nod and say, Yes, he also has some portion of the logic of the pattern. *Ta ye yo li.* They would discuss for hours or even days until an agreement was reached between all of them.[28]

As the senior member of the social service departmental family, then, Ida mediated between members of the family, between members of the greater PUMC community, and between the community and outsiders. Perhaps her model for matriarchal mediator was her friend, Old Madam Yin, whose story Ida would later write. Each was a "busy, responsible, and gracious woman with a taste of power in her own sphere." Ida admired and emulated Madam Yin's keen sensitivity to interpersonal relations and the exquisite tact with which she mediated conflict and circumvented future crises.[29]

Ida saw herself in a similar role at the hospital. Many of her hospital vignettes portrayed herself as mediator, her tone of frustration about the doctor-patient gap mixed with a sense of accomplishment for bridging that gap.[30] She explained to the American doctors that a Chinese father didn't want to take his son home from the hospital because he could not feed the boy. She intervened between a doctor and his technician who refused to feed the mice correctly until the reasons for the procedure were explained to him. She gained the confidence of a woman patient by talking with her in the flat Shandong intonation. Her "Shandong friend" credited Ida, not the doctors or hospital, for saving the lives of her entire family. The daily tasks of arranging adoptions for babies, seeking jobs for patients or their relatives, and ordering caskets for indigent patients who died were all seen by the Chinese, and Ida herself, as mediating or go-between functions. Of a man whose wife's funeral she arranged and whose children she placed temporarily in foster care, Ida remarked, "As so often happens, he then clung to me as to an elder of his own family."[31]

Dr. Joshua Horn, writing about health care delivery in the People's Republic of China, reported that patients often selected their own representatives to convey their opinions and suggestions to the doctors, nurses, and orderlies.[32] In the model American hospital of the 1920s and 1930s, the patients' representative was Ida Pruitt. The patients called her Pu Jiaoshi, "Teacher Pruitt," as they respectfully kowtowed to her. (She tried to stop them before their heads reached the floor.) "Teacher" was an honorific title reflective of Confucianism's high estimation of education. That Pu Jiaoshi was matriarch, mediator, and teacher to the patients is clear in the case of the marriage of a former woman patient to the father of two child patients. Ida made the arrangements for the marriage and accordingly was paid the ceremonial call the next day normally made to the bride's parents the day after the wedding.[33]

Other hospital personnel and community leaders also provided support for society's indigent. In the above case, the attending physician gave money to the man towards his wife's funeral. The Taoist Red Swastika Society provided the coffin, and the man's landlord contributed toward the expenses. But the role of responsible elder of those without family was played by no one more fully than Ida—a dowager before her time.

Ida's childhood in a missionary family living in an interior village only partially explains Ida's adoption of the Chinese matriarchal role model and the mediator function at the PUMC. Many other missionary children were products of the "American villages in the midst of China," as Ida called the mission compounds. Yet few became as bicultural as Ida; few took on the Chinese roles as naturally.[34]

Ida perhaps knew the Chinese roles better than most Americans because she spent more years completely immersed in the hinterland than did most missionary children. Children born to missionaries before Ida's time were sent to America as young as age six or seven to be raised and educated by relatives or home congregations. By the time Ida's younger brothers were school age, the China Inland Mission School (CIM) for missionary children in Yantai replaced America as the place missionaries sent their children. Ida was caught between these two periods. Anna, her mother, resisted the custom of sending her children away anywhere to school and, except for brief periods at the CIM school when they were ten and twelve years old respectively, taught both Ida and John at home. Thus, Ida more naturally played Chinese roles in her position at the American medical institution because she was in much longer and closer contact with her Chinese amah, the servants, neighbors, and general community than were most missionary offspring. "Dada" was the more significant a model for Ida because of Anna's busy schedule with the boys' school and her intellectual, seemingly cold temperament. "Dada" added an emotional quality missing in the Pruitt kids' lives.

Despite Ida's self-concept as a mediator and her less conscious identity as family matriarch, Ida knew that these Chinese roles were limited, although she couldn't always define the boundaries between American and Chinese roles. As the years passed and her experience within both Chinese and Western communities increased, she realized she was neither fish nor fowl, neither American nor Chinese, and not even a typical missionary kid.

Among caseworkers at the hospital and students at Yenching University's Sociology Department, where she lectured, Ida was considered Chinese "with the face of a foreigner."[35] However, Ida felt estranged from the Chinese doctors in two ways. First, they were sophisticated urbanites and she was from a village in the hinterland. Second, although she felt more identified with 95% of the people of China than did these urban sophisticates, her skin betrayed her as American.[36] In the country united by race and culture longer than any other still extant nation, a white-skinned, "long-nosed" person remained a "foreign devil" despite her mastery of the language or customs.

Ida painfully acknowledged her separateness from her "motherland," China, as well as her "fatherland," the United States. Even as she played Chinese roles at the PUMC, she sought the advice of Mr. Wang, her Mongolian staff person, about intricacies of Beijing life and customs with which she was unfamiliar. Her close observations and formal interviews of the patients taught her much. She applied herself to the formal study of Chinese folk culture as well as high culture. Yet Ida knew that some clients would never feel comfortable with either a "foreign devil" or young, educated Chinese social workers. In these instances, she used "coolies," rickshaw pullers, to make connections with these patients.

Ida never felt truly included in the Chinese community of her childhood, which no doubt contributed a great deal to her bitterness toward missionaries. Only as an adult in Beijing, did she finally feel accepted by a Chinese family, that of Wu Yong (Wu Yuchuan), whose story she translated.[37] One evening, Ida sat with the family as the children recited the story of the famous poet, Li Taipo, who drank to the moon on the prow of a boat, unable to tell the moon from its reflection. "And even as the magic of the moon was upon the poet, so was the magic of the family on me, and I was one of them. The curtains had opened, I had entered China, and the curtains dropped together behind me." Momentarily, Ida achieved the welcoming acceptance her mother and all the nineteenth-century missionary women had sought through their obtrusive "visitations" to Chinese women's homes.

As interpreter and mediator between the American and Chinese peoples and cultures, Ida played an essential role at the PUMC, as is clear from both the medical reports and the patients' responses to her. Yet, except for brief periods, the chief of social service remained apart from both worlds, able to explain one world to another, but a citizen of neither.

It may be that the role of mediator was the only one Ida could play, estranged as she was from both the Chinese and her American medical colleagues. But among the American and Westernized Chinese medical staff, the mediating role was not needed, and Ida's stance of departmental dowager was poorly received. In his 1923 formal evaluation of the Social Service Department, Roger Greene was not only concerned about the relative merits of medical social work and public health nursing. He also felt that "grave questions" remained about Ida's ability to "develop work in an original and constructive manner." Greene admitted that the department served a valuable function. Some of the staff physicians had even called it "indispensable"; only the Optometry Department reported receiving no benefit from social service.[38] The concern of Greene and others lay in the chief's weakness as an administrator. Her work was not clean-cut; her record-keeping was careless. She had an easy-going style in the management of the Women's Hostel. And, her minute taking at committee meetings was inaccurate.[39] These were not light charges in a period when social work struggled to be accepted as a profession by taking on the attributes of order, efficiency, and specialization of skills.

Ida knew she kept sloppy records. Her work was with people, not paper, as her superior in Philadelphia had remarked. She never let any of her secretaries decide who should see her and who was turned away. Personally attending to all callers was a most inefficient use of the department chief's time, but Ida explained, "Often the people most unimportant to the world were the most important to me."[40]

Criticism of Ida continued after 1923, mostly in the form of confidential internal memos between administrators in New York and Beijing. These memos referred vaguely to Ida's "outspoken," "antagonistic," even "outrageous" temperament which grated upon that of the medical superintendent, Dr. J. Heng Liu, as well as unidentified "many others," Chinese and American staff alike.[41] Ida knew she had a temper. When a candid staff member told Ida how difficult she was to work with, she responded, "The picture he paints of me is pretty dreadful. If true it's high time I did something and I know it is at least partly true."[42]

These criticisms brought Ida to the brink of dismissal in 1925. The administration seriously considered not renewing her contract in 1927 after her 1926 furlough. Only because of Ida's familiarity with the conditions and language of China was her contract finally renewed before she left for her furlough, but she was told in no uncertain terms that it would be for a two-year period and not the customary four-year term. Her future at the PUMC depended on her ability to "enlarge her point of view" while on furlough, and generally revise her attitude toward work. Meanwhile, Dr. J. Heng Liu planned to study medical social service elsewhere with a view to reorganizing the Social Service Department (renamed the Division of Medical Social Service).[43] Ida seemed to take this criticism of her work and threat to her job as a challenge. As she left for the United States, she wrote to the New York office of the PUMC that she looked forward to reorganizing the department for greater effectiveness after studying American hospitals.[44] After touring a number of the best-known medical social service departments throughout the country, Ida settled in to study and work with Janet Thornton at the Presbyterian Hospital in New York City.

Much depended on Ida's work with Janet Thornton. Roger Greene was charged with evaluating Ida at year's end to judge the extent of her "enlarged views" and "change in attitudes." Margery Eggleston, assistant secretary to Edwin R. Embree of the China Medical Board, interviewed Thornton.[45] Ida was asked to submit a report of her study of hospital social service in America.

Greene considered the report excellent. Through her writings and discussions with him, Ida's views clearly seemed "enlarged." She asked for additional Chinese staff to handle special cases, as well as another American instructor of social work. She requested an advisory committee composed of three clinical department heads to suggest ways to make the social service more useful to the clinics. Thereafter, workers were assigned to specific wards and clinics.[46] Eggleston, who was not one of Ida's sympathizers, reported that Janet Thornton's evaluation of Ida was very positive. Thornton praised Ida as knowledgeable and hard working. Her judgment was sound and reliable; her heart was very much in her work. Ida was kind to patients and obviously deeply attached to the work in Beijing. Thornton recognized that other hospital staff might have trouble getting along with Ida due to her "good many odd little mannerisms." But at Presbyterian Hospital, Ida proved to be a congenial colleague. She advised Eggleston that considering Ida's knowledge of the language and customs of China, the PUMC would do well to retain her services.[47]

Ida completed her two-year trial period from 1927 to 1929 and another two-year reappointment from 1929 to 1931. Thereafter, the hospital must have been satisfied with her performance for she was offered the customary four-year contract in 1931. In reappointing her,

Acting Medical Superintendent S.T. Wang notified her that her title had been changed from "Medical Social Service Worker" to "Chief of Hospital Social Service."[48]

The administration's criticism of Ida Pruitt as medical social worker clearly was leveled at Ida, personally, as well as toward the Social Service Department. Ida's personality and relationship with the medical staff were under attack from at least 1923 until 1931, and probably continued thereafter.[49] Much of the dissatisfaction with Ida may be traced to differences between the administration's expectations of her roles and functions at the PUMC and Ida's own views. They put a priority on her executive ability; she focused on mediating relationships. By common agreement, Ida was superb at helping patients and physicians to better understand and cooperate with each other, and this ability ultimately made Ida indispensable to the hospital. But the administration was ready to fire her over her admittedly poor record-keeping.

Ida's temper was the other source of criticism. However good she was at facilitating relationships between staff and patients, her own relationships with the staff and administration were far from perfect. The administration and staff expected a professional colleague. Because she was a woman, perhaps they expected a somewhat deferential colleague. Instead, they got an outspoken "Chinese" grandmother/mother-in-law. Whether or not the administration would have reacted to a male administrator's temper in the way they reacted to Ida's remains in the realm of speculation. What is clear is that Ida's bossy personality was more appropriate for the matriarch of a large, traditional family than for a woman administrator in an American, democratic-style, reformist institution.

A "Dangerous" Woman

When Ida accepted the position of medical social worker at the PUMC she was thirty-three years old. She imagined herself meeting handsome young doctors, "cutting a social swath" in Beijing's foreign community, and eventually marrying. She didn't understand that, for a number of reasons, her professional status in public life set her on a career track that generally did not intersect with the marriage track in the private sphere.

Different cultural expectations and the PUMC's policy against hiring "marriageable" women were the most blatant obstacles to Ida's ability to combine a professional life in the public sphere with a fulfilling personal relationship. Subtle psychological factors also came into play.

Early generations of American professional women in positions of authority frequently were forced to choose between career and marriage. The China Medical Board, Inc., which oversaw the hiring of PUMC professional staff, rejected a number of women as Ida's assistants or replacement solely on the grounds that they were attractive enough to marry. The reason given for this policy was the assumption that, once married, women quit their careers to become wives and mothers.[50]

Ida was described as a good-looking, outgoing woman by some, while others saw her as unattractive.[51] Some hospital personnel talked about her as a "flirt," or suggested that she was a "dangerous person" who threatened marriages. Ida didn't—couldn't—give up her sexuality when taking on a professional identity. She openly enjoyed male companionship and identified herself through her relationships with men to a far greater extent than she realized.[52] This may have added to her department's controversial reputation and her own tenuous position at the hospital.

Ida carried on a tempestuous love affair with an associate professor, Canadian doctor John F. "Jack" McIntosh, who almost became her undoing.[53] Ida remembered life before meeting Jack as terrible and barren compared with the happiness and desire she experienced in his company. After being introduced at a Christmas party in 1928, she was immediately attracted to the younger man's intellect, emotional sensitivity, and strong physique.

During the following years, the Western community in Beiping (renamed from Beijing in June, 1928, when the Nationalist government moved the capital to Nanjing) grew to know Ida and Jack as a couple. Together, the two socialized with other couples and explored the Western Hills. They made joint travel plans and corresponded almost daily when traveling alone. Each made occasional, flirtatious references to their shared physical passion.[54] At age forty, Ida had fallen in love as never before.

Jack's love and encouragement initially stimulated and calmed Ida.[55] Buoyed by his support, she tried her hand at creative writing, one of her loves in childhood and at Cox College. She wrote three fictional accounts of Chinese rituals and beliefs, which were published by *The Atlantic Monthly*,[56] and translated *The Flight of an Empress*, by Wu Yong.[57] All received both popular and critical acclaim.

As Ida confided her fears, frustrations, and depressions to him, however, Jack responded defensively by disparaging Ida's emotions as "silly" or "coocoo," calling her "my midget," "a good girl," a "duck," and other diminutive terms.[58] To this, she asserted that her letters were not silly, but rather an honest sharing of feelings. Although Ida still deeply desired Jack, his condescension compelled her to demand respect:

> I am neither a child nor a toy, but I am a companionable woman ready to give generously.... Do you really believe that women should be treated as inanimate objects are treated, to be for the pleasure of the male? You begin to make me realize why there is a feminist movement....[59]

As Jack pushed Ida away, she clung to him with ever-greater ferocity. She became desperate for an intimate personal relationship at all costs.[60] Her letters swung between psychological blackmail and self-recrimination. She begged his forgiveness, then justified her behavior. Convincing herself that living with Jack would resolve their difficulties, Ida renewed her plea for marriage. For a marriage to work, each person in a couple must give up something, Ida reasoned. To become a wife, she would give up her profession and China, which had been her lifeblood.[61]

Ida followed Jack to North America, clinging to the hope of marrying him in Montreal. Her household belongings were stored, ready to be shipped from China to a new home in Canada. Possibly to forestall Ida's emotional breakdown, Jack agreed to consider their future together after she promised to give him time and space apart from her. So Ida arranged a study tour of social work schools in Boston and New York, began a new writing project, and settled in to wait for Jack's decision.

Whether psychoanalysis was a part of Ida's social work training at the Massachusetts General Hospital in 1920, or whether she was introduced to Freudianism only during her 1932 study tour, this much is certain: As she struggled to understand the painful dynamics between herself and Jack, Ida found psychological concepts to be distinctly helpful.

The dissonance between Jack's tender letters and rejecting behavior ripped Ida apart. The more she struggled to understand him, the more confused she became. She tried to apply psychological principles to Jack's behavior and wondered if latent homosexuality explained Jack's ambivalence toward her.[62] Her mind ran in circles and threatened to disintegrate. In her own letters to him, she swung between anger and remorse.

For his part, Jack felt genuine affection for his "Pu" (a reference to

Pu Ai-de, her Chinese name), yet recoiled at her intense emotionality. Where was the "sensible, reasonable" woman he loved? He dismissed her urge to psychoanalyze him as silly and irrelevant to his life.[63]

Thus began the 1932 Christmas season for Ida. She had spent the four previous holiday seasons with Jack. Living alone in a small Boston rooming house, she looked forward to a fifth Christmas together. But he refused to see her, saying only, "It would be too hard for both of us—and I haven't the courage for a third parting."

Ida responded to his rejection with an emotional, five-page outpouring of love and anger. She begged him to change his mind, but in the end she found herself wandering in a strange country alone, disintegrating and unable to write.

As the fabric of her personality unraveled, Ida worried about her own possible sexual dysfunction. Was she "too heavily sexed"?[64]

On the day of Ida's forty-fourth birthday, just two days before Christmas, she found herself in the office of Dr. Marianna Taylor, a psychiatrist in practice at the Boston Psychopathic as well as the Massachusetts General Hospital. Ida had taken considerable care to chose a psychiatrist with some knowledge of psychoanalytic principles over a "rabid" Freudian.[65]

Ida's purpose in seeking psychiatric help was to sort out her emotions toward Jack. Taylor assured Ida that her difficulty lay not in any abnormal sexual needs but in Ida's domination by her mother and consequent emotional immaturity.[66] Immediately, Ida felt both relief to find a name for her problem, and thus the promise of a solution, and remorse that she had wasted over twenty years of her adulthood.[67]

Twice weekly over several months, Ida explored her childhood and her relationship with Jack, as well as her own future. The two-hour sessions left her upset and depleted, nauseated for weeks at a time, and suffering from headaches, tooth aches, diarrhea, and excessive menstruation. A little internal demon seemed to struggle against exposure, as Ida confronted her "wretched" childhood. "I must have been a horrid little kid and not made use even of the very few opportunities I had."

By the second session, Ida had dissolved her bitterness toward her childhood, recognizing that she had spent her early years living in a fantasy created by books and paper dolls. One reconstructed childhood memory was of her parents' dismissing a poem of hers. When Ida realized that her parents probably did not even see Ida's poem, she overcame a writer's block.

A new understanding of her behavior toward Jack also crept into her voice.[68] In a tone of acceptance, Ida wrote:

> I am feminine in my temperament, but because of my lost [years] in interior China, I never learned the feminine technique of piquing the male. In my twenties I had many men wanting to marry me because I did not care for any of them and so treated them indifferently. But when I really loved a person I could not treat him indifferently. So I pestered you my darling, and lost you.[69]

Ida became an enthusiastic proponent of the psychoanalytic method. Her attempts at analyzing Jack were quite confrontational as well as unsolicited. Seemingly unaware of their power to wound, she tossed around phrases such as "mother-fixation," and "dislike, fear and hatred of mother."[70] They cut Jack to the quick.[71]

Dr. Taylor diagnosed Ida's hurtful behavior toward Jack as a manifestation of her unconscious fear of marriage. Ida had suspected as much, although she was loathe to face the truth.[72]

Convinced that the key to future happiness lay in her psychological maturity, Ida requested permission from the PUMC to extend her study leave in order to continue working with Dr. Taylor. After six weeks' intensive psychotherapy, Ida became aware of herself as:

> [a] little girl of two, sitting at the gate of my emotions ... not allowing them to function.... She had just cause for her attitude and it is too bad that life did what it did to her but there is no need for her to cramp me. When I think of how many years that little girl has been unhappy inside of me and how much she has damaged my life, it seems a great waste. But ... the only thing is to go ahead now and live fully.[73]

Although Ida still hoped for a future life with Jack, no longer was she miserable without him. Ida's psychological insights broke through the fear and passivity that had blocked her fill enjoyment of daily life. She experienced newfound joy and courage; she laughed freely. Physical ailments disappeared.

Jack noted the change in Ida's letters. A new maturity replaced her vague, false tone. No longer did she seek his counsel or lambaste him with psychobabble. In an ironic twist, Jack began to ask her advice. However, by this time, Ida had none to offer. She praised psychiatry as helpful to her own development, but recognized many other paths to a fulfilled life. "The only requisite is to see the truth, the truth about the world and about oneself."

Jack referred to her transformation as a "conversion" experience. Ida resisted the religious connotation associated with "conversion." Rather, she saw the process as "integrating and balancing the body, mind, and emotions." By February, Ida began to gain a new sense of her life's direction independent of Jack. No longer did she define herself only in relationship to him, or any male. Tentatively, more sure of her goal than how to reach it, Ida decided to move away from social work toward research about Chinese folk beliefs.

> What I want to find out is the faith in the hearts of the Chinese that makes them, the old Chinese, able to live and carry on for thousands of years, the faith which lost is making the young Chinese commit suicide.... The Chinese religious festivals and religious dances and the faith behind them ... will not be Daoism nor Buddhism, nor Confucianism nor even animism. It will be Chineseism.[74]

She set her sights on the stilt and tiger dancers and on the religious societies among the journeymen of Beijing. At funerals, she had seen them beating drums with real, mystical emotion to accompany the soul to heaven. Several scholars at Harvard University encouraged her research, even dangling the possibility of a Harvard-Yenching fellowship before her eyes.

Meanwhile, she could best promote the PUMC Social Service Department by developing a method of training new caseworkers. She would arrange for supervisory visits by American social workers, then devote herself to folk research. No longer did she see life as a duty. Life was to be lived fully and with abundance.

Feeling confidant and looking forward to her life's new direction, Ida terminated her work with Dr. Taylor and prepared to sail for China in early March. The thought of returning without Jack was wrenching. She missed their physical intimacy and, more importantly, having someone to "actively love." But she remained convinced that, at least temporarily, their paths lay apart.[75]

6

Ida's Open Door in Beijing:
Beyond Missionary and Social Worker

Reflecting on her life, Ida used a metaphor from one of her favorite hiking trips, the pilgrim's climb up Shang Fang Shan, in the Western Hills outside of Beijing. Her life's path, like that of the pilgrim, had been one of innumerable twists and turns around blind curves and precipitous drops before reaching the wide mountain valley. Some periods had been as black as the inevitable storm clouds over the great mountain. Although storms would come again on Ida's life-long pilgrimage, the clouds cleared as Ida returned in early 1933. She felt that her pilgrimage had taken her to the wide valley of her life where the journey was less arduous.[1] No longer emotionally crippled by the past, Ida applied herself to the Social Service Department and to her writing. During her remaining years in China, she made groundbreaking contributions both as a leader in social work education and as a unique chronicler of Chinese women's stories. But first, she needed a home of her own.

Ida's first project upon returning to Beijing was to find the house of her dreams. Since childhood, Ida viewed houses as she believed the Chinese understood them, like the "outermost covering" of the inhabitants, "more permanent than the clothes we wear ... [or] the flesh and bones of [our] bodies. One would be naked without a house."[2] Yet for the first decade of her life in Beijing, Ida lived in temporary housing situations, "naked" in her impermanence.[3]

After touring numerous Chinese structures made unsatisfactory to Ida by their Western remodeling, she almost despaired of finding an authentic Chinese "compound" house: a traditional structure having a square ground plan around a main courtyard, surrounded by freestanding wooden pillars that supported tiled roofs. A covered arcade thus connected the wings on all sides of the house. The entire compound was secluded from the street by thick walls of brick and plaster.[4]

Finally, her rickshaw puller took Ida about two kilometers north of the Beijing train station to Xiao Yang Yibin Hutong, the "Little Sheep Alleyway that Delights Guests."[5] He trotted past a lively little temple with orange strips of cloth, burning incense, and a priest beating the traditional, deeply resonating gong. Ida's heart warmed at this scene straight out of her childhood village, a street unmarked by foreign influence. Heavy double doors opened directly from the *hutong*. Inside, a tiled "spirit screen" hid the main courtyard. As Ida sidled past the screen and into the front entrance court, filled with flame-colored crab apple trees, white lilac trees, irises, and forsythia, she gasped. At the second gate, she knew she had found her home. Her delight grew from room to room. "Everywhere was the rhythm and harmony of a house well planned and well built." This compound would be Ida's outermost garment, adding much needed rhythm and harmony to her soul.

If she had not decided on this house because of its perfect lines and proportions, the little temple, the courtyards and most of all, the paper-covered, lattice windows, Ida's mind was made up by the arrival of a Westernized Chinese couple who spoke of replacing the lattice windows and traditional doorframe with glass windows and a Western-style doorframe. She could not bear to think of desecrating the perfect rhythm with hard, broken European lines that would clash with the home's front! "I could not let one of the few unspoiled houses be spoiled by ignorance and a set of false values. I would keep one house pure for all to see what a really good Chinese house was like, and I would enjoy it myself."[6]

Ida set to work repairing the house on Xiao Yang Yibin Hutong, taking great care to restore the original Chinese design. The papered windows, white washed walls, furnishings from Chinese antique shops— all were intended to preserve the Chinese patterns. Ida's only accommodations to Western living were electricity and plumbing. Ida's evident pride in preserving part of traditional China lingered long after she left Beijing. She remembered that of the Westerners living in Chinese compounds all over Beijing in those days, only she and her friend, Bob Winters, refrained from remodeling.[7]

Ida, never the American reformer, resisted changing the pattern of Chinese homes—the people's outermost layer—as she objected to the missionaries' attempts to convert people's innermost layer—their souls. Seeing the importance of an American-style home to her mother and other missionary women's evangelical work, Ida was aware of the relationship between preserving the Chinese compound and defending the Chinese way of life.

However, in adding plumbing and electricity and changing the use of some parts of the compound, Ida distinguished between the essence of the building—embodiment of Chinese culture—and its use, echoing nineteenth-century reformer, Zhang Zhidong's famous slogan, "Chinese learning should remain the essence, but Western learning be used for practical development."[8]

Her friend, Old Madam Yin, came to assess Ida's home after the completion of the renovations. In roaming through the courtyards and among the various houses, she was disturbed by the height of the trees that interfered with the favorable influences from south and east. She was also upset by Ida's failure to sleep in the Main House, where the master of the house should live, and by other of Ida's changes in the buildings' uses. Ida realized that, despite her best efforts to preserve the Chinese atmosphere and harmonies, she had offended their sense of fitness as much as the people who remodeled the houses had offended hers.[9]

Ida's home in Beijing then, was as full of contradictions and ambivalence as was the rest of her life. Her identification with the Chinese people and culture was expressed in beauty and harmony through the compound on Xiao Yang Yibin Hutong. Yet her home was no more Chinese than was its master. Rather, it was a blend of peoples and cultures, a mixture of both worlds. As the outermost of Ida's layers of identity, this home expressed Ida's bicultural personality and, in so doing, gave harmony to her American/Chinese soul.

Sitting in her courtyard shortly after moving in, Ida looked up, past the rippling green tile of her own rooftops, to the deep blue sky stretching to infinity, which so many others in Beijing also treasured.[10] "I and about a million other people in Beijing had each our own piece of heaven."

The origins of her house were of compelling interest to Ida. According to the former landlord, it was built about 1890 by a paymaster in the Bordered Yellow Banner, the Palace Guard. But Ida preferred the story told her by "one who was as fond of a good tale" as she was. According to this account, the house was built by the provincial governor at the time of Emperor Tongzhi (r. 1862–1875). The daughter of the house, Alute, was married to the Tongzhi Emperor. On the orders of the Empress Dowager, Alute had been a faithful wife and followed her husband into death. Ida enjoyed contemplating little Alute playing in the courtyards, imagining that the gracious and harmonious courts had helped give Alute courage in life and death.[11]

Other stories about the house circulated among Ida's servants. A suicide ghost was rumored to live in the compound, bound to the site of death until able to persuade another hapless person to take her own life. "Have you seen her?" Ida always asked in a hopeful tone.[12] Her great-grandmother in Tallmadge, Ohio, had seen her father after his death, as well as several other apparitions.[13] Ida's mother, Anna, dismissed such stories as superstitions but Ida loved to collect such tales as a way of learning about the thoughts and ways of the people. The traditional and contemporary Chinese folk tales that she gathered fired Ida's imagination. Later, these tales became the basis for her short stories.

Ida reintegrated her life, balanced its public and private spheres, and added a deep, emotional component to it in the most natural way she knew—by establishing her own home. Her Chinese compound gave her most external layer of identity a balance that she internalized. The building's history fired her imagination. The architectural mixture of East and West was replicated in her social relations. She established a uniquely multinational household that comforted her even as she nurtured her "family" members. Her home later provided her the opportunity to aid the Chinese people's underground struggle against Japan, giving Ida the important cause that in 1933 she had felt lacking in her life.

Ida governed her household at Xiao Yang Yibin Hutong like she administered the Social Service Department at the PUMC, according to the "working" religion of the Chinese people: "Every responsibility has its corresponding privilege and every privilege its corresponding responsibility." The duty of those in middle years, like Ida, was to cherish and raise the children while honoring and caring for the elderly. She fulfilled her duty to the next generation by adopting several orphans and welcoming other young people into her family.

Ida's commitment to follow the Chinese ethical system in her home required a careful understanding of those with mixed cultural identity such as her own. Sitting in the courtyard one day, Guijing, the little orphan whom Ida had rescued from prostitution and whom Ida renamed as "Mei Yun" in her writings, looked down at her golden brown arms and told Ida, her "Gugu," that she wished her skin were white. Ida angrily asked herself what had she and her family done to her; what had all the Westerners done to make the Chinese lose the sense of rightness of their way of life and their very skin color. Then Ida realized that she, like Mei

Yun, was unhappy with her skin color. She often sensed a discrepancy between her outer American appearance and her Chinese feelings.

Mei Yun's women friends were Chinese; her men friends were Western. Ida knew that Mei Yun would not be happy with either Chinese or Western men. Speaking for Mei Yun, for other women of mixed cultures, as well as for herself, Ida wondered how she could live with a husband brought up completely in either Chinese or Western culture. As Ida saw it, the heaviest stresses in mixed marriages lay on the wife, who must completely accept her husband's values. The marriage's success depended on the wife's understanding of herself, her husband, and the complicated mixed pattern of their lives. Ida could not see Mei Yun accepting either Western or Chinese values uncritically.[14]

Ida's concern for the psychological sufferings of Mei Yun and the other young people of mixed culture to whom she opened her home and her heart were also expressions of her own sense of isolation. She felt an intuitive understanding only from other bicultural people. Culture clash was a factor in Ida's unfulfilled longing for a deep relationship and motivated her to help Mei Yun find a spouse of equally mixed culture. Ida determined that the young "overseas" Chinese doctors at the PUMC were perfect for Mei Yun. Raised abroad, they looked Chinese but could neither read nor speak their national language. Nor were they familiar with the Chinese ceremonial pattern. Their identities were as mixed as Mei Yun's. So, playing the time-honored Chinese role of matchmaker, "Gugu" began to give parties for the new doctors and included them on her Sunday excursions to the Western Hills outside of Beijing.

One day Mei Yun came into Ida's office. "Dr. Sun asked me to go to the movies with him." A look passed over her face that Ida had never seen before and Ida began to taper off the special parties.[15] Mei Yun later married the overseas Chinese doctor and returned with him to Canada.

Ida felt she had not done her duty as matchmaker for another of her "little girls," as she called her social work students and adopted daughters. Jing Feng was a student at the Chefoo Mission School when Ida began supporting her.[16] Jing Feng's mother worked as a live-in amah and therefore could do nothing for her own children. Her grandmother, Old Madam Ning whose story Ida later recorded, worked during the day but returned home several hours after Jing Feng and her sister were dismissed from school. After a friend in America reneged on her agreement to support Jing Feng's studies at the mission school, Ida took over responsibility for the girl.

Ida sent Jing Feng to study at Yenching University, followed by the School of Nursing at the PUMC, then a period of study in America. Jing Feng became a nursing instructor at the PUMC from 1930 until 1936.[17] She and her friends were intelligent, able, and interesting young women.

Ida later learned that Jing Feng and her two friends were active in the student movement against the Japanese occupation of China, which had begun its course with the 1931 invasion of Manchuria. After the Japanese occupied Beijing in July, 1937, Jing Feng made the painful decision to leave her position at the PUMC and her family in Beijing in order to volunteer as a nurse in unoccupied Free China. To make the dangerous journey across Japanese lines, she planned to dress as an amah or peasant woman. Old Madam Ning, her grandmother, was afraid that the soft hands of her educated granddaughter would give her away to the Japanese.[18]

Ida surely supported Jing Feng's patriotic efforts, since she also helped the anti-Japanese underground. But her main focus was that of a mother, a grandmother, or an aunt. Ida worried that she had not done her duty in helping Jing Feng meet an appropriate boyfriend, regretting that she had not introduced Jing Feng to some of the serious students at the PUMC. She tried to make up for her oversight by thinking more actively on behalf of Mei Yun. Ida, although reconciled to life as a single, professional woman, shared the feelings of Jing Feng's grandmother that marriage and family are women's most important priority:

> She says that marriage is not necessary to working for the country. That is new talk. We all know that the family is more important than anything else.... How can there be a country if there are no families and children? The generations stretch back thousands of years to the great ancestor parents. They stretch for thousands of years into the future.... A woman stands with one hand grasping the generations that have gone before and with the other the generations to come. It is her common destiny with all women.[19]

Jing Feng's destiny was neither to travel to Free China nor to marry. Her grandmother dreamed the same dream that had foretold the death of the old grandfather many years previously. She interpreted the dream as meaning a family member must die and hoped she, the eldest, would be the one taken. But the dream was meant for Jing Feng. She died, not at the hands of the Japanese as her grandmother feared, but from typhoid Ida always felt pain when asked about Old Madam Ning's granddaughter and divulged to few that the girl had become like a daughter to her.[20]

Ida's house at Xiao Yang Yibin Hutong became a home to others.

She Huichen (She Huizhen), a young social worker whom Ida first knew in Yantai, felt a provincial bond with her boss. When Huichen came to Ida in tears, suffering from loneliness, Ida invited her to live in her compound. She Huichen always maintained contact with Ida and valued her as the family with whom she lost contact after the Communist victory. She joined the efforts of the Shanghai Municipal Council to control the abuse of child labor in the burgeoning industrial factories. Later, she took charge of the refugee relief program in Hong Kong, and helped pioneer the social work profession there.

Others of mixed cultural background became a part of Ida's home. Francis Hsu, a Westernized, educated Chinese who worked in the Social Service Department, particularly needed a blending of East and West in his home environment, in Ida's view. He later became a noted anthropologist at Northwestern University.[21]

Twelve-year-old Tony Schada was of Italian-Chinese origin, which caused him no end of troubles at the various schools he attended before being dismissed on disciplinary grounds. His Chinese mother struggled to maintain her family after his Italian father, a sailor in the American navy, was forced to return to the United States to collect disabled veteran benefits. He faithfully sent money to his Chinese family, but this didn't help his son, Tony's adjustment to his peers. When his mother could cope no longer, Ida invited the boy to live in her multicultural household. He called Ida "Gugu" and considered the older girls his sisters.[22] Tony eventually fulfilled a lifelong dream by joining the American navy.

Tania, who was renamed "Sonia" in Ida's essays, was another story. The fifteen-year-old orphan from the Soviet Union had been matched to a Russian in Tianjin, China, by her foster family. When that arrangement fell through, she found her way to Beijing and supported herself by dancing in a cabaret. She met Ida by way of a Russian vocal instructor in Beijing whose voice training offered Tania an alternative to the life of prostitution that inevitably would have followed from cabaret dancing.

Taken by the girl's persistence, self-reliance, and general strength of character, Ida paid her bills at the cabaret and supported her ambition for a better life. Ida arranged for Tania to attend the French Convent School in Tianjin. She then worked toward the Cambridge University entrance examination. Holidays were spent at Ida's American/Chinese home.[23]

Tania studied at Yenching University in Beijing, then Columbia University. After receiving her Ph.D. in Russian language and literature, she taught at Swarthmore College in Pennsylvania for many years, where she lived with her husband and four children. After Ida's retirement in Philadelphia, Tania incorporated Ida into her family and was at her bedside during Ida's final illness.[24]

As mistress of her household and one in her middle years, Ida's responsibilities extended beyond her adopted daughters and other boarders to her servants. The larger area and growing family at the new home required the customary three servants, which soon expanded to four as Ida took in Old Madam Yin's former servant and "almost-daughter."

Yang was an eighteen-year-old cripple when Ida met him at the PUMC. His age and withdrawn personality made Yang resistant to learning a trade. The social work staff despaired at helping the boy become self-sufficient. Mr. Wang suggested that Yang might best become a retainer or house steward. "But who would take a lame boy with a stubborn disposition for a servant?" Ida asked rhetorically, knowing full well that she would do so.

Yang began working for Ida years before she moved into her "dream" home and began assembling her multinational family. He somehow belonged in such an unconventional household, although he did not share the mixed cultural background of Ida's other family members, and in fact, showed no sign of new thoughts at all. Neither did he call Ida "Gugu," as did her adopted children. But Ida was like a father and mother to Yang. To him, she embodied all that the PUMC and the Social Service Department had done to give him a prosthetic limb and life, itself. The other servants, Big Li, the washman, Little Li, the rickshaw puller, and He Jie, the maid, had a contractual relationship with Ida; Yang considered himself her personal retainer.

Ida readily reciprocated Yang's sense of personal responsibility toward her. She accepted the invitation to attend his wedding, urging Yang to bring his wife to live in the servants' court of her compound. Altogether, Ida knew Yang and his growing family for fifteen years.

Yang guarded Ida's home against fire, camels, intrusions by neighbors, and theft. He defended her ways, refused to cook in any way but hers, and displayed a personal devotion to Ida.

When Ida was preparing to leave Beijing for the last time in 1938, she, as the faithful master, had Yang's future to consider as well as her own. Yang was a good enough cook to take any job with a Western-family, or bake for a foreign bakery. However, the Japanese occupation had greatly diminished the demand for Western-style cooks and bakers. How was Yang to support his wife, children, parents, and brother's family, all of whom Ida was indirectly aiding through her employment of one servant?

Ida knew the family was trying to redeem some of the land they had been forced to sell in order to survive. Yang eventually asked Ida for a two-hundred-and-fifty-dollar loan.

> A loan! He knew it was not a loan ... but a gift. He knew that I knew the responsibilities of the master to the servant even as I had known the responsibilities of the servant to the master.... We both knew that the longer the relationship had lasted the greater the mutual responsibilities and privileges. The words each of us said were like the peaks of mountains showing through clouds but the mountains could be guessed....
>
> "I will bring you the money tomorrow.... Get [your land] back. May your family prosper in the home of its ancestors."

Yang did not thank Ida for her "loan." The relationship was of master and servant, too close for thanks.[25]

During the six years that Ida lived at Xiao Yang Yibin Hutong, which she always considered her real home, she kept an "open house." Yang never knew exactly how many people to expect for dinner, although Ida tried to notify him in advance. Ida liked people to drop in for tea or cocktails. She held big parties, once employing a former chef of the Russian Czarist officials in Port Arthur for the occasion.[26]

Guests were greeted by Ida's five cats, seven Pekinese and Tibetan lion dogs, and the inevitable kittens and puppies. "Yuzi," was Ida's favorite. A gift to Ida from a palace eunuch, Yuzi's ancestors lived in the Forbidden City. The little black Pekinese, whose name translates into "Jade," accompanied Ida on excursions, sitting on her lap or walking with her on hikes in the Western Hills. Ida's guests were Chinese, American and European, men and women, boys and girls. Her Sunday breakfasts of waffles and maple syrup became a salon, of sorts, for academics and others traveling through Beijing.[27] At the last Christmas party Ida gave before leaving Beijing in 1939, she counted sixty-one people of eleven nationalities.[28]

Many of Ida's Western guests considered Ida the only authority on the Chinese people. For others, her courtyard epitomized Old Beijing.[29] During her eighteen years in Beijing, Ida succeeded in "cutting the social swath" that she had imagined in 1921 from her lonely vantage point in Boston.

But among her guests, she most valued her Chinese friends, neighbors, clients, vendors, laborers, priests, children, and others who passed through her home. Many became material for Ida's fiction. She felt especially privileged to be invited into the inner courtyards of Chinese compounds and her friends' lives. Old Madam Ning's son warned her not to tell a foreigner so much about the Chinese. But the old woman considered Ida her friend. "I can tell you everything. When my heart is too full I can come and tell you, and then I am at peace.... I know your heart and that in your heart you are like us and that you understand."[30]

For several years, Old Madam Ning visited Ida three mornings a week. Initially, she came to recount stories about the old days, which Ida recorded on her typewriter as she talked. The sessions completed, the old Chinese woman and middle-aged American woman continued to visit; they had become friends and enjoyed spending time together.[31]

One day Ning came at teatime instead. Ida's other cherished friend, Old Madam Yin, happened to be visiting. Ida wondered how the wealthy old woman, who had never known want in her life, and the poor old woman, who had fought and begged to stay alive, would get along. "The one had the air of command and resources about her and the other the unselfconscious self-respect of a woman who has done all her life that which she had to do and enjoyed it in spite of everything." How would they establish precedence?

Old Madam Yin began by asking Ning her age, using the formal phrase for this common question. Ning was sixty-eight. Yin could claim only sixty, so Ning took the seat of honor. As they ate, they continued sparring, comparing the number of their sons and grandsons. Honors about even, they chatted away while Ida happily listened.[32]

Ida knew and honored her responsibilities as a neighbor and resident of Xiao Yang Yibin Hutong. She sent the customary amount of money at the regular intervals to the little street temple. To the concerns of the next-door neighbors that her remodeling efforts ignored some principle of *feng shui* and therefore threatened the life of their eighty-five-year-old mother, she responded by modifying her architectural plans. She responded to unfortunate neighbors whose adobe houses had melted in the rains by opening the double doors of her "gate cave," the covered entrance to one of the courtyards whose high roof offered shelter. After the rains subsided, she visited them in their tenements, taking medicines for their feet, which had developed sores from standing so long in the floodwaters.[33]

What to her mother's generation was Christian charity, motivated out of a desire to show God's love to the "heathen," was to Ida only her responsibility as neighbor, friend, employer, or "Gugu." She admitted that such duties were inconvenient at times. "But friends are friends and it would be a dreary world in which we could do nothing for them."[34]

Ida surrounded herself with the Chinese art and architecture that gave form to the values by which she lived. She loved her adopted daughters, cherished her old Chinese women friends, provided "toeholds" for those of mixed cultural backgrounds, and fulfilled her responsibilities toward her servants and neighbors. She recalled these six years as the best of her life. By nurturing others of mixed culture and restoring a traditional Beijing courtyard home, Ida created and nurtured her private life. Her depression lifted and she was able to reinvigorate her public role at the PUMC.

Ida had traveled far from her childhood in the village of Huangxian among Baptist missionaries. Yet occasionally she heard echoes from the past above the noises of Beijing and the voices of its inhabitants. They came to her distorted almost beyond recognition, as echoes do.

The nineteenth-century missionary strategy, captured in the slogan, "women's work for women" was one of those echoes. Though she rejected Christianity, avoided the missionary community, and disagreed with their exclusive focus on women, Ida's work at the PUMC largely concerned women and children. As chief of hospital social services, Ida played almost all of the missionary women's roles: teacher, nurse, and mother.

In Ida's home at Xiao Yang Yibin Hutong there were other echoes from her childhood. Her parents' missionary "home with an open door" remained the policy of Ida's home. Ida's Chinese architecture and interior design communicated her life's goals and values as consciously as her mother's American furnishings and remodeling reflected her American Christian values and evangelical goals. No wonder Anna was conspicuously silent when she saw Ida's Chinese compound; she understood the point of her daughter's surroundings.

There were also echoes from a distant past. Ida's identification with the grandmother role in both her home and at the PUMC not only arose from her Chinese women role models but from her own foremothers. "The Grandmothers' Window," an essay written by her Aunt Myra, recounted the story of the family's pilgrimage from Connecticut to Ohio in 1818. From the journey to Ohio, which seventy-three-year-old Sarah Fellows undertook largely on foot, to her own generation, Myra told the history of the women in the family. Throughout the story, almost as an organizing theme, was the grandmother sitting by the big, bay window overlooking the village green. Throughout five generations, family members seemed to orient themselves around the matriarch. Anna Pruitt read Myra's essay to her children in Huangxian. Surely it was no coincidence that her daughter cast herself as the dominant figure of a large family.

There were other echoes from her past that Ida heard but chose to ignore. Timothy Lin, an Anglican priest whom she knew from Yantai days, candidly voiced his concerns about her religious life. By this time, Ida had disavowed having any religion, but did not mind an old friend speaking his mind. However, the irony of a Chinese convert to Christianity attempting to convert the daughter of a Baptist missionary did not escape her.

Ida developed a sense of non-religious spirituality. On her explorations of Beijing's *hutong*, she sought out and studied the little temples and shrines, talked with the priests and monks, and drank in the beauty with all of her senses. When a Daoist priest in Yantai spoke to her in a pavilion overlooking the sun rising through the morning mist over the ocean, Ida felt a spiritual uplift. Hearing the rise and fall of cadences across the rooftops in Beijing, as services were sung at one or another of Beijing's myriad little temples, Ida often would shut her eyes and feel that this was traditional and as it should be.

But even though Ida avoided the missionary community and fled all suggestion of Christian proselytizing and its modern, secular variations, the echoes followed her. Her strangest experience of this sort was the case of the evangelical Buddhist. On one of her explorations of Beijing, Ida wandered into one of the largest and oldest temples in the city. After touring the premises and eating a sumptuous meal of bean curd prepared in the Buddhist tradition, Ida and her friends were invited to a religious service. After a few minutes, Ida realized she literally was attending a prayer meeting such as the countless Wednesday and Sunday evening services from her childhood. A man in civilian clothes, head unshaven, was addressing the audience in place of the robed monks. To her astonishment, the lecturer was urging his audience to repent and trust in Buddha. "I groaned within.... How well the missionaries had done their work!" A choir began to sing a tune only too familiar to Ida, an old Christian hymn. She slipped away, unable to enjoy the show with the rest of the crowd.

But, like the Christian missionaries from whom they borrowed their methods, the Buddhist evangelicals persisted in their conversion efforts. A young monk visited Ida at her home one Sunday morning. Over Ida's waffles, whipped cream, honey, and coffee, he preached salvation through the Lord Buddha, directly echoing words out of her past. Ida's efforts to learn about the temple, the abbot, or the women's aid societies got her nowhere. The more Ida thought of the whole matter the angrier she became.

> But even as my anger grew I knew that I was paying for the sins ... of my parents. How many times had my mother and the other missionary women visited in Chinese homes, and, sitting on their *kang* (beds) and drinking their tea and bowls of poached eggs, tried to convert them to Christianity when all that the Chinese women wanted was to see how the strange creatures dressed and to ask questions about the people in their families. These Chinese women had been bound by the laws of hospitality not to throw my mother and the Bible woman out even as I was bound and could not tell this young man to go about his business elsewhere.[35]

7

Writing: "The Road to My Heart"

I f Ida's home developed the private sphere of her American-Chinese life, her Chinese folk studies and writing provided a creative expression of her bicultural identity. In the black moments of depression while in the United States, Ida felt torn between her need to support herself and her life-long desire to write. Returning to Beijing and establishing a home at Xiao Yang Yibin Hutong, Ida continued to observe the life around her more as a writer than as a social worker. She translated a friend's story, interviewed Old Madam Ning, and recorded Chinese beliefs and customs.

Ida was a friend of many years with the family of Wu Yong, author of *The Flight of an Empress.* During the violent Boxer Rebellion against foreigners and Chinese Christians in 1900, Wu was a fledgling magistrate in the city of Huailai, north of Beijing in Hebei province. He had the unusual distinction of being the first official on the scene to offer decent food and clothing to the Empress Dowager Zu Ci (Cixi) and her entourage as they fled Beijing during the Allied Forces' counter-attack.[1] His great sense of duty, responsibility, and virtue as a Confucian official impressed the Empress Dowager sufficiently that she charged him with arranging the logistics for the Sacred Chariot's remaining journey. Further, she gave careful consideration to his ten-point resolution to the conflict with the foreign powers.

Wu began his account in 1897 as a very young district magistrate who worked "faithfully and with my whole heart." He described the Boxers as the Eight Symbol Religion, a sect that practiced charms and exorcisms and cheated and seduced the country people. He explained their appeal as a reaction against the Christian missionaries, whose protection of Christian converts interfered with the Chinese government's prosecution of criminal suspects. Therefore the hatred of the Christians became as intense as the pain of a sword thrust.[2] Throughout the book, Wu Yong expressed the Chinese people's opposition to the "unprincipled and overbearing" missionaries, and by extension, all foreigners. That foreigners wielded power over their once great civilization caused the national face to "drop into the dust."[3]

Ida knew that her own parents strongly opposed the Christian practice of protecting criminals from Chinese law. Realizing her parents were atypical, she deeply resented most Christian missionaries for interfering in Chinese government and empathized with popular Chinese antipathy toward Westerners. By translating the old scholar's story, Ida gave voice to a proud people.

Wu's inside stories about intrigue at the imperial court, horse thieves and his adroit handing of the Boxer threat mesmerized his audience of government office workers. They "sat in a circle hugging their knees.... Their hearts and their spirits were concentrated in their ears...." The transcriber, Liu Kun, was among the audience. He considered Wu a "very gentle and honest person, and ceremonious, like an old scholar."[4]

Ida's decision to translate her old friend's story was very much in keeping with her urgent desire to study and record the traditional faith behind Chinese customs and beliefs that preserved their civilization for thousands of years, which she feared was being lost. Magistrate Wu Yong personified the best in the Confucian scholar class, which had ruled China through its many dynasties.

He described the delicate position of a magistrate:

> During these two years I had been very careful in all details, reflected deeply, and prayed for the right outcome of all lawsuits. I was not avaricious and not careless and I used punishment with reason.... Those who should have been imprisoned I forgave if the sin was light.

He believed he treated people generously and the people liked him as a magistrate. Favorable public opinion protected him from the Boxers, who had stored up much anger against judges. Wu Yong was surprised by the gentry's support. "If I had had the least secret motive, or twisted the law, and thus established an old hate with the people, this friendship would long since have vanished. To be a magistrate in this troubled world is perilous."[5]

Ida's friendship with Wu Yong and her translation of his story no doubt influenced her understanding of the importance of responsibility and duty toward her own hospital and household staff. Her future writing and public lectures about China invariably stressed these same virtues.

From the social casework files at the PUMC hospital, Ida crafted short vignettes for each of the six issues of the progressive magazine *democracy: a far eastern half-monthly of fact and opinion.*[6] "Husbands and Wives" presents four cases as dialogues between the patients and Ida, as well as Ida's sense of the problems and the cultural component of each patient's illness. Ida took this opportunity to share with her Western audience a few emotional and physical qualities of Chinese marriages that, although arranged, became very happy.

Among the four chosen examples, one case focused on the first wife, who had encouraged her husband to take a concubine in order to perpetuate the family lineage. The other examples concerned a second wife and two only wives. Using these common Chinese citizens from both rural and urban backgrounds, Ida explored individual variety within Chinese tradition and the confusion wrought by modern values.

In addition to realistic dialogue, the stories are rich with descriptive detail about the patients and their families' demeanor, clothing, and interactions. The beloved second wife whose life and health were ruined by the sudden return of the first wife from the countryside approached Ida:

> ... carrying the shapeless hospital garment with grace, and the hospital slippers did not flap. She walked with the slow-stepping dignity and straight-backed swing so characteristic of the Manchu women who have worn the high winged headdress and the stilt-soled shoes. She greeted us with the formal courtesy of many generations and sat on the offered chair ready to discuss graciously any treatment the doctor might have to offer.

Ida's own empathetic imagination came into play in her writings about hospital cases. Although Ida admitted not being able to communicate with a Cantonese-speaking patient, she imagined that the girl "lay and wondered why the world, which had seemed such a pleasant place, should have become so unpleasant." On another occasion, the patient's husband was described as "a not very robust soul [who] let his claim to be a scholar exempt him from every other need. Quotations and references could probably be got from him, but not much, one would think, in the way of judgement [sic] or initiative."[7]

Ida discovered that "the road to my heart was through my imagination."[8] Chinese poetry expressed the identity she began to build during psychotherapy with Dr. Marianna Taylor in Boston—not as wife or lover but as an autonomous woman writer:

> I thirst ... But none of the proffered cups
> Can slake that thirst ...
> "Oh who shall I mate with?" ...
> My body is beautiful
> But who has sat by the China sea ...
> Or on a peak at dawn and
> Been taught the mysteries of Tao?[9]

Through the writing process, Ida sublimated her sexual passions and developed close relationships with Chinese people that proved impossible in reality. She discovered a deeper dimension to life than either the Christian church or marriage had offered her. Speaking to herself, perhaps through a fictional or dream character, she clearly juxtaposed romantic love and love for China: "Foreign men are only on the fringe of your life. Your life must be with Chinese. You should cultivate the people your life will be with."

Ida loved to imagine that she had been Chinese in a former incarnation. She retold the Chinese belief that the souls of those who have been much to each other through the tens of thousands of years would reunite every five hundred years. Ida's own Western lovers must have paled in comparison to her union with the souls of the Chinese people. Perhaps she had been an artisan who created the glorious Imperial Palace or a citizen of the Ming dynasty who accepted his world happily, without a thought for changing it.[10]

Ida's stories captured the sensuality of the daily lives of the common people and of the city, itself. According to legend, the city was built to resemble a mythical person, "No Cha," with three heads and six arms. Each building and open space was situated to represent a specific body part. Ida's stories gave No Cha a voice: the sounds of the people, animals, and vehicles, the daytime noises of work and play, the wail of prayers at night, all blending into a great symphony. The pungent fragrances and foul odors, the colors and the forms of "No Cha" all gave Ida "abundant joy in life," as lovers do.[11]

Before her furlough in 1932–1933, she had already published several essays in the *Atlantic Monthly*, as well as in professional medical journals.[12] In her *Atlantic Monthly* article, "Day by Day in Peking," Ida described the crudity of the coolie theater compared with the pleasure of listening to the most ancient of the arts, the storytellers, and then imagined the emotions of an old man in the audience who "leaned back, closed his eyes, and with an expression of perfect joy on his face beat time to the music." In her essay, Ida conducted her reader through a day in Beijing. Starting from a description of the sights, she moved on to comment about subjects as diverse as the Chinese so-called lack of initiative, women's social position, crime and punishment.[13]

"New Year's Eve in Peking," also published in the *Atlantic Monthly*, began lightly as did "Day by Day," portraying scenes of street markets laden with produce, game, fruits and vegetables, and baskets of seafood. "Snails ... still crawl sluggishly.... Great tubs of water contain big fish and little fish ... and eels slithering." Peddlers sold fish-shaped lanterns of red and green and yellow, children's toys, and candy to sweeten the lips of the kitchen god prior to his yearly report to the Heavenly Emperor. For many nights before New Year's Eve, firecrackers exploded continuously throughout the city, "a bombardment of joy."

"Like an insistent theme carried by ambitious piccolos," another, quieter sound could be heard by those who listened carefully— housewives' endless chopping of meat and vegetables for the New Year's dumplings.

> This chopping in the dark hours symbolizes to many a man and woman all that is most dear in the home. They speak of it in the hushed voice used for sacred things. And when this sound is mentioned there can be seen, in the face of a weathered man, the small lad tense in the New Year atmosphere as, lifted out of himself, he watches the elders busying themselves ... hanging the ancestral portraits, preparing the offerings, donning their best clothes. And always the mother is chopping, chopping the food that shall last them many days.[14]

Through Ida's pen, the Chinese New Year's Eve festivities drop their exotic quality and take on the same childlike excitement and family spirit as an American Christmas; the mothers' endless chopping is like American mothers' baking of endless batches of cookies.

In this essay, Ida went beyond depicting universal human emotions through common daily customs and habits. She moved on to the most central of Chinese religious rituals—ancestor reverence. As a guest of a former high-ranking Manchu official, probably Wu Yong, Ida was invited behind the spirit screen to observe the family's private worship of the ancestors and of Heaven and Earth.

They gathered in the common room, newly transformed into a shrine by offerings, scrolls, and pictures of the family patriarch's grandparents,

parents, and three deceased wives. The change in the room went deeper than the rearrangements.

> It was as though these people whose descendants had gathered to do them homage, whose presence had been invoked, had come, and these their [sic] descendants knew it. The family stood in calm dignity, respectful and aware in the presence of their ancestors who, living on the other side, had come to visit them.

Ida went on to describe the family ceremony of offering food, and kowtowing to thirteen generations of their ancestors and the younger generations kowtowing to the older. "Space and time had been annihilated. There was no barrier between the dead and the living, between the seen and the unseen."

She was careful to explain that the ceremony was not a worship of gods or pagan idols as the missionaries charged, but the veneration given to members of a family who now live elsewhere. The veneration was the same as that given by the younger generation to the elders. The spirit, which Ida and perhaps the family felt, was not that of supernatural beings but of great thoughts and of the family, itself.

Ida's joy in writing came from imagining the patterns in peoples' minds from the patterns of their rituals and social relations. Her goal, like that of ancestor reverence, was "to overcome space and time" between her Chinese subjects and her American audience. Her writings, like her mediation work at the PUMC, became a bridge between peoples but on a more profound emotional level than she could achieve as a social worker.

Ida's literary reflection on the Chinese spirit led her to a re-examination of the religious spirit she had rejected along with her missionary past. In all of her translations and writings, Ida used descriptions of Chinese scenes as metaphors for expressing the people's inner thoughts and feelings. Her essay "New Year's Eve in Peking" most directly and concretely conveyed the deepest beliefs of the Chinese. This piece was remarkable also for divulging Ida's own reactions to the Chinese ritual. "I felt my throat tighten. Surely we were in the presence of unseen beings.... My thoughts had soared."[15] This was the writing of an insider, one who participated in the ceremony and found meaning in the ritual.

As she studied Chinese literature, wrote short stories, translated books and recorded Old Madam Ning's life, Ida observed that most of China's honored writers, most revered sages and most beloved poets of all historical periods addressed what they considered the right way for people to live and fearlessly condemned the wrongs of their time.[16] Ida came "to realize that religion was not the ritual or even the theology of any given faith but the way of life of the people...." She saw that the ritual, pageantry, priesthood, and theology of religion were expressions of people's pattern of feelings, their thoughts about the universe's creation, their ethical system, and other unanswerable questions.

She found Chinese religions to be more meaningful to her than Christianity. She shared Confucianism's agnosticism about an afterlife and the supernatural, lived by its "five cardinal relations" based on family relationships, and found peace of mind from its emphasis on self-acceptance. She considered herself even more the Daoist than the Confucian, perhaps because of its dialectical philosophy of action/non-action (*wuwei*), or maybe because of her love of little temples on misty mountains. But beyond these religious forms, Ida most valued Chinese eclecticism that accepted many apparently contradictory beliefs. To her, the Chinese way was one of acceptance of self and other people; the Christian way was one of impossible striving for perfection over one's own sins and judgment of the sins of others. Of the two philosophies, only the Chinese way offered Ida a means to integrate her disparate Eastern and Western selves.

In her Chinese eclecticism, Ida even came to terms with Christianity in her later years. She worked with the missionaries on behalf of China during World War II, and accepted her mother before Anna died. Reflecting on religion in 1966, Ida said, "Mankind, whether feeling helpless or arrogant, whether seeking to wear the armor of ritual or to walk forth armed only by science, needs *a restatement of that which is in his heart*" (emphasis hers). She considered religion to be this restatement and therefore a universal element in all people. While Ida gave due respect to the powers of science, she believed that the greatest power known to humankind is one's own mind and emotions.[17]

Writing Chinese Women's Lives: The "Lao Taitais"

During the late 1920s, before leaving Beijing for a sabbatical in New York, Ida had interviewed Old Madam Ning (Ning Lao Taitai), an elderly Chinese working class woman from her hometown in Shandong province. Ida met Old Madam Ning through her son's employer. She initially sought Ning out for her knowledge of old family customs and folk tales, particularly those concerning childbirth, marriage, and death. The elderly Chinese woman and middle-aged American woman struck up a friendship, perhaps because they shared the thick Shandong provincial accent and had each lived in Penglai and Yantai.

Over breakfast three days a week for two years, Ida listened to the elderly woman's stories and simultaneously typed the English translation. By way of illustrating the old customs, Ning told about her own life of hardships and ever-declining fortunes. The daughter of a small shopkeeper, Ning was married at age thirteen to a much older man who became an opium addict. He sold their possessions and young daughter to support his addiction, forcing his wife to beg for food in order to survive. Ning eventually left her husband and worked for years as a servant of Chinese officials and Western missionaries. Ida portrayed Ning as a woman whose gift of humor and of seeing things as they are overcame her bitter destiny. Old Madam Ning's strength of character and dignity in the face of adversity represented the finest of the Chinese spirit. The book's title, itself, honors China's women as heroines. As daughters of Han, they become female counterparts of *hao hanzi*, virile sons of the Han race.[18]

Pruitt allowed Ning's voice to speak throughout the book. In organizing the countless customs, tales, and beliefs around the chronological structure of Ning's life, Pruitt gave continuity to the elderly woman's life, yet maintained the fragmentary, unsettled, anxious sense in which Ning experienced her life unfolding. Brutality and tenderness, weakness and strength, coexist on each page. It is a sympathetic but unsentimental presentation.

In one example, Ning told of childhood beatings by her mother. "She broke a broom over me. She broke a stool beating me. I screamed and said that I would not do it any more. She said, "The more you say you will not, the more I will beat you." Ning tempered the brutality of this story with comical descriptions of her own misdemeanors, and of the chickens who divulged those misdemeanors to her mother. ("… the chickens did not give us face.")

Ning's presentation was neither a defense nor a condemnation of her mother for the beatings, but simply a comment on the difficulties and heartaches between mother and child. The passage ended: "My mother was sorry that she had to beat me. My mother loved me. And after that I needed no more beating for I knew that my mother loved me and I was beginning to have the reason of a grown person."[19] Likewise, in a passage about foot binding, Ning's tone is that of recounting to a close friend the love and care which motivated her mother to bind her daughter's feet.

> My feet hurt so much that for two years I had to crawl on my hands and knees. Sometimes at night they hurt so much I could not sleep. I stuck my feet under my mother and she lay on them so they hurt less and I could sleep.... A girl's beauty and desirability were counted more by the size of her feet than by the beauty of her face.[20]

Ning felt no need to justify or condemn the painful practice or her mother's role in perpetuating it. Nor did Ida, as Ning's biographer, feel any need for editorial comment on the practices of foot binding and child abuse.

Ida's presentation of Old Madam Ning was a striking departure from missionary woman's writings about Chinese customs. The publications of Ida's mother and other nineteenth-century missionary women centered around lurid stories of Asian womanhood brutally oppressed by an evil, male paganism. This emphasis inspired financial contributions and recruited new missionaries.[21] Anna Pruitt's reaction to her daughter's presentation of Chinese womanhood in *A Daughter of Han* was to call it a "huge dose of unvarnished heathenism ... [and] a direct call to increased evangelistic effort."[22] She failed to see the extent to which Old Madam Ning had succeeded in responding to hardships and ill-treatment with strength, compassion, and resourcefulness.

Ida might well have carried on the theme of victimization, oppression, and sexual submission expressed in other Western literature about China, including her mother's books, articles, and letters. Much of her writing drew on the Chinese who came as patients to the PUMC hospital and became her clients. From thousands of Social Service Department cases, she could have chosen as her subjects any number of women with tragic life stories. For example Pai Shun-ke, like Ning, had a husband whose opium addiction had brought the family to ruin. Pai attempted suicide, while Ning struggled to survive. In spite of social sanctions against women appearing in public, and ridicule by friends and neighbors, Ning forced herself out on the streets to beg for food.

Suicide and begging were both ways that Chinese women traditionally solved their problems. Missionary women and novelists focused on the suicides and other forms of victimization, not the ways women overcame adversity and built successful lives. Ida resented this distorted emphasis. In her fiction and nonfiction stories, as well as her biography of Ning, Ida wrote about women who participated in shaping their fate within Chinese tradition. She clearly chose to portray a very different sense of the ordinary Chinese woman. Ning is the representative of everywoman in China; she gives a heroic dimension to her sex.

The most poignant example of Ning's struggle against victimization is her reaction to the news that her husband had sold her daughter. "I jumped out of bed.... I seized him by the queue. I wrapped it three times around my arm. I fought him for my child. We rolled fighting on the ground." They searched for the child the night through, Ning's hands grasping her husband's queue. They finally found the little girl in a house of dealers who trafficked in prostitution. Ning demanded to see her daughter, took the child into her arms, and started to leave. The proprietor barred the door.

> "Then," I said, "I will stay here. My child is in my bosom. Mother and child, we will die here together." ... "They tried to frighten me.... I was young then, and salable. But I said, "No. I have another child at home. I must go to that child also." After some negotiations about repayment of the child's selling price, the dealers let the mother and daughter go.[23]

Ida's spirit was as indomitable as Ning's. As a child, she survived the hard life in the Chinese interior, which spelled death to many missionary women and children, including members of her own family. She navigated her way through political infighting at the Rockefeller hospital and in the anti-Japanese underground. In later years, as the American executive secretary of Indusco, she waged constant battles against the Henry Luce forces to protect Indusco's interests within the United China Relief organization. Even those who knew her tender side recognized that Ida was nothing if not tough. In choosing Old Madam Ning as her literary subject and friend, she sought out a woman as resilient as herself.

During the late 1920s—the period in which Ida interviewed Old Madam Ning—Ida struggled against her tendency toward dependent passivity in her love relationship with Jack MacIntosh and in her position at the PUMC hospital. Private writings from that time period express a self-image torn between the Chinese and Western cultures, and between the traditional missionary and modern professional sense of womanhood. In 1932, while in the United States, she pulled herself out of an immobilizing depression by means of psychiatric counseling. After returning to Beijing the following year, she continued her recovery and built a fulfilling life. She established her own home, an architectural hybrid of Chinese and American design, and filled it with a multicultural household.

Studying and writing about Chinese life and customs became the key to Ida's strong identity and satisfaction. She described the writing process as "firing my imagination," something that her professional social work career or, indeed, her relationships with Western men failed to do. She experienced an almost mystical connection with her Chinese subjects and with eternal Chinese values. Her *Atlantic Monthly* story about a Chinese family's New Year's Eve celebration describes her sense of communion with the departed ancestors.[24]

The traditional Chinese understanding of the close proximity between the material world and the ancestral realm best expressed Ida's sense of deep connection, bordering on identification, with the subjects of her writings. This sense of connection is common to biographers irrespective of the gender of writer or subject, but may be most pronounced between women authors and their subjects.[25]

Ida often imagined that she had been a Chinese in previous lifetimes. Writing about Old Madam Ning and other Chinese women allowed her vicariously to become Chinese. Her concern to record the traditional Chinese popular culture even as it fought a losing battle against modern Western culture was an extension and expression of the battle waging within her. As Ida immortalized Old Madam Ning, her own spirit revived and strengthened.

Ida's models of womanhood, which she drew upon in constructing her mature self, were "Dada," the Chinese nurse who raised her until age six, as well as her own mother. "Dada" exerted a dominant influence in Ida's childhood. She taught Ida that it was the quality of being human that was important. "So was built up in me, as in Chinese children, the conviction of the dignity and worth of the human being."[26] "Dada" was the children's teacher and ally, the mother figure who provided the warm, emotional nourishment for Ida.

Perhaps the later act, as an adult, of setting down on paper the life of Old Madam Ning, another dignified Chinese woman from a village in Shandong province, renewed Ida's taste for life and asserted her connection with the culture of her mother figure.

Literary critic, Bell Gale Chevigny, focuses her gender analysis of autobiography on the mother-daughter dynamic. She suggests that a woman author's bond with her woman subject symbolically reflects her internalized relationship with her own mother and in part reshapes that relationship. The author's writing is influenced by the nature of her relationship with her mother. At the same time the author, by writing about her woman subject, has "recreated" her mother in a way that nurtures her own autonomous adult self. The research and writing about her woman subject enables her "to know a precursor" in ways she could never know her own mother.[27]

Chevigny's theory of women biographers and their subjects may be faulted for seeming to imply a stronger or deeper relationship between women than between male biographer and subject. Further, one may question Chevigny's assertion that the theory encompasses, with slight translation, biographers whose bond is strongest with the parent of the opposite sex, or whose subjects are of the opposite sex. These considerations aside, Chevigny's theory offers an insightful explanation for the strength of Ida's biography of Old Madam Ning as well as for the strength of her feelings toward Old Madam Ning and wealthy Old Madam Yin. Obviously, it is not adequate to explain Ida's strong bond with Chinese male characters in her other essays.

The pictures that Ida painted in her unpublished writings about her mother and her Chinese nurse stand in stark contrast to one another. The American woman was absorbed in her work with the Chinese and used her daughter to provide emotional comfort otherwise lacking in her life; the Chinese woman was warm, nurturing, and emotionally available to the little girl. Anna's affection typically was expressed by reading to the children; "Dada" care for their physical needs, played with them, listened to them. Ida loved her.

Ida's biography of Old Madam Ning not only symbolically reflected her internalized relationship with her Chinese mother figure but helped to "recreate" or "repair the reality" of her difficult relationship with her biological mother, in Chevigny's terms.[28] Through Ning's life, Ida could make her own mother look, dress, and act Chinese, as she had longed to do as a child. Through the character of Ning, Ida accepted her mother's strong personality while infusing her mother with "Dada's" sensitivity to human relations. The missionary woman's moral rectitude lost its harsh, judgmental tone and took on the Chinese sense of moderation and pragmatism in Ning's ethical system.

While symbolically changing some aspects of Anna Pruitt, the narration of Old Madam Ning's life affirmed other aspects of Ida's mother. Ida's tribute to a strong Chinese matriarch was at once a memorial to her family matriarchs. Her maternal relatives structured their family history around "the grandmother's window" in the Tallmadge, Ohio homestead.[29] Reading Aunt Myra's view of the family story, it seems that successive generations of women sat by the grandmother at her window, while the men folk faded into the background of the family narrative. Anna Pruitt perpetuated her matriarchal family structure as the dominant force in the Pruitt family home in north China. Her husband, C.W. Pruitt, withdrew to the life of biblical scholar and Chinese translator; Anna managed the children and servants as well as the mission school and medical clinic, and she organized activities involving Chinese Christian converts.

Although the particulars of the Pruitt family home and relationships were different from Ning's, the matriarchal structure was similar. Ida grew to emulate, if not appreciate, her mother's managerial abilities. In her childhood fantasy play with paper dolls, Ida marshaled great families of women, children, and grandchildren, but there was never a father present.[30]

As chronicler and editor of Old Madam Ning's story, Ida Pruitt affirmed her family structure while transforming her relationship with her mother into one that met her need for nurturing. By combining her American and Chinese mothers into the person of Madam Ning, and by organizing the disparate parts of Ning's life into a whole, Pruitt resolved the conflicting American and Chinese aspects of her personality. Her writing, even more than psychotherapy, the establishment of her home in Beijing, or her professional success, ended her periods of depression and promoted her sense of wholeness.

Chevigny explains this process as the author's final separation from her mother, or in Pruitt's case, two mother figures, in order to become an autonomous adult woman. Chevigny is convinced that women writing about other women in biography are as daughters writing about foremothers. A woman writes a biography in an attempt to know her mother both intimately and separately from herself, and thus to recognize herself as separate. As an author of women's biography, a woman may be subtly constructing her own autonomy separate from her male-identified roles.[31]

Ida began to authorize her autonomy by publishing several short stories in *The Atlantic Monthly* in 1931–1932 while on sabbatical in the United States. *A Daughter of Han* completed the process by which Ida overcame the child-like dependence and passivity fostered by both her own overbearing mother and her loving Chinese nurse. After returning to

China from the United States, she began to organize the fragmented notes of interviews conducted in the late 1920s. As she moved into place the disconnected pieces of Ning's life, her own life took shape, as well. Ida organized the Social Service Department into the model for the practice and teaching of medical social work throughout China. She became the matriarch of a family consisting of adopted daughters, servants, friends, guests, and a lover, but no permanent man. After the Japanese occupation of Beijing, she played an important role in the anti-Japanese underground. Perhaps Pruitt drew on Ning's spunk in conquering her bitter fate as she struggled to assert her autonomy against strong international and intra-psychic forces that threatened to overwhelm her.[32]

As Ida was finishing her biography of Ning, the Rockefeller hospital was responding to Chinese nationalistic concerns by replacing its Western staff with Chinese and the Japanese were encroaching on ever-larger areas of China. Ida anxiously sought other positions in China, Hong Kong, and the United States, and began to reassess her skills and resources. In such troubled times, with individual, national, and cultural survival at stake, the telling of Ning's story became more urgent than ever for her. Saving Ning's story held a meaning beyond the social and political acts of rescue or the sentimental act of preserving the memories of a dying tradition. At an intuitive level, Pruitt knew that writing the biography was helping to restore her own depleted spirit. In saving Madam Ning's life, she saved her own.[33]

Ida's second biography, *Old Madam Yin: A Memoir of Peking Life, 1926–1938*, was begun during the same period in which she was interviewing Ning for *A Daughter of Han*. The initial writing served the same purpose as did Madam Ning's biography. In fact, as Ida describes her, Madam Yin embodied the wholeness that Ida sought. "There was vibrancy in her whole person that seemed to go from her toes to every hair lying so smoothly on her head. She was a complete person, in harmony with herself and her world."[34]

Old Madam Yin is a sympathetic yet unromantic reminiscence of Chinese upper class, as experienced by the matriarch of a large family. Ida first met Madam Yin at the PUMC when the older woman sought out the hospital's adoption services for her daughter-in-law.[35] The friendship between Yin and Ida unfolded during strolls through Yin's magnificent courtyards and gardens and social gatherings with Ida's Western friends. Madam Yin sought out her American friend to help her navigate through the foreign hospital and to make sense of the strange ways of her

European daughter-in-law. On one occasion, Madam Yin noted the similarities in their personalities: "I like you. You and I are alike. We both like people and we both like to have a bustle going on around us. Also we both like to manage other people's affairs."[36]

Another day, Madam Yin complained to Ida about Western women, then suddenly remembered Ida's origin. "Of course, you are more like a Chinese," she hurried to explain.[37] Ida reveled in such moments when Chinese friends let down their cultural barriers and shared their family ceremonies and personal confidences with her. Through her close friendships, Ida vicariously fulfilled her fantasies of being Chinese. Madam Yin embodied the finest of the civilization that Ida loved as her own.

Did Ida's deep love for Chinese civilization and its representative, Madam Yin, perhaps lead to identification, impinging on her biographical responsibilities? As Leon Edel warns, "biographers must struggle constantly not to be taken over by ... or fall in love with their subjects."[38] Ida's need to become a part of the Chinese civilization may have marred an otherwise extraordinary glimpse into the private gardens of a Chinese matriarch's home and psyche. The reader remains unsure how much is Madam Yin's psyche and how much is Ida Pruitt's. Which woman's view of Chinese civilization are we glimpsing?[39]

In contrast to the first person narration of Madam Ning's tale, Madam Yin's story is told in Ida's voice and Ida remains a dominant figure throughout the book. She is more honest as an author for showing the reader the lens through which she views Yin's life; it is unabashedly the lens of friendship. Its rose-colored hue adds an unrealistic color to Madam Yin's life. Whether it distorts the Chinese woman's life more than the tinted lenses of strangers distort their so-called "objective" reporting is doubtful, however. In much greater detail than a strange biographer could do, Ida's lens of friendship explores Madam Yin's "covert mythology," to use Edel's term. Edel urges the biographer to look for her subject's self-concepts and underlying life patterns by studying the patterns and modes of her public works.[40] In the patterns or forms of Yin's dress, manner, and speech, her design of courtyards and interior rooms, in every lift of the eyebrow and choice of painting, Ida finds the character of Yin's personality and Chinese civilization, although she might over-interpret the minutiae of Yin's daily life.

It is the biographer's sensitivity toward her subject's "covert mythology" without merging it with her own mythology that Ida mastered in *A Daughter of Han*. Arguably, more than any other non-Chinese author, she entered into Chinese society and the mind of Madam Ning without losing her separate sense of self as observer.[41] However, by the time Ida edited her memoir of Madam Yin for publication in 1979, at age ninety, her foremost task no longer was to record another life but to reflect on and evaluate her own life's "covert mythology." This mythology included a restatement of her sense of womanhood as a capable family manager. Further, Ida's myth required an affirmation of the Chinese civilization at its finest. Madam Yin played the managerial role superbly and embodied her civilization in a way impossible for the earthy Ning. "When she entered a room, there was no jar of the harmonies ..., no breaking into the pattern...."[42] Finally, Ida needed to see herself as a part of that oldest living civilization. By inserting herself throughout Yin's story, she affirmed her own place in Chinese history. *Old Madam Yin*, even more than *A Daughter of Han*, was an autobiographical act.

Why didn't Ida approach this autobiographical task directly? *A China Childhood*, written in numerous drafts over many years of retirement, is the only published portion of a much larger attempt to chronicle her life in China. American presses repeatedly rejected the entire manuscript. *A China Childhood* finally was published in a much-abbreviated version in Taiwan and consequently is almost unknown in the United States.[43]

Why was the successful biographer so unsuccessful as an auto-biographer? The quality of Pruitt's autobiographical writing is inferior to her biography and fiction. Where there is rich detail about the Chinese, there is silence about herself. Flashes of insight into the Chinese subjects' psyches and cultural patterns are replaced by lengthy travelogues of her journeys throughout China and poetic descriptions of Beijing. Her work as chief of social service at the PUMC, one of only two women in administrative positions at the most prestigious hospital in China, is missing altogether. She offers, instead, insightful, imaginative accounts of her patients' lives outside the institution. Her passionate and, at times, heartbreaking love affairs are censored; her social life becomes breakfasts followed by hiking expeditions, genteel cocktail hours in the courtyard, and occasional large parties.[44] The writing is rambling and unfocused.

Her fascinating life among both the rich and famous and the down and out in Beijing, as well as her well-developed interpersonal and interior life certainly provided material for a publishable autobiography. Instead, these were confided to private diaries and essays.

There probably are a number of explanations for Ida's hesitation to write about her own life as she had written about others. She no doubt considered the personal and political aspects of her respected position among American supporters of the People's Republic of China, including former China missionaries. She did not want to jeopardize her legitimacy as a vocal advocate of a controversial cause.[45]

In addition to personal and political considerations, gender differences probably affected Ida's writing about her life. Elizabeth Winston shows that American women autobiographers before 1920 "understated their achievements, disclaimed interest in personal recognition, or stressed the broad historical value of their life stories."[46] In her unpublished drafts of her eighteen years in Beijing, which she titled *Days in Old Peking*, Ida's writing conforms to these patterns. Nowhere in her manuscript did she describe or evaluate her own work at the hospital. With the exception of social work issues discussed in her annual reports and professional social work articles, Ida's writings are an escape from her professional concerns into personal ones. Yet, her autobiography, by focusing on her personal, non-professional world, is not the more intimate. She explores the unspoken emotions of her Chinese subjects in exquisite detail but is silent about her own relationships with family, friends, and lovers. Even Ida's childhood account, as published, is devoid of the emotional substance of her familial relationships and her fantasy world. Several chapters of these were included in earlier drafts but were excised in the final version.

A China Childhood became an artful account of an American child growing up in a Chinese village who reveals little about herself and much about traditional Chinese culture. Earlier versions were disorganized, unfocused, and rambling. Chapters appeared more like individual essays about Chinese servants, neighbors, villagers, and Christians than chapters about a family. In the final version, Ida consciously used the pattern of the Chinese house or compound as a metaphor for the Chinese way of thinking, for which she held such a strong affinity. The work acquired a harmonious shape, but lost the emotional depth expressed in earlier drafts.

A final consideration in the evaluation of *A China Childhood* is Ida's life stage at the time of editing. The substance and structure of early drafts reveals her effort to clarify her identity as a person pulled between cultures, historical periods, and worldviews. The final manuscript projects an already clarified, affirmed and authenticated self-image. It was written by a woman who, in her retirement years, had resolved these questions and who was trying to get her work published after many unsuccessful efforts. The quality of her work may have suffered for her adherence to preconceived notions of autobiographical form, notions that publishers shared. It is both fortunate and ironic that Ida did not allow preconceived notions of biographical form or even numerous publishers' rejection notices to interfere with her recording of Chinese women's lives. It seems that she could assert the identity of traditional Chinese women with more confidence than she could assert her own identity as a woman born in the margins between cultures and historical periods. She stretched the limits of the conventional biographical form for Chinese women but lacked the confidence to stretch the standard autobiographical form to include her own life.

In *Orientalism*, Edward W. Said's now-classic exploration of the dominant Western literary constructs of Asia, he reveals:

> [The] very large mass of writers, among whom are poets, novelists, philosophers, political theorists, economists, and imperial administrators, [who] have accepted the basic distinction between East and West as the starting point for elaborate theories, epics, novels, social descriptions, and political accounts concerning the Orient, its people, customs, "mind," destiny, and so on.[47]

His 1993 follow-up study, *Culture and Imperialism*, extends the analysis to European and American writing about other parts of the world. Said notes stereotypes of "the mysterious East" and the "mind" of entire cultures, among other rhetorical figures and devices used by all the Western discourses.[48] Works of literature produced in the First World invent and "orientalize" imaginary, stagnant Third World cultures that experience no social change or political unrest. Non-whites are essentialized and subordinated to the superior European/American power-holders.

Scholar Zhang Longxi applies Orientalism to China, citing European writers from the Enlightenment to Michel Foucault, as well as Harold R. Isaacs' analysis of American images of China.

> The image of China in the Western eye ... has always been historically shaped to represent values that are considered different from Western ones. China, India, Africa, and the Islamic Orient have all served as foils to the West at one time or another, either as idealized utopias, alluring and exotic dreamlands, or lands of eternal stagnation, spiritual purblindness, and ignorance....[49]

Ida's publications about Chinese women and men, written during the 1930s, depart from the Orientalism of European and American writers. She replaces their caricatures with portrayals of realistic individuals, ranging from a young district magistrate to an elderly beggar, privileged first wives to beloved only wives. None are subordinated to the Westerners. Old Madams Ning and Yin are very much the equals, and at times moral superiors, of the white race.

"Ida's" China, though possessing enduring cultural patterns and values, was anything but "frozen and timeless," as it has been for Foucault and Western writers for hundreds of years. The characters in her books and short stories were affected by the political and social changes and responded as best they could within the patterns of their tradition. Madam Ning's life unfolded amidst the tragedies of the late nineteenth century, such as opium addition and an economy in crisis. For a time, she worked for the foreign missionaries. Madam Yin's children and other young people challenged traditional Chinese social conventions between the sexes. Her son even married a foreign woman.

Ida describes traditional customs in colorful, but not exotic detail. She recounts occasional mystical experiences in universal terms such as cooking for holiday meals and remembering deceased relatives. The reader feels closer to the Chinese, rather than seeing them as inscrutable or ignorant.

Said points out that even contemporary Western critics of imperialism cannot understand that "India, Africa, and South America also had lives and cultures with integrities not totally controlled by the gringo imperialists and reformers of this world.... [They] argue that the source of the world's significant action and life is in the West...." These authors lack the political willingness to consider any alternatives to imperialism; they fail to comprehend and engage with other societies, traditions, and histories.[50]

Ida's writings distinguish themselves from those of Western critics as well as supporters of Western imperialism. Her stories of ordinary men and women do not revolve around their interactions with Western residents of Beijing, not even the missionaries and reformers among whom Ida worked. Rather, her work foreshadows that of postcolonial scholarship since *Orientalism* was published in 1978. "Such works are feminist, but not exclusivist; they demonstrate the diversity and complexity of experiences that works beneath the totalizing discourses of Orientalism; they are sensitive but not maudlin about women's experience ...."[51]

In her 1946 review of *A Daughter of Han* in the *Saturday Review of Literature*, Alice Tisdale Hobart noted with pleasure how publishers' attitudes had changed since 1925. "There is no sale for a book that presents China with realism [in 1925].... The public has been too long fed on the Fu Manchu type of Chinese. Americans want only China picturesque or villainous." To Hobart, the publication of Old Madam Ning's life was testimony to the greater public interest in China by the mid 1940s.[52] She may not have been aware of the manuscript's rejection by many publishing companies before Yale University Press accepted it. Roberta Yerkes, Ida's contact at Yale, confessed that she had "no idea what the market for this book will be, because I have never seen anything like it...." But Yale was willing to gamble on the "unique material." By 1967, Stanford University Press's decision to reissue *A Daughter of Han* was less of a gamble. Oral history and women's history had both come into their own; some Americans were questioning their nation's attitudes toward the world. Through Old Madam Ning's story, *A Daughter of Han* challenged Orientalism and became one of Stanford's top bestsellers for many years.

8

"Gung Ho" for China

Ida's multicultural household in Xiao Yang Yibin Hutong was home to a young investigative writer from New Zealand when he was in Beijing. Jim Bertram grew quite fond of the older woman over twenty years his senior, whose command of the Chinese language and intimate knowledge of Chinese society and culture fascinated him. Ida, in turn, believed fervently in Jim's greatness as an author whose books would help China and the "world's idiocy." Their mutual admiration eventually turned passionate.

Jim's love for Ida was laced with ambivalence. While away, he anticipated their reunion with tremendous excitement. He described her as "a mixture of business-like detail ... [and] the other you, so impulsive and warm-hearted and forth going [sic], so recklessly loyal, and (quoting Auden) 'able, at times, to cry'." He felt uneasy about his own "cold, inadequate" notes to her "wide open mind and ... fanatic heart."[1]

Japan's ever-expanding occupation of north China and the growth of Chinese Communist-led resistance beckoned Jim away from Beijing ever more frequently. Jim's absences haunted Ida. In her mind, Jim had replaced Jack as the first man to whom Ida could give herself completely, the kind of man she could have married if they had met earlier and been closer in age. She confided to her personal diary that she sometimes strongly felt his presence with her. "After going to bed a feeling of bliss of his soon arrival. He almost came into the room. I almost touched him. Knowledge of his love." In her letters to Jim, Ida confessed her deep pain and loneliness in his absence.[2] Although she no longer defined herself in relationship to a man, Ida remained emotionally vulnerable to love and loss.

A Deepening Shadow

A deepening shadow began stretching across China as the Japanese invaded and occupied Manchuria in 1931. The shadow lengthened as Suiyuan, Chahar (both part of Inner Mongolia now), and Jehol (now Rehe) fell to the foreigners.

On July 7, 1937 Ida and her Western friends had planned a dinner party and paid little heed of martial law in Beijing. Martial law had been proclaimed every time the various Chinese warlords exchanged positions in the power struggles of Chinese politics during the 1930s. Westerners had generally considered these internecine wars as "brawls"; martial law didn't apply to them. This time, however, was different.

The dinner party was called off, as some of the men went out to the Marco Polo Bridge to check out the incident at first hand. Ida dined with a friend on the roof top restaurant at the Beijing Hotel. She only realized the seriousness of this event when she attempted to return home later in the evening, only to find herself alone on the normally busy main streets of the city. "How small I felt bowling along alone, in the middle of that wide expanse. How still everything was, as though the great wide city was holding its breath and that we only were moving."[3]

Turning from the Street of Eternal Peace (Changan Jie) into Hademen Street, suddenly Ida's rickshaw was stopped at bayonet point by a soldier from the regular army. His discipline and precision of actions, so unlike the half-hungry, poorly equipped warlord mercenaries Ida was used to, told Ida he meant business. Only after his commanding officer interrogated Ida was she allowed to continue, accompanied by another soldier. Never again did she disregard the announcement of martial law.

In the weeks that passed before the final Japanese occupation of Beijing, Ida and her friends gathered after work in her courtyard to drink cocktails of canned grapefruit juice and vodka and catch up on the latest rumors. Friends who lived outside the city would spend the night in Ida's compound when they joined the party. Jim Bertram had recently returned from visiting the Communist Eighth Route Army headquartered in Yan'an, Shaanxi province. He shared with Ida a poem that a guerrilla had found on the body of a dead Japanese soldier. "There is no end to this land of mud. There is no end to my longing for home...."[4]

Ida was overwhelmed by the realization of war's irrationality and by the inevitability of unhappiness and suffering for both warring parties. She couldn't sleep. The comforting rise and fall of Beijing's human voices each evening had grown silent, replaced by the booming of guns in the night.

One morning in early August, an American marine interrupted Ida's breakfast to advise her to seek safety in the United States Embassy. They expected the Japanese to take Beijing that day. At first, Ida refused to go. Then, realizing that her home was situated in the line of fire between the Chinese barracks and the Japanese army, she recognized that the street fighting might jeopardize Guijing and Tania. The Rape of Nanjing had not yet occurred, or she would have been frightened enough to seek asylum at the embassy immediately. Instead, they gathered together a few toiletries, stopped by the hospital, and rode on their bicycles through the city streets, once again deserted, to the American Embassy. Ida did not say goodbye to the servants. She did not like leaving them, and could not protect them in case of trouble. But she could not push aside the thought that, because of her own privileged status, she had abandoned some members of her household.

At noon, Beijing was declared an open city. The Chinese commander had not carried out his promise or threat to defend the city to the last man. Lives were saved and the city's architectural wonders were preserved. But the normally gay people of Beijing looked gloomy. Citizens forced to carry banners in the "victory parade" had long faces. Tears ran down the faces of school children as they marched in the parade. They carried little pennants saying, "Japanese and Chinese are One Race." But as they walked, they tore tiny strips off the pennants. There would be nothing but bare sticks when they arrived at the reviewing stands.

The surface of Ida's life went on as usual under Japanese occupation. Western residents of occupied Beijing rang in 1938 with a costume party and dance, at which presided special guest, Tibetan Buddhist monk, Delawar Gegan. Although he refrained from dancing, the bemused lama threw confetti with Ida and the other revelers, as all tried to forget the strict search that cars, buses, and pedestrians had been subject to that day.[5]

New Year's Day newspapers brought the war back quickly enough with reports of the Japanese demands for peace and references to "the sublime destiny of the Yamato race." Reports came in the following day from Nanjing of Chinese bound together in bundles of 250 and machine-gunned. Gradually, the full extent of Japanese atrocities in Nanjing became known: Foreign observers estimated between 20,000 and 80,000 females were brutally raped. Between 200,000 and 300,000 people were killed altogether. The city lay in ruins, destroyed by fires, robbery, and unbridled havoc.[6]

After seeing *Captains Courageous* on January 3, Ida dined with friends and heard reports that Chinese "irregulars" had picked off many Japanese shopkeepers and police on December 31.[7] ("Irregulars" referred to the anti-Japanese resistance fighters, not the regular Nationalist troops. According to many, Chiang Kai-shek was saving his troops to fight the Communists.) Soon, she learned that over 2,000 Chinese irregulars in Beijing were beginning to frighten the Japanese, who arrested over 100 Chinese possessing incriminating letters or telephone messages during the last week of 1937.

Stories circulated of Japanese burning women and children, of both Chinese and Japanese armies in turn looting the town of Taiyuan in nearby Shanxi province, of the killing of three American missionaries. Word spread about the Communist Eighth Route Army, as well.

By January 12, the PUMC received a few victims of the Battle of Fangshan, outside of Beijing. As always, Ida tried to talk with the wounded, who told her of the Japanese setting fire to peasants' houses, barring their exit, and watching them burn.

Ida's home, social life, and work at the Rockefeller Hospital took on new meaning, as her passion for preserving the Chinese ways became a struggle to defend China's national integrity and save individual lives. She built a big bonfire in her back garden to help her Chinese friends burn their modern books after the Japanese began house-to-house searches and imprisoned anyone possessing books on America or in English.

The arrest of many hundreds of anti-Japanese resistance activists continued. In her diary, Ida expressed worry about the arrest of her Chinese friends in the underground. The home that had given harmony and balance to Ida's life became a lifeline for her Chinese friends. Her rooms filled with refugees from the Japanese, as her parents' compound in Huangxian had filled with refugees from the first Sino-Japanese war. In 1937, as in 1894, the privileged status and extraterritorial rights of Westerners protected their Chinese friends for a while.

Huang Zemin, which Ida knew was a nom d'guerre, lived at Hsiao Yang Yibin Hutong for eight months, during which time he taught at a day school for refugee children which the Social Service Department at PUMC had organized. The job enabled him to register with the Japanese. His real work remained a secret, but he always knew the latest war news, so Ida speculated he was involved in intelligence gathering. Her guest knew that he must invent a realistic reason to justify his lengthy stay in the home of a foreigner. So the multi-ethnic, multicultural family grew again, as Ida became "Gugu" to the son of a "dear friend from Shandong province." Ida cashed large checks for her "adopted son" while he lived in the protection of her home. In 1959, she was reunited with him in Jinan, the capital of Shandong province. His name was Chang Lei, the chief judge of the province.[8]

Ida never learned the real identity of another of her guests. He had been a general on the Long March of the Communists out of Jiangxi province as they fled Chiang Kai-shek's troops in 1934. Deng Yingchao (Mrs. Zhou Enlai) sometimes visited "Ida's general," smiling a "thank-you" to Ida across the courtyard.

One day Ida went to the train station to see off her friends, Jim Bertram and Edgar Snow to Tianjin. As was customary, two attendants followed behind the two Western men, carrying the baggage. There, dressed in traditional blue servant gowns, were Ida's guest and Deng Yingchao, squeezing into the third-class compartment of the train among the other servants and peasants. As the train pulled out of the station, out of Japanese-occupied territory and into "Free China," that was the last Ida ever saw of "her" general.[9]

The guerrillas needed medical supplies. Ida's position at the Rockefeller Hospital allowed her to obtain supplies requested by the guerrilla doctor. Ida wrapped the medicines as if they were milk powder or halibut oil ready for foster mothers to pick up. Then she placed the packages in her office and hoped the guerrilla messengers would not be recognized by their straight shoulders held so purposefully. Sometimes the messenger would say briefly, "A sick man." Ida accompanied him to help the so-called "peasant" or "artisan" through the examination and registration process. She soon learned that the hospital admitting staff was intensely patriotic and protective of the irregular guerrilla soldiers. They never questioned the made-up names of those who were wounded while "watching the crops to keep off the thieves."[10]

Ida understood that discretion was of utmost importance in underground work. Even her private diary entries maintained the fiction of her neutrality. A customary Sunday afternoon picnic in the Western Hills recorded details of the picnickers' encounter with Japanese soldiers, but was conspicuously silent on the purpose of the picnic. Only in an autobiographical essay written many years later did Ida admit that the picnickers' mission was to make a delivery to the resistance forces.

As feared, the picnickers were stopped by a Japanese soldier. He refused to allow them to continue toward their alleged destination, a temple near the guerrilla stronghold. "Too many bandits. Not safe," was his explanation. Ida, always ready with the name of yet another temple, asked if that route was safe from the "bandits." The picnickers were allowed to proceed and successfully delivered their cargo. Ida's only regret was that she could not explore the new temple.[11]

At the time, Ida thought that she and her friends were only smuggling medicines to the underground. Only later was she told that a radio vacuum tube, printing press, revolvers, and explosives for the anti-Japanese resistance fighters lay under the sandwiches, deviled eggs, and fruit.[12] As a long-time foreign resident of Beijing who constantly moved between the Chinese and Western communities, Ida consciously used her privileged status to help the underground raise much-needed funds. The main source of income for the guerrillas was obtained by robbing the imperial tombs outside Beijing. Ida wished that a trained archeologist had opened the tombs, but "war supercedes all and is no respecter of science." For the local patriots, she sold strings of semiprecious stones, translucent jade bowls, and other goods "taken from the ... dead that the living might continue to live in their own land."

In the midst of her underground activities, Ida continued a busy social life of teas, cocktails, and dinners with a wide variety of friends. Although she enjoyed both Chinese and Western theater, her spiritual sustenance came from traditional Chinese culture. Viewing Chinese ceramics "took my heart into my mouth."[13] An exhibit of "Nellie," a Pleistocene recreation of a Paleolithic era skeleton, gave Ida a long view and courage to face the coming world war.[14]

That summer of Japanese occupation, Ida's dreams reflected both anxieties of the day and a deeper steadiness. Disturbing images haunted her—the PUMC administration, friends' hurt feelings, battles between White and Red Russians, shootings, lost pocketbooks, and a plane trip/turned pleasure cruise to Texas. Her worst nightmare was to have no contacts with men after returning to live in the United States.

However, most of her dreams contained a kernel of self-confidence and serenity. In one especially vivid dream, "a great muddy sea was coming in. In the midst of it was a mountain of red mud—I knew it would catch us and overwhelm us but though I knew I should be, I was not afraid."[15]

Ida's primary contacts with the resistance forces were Jim Bertram, Edgar and Helen Foster ("Peg") Snow, and the "Shanghai liberals" associated with Sun Yat-sen's widow, Song Qingling. Through them, Ida also first learned of the Chinese Communist Party and its Eighth Route Army. Bertram and the Snows had all traveled to the Communist guerrilla base in Yan'an and had written about their experiences.[16] Snow had interviewed their leader, Mao Zedong, and later wrote *Red Star Over China*.[17]

Ida realized that Communists were very active members of the anti-Japanese irregular forces that she supported. She never felt the need to justify her cooperation with the Communist. "They were helping the Chinese people!" she merely shrugged impatiently when asked about her communist sympathies. Ida needed only to see that they, more than the Nationalists under Generalissimo Chiang, were fighting to oust the Japanese from their territory. Eighth Route Army soldiers were adhering to Chinese ways, instead of following Soviet dictates, or depending on American economic and military support, which Chiang pursued. The Communists seemed to be China's real nationalists, and so were winning the trust of the Chinese peasantry.

As a member of a prestigious American medical institution, Ida's privileged status protected her from arrest by the Japanese. She gave strict instructions to her social service staff to lead the Japanese to her if they were ever questioned. Ida saw no nobility in her instructions. Even when recording these adventures in her memoirs, Ida brushed over them lightly while dwelling on detailed descriptions of the Chinese countryside, people, and temples. Her consciously constructed identity emphasized her biculturalism, not Chinese nationalism or her anti-imperialist politics.

Jim Bertram indicated that Ida's role in the resistance movement was not so minimal, suggesting that her efforts on behalf of the anti-Japanese underground were one reason that Ida had to leave Beijing. Two of the underground student leaders who frequented Ida's house were arrested. If under prolonged torture they divulged information about Ida's "safe house," many more patriotic activists were in danger. By late March of 1938, the Japanese had become suspicious of Ida and her friends. Soon her worst fears were confirmed when she learned that one of the men had talked. Ida's house guests quietly moved to safer quarters in Beijing. Her home became less dependable to the underground network.[18]

In Hong Kong a year later, at a cocktail party Ida met a British officer whom she had known casually in Beijing. The officer asked her, his eyes twinkling, "What are the guerrillas doing for medicine now that you have left Beijing?"

"How did you know about that?" she admitted. "Oh, it is my business to know about such things. There are lists in Beijing in which your name appears." Ida then responded, "That is overrating my contribution."[19]

If Ida discounted her role in the nationalist movement against the Japanese, she nonetheless was deeply affected by the growing Chinese nationalistic assertion against all foreigners. She could see the handwriting on the wall when her contract at the PUMC was not renewed for the customary four-year term after 1935, but rather, for two consecutive appointments of two years each, 1935–1937 and 1937–1939. In the reappointment letter of 1937, J. Preston Maxwell, acting director of the PUMC, informed Ida that she would not be renewed thereafter.

The reason given by the Rockefeller Foundation for not retaining Ida was the PUMC's financial stabilization program that required the retrenchment of faculty and staff, especially since "Chinese are available adequately trained for our needs." Maxwell made special note of a minute by the hospital committee that stated their appreciation of Ida Pruitt's "long and faithful service to the College."[20] In corresponding with the director of Medical Services at a Hong Kong hospital, the acting director of PUMC, H.H. Loucks, praised Ida as "the ablest, best trained and most experienced social worker in China." He regretted the loss of her services to China but presumed that the Hong Kong hospital would not consider hiring a Westerner to develop their social service department.[21]

Ida felt that the real reason for the non-renewal of her contract was the long-standing feeling among the hospital administration that any minimally trained public health nurse could conduct social service work. Her feeling was shared by some social workers in America who, in the 1930s, were still sensitive to the suggestion that their main value lay in the compassionate, "womanly" arts for which little training was necessary.[22] Ida also wondered if the hospital administration wanted a social service chief who they could better control. However, this suspicion may have been colored by Ida's hurt feelings since her appointed successor was none other than Miss Yu Ruji (Ju-chi), whom Ida recruited, and had sent to the New York School of Social Work.

If there was any sustained bitterness in Ida about her dismissal, she did not express it. She tried not to take the decision as a personal rejection as had her father. He had interpreted the student nationalistic rejection of missionaries in the 1930s as a personal affront and had died a deeply disappointed man.

Always the champion of the Chinese people's rights and confident of their ability to manage their own affairs, Ida was genuinely glad for the turnover of the PUMC to Chinese administration, even if it did hurt her own position and, admittedly, her ego. On October 10, 1938, the twenty-seventh anniversary of the Chinese Republican Revolution, the entire twenty-six member staff of the Social Service Department signed a "Bon Voyage" letter and presented Ida with a bracelet by which to remember them. Leaving the city and the people she had loved for almost eighteen years was much more painful for Ida than she had imagined, although she was given over a year's notice and intellectually agreed with the decision. Packing and delegating responsibilities took two solid months' daily work. For one full month, Ida dreamed of Beijing nightly, as she began to heal from the deep losses.[23]

In December, as she sailed to Shanghai on a small coastal steamer, she had little idea where her future lay but faced the unknown optimistically. In letter after letter to American leaders in the medical social work profession, Ida insisted that she could best contribute to the war's effort by working in China. Tentative plans of either establishing a national school of social work with a small group of other social workers or working for a Quaker orphanage had both fallen through. Reluctantly, she considered further training and temporary employment in the United States.[24] Perhaps Ida recognized the essential place of China in her identity formation. She experienced her departure from Beijing as a painful process but perhaps necessary for her further self-development. En route to Shanghai, Ida wrote:

> I have clung to the warm, round womb of life in Beijing, knowing that the forces that must needs push me out were stronger than I to stay, and as inevitable as the end of pregnancy. And the wail is the natural way to greet a new world…. I wonder if I am now fully born.[25]

During late winter of 1938 and the following spring, Ida's letters to Jim reflect her growing sense that their lives were diverging, even while she hoped for his return to Beijing. After receiving his cursory telegram stating he would be traveling to Britain and the United States instead of returning to her, she struggled to support his decision. Jim's subsequent letter spelled out the political reasons behind his plans: "a growing indignation at British policy" that he hoped to influence directly as well as by writing about the anti-Japanese initiative in north China.[26] Another letter soon followed in which Jim gently broke off his sexual relationship with Ida: "I shall never forget how grand you have been, in so many ways.

And I am sure that we shall meet again, in a continuing relationship but better, I think, as friends, on a common ground that is safer footing than this other.... You must believe that this is deeply-thought."[27]

Ida's heart ached "for the love that I want from you and cannot have and ... for the love you need and won't let yourself have."[28] Despite the sexual impasse in their own relationship, she reaffirmed her own faith in the ability of "sex for bringing two people who love each other closer than anything else." After confiding her belief in their linked destiny, she affirmed that he had given her "newfound courage to face an unknown future."[29] But from the April day when she last saw Jim until the following December, when she left Beijing, she struggled to find her own new place even as she continued resettling Chinese displaced by war.

Her dreams revealed that, even as her self-definition could no longer reside totally in China or depend on her relationship with Jim, her sense of self was secure. On one occasion, after struggling with feelings of pain all evening and into the early morning, Ida dreamed she was standing on the shore of a lake. The surface was smooth with little ripples leading to an American-style house, surrounded by trees, on the opposite shore. Light shone from the windows. "And my heart told me that the name of the house was serenity. The home of my soul."[30]

The Chinese Industrial Cooperatives

One hot June afternoon during Ida's last summer at the PUMC, a stranger hand-delivered a fat package. (This method of mail delivery was a common procedure used for circumventing the Japanese censors.) Journalist Edgar Snow and his wife, Peg had sent her a booklet about the new Chinese Industrial Cooperative (CIC) movement, also called by its cable name, "Indusco."[31]

By 1942, the movement's slogan, "gung ho" became another nickname for the CIC cooperatives. "Gung ho" is an anglicized spelling of "gong he," the Chinese word for "work together." The full Chinese name of the cooperatives was *Zhongguo gongye hezuoshe*. The word was soon brought into the American lexicon by a wartime film about the Second Marine Raider Battalion, which used the expression as a rallying cry. Lieutenant Colonel Evans F. Carlson, the commanding officer of the Second Battalion, had toured the CIC cooperatives in 1940 and later spent several months with the Communist Eighth Route Army in the northwestern war front. To Carlson, "gung ho" epitomized the spirit of both the CIC cooperatives and the early days of the Communist movement.[32]

Ida's work was neglected for the moment as she read the materials with growing excitement. Here was a carefully designed proposal for refugee employment and anti-Japanese resistance. Crafted by economists and engineers, the project put refugees and older war orphans to work in small, mobile factories and workshops throughout unoccupied China. As self-supporting workers no longer dependent on charity, they would resist Japanese economic domination by manufacturing products currently bought from the Japanese—consumer goods such as toothbrushes and soap and military items such as blankets for the soldiers.[33]

Peg Snow, her husband, and Shanghai factory inspector Rewi Alley, became the driving force behind the CIC movement after surveying the Japanese destruction of seventy percent of China's factories during the three-month battle for Shanghai. They blamed the Chinese government for failing to transport the small modern industrial plants to the interior, thus creating refugees from the hundreds of thousands of workers and their families. (The government was evacuating heavy industries and arsenals but abandoned textile mills and consumer industries.)[34] Among the early supporters of the Industrial Cooperatives were Shanghai banker Xu Xinliu (Hsu Sing-loh), editor and publisher Hu Yuzhi, economist Chen Hansheng (Hanseng), and the Song (Soong) family (Finance Minister H.H. Kong, banker-government leader T.V. Song, Madame Chiang Kai-shek, Song Ailing, and Madame Sun Yat-sen [Song Qingling]).[35]

Western supporters included Yenching University economics professor, Harry Price, who educated Peg Snow about cooperatives, British ambassador Sir Archibald Clark-Kerr, British consul John Alexander, publicist J.B. Powell, and YWCA leader Talitha Gerlach. The uneasy alliance of representatives and critics of the Nationalist government was essential for the cooperative movement's success but soon became the source of constant sectarian infighting. The foreign leadership at the inception of the CIC movement was always a sensitive issue, as well.[36]

The core technical staff consisted of the "Bailie Boys," American-educated engineers who had received advanced training by the Ford Motor Co. Many converted to Christianity under the influence of iconoclastic missionary Joseph Bailie, whose motto "hungry Christians cannot be good Christians," inspired his work in rural educational, medical, and economic development.[37] In late August, Bailie Boy Lu Guangmian and Rewi Alley set up the first four cooperatives—a blacksmith foundry, soap/candle shop, stocking knitting shop, and a printing press—in Baoji, Shaanxi province. Within two months, forty cooperatives were operating successfully.[38] J.B. Tayler, chair of the Committee on Credit and Economic Improvement of the China International Famine Relief Commission (CIFRC) and professor of economics at Yenching University, where he worked with the Rockefeller-sponsored North China Council for Rural Reconstruction, later established the Gansu Science Education Institute. From this base, then from Chengdu, he traveled extensively for the Chinese Industrial Cooperatives, organizing training courses for cooperative leaders.[39]

Ida seriously considered the Snows' invitation to join the CIC movement after leaving the PUMC but struggled with internal misgivings. On the one hand, the notion of cooperative industries seemed too idealistic to Ida. She was aware of the shortcomings of credit and consumers' cooperatives, as well as early producers' cooperatives.[40] On the other hand, the cooperatives resonated with Ida's worldview. In the agricultural village where she lived as a child, Ida perceived a philosophy of life that emphasized the responsibilities and privileges of each individual to the social group. She feared the concern for group welfare would be destroyed by competitive industries based in large cities that concentrated the nation's wealth into the hands of the few.[41]

Ida's enthusiasm for the CIC movement was based on its potential to organize Chinese industry on a traditional cooperative basis. Refugee employment and anti-Japanese resistance, the motives of the Gung Ho founders, were essential but secondary in her mind. The CIC movement resonated with Ida's worldview, shaped in her childhood home of Song Family Village, Huangxian. Although the cooperative movement appealed to her, Ida had grave reservations about the viability of the CIC. She doubted the Nationalist government's pledge of support would materialize, misgivings that proved all too true during the years to come. On a more personal level, the invitation to join the movement made clear that Ida would have to raise her own salary from fund-raising campaigns in the United States. Ida suspected that in 1938 the American people were not yet "public-spirited" enough to donate much aid to China. As for funding by American philanthropy, Ida revealed a moment of bitterness toward her long-time employer: "The Rockefeller [Foundation] likes to bet on sure things and to desert those that are in trouble."[42]

Even at a distance, Ida's sense of American public opinion was not far off the mark. During the 1930s, as Japan encroached further into Chinese territory, the U.S. government spoke out against Japanese aggression as immoral while continuing trade in oil and scrap iron. Few war materials were sold to China and no loans were granted until 1939. The attention of the U.S. government, press, and public was focused on events in Europe and didn't perceive that American national interest was at stake in Asia as well as in Europe.[43]

Some Americans, notably the "Committee for Non-Participation in Japanese Aggression," composed of former China missionaries, spoke out after the Marco Polo Bridge Incident in 1937, and Roosevelt's "Quarantine Speech" of October 1937 included the Japanese in the "epidemic of world lawlessness." However, trade with Japan continued until September 1940 when Japan signed the Tripartite Pact with Germany and Italy. Only then did Americans recognize the worldwide nature of the war.

Once in Shanghai, where, for the time being, the international settlement remained "an island in a sea of Japanese occupation," Ida discretely inquired about the CIC. In an atmosphere of intrigue and political assassination, she found the leadership meeting secretly around town. Discouraged by the air of mystery and lack of information about the cooperative movement, Ida seized an opportunity to travel for six months with the Red Cross into Free China before returning to the United States.

In early December, the group boarded a small riverboat—larger vessels had been sunk to make the boom across the Yangtse to retard the Japanese advance—and steamed down the coast to Wenzhou, Zhejiang province. They changed to a launch, then to several boats, and for three days sailed past scenery reminiscent of Song dynasty landscape paintings before reaching the town of Jinhua. Coincidentally, New Zealander Rewi Alley, a principal organizer of the industrial cooperatives, was also passing through. Ida's plans for the foreseeable future soon crystallized. Recalling her first encounter with Rewi Alley, whose larger-than-life reputation already intrigued her, Ida remembered a short, stocky man with a huge, jutting nose and red hair sticking straight up, wearing baggy knickers of rough tweed. Looking past his shy smile and into his blue eyes, Ida saw a man of integrity. Her reservations about the viability of the CIC evaporated. Rewi recalled Ida as a "short, determined figure" whose patience and determination became a "tower of support" for him throughout the years of work for the Gung Ho cooperatives.[44]

The two talked all day on the mission station porch. That evening, the Red Cross tour boarded the train for Nanchang, Jiangxi province without Ida, as she started the journey back to Shanghai with Rewi's report of the cooperatives.

Rewi accompanied Ida from Jinhua to Wenzhou by bus, a journey of two days. Ida recalled an incident from the first day that gave her an insight into Rewi's character. In her retelling, the incident also reveals the genesis of Ida's conscious awareness of her own privileged status as a white, Euro-American woman among a colonized people.

A woman nursing a baby sat in the seat behind them on the crowded bus. Ida opened the window to freshen the air. Rewi took in the scene, and then closed the bus window, explaining the cold air and wind would harm the infant.

> One of my rare angers began to rise. He had not even consulted me.... I was not as important as a peasant woman. Then I realized that to him we were both women—one with a baby and one without, one who had her breasts bare to nurse her baby and the other ... warmly clothed. And I realized that for the first time in my life I was seeing in operation that which I had been taught as a child, that which I had *thought* [King's emphasis] I believed and practiced, that it was not the station in life, nor the color of the skin, nor the degree of relationship, that should determine one's actions toward another, but the needs of any person in any given situation....[45]

As a white woman in a colonial setting, Ida received preferential treatment from foreign men. Chinese of both sexes deferred to her and other whites as colonial agents. Ida would then "graciously concede" to Chinese women, for she prided herself on thinking of others. Rewi was the first man she had met who did not adhere to colonial conventions.[46] Ida's anger at him melted away as she faced her own unconscious assumption of privilege as an expatriate woman in China.

During those endless hours bumping along on the bus, eating dumplings by the side of the road, and waiting in bus stations, Rewi told Ida something about his past and his reasons for accepting the Chinese government's invitation the previous summer to join the Gung Ho movement. Even more than for Ida, the movement gave Rewi a way to respond to China's wartime crisis that was consistent with values from his childhood and youth. His father, a teacher and farmer in Christ Church, New Zealand, spoke out against large estates and land speculation during the severe depression of the 1880s and wrote pamphlets advocating agricultural cooperatives and "factory farms."[47]

Rewi and the other Alley children considered their father a "cooperative crank. As children we ate, slept and drank cooperatives until we were sick of the word.... But some of it stuck you see."[48] During World War I, Rewi served in France with the Australian and New Zealand Army Corps (ANZACs). In the trenches he experienced "a big, anonymous brotherhood"; without question, soldiers shared everything with the group.[49] During the Allies' final advance, the New Zealand division became the shock troops. During an assault on Bapaume, Rewi suffered a smashed pelvis while trying to retrieve wounded comrades under enemy machine-gun fire.[50] Initially left for dead, eventually Rewi was pulled out of a shell hole with a pile of corpses.[51]

Having barely survived the world war, Rewi bought an isolated New Zealand sheep farm. With a friend, he spent six lonely years fighting the elements and international wool prices. But Rewi yearned for a wider world. Reading the *Auckland Weekly News*, he learned of the Chinese nationalistic movements and battles between Communist and Nationalist forces. He sold his share of the farm to the friend, then, in April, 1927, he sailed into the Shanghai harbor. Just days before, Nationalist leader Chiang Kai-shek had ended a united front with the Communists by slaughtering thousands of striking factory workers.[52]

Rewi soon found a job with the fire department of the Shanghai Municipal Council, the governing body of the foreign concessions. In this capacity, he inspected many of the Shanghai factories, and eventually was appointed chief factory inspector of the industrial section of the council.[53] One of his worst experiences as factory inspector was to see the treatment of child laborers in unbearably hot silk filatures.

> The children, many not more than eight or nine years old, stood for twelve hours over boiling vats of cocoons, with swollen red fingers, inflamed eyes, and sagging eye muscles. Many would be crying from the beating of the foreman, who would walk up and down behind their long rows with a piece of No. 8 gauge wire as a whip. Their tiny arms were often scalded in punishment if they passed a thread incorrectly.... Conditions of work in many other factories were no better than in silk filatures....[54]

As Ida listened, she thought of similar accounts by the Shanghai Municipal Council's social workers who she had trained and of her own factory tours. She realized that the abuses of child labor were part of industrialization's history worldwide, and that neither the modern contract labor system nor the traditional apprenticeship system protected workers from abuse. Her discussions with Rewi reinforced in Ida's mind the connections between her experiences as a social worker and the worldwide imperial system. China's semicolonial status, whereby industrial profits were exported to Japan and Western nations, made fortunes for Chinese comprador merchants but destroyed the traditional handicraft economy of Ida's childhood, an economy that had employed artisans full-time and farmers in the off-season for centuries.

Yet here, sitting beside her, was a man who was creating a humane industrial system away from the crowded, filthy, dangerous conditions of large, urban factories. In the little cooperative industries, begun with CIC capital, no rich owners or domineering managers brutalized the laborers. Workers showed pride in their factories, which they managed through their own representatives, and in their products, so desperately needed by both soldiers and civilians. Rewi talked about the alternative model of industrialization offered by Gung Ho cooperatives, whereby village-based industries improved upon, rather than destroyed traditional handicraft production, where workers enjoyed clean air, sunshine, and the freedom to work for themselves. As she listened, Ida integrated Rewi's vision into her own worldview, shaped by her childhood understanding of both Chinese village economy and Christianity.[55] "'One for all and all for one' ... was their motto.... It sounded like a modern golden rule, one for the industrial age.... It fitted with what I had learned in my childhood of what Jesus had taught."[56]

On December 12, Ida and Rewi parted in Wenzhou, he to organize a cooperative of disabled soldiers back in Lishui, she to further investigate the cooperatives in the southwest and southeast and submit reports to the Shanghai CIC Committee, then to organize support committees abroad. But Ida longed to participate in organizing the Chinese villagers into little cooperatives and accepted her overseas assignment under protest. "Oh, you'll be back in six months," he reassured her. Neither realized that, once back in the United States, world events would conspire to prevent Ida from ever again calling China her home.[57]

Filled with the feeling that all her life's work had prepared her to join the Gung Ho movement, Ida steamed back up the coast from Wenzhou to Shanghai. After submitting Rewi's progress report to the Shanghai committee, she continued to Hong Kong, stopping in Shantou (Swatow) on New Year's Day, 1939. The weekend was spent touring a sugar refinery bombed by the Japanese, hoping to secure its centrifugal extractor for a cooperative refinery. In Ida's enthusiasm for her task, her diary failed to mark the contrast with the previous New Year's Day or even her reunion with Jim Bertram in Hong Kong.[58]

Strictly Confidential

Armed with Rewi's lists of machinery, materials and technical staff to procure and publicity to organize, Ida landed in Hong Kong in early January, where she organized and chaired the Hong Kong Promotion Committee of the CIC.[59] Key supporters included Anglican Bishop R.O. Hall, Muriel Kane, wife of the finance secretary of the Hong Kong government, and Madame Sun Yat-sen, who became the honorary chair. Hong Kong banks funded a small CIC office from which machinery was shipped to the interior through Shantou and publicity was mailed overseas.[60] When Ida left for the United States in July, Chen Hansheng, the secretary of the International Committee for Chinese Industrial Cooperatives Productive Relief Fund (ICCIC, later referred to as "International Committee for the Promotion of the Chinese Industrial Cooperatives"), became acting chairman of the Promotion Committee. The two committees merged for all intents and purposes.[61] Essentially, the purpose of the International Committee was to reassure overseas contributors that their donations would reach the cooperatives, rather than line the pockets of sticky-fingered bureaucrats. Overseas Chinese supporters in the Philippines were particularly adamant that their donations not support the Nationalist party, but the Nationalist-Communist United Front against Japan.[62]

Westerners living in China were well aware of the Nationalist government's faults. The consul general in Hangzhou reported in 1938 that Chiang Kai-shek was "conserving and later will probably withdraw its best troops and equipment to ensure its transcendency in domestic politics." The State Department received reports of severe repression.[63] American journalists knew of the rank corruption, graft, cowardice, greed, and administrative stupidity of Chiang's regime, but withheld their information from the American public until 1944 for fear of sabotaging the delicate Nationalist-Communist United Front against the Japanese invasion.[64] CIC activists knew that the Nationalist government's sponsorship of the industrial cooperatives was both necessary and dangerous. Long-time British missionary Ralph Lapwood, who worked as a CIC inspector and statistician, saw first-hand the "borrowing" of CIC funds by Nationalist officials assigned to the CIC Central Headquarters in

Chongqing, the growing staff of Chiang's relatives and political supporters, and the vile treatment of CIC field workers. H.H. Kong, who at various times served as president and vice-president of the Executive Yuan, as well as finance minister of the government, was tolerated by cooperative activists as the "least vicious" choice for president of the CIC.[65]

Ida was aware of the inherent tensions within the CIC leadership structure. In her initial meeting with Rewi, sitting on the mission porch in Jinhua, she was given confidential information about a $50,000 bribe demanded by a high-level CIC administrator.[66] She was also the person Rewi depended on to report to the Shanghai committee the major roadblock obstructing new cooperatives: the government's failure to release much of the promised $5 million (Chinese National Currency or CNC).

The government's corruption and its reluctance to make good its promises of support can best be understood in the context of Nationalist Party faction-fighting. Factionalism, rather than policy differences or public opinion, dominated political struggles in Republican China. Of the three largest factions, the Political Science Clique and the C.C. Clique (C.C. for the Chen brothers, Chen Guofu and Chen Lifu) found opportunities to profit from the cooperative movement generally, and the CIC movement in particular.[67] From a banker who mistakenly took Snow for a sympathizer, Edgar Snow learned the "nauseating details" of the Political Science Clique's scheme to profit from the foreign-financed cooperatives. This insider's view of the CIC headquarters became the framework through which Snow, his wife, Rewi Alley, Ida Pruitt, and others CIC activists in the "Rewi faction" interpreted the politics of wartime China relief work. The conspiratorial rhetoric sometimes conveyed by the Rewi faction's correspondence, and the vehemence with which they fought to keep the International Committee independent of the Central Headquarters can be traced to Snow's inadvertent discovery.[68]

The Rewi faction's only hope for salvaging the original vision of the cooperatives was to direct overseas' contributions through the independent ICCIC. Before her departure to the United States, Ida candidly wrote E.C. Carter of the Institute of Pacific Relations that the ICCIC "is purely and simply an organization to receive and send out money for and to Rewi Alley." During subsequent political struggles within the China aid community, Ida may have regretted her candor.[69]

In the spring and summer of 1939, during the C.C. Clique's takeover of the cooperatives, Ida visited the CIC Central Headquarters in Chongqing, met with Madame Kong and Madame Chiang, toured cooperatives in Jiangxi, and wrote promotional literature. She continued to put herself in the traditional Chinese mediator role, as she had done during her eighteen-year tenure at the PUMC and through her creative writing. The Gung Ho pamphlets always gave the government leaders a prominent position. One of Ida's essays describes Madame Chiang as "a true Chinese woman who sees the traditional possibility of her high place."[70] Yet in her private correspondence with Rewi, she must have sounded discouraged, because Rewi responded, "Don't be depressed about all this," reminding her that the cooperatives were "a show worth keeping up, in spite of all the opposition.... We knew it would all stack up something in this way."[71]

Ida's 1939 investigative tour of southeast cooperatives and the Central Headquarters in Chongqing garnered much of the information and many of the statistics reported in the Gung Ho literature of 1939. Her photos of sandalwood vessels crafted by the boat-building cooperative, and spinning and weaving cooperative members clustered around the spinning wheels, both in southern Jiangxi province, graced the promotional pamphlets.

Ida's promotional writings took special note of gender relations among the cooperative workers and reflect her identification with traditional China. Even the seemingly modern theme of women's equality harkened back to early Chinese history, to which Ida traced the roots of capable women performing public responsibilities. Her essay, "China's Women Unbind Their Feet" links the sexes across both space and time in the cause of freedom from conquest by Japan.

Deeper dimensions of Ida's being that were nourished by her work with the Gung Ho cooperatives were revealed only in her private essays. The legendary limestone karsts of Guilin city evoked musings about China's ancient civilization. She experienced rural Chinese cooperatives with all her senses and vividly recorded the body language of workers, the rhythms of their labor, word images of the manufacturing processes, and occasional over flights of enemy bombers.[72]

While Ida toured the cooperatives of southeast China, Rewi was appealing to E.C. Carter, secretary general of the Institute of Pacific Relations in New York, for financial support for Ida's work in the United States and in China after her return. "She has worked like a slave for us for the past year, on a voluntary basis [and] ... is in no position to carry on indefinitely on her own slender resources. She has allowed our job to exploit her to the fullest, and has a pretty thorough grasp of what is being carried on at the moment."[73]

Ida wrote nothing about her personal financial concerns, even in private jottings. These contained descriptions of summer rainstorms, gentle breezes on the beaches, and an unusual concern for an appropriate summer wardrobe. She chose two practical black-lacquered silk dresses that modestly stood off from a body perspiring in the summer heat. Her musings ended by linking her own split identity with the great causes of the day:

> It was time for me to go to my Fatherland and tell the big hearted people there about the brave people of my Motherland, people bombed and harried by the invader, neglected and harried by their own government, who were not only holding their ground but were building all the time toward their own future and the future of their country, toward the time when they would also be one of the Nations of the World that was being forged by the machine and man's conquest of nature.[74]

9

Organizing in America

I da saw her mission in America as crucial for the CIC and China's resistance against Japan. As her ship crossed the Pacific toward San Francisco in August 1939, America's attention was focused across the Atlantic on the gathering war clouds. Although Americans clearly sympathized with Britain, the prevailing sentiment was isolationism, spawned by post World War I disillusionment about collective security. Few were willing to become embroiled in struggles among European countries. Fewer still saw a connection between the German advance in Europe and the Japanese advance throughout Asia, or felt that Japanese aggression threatened either Europe or the United States. Despite overwhelming emotional support for China's plight, most Americans were unwilling to provoke Japan by cutting off trade. For two more years, until the summer before Japan's attack on Pearl Harbor, the United States continued to sell Japan large quantities of oil, steel and scrap iron.

The CIC founders, particularly Edgar and Peg Snow, argued strenuously for American government aid to the industrial cooperatives as the ideal way to help China without provoking Japan, thus satisfying the objections of isolationists and anti-embargo groups. Seen from this strategic vantage point, Ida's task of organizing American CIC support committees was critical, not just for the success of the cooperative movement, but also for China's national salvation.

Ida's first months in the United States, during the autumn of 1939, were spent renewing family ties with her parents and brothers as well as making political contacts and publicizing the cooperatives. Ida was glad to be near her adopted Russian daughter, Tania, who was living in New York, but she seemed to feel uncomfortable in the mother role. Although they lived in the same city, she and Tania saw little of each other. Both the young woman and her middle aged "Gugu" struggled to balance the demands of their work and personal lives. Their distance involved more than the typical time pressures of work and school, however; Ida believed her own "type of life" had little to offer a young woman.[1] Tania, on the other hand, seemed to value Ida's involvement in her life. She sought out "Gugu" for advice about her love life. When Ida failed to offer any, preferring to bolster Tania's confidence in her own decisions, one wonders if Tania yearned for a closer emotional connection.[2] Ida's conscious self-restraint in the mothering role clearly was a reaction against Anna's suffocating overinvolvement with her teenage daughter. Ironically, in her effort to avoid making her mother's parenting mistakes, she took on her mother's aloof, intellectual affect.

Ironically, as a grandmother, Anna developed a warmth that Ida felt she lacked when caring for her children.[3] Ida's adopted Chinese daughter, Guijing, always kept in closer written communication with Anna than with Ida.

Ida visited her parents briefly at the West End retirement home in Atlanta in late September, where C.W., though frail, held the unsalaried position of superintendent. C.W. called his daughter "the Queen of China" in obvious pride.[4]

Ida was surely amused to see her vigorous mother in her new base of operations. Anna's only complaint was that life among the "snuff-dipping cracker variety" of women lacked excitement. Uncomfortable "so far from the maddening crowd,"[5] Anna led the Friday night prayer services as well as the Sunday school lessons. Believing that games help to keep the mind alert, she also organized the "anti-Cobweb Society."[6]

Sitting under the trees at the retirement home, during Atlanta's cool autumn weather, they must have reminisced about the old days and friends in China. Anna shared Guijing's recent letters from Beijing. They certainly discussed world events; these topics continued in future correspondence. Shandong province had been occupied by the Japanese since January, 1938. Ida learned that the city fathers of their hometown, Huangxian, decided to tear down the city walls, fearing a Japanese siege and blockade of food.[7] Yet a remaining Baptist missionary boasted of 441 baptisms in Huangxian in 1939.[8] Yantai suffered both drought and flood, after which dysentery and typhoid predictably followed. The hospital was overcrowded like never before and all public health services had broken down.[9]

Western newspapers' reports of the war in China, which relied on press conferences and official communiqués, were notoriously inaccurate,[10] so the elderly Pruitts no doubt were interested in their daughter's "inside information" about the Japanese occupation. Ida's closest contact was Jim Bertram, who saw the effects of Japanese terrorism at close range during his yearlong travels among the Communists in north China, 1937–1938.[11] Another reliable source was a detailed, confidential report by a young English instructor at Yenching University, Michael Lindsay, who had just returned from a two-month journey in Communist-administered areas. Both Bertram and Lindsay were free to travel and talk with the population without the official constraints imposed on professional journalists by Communist, Nationalist, and American governments.[12]

Lindsay told of Japanese soldiers' intentionally burning entire villages and leading male villagers through the streets with a wire threaded through their jaws and then buried alive. Captured Japanese documents referred to the continuing rape and assault of civilians. Hearing Ida's news of China's suffering under Japanese occupation, C.W. prayed that Japan would not conquer China and urged Ida not to return to China until the war's end.[13]

Trying to absorb the horrors inflicted on the people whose lives they had shared for almost fifty years, the elder Pruitts listened intently to Ida as she explained the CIC's strategy to aid refugees. Anna jumped at the chance to find a concrete way to help China but couldn't resist the occasion to remind her secular daughter that working together with God "is the alpha and omega of true cooperation."[14] In future letters to Ida, she often included lists of possible CIC contacts and small contributions from churchwomen.[15]

Anna's attempts to evangelize failed to upset her daughter, a sure sign that Ida had finally become emotionally independent of her domineering mother. She was pleased that Anna was devoting some of her boundless energy to the cooperatives. After leaving Atlanta, Ida wrote, "It has been a real blessing to have been with you. You have given me some of your courage for life ... and I go back to the struggle to help the Chinese with a stronger spirit than when I came." Singling out her parents' love and gentleness as qualities that most strengthened her, Ida felt rejuvenated for the work she preferred over any other.[16]

She set about organizing American CIC support committees as she had done in Hong Kong. A Hollywood, California Committee in Aid of the CIC was formed and chaired by noted author Lin Yutang. Its members included several executives of Warner Brothers and Paramount studios, a representative of the Chinese Consulate, a Chinese restaurant owner and the chief of Immigration and Housing. Ida's contacts in Boston included a number of academics such as Professor Ernest Hocking, China scholars Olga Lang and John King Fairbank, Japan scholar Edwin Reischauer, members of the Eastern Cooperative Wholesale organization and Ida's former social work mentor, Ida Cannon. Philadelphia, Cleveland, Princeton, Rochester, San Francisco-Berkeley, Washington, and, of course, New York were early centers of Ida's organizing, as well.

The primary appeal of the CIC—to give Chinese refugees the skills to rebuild their lives—was a humanitarian one.[17] In contrast, the strongest single group to lobby Congress and the Roosevelt administration on behalf of China was the American Committee for Non-Participation in Japanese Aggression.[18] The committee's goal was to rally American public support for an embargo on the sale of war supplies to aggressor nations. Concerned that Americans would not be moved by the plight of China, the Price Committee argued that Japan's aggression in Asia threatened American self-interest.

Publicity was Ida's other goal. Ida's October, 1939, publication in *China Today*, a monthly publication of the American Friends of the Chinese People, edited by Max and Grace Granich, continued the public relations momentum started by Pearl Buck and other supporters.[19] As in other Gung Ho literature, Ida credited patriotic Chinese citizens as the original CIC leaders. Her article emphasized the concept of decentralized industry, linking it with traditional Chinese peasants' handicraft industries and social organization, as well as to initiatives by Henry Ford and experiments in Scandinavia and France. She laid out the strategic implications of the 12,000 to 15,000 cooperative units spread throughout fifteen provinces in China's fight to resist Japan's invasion. After enumerating the many technical, military, socio-economic and motivational advantages of cooperatives, Ida's article acknowledged the contributions by overseas Chinese, the Chinese government and Chinese financial institutions, then confronted her American audience with her main message: "If the industrial life of China is to stand the shocks of the war there must be foreign support also." She appealed to the "natural generosity" of the American people as well as their business sense. "As little as ten dollars will change a destitute human being into a workman supporting himself and his family and owning a share in his business.

This is permanent relief." She ended by evoking the vision of China as a free and prosperous nation accepted on a par in the international community.[20]

Ida published a longer article in *Survey Graphic*.[21] *The New York Times* interviewed Ida in March and wrote up the CIC the following summer and autumn.[22] Throughout the war years, the CIC continued to make the news from time to time,[23] although after 1942 most of the publicity focused on the umbrella organization, United China Relief, in which the CIC became a participating agency. Ida learned that the war in Europe always took precedence in the press, which considered the Chinese cooperatives lacking in drama.[24]

During Ida's first months in America, Jim Bertram wrote her from China, Vietnam, the Philippines, and Australia. His letters became self-absorbed and angst-filled in October, as he confided in desperate tones: "Ida darling (and my God don't I mean it!) ... You are the only person in the world I can talk to ... and I would give $1,000,000, if I had them, to be talking with you now over a cup of American coffee." The tone of Ida's response several months later was compassionate and self-confident, but detached. She reassured him of her love and hoped to see him again on the "same pilgrim path," a metaphor from the days of their long hikes in the hills around Beijing.[25] When, in early 1940, Ida learned of Jim's enlistment in the ANZACS, she reiterated the symbols of life as a journey and humankind as pilgrims. "I am sorry, but we must each walk the road that is in us to walk...."[26] She felt her own life's journey was beginning a difficult stretch through the maze of American and Chinese political factions and must have been comforted by seeing the struggles in vaguely spiritual terms.[27]

Clearly, the emotional roles between the two former lovers had reversed, as Jim revealed his raw neediness and Ida responded with restraint. Ida's leadership role in the CIC gave her a sense of purpose stronger than the love of Jim Bertram or Jack MacLeod. Ida's passions found a new, larger focus: the movement for rehabilitating the Chinese common people, which she identified with the movement's key field organizer, Rewi Alley. She became Rewi's most steadfast correspondent, informing him of every new organizational development and always inquiring about his health. Rewi appreciated Ida's frequent letters to him and regularly reciprocated with personal letters and copies of his correspondence to other CIC staff.

After attending a meeting of twenty-two cooperatives affiliated with the Women's Department, Rewi expressed his sense of the cooperatives' importance.[28]

> Small sheds [were] built over water races, which turned the water wheels installed beneath, and ran the cotton spinning and cotton carding machines installed.... No cost in power, and a very good 16-count thread being produced. That is progress—the very thing the CIC is striving to do. *To bridge the old and the new, and to make livelihood possible in the villages* [M.K.'s emphasis]. The cotton used was grown alongside the small mills. The yarn was dyed and woven into multi-coloured cotton cloth, in a temple alongside which had been converted into a cooperative.[29]

Ida and Rewi viewed the cooperatives differently than did most activists in the movement, who emphasized the immediate needs of the refugees and their function in the anti-Japanese resistance. Neither did the two object to the use of a religious building for economic gain, as would some sinophiles. They shared a common vision of small cooperative industries in rural villages as bridges between traditional and modern economic systems. Ida, herself a bridge spanning her two countries, cultures, and historical periods, had found a soul mate.

Rewi acknowledged Ida's critical role in developing American support for the cooperatives and planned for her to return to China within the year. Never did he end a letter without words of comfort, support, or affection.[30]

Ida hoped quickly to organize American support for Gung Ho, and then return to China. She found a place to stay on 93rd Street with another China activist, Maud Russell. Russell headed the Committee for a Democratic Far Eastern Policy from 1945 to 1951, and then edited the *Far East Reporter* for many years. The housemates shared a commitment to China, but seldom socialized together.[31]

Ida enlisted E.C. Carter of the Institute of Pacific Relations and publisher Henry Luce as key supporters of the American committee. But neither shared Ida's sense of urgency to help Rewi. The slow pace of establishing an organization greatly frustrated her; New York, "a dreadful city [which] pulverizes and dessicates [sic]," left her embittered. Despite visiting Washington and promising discussions with New Dealers about aid to the cooperatives, Ida remained unhappy in America and reinforced her identification with China.[32] "There is so much here, enough for everybody and for all the rest of the world. Why can't we find a way to give everyone the good life?"[33]

As 1939 drew to a close, Rewi's letters foreshadowed financial and political problems that would haunt the cooperatives and the entire China Aid community throughout the anti-Japanese war and into the Chinese civil war. He spoke obliquely of "scoundrels" in the Chongqing CIC Central Headquarters who mismanaged funds in a climate of hyperinflation and channeled government donations into private bank accounts. Nationalist government-appointed staff members in the CIC headquarters withheld funds from CIC cooperatives in the Communist guerrilla-controlled northwest region. Rewi stood decidedly on the side of supporting the guerrillas, complaining that the others had forgotten that "without the guerrillas fighting it would not be possible to hold [their cooperatives in] Baoji...." He later reported that the only industry organized on the front lines was sponsored by CIC.[34]

In fact, the Communists had begun credit and producers' cooperatives in the Northwest Border Region of Shanxi-Gansu-Ningxia provinces and expressed strong support for the CIC movement. Mao Zedong wrote to the ICCIC in Hong Kong to express his interest in receiving CIC help to build cooperatives in the guerrilla regions: "If we struggle hard, and if China and her foreign friends cooperate together, there can be no doubt of our final victory over the Japanese! With national anti-Japanese greetings...."[35]

Rewi soon visited the Communist capital of Yan'an, situated in the province of Shanxi, and reported to Ida that the CIC cooperatives were an integral part of the new society he found there.[36] However the CIC headquarters in Chongqing failed to make a second capital loan and the thirty CIC enterprises established in 1939 soon closed or were absorbed by the Border Region's cooperative movement.[37] By 1941 even the overseas Chinese contributions sent by way of the ICCIC had ended.

Indusco: The American Committee in Aid of the Chinese Industrial Cooperatives

As 1940 dawned, Ida became increasingly discouraged by America's inaction over Japanese aggression in Asia.[38] America's trade in oil, steel and scrap iron with Japan was brought home all too graphically to Ida when she learned that Rewi's jeep had been the target of a Japanese explosive which still bore the name "Toledo, Ohio." (Luckily, the bomb was a dud; it later was made into a gong.)

Ida still estimated the time necessary for organizing an American CIC support committee in terms of months. She was very impatient in the

United States and felt her real life was in China. But Rewi had decided the movement badly needed Ida in the United States. She must have objected quite strenuously, for by May Rewi was urging her just to "hold on for a month or two, do your damndest. It might do much to save the situation here." Rewi worried about the rising support for fascism in China and the popular fear of anything that appeared leftist. The CIC, which some people accused of being "red," had to produce results soon to prove its usefulness. Although he sympathized with her desire to be in China, he considered Ida's role in the United States essential, especially after receiving feedback about her splendid lobbying in Washington.[39] Rewi's pressure came as America's attention was riveted on Europe. Hitler invaded Denmark and Norway in April, followed by Belgium, the Netherlands, and Luxembourg in May and half of France in June. Germany controlled the continent and Britain was isolated. The only major American group lobbying on China's behalf, the American Committee for Non-Participation in Japanese Aggression, redirected its appeal from China's welfare to America's own defense needs.[40]

A few national leaders understood the connection between events in Europe and Asia and argued for U.S. assistance to the Chiang government. A Japanese conquest of China would have facilitated Japan's alliance with Germany as well as increased the chance of a world war. Further, denying China assistance would enhance the Soviet-Chinese connection, since Russia was the only country that extended financial support to the Chiang Kai-shek government.[41] U.S. aid to China would pin down the Japanese military and discourage its advance into Southeast Asia, as well as woo China away from the Soviet Union. A major concern about aid to China was possible repercussions from Japan.

Ida and other friends of China, urged on by the Snows from the Philippines, lobbied the American government to direct $5 million of its China aid toward loans administered by the CIC.[42] A distinguished list of sponsors petitioned the Roosevelt administration to lend economic aid to China through the CIC.[43] The CIC supporters argued that the U.S. government could avoid provoking Japan by channeling its support to Free China's economic infrastructure instead of its military. Additionally, a U.S. government loan to the CIC would serve the political purposes of the Snows, Ida, and others within the CIC movement who were increasingly alarmed by the Chinese government attempts to undermine the original intent of cooperatives.

Ultimately, the Roosevelt administration gave nothing but moral support to the Chinese Industrial Cooperatives. Early in 1940, Eleanor Roosevelt endorsed the cooperatives in her column, "My Day."[44] Both Eleanor Roosevelt and Lauchlin Currie, a presidential advisor, became members of the advisory board.[45]

Even before Roosevelt's response, the Snow-Pruitt-Alley faction realized the independence and integrity of the cooperative movement would not be safeguarded by an American government loan and turned its attention toward securing the support of the American public.[46] The Snows and Rewi urged Ida to remain at the helm of Indusco, although she was receiving neither salary nor expenses.

Edgar Snow chided Ida for wanting to return home to China: "You are getting some romantic ideas about China as 'the only decent place left' etc; distance lends enchantment I fear."[47]

Words failed Ida when she tried to explain to Rewi and the Snows why she yearned to return to China, her nurturing "motherland," or why she so disliked the United States. But she was convinced that the cooperative movement could help the Chinese people and that her most effective place was America. Once again, Ida put aside her dream of returning to China.

While riding the bus on one of many speaking tours, Ida read *The Secret of the Golden Flower*, a Chinese esoteric text traceable to a Daoist adept in the Tang dynasty. Leaning back in her seat, trying to "think out" her problems, she drowsed off and dreamed of a white and green-shuttered colonial-style house, a common image in her dreams. To Ida, a house represented one's "outermost covering ... more permanent ... than flesh and bones...."[48] Previously, the colonial-style house appeared on a grassy bank in front of a clear lake, but that day the house took on legs and began to run. Ida believed the significance of the running house was a sign of her psyche's mobility.

The house of Ida's psyche was a colonial American one, not her cherished Chinese courtyard homes. Ida's organizing trips through the Midwest and New England tapped into her deep connections with Connecticut and Ohio ancestors as well as her own parents' lives. Her tours became secular itinerations reminiscent of her father's regular travels through north China, preaching the gospel and establishing Christian missions. Other organizing tasks, notably her correspondence, publicity, and even a series of children's pamphlets for "Our Global Community Series," drew on her mother's lifelong discipline of writing letters, essays, and children's literature. The painful process of being forced from the comfortable womb of Beijing in 1938 had led Ida to her American roots.

1940 was an election year. The only evidence that Ida followed the presidential conventions that summer was a clipping of Dorothy Thompson's *New York Herald Tribune* column "An American Platform," written on the opening day of the Republican Convention in Philadelphia.

Several basic themes of Ida's life found expression in "An American Platform": first, Ida's frustrations with her country's great wealth and power; second, her commitment to empowering the common people to which she devoted her professional life at the PUMC and now her unpaid organizing of industrial cooperatives; third, her longstanding appreciation of the role of self-support in giving people dignity. Thompson's words were an affirmation of Ida's own convictions:

> that the resources of this nation, of this soil upon which we all live, whether in public or in private hands, shall be recognized as communal wealth ... that every man and woman shall have the necessities of life, consisting of decent food, clothing and shelter, provided they are willing to work; that they shall be free in their choice of work, but encouraged and assisted in retraining, if their choice lies in an overcrowded field.[49]

The assignment facing Ida in the summer of 1940—to arouse the American public's support for China's survival against Japan—may have appeared less daunting with Dorothy Thompson's vision of America before her: "We swear that wherever men suffer from any cruel humiliation on this globe that [American] flag shall be for them the symbol of faith, hope and charity." The final sentence of Thompson's vision was to be the most daunting of all: "We swear that never shall [the American flag] be a symbol of terror and oppression."[50] During the decade of Indusco work during World War II and the subsequent Chinese Civil War, the foreign supporters of China disagreed vehemently about the sources of terror and oppression in China and the proper role of "friends of China" in the struggle. Ida stood clearly with those who criticized the position of the American government.

Between Ida's publicity tours, she organized the fledgling New York office, recruited a board of directors, and conducted meetings. The September 4th minutes of the Indusco executive board record the payment of a salary to Ida for the first time. Her official position was designated "representative from China," for which she was paid $250 per month for six months.

Ida soon found herself to be a central player in an ongoing battle between the original founders of the CIC and the supporters of the Nationalist government officials occupying formal CIC leadership. This deeply divisive factional struggle was fed by the large sums of foreign donations to the CIC. Taking on many forms through the war and post-war years, the factions permeated all China aid work and paralleled the Nationalist-Communist struggle for United States government support.

Ed and Peg Snow were key strategists in the faction derisively called "The Rewi-Ida Axis" by the opposition. Most of the original field engineers played supporting roles in the movement for genuinely worker-owned, democratically managed cooperatives, controlled at the local level according to specific regional conditions. Supporters of high-level CIC leadership, namely H.H. Kong and Madame Chiang Kai-shek, were concerned primarily with centralized coordination and the cooperatives' bottom line.

The battle for control of American contributions was soon joined in the person of Harry Price, the unpaid executive secretary. Price dominated the meetings with his talk of building one big committee to oversee political, educational, reconstruction, and other types of aid. His committee of overseers would be based in China and led by three Chinese government representatives and three Americans. Speculating that Price was being paid by the Chinese government, Ida realized that if he headed the American Indusco office, he would destroy the carefully crafted nonpartisan position of Indusco. She resolved to stay and "throw my weight around ... until there is someone better."[51]

United China Relief

The ICCIC remained under siege as Harry Price continued pushing for centralization of CIC management and all American funds under the Chinese government. U.S. Lieutenant Colonel Evans F. Carlson, who worked with the cooperatives in 1940 and who popularized the expression "gung ho" in the United States, reiterated the importance of the independence of both the ICCIC and the American Indusco Committee:

> There is a vast gap between the bureaucrats and the earnest, self-sacrificing men and women who are actually making CIC work in the field. Independent foreign support is the most important factor in bridging that gap, giving support and encouragement to the field workers and in assuring that

the administration of Gung Ho will remain non-political, non-partisan, honest and constructive.[52]

Other CIC supporters disagreed with Carlson, who clearly belonged to the "Rewi-Ida Axis." Although missionary George Fitch acknowledged the cooperatives as the most effective form of American aid to China, he advocated establishing a single committee, based in China's wartime capital, Chongqing, Sichuan province, as the channel for all American funds and contributions. This committee would designate a given percentage of its funds for the industrial cooperatives. In turn, a strong CIC Central Headquarters in Chongqing under H.H. Kong's leadership would distribute the funds to individual cooperatives, bypassing the International Committee altogether.

Harry Price and George Fitch were not alone in their ambitions to form a single committee to coordinate all American aid to China. Former China missionary B.A. Garside brought together representatives of fifteen China-related organizations in late July to discuss increasing U.S. government and Red Cross funds designated for China relief, and to petition President Roosevelt to stop material aid to Japan. Staff members from five groups formed the organizing committee: the Church Committee for China Relief, the Committee for Nonparticipation in Japanese Aggression, the American Bureau for Medical Aid to China, the China Aid Council, and the Associated Boards for Christian Colleges in China.[53]

Ida attended the original meeting to discuss coordination of China aid but was not informed of subsequent meetings, although Indusco's board officially appointed her as their representative. Initially, she believed that the organizers excluded her because her Chinese personality did not fit in with American organizational behavior. As time went on, however, the political motives behind her exclusion from China relief decision-making circles became evident. Determined not to be squeezed out of the coordinating committee, Ida firmly requested that she be notified of each committee meeting and fought fiercely for her convictions.[54]

Fund-raising for the umbrella organization, which was named United China Relief (UCR), got off to a slow start. Indusco continued its own activities, including the provision of technical information and personnel for the cooperatives, public education about the cooperatives, and fund-raising.

In January of 1941, Peg Snow arrived in California from the Philippines and seems to have "hit the ground running" for Indusco. After presenting lectures to groups of Berkeley students, Chinese Americans, and the YMCA, Peg had tea with Mary Pickford and Buddy Rogers and with movie producer Samuel Goldwyn. Goldwyn led a Hollywood committee on war relief. He agreed to include China in his appeal but insisted on working with "somebody important." As Peg left his office, he added, "Get Henry Luce.... He'd be the man."[55]

In 1941 Henry Luce, publisher of *Time, Life,* and *Fortune,* was "probably the white man most important to the survival of hard-pressed Nationalist China," according to his biographer W.A. Swanberg.[56] Time-Life, Inc. had strongly supported the Chinese struggle against Japanese aggression since 1936 and named President Chiang Kai-shek and Madame Chiang *Time*'s Man and Wife of the Year for 1937.[57] Luce joined the board of directors of UCR, personally contributed impressive donations, and solicited contributions from business leaders and readers of *Time, Life,* and *Fortune.*

Luce and other UCR board members considered Hollywood hype all well and good to generate public sympathy for China, but they much preferred soliciting large gifts from a few generous donors. According to Ida, John D. Rockefeller, III and Henry Luce stated on record that the big givers should decide on the distribution of the contributions. All the agencies resisted this infringement on their freedom to determine the use of their portion of UCR funds. Two other UCR participating agencies, the American Board of Medical Aid to China and the China Aid Council, warned Ida of the danger of being swallowed up by UCR and urged Indusco to join forces with them in a nonreligious China aid coalition.[58]

Ida leaned toward withdrawing from UCR. She judged from the UCR literature and speeches by members of the board of directors that men like Luce and Rockefeller were interested in "getting a footing in China and control through investments and trade," not in supporting Chinese-owned grassroots enterprises such as the cooperatives. Throughout the life of the UCR, and its successor after the end of World War II, United Service to China (USC), Ida struggled against its tendency to bypass Indusco and channel Indusco's share of the relief funds directly to its own advisory committee in Chongqing, which disbursed the funds to the corruption-ridden CIC Central Headquarters. Indusco considered withdrawing from UCR/USC many times. The main motivation for tolerating UCR's constant encroachments was to avoid being labeled "leftist" and isolated from the American public. For its part, UCR tolerated Indusco's presence because of its popular appeal.[59]

Ida's aim was not pure relief for the Chinese people or investment opportunities for American business. Always the little man and woman's advocate, always the cultural mediator, her goal was to build three things: the cooperatives, nonpartisan Chinese-American relations, and American understanding of "new guard labor relations and democratic processes." Her ideal constituencies were unions, radicals, and socially conscious groups.[60] The absolute dollar amount of aid raised for China was less important to Ida than its wise allocation.

Even Indusco's executive secretary, Harry Price and his assistant, Helen Loomis, seemed intent on merging Indusco with the UCR. Loomis denied Indusco board members the right to see UCR minutes, curtailed discussion at board meetings and controlled access to the executive secretary. Ida, whose position at this time was "representative from China" or "field secretary," fought for open discussion at board meetings as "the only healthy way to work" and argued for opening the minutes of the UCR Coordinating Committee and Joint Committee to the Indusco Board.[61] Eventually, Ida and other Indusco board members sympathetic to her position had Price and Loomis replaced.

The UCR never could quite pin the label "Communist" on the industrial cooperatives but remained uneasy with the radical-sounding movement that sought to organize American workers, minorities, and women on behalf of Chinese workers. UCR's leaders were well-appointed Republicans, whereas Indusco was supported by the Roosevelt New Dealers.[62] The UCR wanted to deliver aid to refugee intellectuals and church-related institutions, not to ordinary farmers and craftsmen. The UCR put great stock in Chinese organizations and leaders who were "pro-American" and educated in the United States; funding for medicine and orphanages was directed away from the millions of needy refugees living in Communist guerrilla-held territory and toward Madame Chiang Kai-shek's organizations in Nationalist areas.[63] In contrast, Indusco carefully crafted its program to support Chinese grassroots economic initiatives that freed them from foreign aid and foreign leadership. Through the ICCIC, funds were channeled into the Communist-held regions occasionally, in accordance with the wartime United Front agreement between the Communists and the Nationalists.[64]

The "Rewi-Ida Axis" was acutely aware of Chinese sensitivity to Western control of funding after a hundred years of imperialist exploitation.[65] They had conceived of the CIC as a strategy for supporting China as a nation and grassroots communities, not a particular political faction.[66] In contrast, the UCR's insistence on working exclusively through the Nationalist government, its emphasis on centralized control of American donations, and the priority given to pro-American funding recipients came dangerously close to what sinologist Owen Lattimore called "charity imperialism." The mutual reinforcement of humanitarianism and European imperialism has been explored elsewhere.[67]

Convinced that supporting cooperatives was the most effective strategy to help the Chinese people, Ida fought for Indusco's control over its portion of American donations with a single-minded determination that earned her the reputation of being a difficult committee member. The UCR continued to edge her out.

Ida suspected that UCR sympathizers on the Indusco board were plotting to oust her. Her fears were confirmed by journalist Hugh Deane, who inadvertently won the confidence of the plotters.[68] Rewi urged Ida to hold on for the future of Indusco, the cooperatives, and postwar reconstruction. "If there is no hope for ... a system of well-organized efficient cooperative units, there is little hope for anything, for what we do is so very elementary and essential. So completely in line with the way things have to be worked from a family system." Heartened by memories of the Chinese families and small villages of her childhood, Ida threw herself into the faction fighting. Within seven months Indusco Chairman Henry J. Carpenter, not Ida, was ousted from the Indusco board for failing to follow the Indusco line either in the United States or in China. But, although she was able to play rough, power politics saddened Ida. "I am not hard-boiled enough for this game."[69]

The fight for control of donations was no petty turf war in the eyes of the Rewi-Ida faction, but a desperate struggle to deliver American contributions to their intended recipients. Government corruption was well known in Beijing before the Japanese invasion. Wartime privations only aggravated the most venal qualities of government bureaucrats, who smuggled luxuries such as perfumes, cigarettes, oranges, and butter into war-ravished Chongqing. Chauffeured automobiles, carrying officials and their glamorously dressed wives to sumptuous banquets, were a common sight in the streets of the fuel-short city.[70] Lower level officials, whose salaries had been cut to one-tenth of their prewar levels by inflation, soon emulated their superiors.

The depraved nature of Chinese officialdom was seen in its most predatory form during the Henan famine of 1942–1943. Journalists Teddy White of *Time* magazine and Harrison Ford of the London *Times* had learned of the famine from missionary letters. In February 1943, after China's most independent newspaper, *Ta Kung Pao* (*Da Gong Bao*), had been suppressed for three days for publishing the only report of the famine, White and Ford set off to see the disaster for themselves.

As the destitute Henanese peasants told White, government exactions were the most horrific aspect of the famine. The officials considered their right to tax as one of the perquisites of office; after their quotas were sent to the higher authorities, surplus grain was sold on the black market. "Even American relief authorities, operating with American money, were forced to beg army officers for the right to buy their private hoards for distribution back to the very peasantry from whom the grain had been extorted." The army officers drove a hard bargain. "Relief money that could buy sixty bushels of wheat in America could buy only one bushel of wheat in China."[71]

The Chinese government used the occasion of the Henan famine to stress the urgency of international famine and disaster aid, while the UCR argued that its own effectiveness depended on maximum cooperation with Chinese government authorities.[72] This strategy was challenged by on of its participating agencies, the American Board of Medical Aid to China, which warned Indusco and the other participating agencies that the UCR's close relationship with the Chinese government would subject the American organization to the "pressure of powerful [Chinese] personalities." Rather than heed these warnings, however, the UCR advisory committee in Chongqing took on greater administrative authority, which it used in close collaboration with the Chinese government. UCR ignored Indusco's demands for "American control over American funds," cut the budget request for the ICCIC, and increased the percentage of funds for direct relief, medical programs, and education.[73] Indusco's repeated requests to discuss the budget with the UCR Allocations or Program Committee went unacknowledged.[74]

During the summer of 1944, as the Allies landed in Normandy to open a second front against Germany, the Japanese continued to advance further into north China. On June 10, a cable from the Allied Labor News reported Japanese troops were overrunning the Gung Ho cooperatives in Luoyang and nearby villages. Ida pleaded one final time with the chair of the UCR program division for funds to evacuate Chinese cooperators, skilled technicians, and irreplaceable machinery from Luoyang, Dongguan, Xi'an, and Baoji—all major sites of the imperiled cooperatives. She was deeply distressed to learn that Indusco's funds were sent to the UCR advisory committee in Chongqing, where they sat for months, devalued by inflation while awaiting committee action.[75]

As the tide began to turn in Europe, the Roosevelt administration launched several historic initiatives that would guarantee American leadership in the postwar world. The United Nations Monetary and Financial Conference met in July at Bretton Woods, New Hampshire, to create an International Monetary Fund (IMF) and an International Bank for Reconstruction and Development (World Bank). The IMF was designed to stimulate world trade and stabilize international currencies, while the World Bank provided the mechanism and resources to finance rebuilding, to generate productivity and to promote trade. In August, representatives of the allied nations met to shape a permanent new system of collective security, which was formalized as the United Nations within the year. Despite protests by small countries, the "Big Five" powers—the United States, Russia, Britain, France, and China—insisted on structuring the organization to ensure their dominance.[76]

Indusco initiated its own postwar program during the fall of 1944, a program that challenged the central tenets of the World Bank and IMF model of development. True to form, Ida argued for the importance of small-scale industry for the Chinese postwar economy, as well as the American economy, and urged that visiting Chinese engineers be shown some small American factories. She was convinced that the modern American model of centralized, urban industrialization featuring heavy industries would inevitably lead to social disintegration. Admitting that the machine age brought "more bathrooms and more steam heat, very pleasant and useful things," and recognizing that China suffered from the lack of these amenities, she still saw "more happiness and more human satisfaction where there were no bathrooms but plenty of books, no steam heat but beauty of the arts and human intercourse." She deeply hoped Chinese modernization would build on traditional family and village patterns of mutual responsibility. Ida's vision of the Gung Ho cooperatives would offer the benefits of industrialization without destroying China's social patterns and spiritual wealth.[77]

As early as October 1944, Indusco began organizing a postwar conference on "The Role of the Chinese Industrial Cooperatives in the Economic Progress of China."[78] Invited participants included the United Nations Relief and Rehabilitation Agency (UNRRA), the U.S. State Department, the Department of Agriculture, the United Food and Agriculture Commission, and the U.S. Army. Other postwar plans were the endowment of the Bailie School in Shandan, Gansu province as a cooperative training center and integration with cooperative organizations in India.[79]

The Asian war ended dramatically on August 14, 1945 with Japan's surrender after atomic bombs were dropped on Hiroshima and Nagasaki. Ida's long years of political maneuvering and public relations building seem to have depleted her. Indusco had consumed her entire life, except for occasional visits from Tania and one additional trip to see her parents. No dream record, diary fragment, or personal essay remains to tell her feelings about the Allied victory. Even the news of Jim Bertram's release from a Japanese prisoner-of-war camp in Hong Kong, where he was interned when Hong Kong fell, provoked only a measured response from Ida: "You have devoted friends here in America and we want you to know how much we think of you … care for you and … hope that you will soon get back into the great fight.…"[80]

Wrangling between UCR and the agencies continued well into 1946. Indusco signed a letter of postwar cooperation with UCR in April, while remaining ever vigilant about UCR encroachment on its authority. By then, however, Ida looked forward to more than sectarian fighting over American aid dollars. Her anticipated six-month organizing trip to the United States had become six years. Now her long exile in the United States drew to a close, as she prepared to return to China.

10

Danger and Opportunity

Return to China

"Tonight I have the pleasure of introducing our listeners to Miss Ida Pruitt, Executive Secretary of Indusco. Many of you will remember that Indusco is the American Committee in Aid of Chinese Industrial Cooperatives." So began Henry Milo's interview of Ida Pruitt on January 29, 1946 at radio station WINS in New York. The first segment of Milo's interview focused on Pruitt's just-published *A Daughter of Han: The Autobiography of a Chinese Working Woman as Told to Ida Pruitt*. The subject then turned to her upcoming tour of the industrial cooperatives. The talk-show host had done his homework about the cooperatives and knew how to personalize the interview for his listeners. Before the show ended, Ida had acknowledged her nostalgia for China and confessed her hope of returning to live there again in the near future.[1]

As Ida prepared for her six-month tour of the cooperatives, however, she came to terms with the fact that the war's end brought her little closer to home. In a letter to Rewi, Ida tried to convince him, and possibly herself, that she didn't mind living away from China. "... Wherever I am needed is the place for me...."[2] Civil war loomed larger in China, the Nationalist government withdrew its funding of the cooperatives and American donations dropped precipitously. Ida and other CIC leaders became desperate. The small Gung Ho cooperatives and the training school for leaders embodied Ida's most cherished principles. She was convinced of their strategic value for resolving China's current economic crisis and its future direction. As the driving force behind Indusco, on which the cooperatives greatly depended for funds and machinery, Ida shouldered a tremendous burden.

She enthusiastically embraced her tour's twofold purpose: first, to report the cooperatives' postwar condition to American supporters, and, second, to voice Indusco's positions at a controversial Planning Committee meeting between the ICCIC and the Association for the Advancement of the CIC (AACIC), formerly called the Central Headquarters of the CIC. Rewi confided to Ida his hope that her visit would "spark up" the field staff who were disheartened by skyrocketing inflation, isolated by transportation problems, and demoralized by a temperamental technician.[3]

In the foggy dawn of May 4, 1946, the S.S. Rattler pulled away from its berth at the foot of 23rd Street in New York harbor en route to Shanghai. Tania and her husband, Cornie, had hosted a farewell party the evening before. The entire Indusco office staff saw her off with flowers and gifts.

On board ship, she passed the time banging out business and personal letters for mailing at the refueling stops. Her first letter was a long, reflective one to Evans F. Carlson of the U.S. Marines. Now a Brigadier General, Carlson had popularized the slogan "Gung Ho" to Americans by naming his raider battalion after the CIC movement.[4] The World War II hero was terminally ill. Ida identified with his forced inactivity; she consoled him, as she did herself: "I am a great believer in 'all things work together for good to them that love the Lord.'" Defending herself against those who accused her of idealism, she revealed her sense of self as bicultural: "I suppose that I am really a mixture of Christian and the 'Da Jiao' of the Chinese, their own inimitable mixture of all that they need from animism, Daoism, Buddhism, and just Chinese. I always feel the presence of a pattern."[5]

Ida's own pattern was quickly to move between personal reflection and social action. Deeply affected by the famine then raging in China and frustrated by her sense of powerlessness, she resolved to take notes and write about her experiences. Her goal as a writer was to convey a sense of proportion, to present China "with character lines and shadings and not just the black and white of Fu Manchu." She considered her American audience to be "a decent and lovable lot but woefully ignorant of what makes the world tick.... They judge those they meet in the world with the same yardstick with which they judge the new man in the filling station ... in their comfortable and dull little towns...."[6]

Ida's five-week enforced respite from political maneuvering and infighting gave her time to read Harrison Forman's 1945 *Report from Red China* and Gunther Stein's 1944 *The Challenge of Red China*, both sympathetic to the Chinese communists. Contemplating the civil war being waged by the Chinese Nationalist and Communist parties, as well as the political struggles within her own organization, Ida linked the two and sought a new pattern to help chart the unknown course.

Ida feared that leftist American supporters of the CIC were impatient to shift their donations to the Communist-governed region in northwest China. She had become increasingly sympathetic to the Communists since working with the anti-Japanese underground in Beijing in 1937 and hearing reports from Ed and Peg Snow, Jim Bertram, and other visitors to Yan'an. She considered the Chinese Communist movement to be a "democratic" challenge to the corrupt Nationalist dictatorship, by which she meant the Communist government in the northwest had won popular support during the war against Japan. Nonetheless, she reminded Indusco co-workers in New York:

> We are non-political and that is the only way in which we can help in the greater political job. In fact we are one of the outposts of democracy for the world. Our enemies see that clearly. That is why they do so much to hinder us.... Any direct political action on our part would endanger that greater usefulness.[7]

Ida attended the CIC Joint Planning Committee meetings and the UCR Coordinating Committee meeting in Hong Kong. Although she appreciated the devotion and courage expressed by Chinese CIC activists at the meetings, and delighted in her lunch with Madame Sun Yat-sen (Song Qingling), she was eager to begin her tour of the cooperatives. After more meetings in Nanjing with leaders of CIC and UNRRA, as well as with Madame Chiang Kai-shek, on June 27 she finally flew to Lanzhou, capital of Gansu province in northwest China.

She rode by weapons carrier along the old Silk Road to Shandan (formerly Sandan), past the snow-capped Qilian Mountains on her left and remnants of the Great Wall on her right. Currently a charming old town of 30,000, Shandan had been a flourishing trading center during the Tang dynasty and boasted a population of 240,000 during the last dynasty. At an altitude of 1,560 meters, high on a deserted plain, Shandan's isolation from the escalating civil war made it ideal as a cooperative training center. Ida traveled well prepared for her month's stay, equipped with personal items as well as those requested by the training center staff: rugs, cigarettes, whiskey, cloth, butter, honey, apricots, baskets, hat, paper, food, postage, tips, and vegetables.[8]

July Fourth was Ida's first full day in Shandan. They celebrated

America's Independence Day by getting the generator going. "... [T]he noise, heard for the first time in the city, was better than any number of fire crackers."[9]

July 6th was "coop day" in Shandan. Ida celebrated at a little party with the training school students, staff, workers, and other visitors, sitting together on the ground in front of a temple. "Outside the moon shone on the dagoba framed between the trees and the roofs of the front temple."[10] She toured the clinic for women and babies, visiting the grave of cooperative leader George Hogg, who had died tragically of tetanus, and observing student self-governance.[11]

The school had been established two and a half years earlier, on Christmas day, 1943 by Rewi and George Hogg as one of several CIC programs to train cooperative leaders. They were named after British missionary Joseph Bailie who, during the late nineteenth and early twentieth centuries, put his religious values into practice by working to improve the Chinese common people's livelihood. Bailie training schools in more accessible areas of Shaanxi had been bombed and closed, their leaders incarcerated by the Japanese. The programs in Nationalist-held regions were undermined by small capitalists who sought to hide behind the Gung Ho name to evade taxation. Rewi and George Hogg thus resolved to concentrate their efforts on the northwest, far from the war front and Nationalist control, and close to the Communist region, where leaders were supportive of the cooperative concept.[12]

Rewi and George Hogg established the Shandan Bailie Training School with the conviction that training in cooperative principles and practical industrial techniques demanded experiential learning about specific local conditions by living in the villages. They were chagrined that many cooperative trainees had their sights set primarily on individual advancement through college and study abroad. Therefore, the 170 Bailie school students were carefully selected country youths in their early teens who planned to remain in their native villages. The Shandan Bailie Training School curriculum was structured to give students responsibility for managing their own affairs and for creative problem solving, as well as training them in the production processes.[13] A Supervisory Council of older students and a trouble-shooting Circuit Committee supplemented the student assembly, which met weekly. Student activities included wall newspapers, debates, and newspaper reporting, as well as the practical running of the school. Order was maintained through the understanding consent of the whole, which required much talking things through.

Rewi believed that cooperative living was built on a foundation of confidence in one's ability to create. Toward this end, experienced technicians established leather works, pottery kiln, glass-making, coalmine, electrical section, machine shop, construction department, transportation sections, rug weaving, spinning, foundry, smithy, and pattern-making shop. Students took responsibility for managing a paper-making plant, tailor shop, business management, and the farm work.[14] Farm plots grew vegetables for the school, including some New Zealand varieties. A pastoral section contained a flock of 700 sheep from New Zealand. A central store kept track of the materials for each department and a free medical clinic treated peasants from far and wide, as well as residents of the school. The following year, a New Zealand doctor and his wife oversaw the establishment of a modern hospital.[15]

Ida saw the Shandan Bailie Training School as an object of beauty. The foundation of the school embodied several of her own principles: dedication to a cooperative form of social organization based in the Chinese countryside and promotion of human development through productive work. She shared Chinese society's emphasis on the needs of the entire group over the needs of any individual and she valued the collective problem-solving process she had witnessed in her childhood village. For two decades at the PUMC hospital, Ida observed the critical importance of productive employment to her clients' well-being. Her month-long visit to Shandan redoubled her resolve to defend the experimental training school in the face of growing opposition.

Ida returned to Lanzhou, as she had come, by weapons carrier. Situated at 5,000 ft. above sea level, with a population of 170,000, Lanzhou was a center of ancient Chinese civilization and had enjoyed an economic revival during the Sino-Japanese War, as the destination of thousands of coastal refugees. Even after war's end and the refugees' return to their coastal homes, Lanzhou was considered an important hub of transportation and communications with China's far northwest and strategically situated in Chinese-Soviet trade.[16]

At the peak of Lanzhou's wartime boom, raw wool was transported by camels from Inner Mongolia and by sheepskin rafts down the Yellow River from Qinghai province. Over twenty wool-textile CIC cooperatives produced army blankets, uniforms, and fur-lined coats.[17] The Lanzhou Bailie Training School had trained over eighty students in technical skills and cooperative principles as well as general education. However the wartime economic prosperity was short-lived, as coastal refugees returned home and foreign imports cut into locally produced consumer goods.

By the time of Ida's weeklong visit, only nine cooperatives, including six wool-weaving cooperatives remained. Touring the cooperatives, she saw the lathes, press drills, a tool grinder and assorted tools, a bench work, foundry, blacksmith, and pattern-making molds that Indusco funds from America had purchased. The far-sighted manager of the Ning War Textile Coop, Mr. Wang Zunsan (Tsunsan), had begun classes in arithmetic and reading for the twelve members and sixty women workers, and provided chess boards and musical instruments for their leisure time.[18]

She was also able to observe the student self-government association, their consumer's cooperatives, and their operation of the cafeteria at the Lanzhou Bailie Training School, which was sponsored by the ICCIC since its establishment in 1942. In a city that feared that its traditional professions and handicrafts could no longer compete with products made by coastal industries, the school was a source of civic pride. Mothers begged the schools' directors to accept their boys as students, knowing that, after graduation, their sons would qualify for new industrial trades.

In Lanzhou, Ida observed first-hand two major problems confronting the cooperative center and all of the CIC cooperatives. The first, lack of cost accounting, was a consequence of the wartime exigencies of the cooperatives that valued rehabilitation of refugees before solid business practices. The second problem was China's political uncertainty, which created insecurity among the rank and file workers and prevented coordination between the various phases of work.[19]

The ICCIC, on whose financial and technical support the cooperatives depended, struggled to respond to these and other postwar realities. In turn, the ICCIC depended on the American Committee (Indusco) for the lion's share of its resources. As the executive secretary, Ida felt the weight of Indusco's responsibility and played a crucial role in the deliberations. Flying back to Shanghai, then on to the annual meeting of the International Committee in Hong Kong, she shared many of her concerns in correspondence with Indusco board members.[20]

Ida worried about the continuing expense and inefficiency of the cooperatives' administrative office, the AACIC, despite the lay-off of many staff members. She was also concerned about the inefficient and contradictory decision-making by members of the International Committee, who had scattered to different Chinese cities. Since Indusco channeled its funds through the International Committee, this problem directly affected Ida's work.[21]

Although Ida strongly supported Rewi and the Shandan School, she seems to have remained circumspect in her comments. She praised master weaver, Reba Esser's value as a morale booster.[22] She also inserted the sober reminder that projected 1947 donations from abroad would be less than 1946, and she worked with two other members on the International Committee's budget for 1947. The decline in foreign donations was a time bomb waiting to explode and rip apart the cooperative movement. Following the annual meeting, Ida resumed her tour of the cooperatives. On the second leg of her journey, through the southeast provinces of Guangdong, Jiangxi, and Hunan, she encountered a few profitable, genuinely worker-owned cooperatives with high morale. However, a very high percentage of the Gung Ho cooperatives had closed down, faced with unrelenting financial pressures from hyperinflation and foreign-made products and lacking clear guidance from cooperative leaders. From a peak of 2,000 in 1940, only 336, with a total membership of 7,000, remained in 1946.[23]

Deteriorating conditions within China underlay all other difficulties in the cooperative movement. The ceasefire between the Communists and Nationalists was broken in early July when Nationalist forces launched a general offensive to capture all the cities and towns in China's northeast. The Communists responded by taking their forces, renamed the People's Liberation Army, off the defensive. On August 19, 1946, after their capital in Yan'an was bombed and occupied, the Communists declared a general mobilization for war.[24] The American-brokered peace negotiations broke down completely, as General George Marshall concluded that the Nationalist government was utilizing the American initiative as a cover for attacking Communist-held regions throughout northern China.[25]

After riding three weeks by weapons carrier and sleeping on dirty blankets in bug-infested hotels, Ida took the train from Changsha to Hangzhou, then booked passage on a Yangzi (Yangtze) River steamer to Shanghai. She reported on the cooperatives in letters to Rewi, who complained, "You are the only one writing."[26] Ida remained in Hong Kong and participated in meetings of the Joint Executive Committee of the International Committee and the AACIC during November and early December. Her wish to return to the United States by air was granted by a maritime strike that immobilized the Shanghai docks.[27]

Throughout 1946, as the little Gung Ho cooperative enterprises throughout northwestern and southeastern China struggled to recover after the anti-Japanese war, UNRRA and China National Relief and Rehabilitation Administration (CNRRA) began their postwar aid projects. CNRRA headquarters rejected an appeal by its own Henan regional office to work with the Gung Ho cooperatives.

The U.S. government contributed US$500 million to UNRRA's China aid program, which was based on the principle of racial, religious, and political nondiscrimination.[28] Yet the 130 million inhabitants of Communist-controlled regions of China, who put up much of the wartime resistance against Japan, saw less than two percent of UNRRA supplies. These consisted of inferior flour, used clothing, canned food, ten trucks, and fifty tons of medical supplies, but none of the government-request agricultural, industrial, mining, or communication equipment necessary for rebuilding the economy.[29] The failure of the United Nations, the Nationalist Chinese government, and American government to prioritize village-level economic reconstruction, which immediately benefited China's rural population and laid the foundation for future self-reliance, gave the Gung Ho cooperative movement a greater sense of urgency and self-importance in China's future.

Toward this end, and after much deliberation, Indusco continued to work as an agency within USC, the postwar name for UCR. Among USC donors, economic rehabilitation was a popular cause. USC paid lip service to the principle of aiding civilians in all areas of China. Yet when pressured by Alfred Kohlberg of the American China Policy Association about the use to which USC funds were put in the Communist capital of Yan'an, B.A. Garside, USC's executive secretary, bent over backwards to assure Kohlberg that the money was designated for very limited medical aid. "Well over 90% of the funds UCR and USC have sent to China have gone into areas controlled by the Nationalist government."[30]

The overwhelming support for the Nationalist areas, even by non-governmental charities, rankled Ida.[31] She remembered the U.S. government's military support of the Nationalists even as the Marshall Mission tried to promote a coalition government during the first half of 1946.[32] She was well aware that United Nations' material aid, as well as USC assistance, was distributed in Nationalist areas.[33] Yet, in her view, civilians in all areas deserved postwar assistance, including the villagers in her childhood home, which was under Communist administration.

Ida believed fervently that decentralized industrial cooperatives offered the best way for Chinese villagers to rebuild their lives and represented a far more effective use of foreign aid funds than material relief for Chinese college professors and Chinese Christians, to which forty-six percent of USC funds were allocated.[34] The U.S.-supported Nationalist government had done nothing to support grass-roots economic initiative, allowing the number of cooperatives to decline from 2,000 to 300 after the war, while the Communist government encouraged the growth of the small enterprises from 51 to 591.[35] Ida began to consider the possibility that the Communists might govern China better than a coalition, even as Communist leaders continued to pay lip service to coalition government, and Chiang Kai-shek's Nationalist forces seemed to have the upper hand.[36]

Interlude with Lao She

Back in New York during the winter evenings of 1946–1947, Ida left behind Indusco's political struggles of the day to spend her evenings among the "old hundred names"—the common people of Beijing. Her journey began in the middle class home of Grandfather Ji (Chi), house number five of Little Sheepfold Street in west Beijing. Every evening, from seven o'clock until ten, she walked through the narrow, almost-hidden entrance of the street shaped like a long, big-bellied gourd and met Mr. Ji's neighbors—the barber, widow, mat shed builder, rickshaw puller, funeral caretaker, policeman, poor poet and the furniture mover with a bent back and large swelling on his neck characteristic of his trade.

With the residents of Little Sheepfold Street, Ida experienced the physical hardships and moral dilemmas posed by the Japanese wartime occupation of Beijing. She listened to the traditional sounds of peddlers hawking their wares, smelled the delectable scents and foul odors of street life, and savored typical Beijing foods. She relived the four seasons—shivering and sweating with the change of weather and celebrating festivals with time-honored customs and rituals.

On Ida's journey back to the Beijing she knew so well and deeply loved, her companion was Lao She, penname of S.Y. Shu. Recognized as one of China's great modern writers, and head of the All China Association of Writers and Artists against Aggression, Lao She has been called one of the "two literary masters of Peking."[37] From 1946 to 1949, he was living in New York on a cultural exchange program sponsored by the U.S. State Department. Lao She was introduced to Ida by a mutual friend, probably John K. Fairbank, whom Lao She had known quite well in Chongqing during the war. Together, Ida and Lao She translated his monumental work *Si Shi Tong Tang* (*Four Generations Under One Roof*) into English.

Since Ida could not read Chinese fluently, their method of work was unusual.

> Lao Sheh [sic] would read to me in Chinese and I would type in English. He knew more English than he would own to. As I typed I said what I was typing. Often he would challenge and correct me. Knotty points we discussed. I remember he especially liked my translation of *laito huatze* as "scabbyheaded beggar."[38]

She remembered Lao She worked patiently, hour after hour, never losing his sense of humor. As the Civil War heated up, however, he became restless to return to Beijing, hoping to record the distinctive peddler calls before they vanished with the old society.[39]

Four Generations Under One Roof, which Lao She titled *Yellow Storm* in the abridged English language edition, was Lao She's biggest undertaking and his longest work to date. The novel depicts the daily life of ordinary citizens of Beijing under Japanese occupation. Each character faces hardships, indignities, and difficult moral judgments. The consequences of those decisions drive the narrative for *Four Generations Under One Roof*.[40]

Within the Chinese literature of the War of Resistance against Japan, which is peopled by heroic fighters and the guerrilla underground, Lao She's novel about the virtues and weaknesses of ordinary Chinese living under Japanese occupation stands alone. He documents the slowly evolving consciousness of national identity and resistance through each stage of the conflict, from the Marco Polo Bridge Incident on July 7, 1937 to the unconditional surrender after the atomic bomb was dropped on Hiroshima and Nagasaki. He salutes the defiant pride of peasants, school children, and urban workers alike.[41] The novel serves as witness to the spirit of hope in a people possessing "tremendous reserves of energy," a people yearning to transform China into "the most cultured and civilized country in the world—powerful, yet peace-loving."[42]

While Ida listened to Lao She's evocative descriptions of Beijing's people and neighborhoods, read in his thick Beijing accent, she returned to her own home in Beijing on Xiao Yang Yibin Hutong. As Grandfather Ji's eye's brightened at the sight of two big locust trees in the center of the street, under which children played with the locust pods and green caterpillars, images of her own crab apple and lilac trees must have filled her mind's eye. Like Grandfather Ji, she had planted pots of pomegranate trees and oleanders in a central courtyard. Like the Ji compound, hers was surrounded by high walls, yet overflowed with family and friends, conveying a sense of comfort and security to its residents.[43]

Ida identified with Rui (Rey) Tang, one of the Ji grandsons who worked with the underground. Several of Lao She's characters, including another Ji's grandson, betrayed those who worked with the anti-Japanese underground. She well remembered using her own home to hide patriotic youth and guerrilla leaders. Ida probably shuddered as she translated, recalling one such youth whose prison confession had revealed her house as part of the underground network.

Lao She's paean to the Chinese peasantry reads like a literary version of the many letters exchanged between Ida and Rewi Alley during the war in which they praised the country people's creative intelligence and reiterated their faith in the grassroots to construct New China. Through Rui Tang's dream of starting a village cooperative, school, and clinic, Lao She even expressed a vision of China's future similar to that of Ida and Rewi and the same strategy for realizing their vision.

Throughout the 600-page epic, Lao She's characters brought to life themes common to Ida's writing: affection for the common trades people of Beijing and respect for traditional Chinese values even while cognizant of problematic traditional elements that encouraged corruption and exploitation. Both authors used their writing to express concern that westernized, urban Chinese were losing their bearings and their deep faith in the Chinese people to shape a great modern civilization. It is likely that her work with Lao She reinforced the themes of her later writing.

Lao She enjoyed working with Ida. "… She knows so much about China that she can visualize all what I read to her at once…." Early readers of Ida's translation considered her English to be "broken" or "queer" and advised him against continuing to work with her. He consulted Pearl Buck, who assured him that a competent editor could correct Ida's mistakes.[44] Perhaps such reservations about Ida's work persuaded Harcourt, Brace, Jovanovich to omit Ida's name from the cover of *Yellow Storm* when publishing the translation in 1952. She protested this omission in a clear and feisty letter to Lao She's editor, David Lloyd.[45]

Critics had no misgivings, however. Lena Waters called Ida's translation a "monumental achievement." Ranbir Vohra compared the translation with the two available parts of the original Chinese novel and concluded "the translation manages to capture the essential spirit of the original."[46]

The positive critical response to her translation of *Four Generations Under One Roof* reinforced Ida's literary interests, a goal she set for herself while working with psychologist Dr. Marianna Taylor. For four short years, from 1933 until the Sino-Japanese war broke out, Ida found new meaning in life by studying and writing about the cultural qualities that sustained the Chinese for thousands of years. In Lao She's novel, these qualities shone through the vicissitudes of eight long years of war and occupation. As his translator, Ida played a role in the literary preservation of Chinese spiritual resilience.

The first two parts of *Four Generations Under One Roof* were published before the 1949 revolution. The third part was published in installments in 1950. All three volumes were published together for the first time in 1979. Only in 1992 was the English language version translated by Ida carefully compared with the Chinese original. *Yellow Storm* was discovered to include thirteen additional chapters with a more complicated plot and more consistent writing style than the Chinese version. Those chapters were translated back into Chinese and a complete edition of *Four Generations Under One Roof* was published for the first time.[47] Even more than she knew, Ida had contributed to Lao She's preservation of popular Chinese culture for future generations.

By this time, the novel was proclaimed to be a "triumph of Lao She's theatrical imagination" whose scope, contents, depictions, depth of thought, artistry and variety of character represent the best of Lao She's work. It is seen as a new model of literary discourse, one that has since prevailed in modern Chinese fiction, on both sides of the Taiwan straits.[48]

Crisis within China Relief Organizations

In 1947 and 1948, China's Civil War triggered crises in the international China relief community and contributed to a climate of paranoia in the United States. USC openly sided with the American government's support for the Nationalist Party. Indusco and two other agencies were appalled by the open partisanship, certain that U.S.-China governmental and nongovernmental relations would ultimately suffer enormous damage. American private donations to China dried up. Since the Gung Ho cooperatives heavily depended on American aid, they teetered on the brink of collapse. Desperate to save the core, Ida secretly bypassed her own organization's channels to send Indusco donations directly to Rewi's school. Although she tried to remain positive and optimistic, she succumbed to the conspiratorial worldview of McCarthyism.

In early 1947, Ida and other activists in USC traveled by train from New York to a USC conference in Junction City, Kansas, where her presentation about the industrial cooperatives received an enthusiastic reception. Executive secretary B.A. Garside credited her for generating optimism in the conference's atmosphere of doubt and pessimism about the political situation in China.[49]

By early March, however, Ida, herself, had become pessimistic, not so much about the Chinese situation as American attitudes toward her mother country. After several speaking tours, she described American public sentiments toward China as "revulsion."[50] A USC evaluation concurred, explaining the American attitude as apathetic about foreign relief and confused by the Chinese civil war.[51] For Americans, who never suffered invasion and destruction at home, the war was over. National attention was focused on a postwar buying frenzy—automobiles, homes, appliances, and later televisions—financed by $140 billion in pent-up wartime savings.[52] People did not want to think about postwar reconstruction, much less another Asian war and its victims.

President Harry Truman's March 12 announcement of a policy, soon known as the "Truman Doctrine," which committed $400 million in United States military aid to containing Communism in Greece and Turkey, garnered wide support from the American people by "scar[ing] hell out of the country," about Soviet ambitions. Fear of rising Soviet Communism also fueled popular support for the Marshall Plan by the following June, which called for $22.4 billion to aid European economic recovery.[53]

Diehard supporters of China urged the U.S. government to give similar assistance to the Nationalist government's fight against communism. Former USC chairman, Governor Charles Edison, tried to convince the Senate Committee on Foreign Relations that "a smart and subtle game is being played by the communists with the objective of diverting American attention to Europe while 450 million Chinese are being brought under communist domination." Henry Luce's publications argued that the threat of communism's triumph in China was just as dangerous to Americans as the Soviet threat.[54] But Truman was unwilling to throw good money after bad in China. After contributing $500 million to UNRRA's China program and extending wartime lend-lease credit by more than $900 million of war surplus property, the U.S. government limited its assistance to the Nationalist war effort.[55]

Americans were even less eager to make private contributions to Chinese war victims. Seven million dollars were donated to USC in 1946, but donations fell precipitously to $1.5 million in 1947.[56] The following year, USC raised less than $1 million.

American relief funds for China dried up as the Chinese financial crisis worsened, leaving the cooperatives and Bailie training schools with very little outside support. In February, Rewi wrote that wheat prices jumped from CNC$2,000 to $17,000 in eight months.[57] The Lanzhou Training School was closed down and the students were incorporated into the Shandan School. Staff of the AACIC was reduced drastically. Valuable equipment and trucks languished in Hong Kong for lack of funds to transport them to the cooperatives.[58]

The financial crisis within USC, played out against a backdrop of civil war in China and cold war in Europe, fanned the flames of conflict among the participating agencies. Interagency conflict had smoldered throughout World War II, the natural consequence of the agencies' differing missions and leadership styles—and threatened to burst into flames during the postwar financial crisis.

Often, Indusco made common cause with other secular agencies—the American Board of Medical Aid to China (ABMAC) and the China Aid Council (CAC)—who all resented the church agencies' receipt and control of the lion's share of the funds.[59] Ida strenuously argued for a greater share of the funding since Indusco had to work harder for its donations than did the ABMAC. The ABMAC contributors were medical professionals and always gave larger gifts than did average-income Indusco donors. USC responded to Indusco's concern by designating $200–$300 more for the Indusco operating budget, a sum which made a significant difference to the budget as well as to the Indusco staff's morale.[60]

The question of control over the allocation of funds underlay all other controversies in USC. Wartime debate between a federated versus unified organizational structure had been motivated by this concern. The postwar financial crisis changed the terms of the discussion for both USC administrators and the agencies. USC administrators debated the merits of USC fund-raising versus a federated foreign service campaign that included Europe. In fact, a consolidated program, American Overseas Aid, took over fund-raising for relief and rehabilitation in both Europe and Asia beginning in 1948.[61] The agencies weighed the value of USC fund-raising versus independent, issue-oriented campaigns. Indusco's decision to remain in USC was provisional, based on their continuing sense that the USC umbrella possibly worked to the advantage of a controversial cause such as the cooperatives.[62]

Yet other factors mitigated this advantage. First, USC's need to domineer its participating agencies created a climate of distrust noted by agencies other than Indusco. Bronson P. Clark of the American Friends Service Committee noted the "bungling" and lack of candor of USC executives.[63]

Second, the nonpartisan mission statement of USC was becoming a sham. USC literature began quoting remarks of Minnesota congressman Walter Judd and an essay by Mrs. Geraldine Fitch which both defended the Nationalist government against charges of corruption and incompetence.[64] Lieutenant General Albert Wedemyer's pressure on the U.S. government to support the Nationalists with more military aid was published by the Boston USC chapter.[65]

Third, the church-controlled Coordinating Committee of the USC in Hong Kong strongly resisted granting Indusco control of its allocated funds. Despite continuous, strenuous objections by Ida and the Indusco board of directors, USC bypassed its own participating agency in New York, Indusco, to forward Indusco's money directly to the Nationalist-oriented AACIC in China.

By October, the abysmal failure of the USC fund-raising campaign brought the struggle for control to an impasse. Accustomed to receiving $24,000 a month since January, Indusco was put on a starvation diet of $2,000 a month for the remainder of 1947. In a 180-degree change in policy direction, USC encouraged its agencies to conduct independent fund-raising. Ida, whose public speaking had been severely curtailed by a USC policy prohibiting independent fund-raising, approached the crisis as "an unparalleled opportunity" to educate the American public about industrial cooperatives and the Bailie Training School.[66]

The dual financial crises within USC and in China generated new conflicts within the CIC movement, itself. A flurry of confidential memos, minutes of specially called meetings, and urgent telegrams flashed accusations and counter-accusations across the ocean throughout 1947, as CIC activists lobbied for or against the so-called "Rewi-Ida Axis." Rewi,

Ida and confidante Peg Snow exchanged frequent letters in which they spoke darkly of the forces of "reaction and fascism" infiltrating their ranks. A sense of alarm filled Peg Snow's letters to Rewi and Ida, as she tried to convince the two that Rewi's life was in danger.[67]

The shrinking pool of foreign donations split the cooperative movement wide open. Rewi and Ida's faction argued that the most effective strategy for promoting genuine cooperatives was to intensify membership education about accounting, technical skills and cooperative principles. Training potential leaders at the Bailie school in Shandan was the linchpin in this strategy.[68] They further proposed that foreign funds should support projects in their early stage before the project became self-supporting and profitable.[69]

The ICCIC was "tremendously impressed with the spirit" of the Shandan Bailie School, but remained committed to the cooperative movement as a whole, citing the advice of Mao Zedong, Zhou Enlai, and Song Qingling.[70] They felt that Ida and other American supporters completely underestimated the extent to which Chinese nationalistic feelings demanded that Indusco relinquish control of American donations.[71] The ICCIC's executive secretary, Peter Townsend, and Hong Kong bishop R.O. Hall, argued for dividing the foreign funds equally between the remaining cooperatives and the Bailie training center and urged Rewi to visit other cooperative centers to give the members and field staff a morale boost.[72] This group also placed greater emphasis on sound business practices: "We must weigh any proposed addition or increase ... in terms of its profitability, its contribution to the movement, and above all, our ability to meet the cost."[73]

Mutual suspicions between Indusco and the ICCIC over the use of diminishing funds continued throughout 1948. Ida and Peg Snow argued for prioritizing cooperative training at the Shandan School, while the Shanghai group defended the equal distribution of donations among all the cooperatives. Indusco accused the ICCIC of withholding Shandan's money, which the latter categorically denied.[74]

As dwindling American and international postwar relief channeled money almost exclusively to Nationalist regions of China, and as both the USC and the ICCIC insisted on controlling Indusco funds, hundreds of Gung Ho cooperatives were collapsing. Rewi feared the worst for the Bailie Training School in Shandan. Ida decided she had no recourse but to circumvent the International Committee that she had founded in Hong

Kong in 1939. Without the knowledge of all members of the Indusco board, Ida surreptitiously sent funds directly to Rewi's school.[75]

Conflict between Indusco and the ICCIC was based on strategic differences but their fundamental agreement on nonpartisanship in China's civil war remained. In contrast, longstanding political differences between USR and Indusco rose to the surface as American donations declined. In early March, Ida reminded the USC of its nonpartisan mission statement and inquired about sending funds directly to the "north," that is, to Communist regions. By then, more than abstract political principles were at stake. The Nationalist government's armies controlled only two regions and were on the defensive elsewhere. Looking ahead to the clear possibility of Communist victory, Ida and others realized that the pattern of American non-governmental donations was sure to adversely affect American relations with China's new government.

While Indusco and a few other agencies within USC responded to the Communists' military advance by reasserting their nonpartisanship, USC contributed to the shift of American China policy to the right.[76] As U.S. elections approached, Democratic and Republican parties both campaigned on a platform of greater support for the Chinese Nationalist Party, which had already received US$6 million in aid. Henry Luce and Walter Judd, moving forces within USC, joined one of the Nationalists' staunchest American supporters, William C. Bullitt, in demanding that Congress appropriate US$1.5 billion to aid Chiang's armies.[77]

A September 1948 USC promotional pamphlet titled "Other Defenses" solicited donations to stop Communism and promote Christianity and democracy in China. Indusco and a number of other USC agencies objected strenuously to this openly political appeal. Faced with pressure from its member agencies, USC was forced to retreat temporarily. Soon, however, USC dropped its veneer of nonpartisanship in China's civil war: "USC and its agencies do not engage in any activity which supports or endorses any group or organization in armed rebellion against the governmental authorities of China recognized by the America government."[78]

After USC's open commitment to the Nationalists, Indusco's board was forced to review its status as a USC member agency once again. Ida and Indusco board members continued to chafe against USC's controlling administration. USC was no more comfortable with Indusco.[79] Garside of USC admitted privately that anyone "pinkish" had been "quietly dismissed" from the staff and that their coordinating committee in China had restricted Indusco's work to Nationalist areas.[80]

By October, Indusco's board voted to withdraw from USC, but equivocated the next month. Some board members hoped that USC public statements would become less political as Communist armies took Manchuria, began campaigns near Beijing and Xuzhou, and moved into Jinan, Shandong, where Cheloo (Qilu) University, a Christian school, was located. Others, including Ida, feared that Indusco's association with USC would brand it as an imperialist in the eyes of the Communists.[81] One of few China-aid agencies that genuinely attempted to be nonpartisan during China's civil war was caught in the crossfire, and Ida's own dream of returning to live in her motherland became one of the casualties.

Ida's lifelong role as a mediator became another victim of the times. Before her involvement in the CIC movement, she always strove for harmony, cooperation, and respect for human differences in her personal and professional relationships. Working with the Luce and Rockefeller forces in American relief efforts during World War II and the Chinese Civil War changed her perspective. She firmly believed that worker-owned cooperatives, initially funded by overseas donations, were the key to refugee rehabilitation. Civilians in Communist-controlled regions deserved help from the American government and public just as much as those in Nationalist areas, especially since the United States was officially a neutral party in China's Civil War and was trying to broker a peace settlement. After all, her birthplace and family home were in Communist territory. Ida's support for the CIC was personal. She imagined each little group of cooperative workers as neighbors from her childhood or clients from the PUMC. The Bailie Training School was most personal of all; Rewi personified all of Ida's ideals and was passing them on to a new generation. Ida ferociously defended the Gung Ho cooperative movement, especially the Shandan Bailie School, against all threats, like a mother protecting her babies. She tried to interest the American public in cooperatives and succeeded until the UCR/USC top leadership withheld Indusco's portion of public donations. When reason and fairness failed to make UCR/USC live up to its own policies, Ida turned to subterfuge and dismissed her opponents in China and in America as "reactionaries" and "fascists."

The rhetoric of "reaction and fascism" was commonly used during the war against fascism in Europe. The Gung Ho activists were among many progressives who continued thinking in such terms. Ida, Peg and

Rewi viewed all centralized bureaucratic structures, not only in China but also in the United States, as seedbeds of fascism.

From today's vantage point, both Ida and Peg sound paranoid for imagining conspiracies and secret agents among their ranks. However, events of the late 1940s created a climate conducive to such thinking. The near-indictment for espionage of U.S. Foreign Service officer John S. Service in 1945 for leaking stories critical of the Nationalist Party to the journal *Amerasia* had been a portent of the coming "red scare." The year 1947 saw the beginning of the crusade against Communists and other "disloyal" Americans. On March 22, President Truman established the federal loyalty program to ferret out federal employees whom the Attorney General designated as "totalitarian, fascist, communist, or subversive." Ida and Peg Snow may have heard of the employee whose job was threatened because "he did all his buying at co-ops and didn't believe in small business," or others whose only crime was membership in the Washington Bookshop Association. Listening to the music of Black opera singer, Paul Robeson, aroused government witch-hunters' suspicions ... and Robeson was a personal friend of Ida's.

By October, Peg wrote,

> People are now very afraid to join anything due to the UnAmerican Committee arrests of Anti-Fascist Refugee Committee and other things. Their names are on a list. However, this membership for Indusco is okay as we are a middle way group and respectable still. We can get lots of people ... all the good liberals who are not anticommunist....[82]

Peg Snow's view of Indusco as a "middle way" organization, notwithstanding, "left-wingers" who opposed the escalating Cold War against the Soviet Union and labor activists who organized collective bargaining were among Indusco's strongest constituencies. Both of these groups were targeted by the Eightieth Congress. The 1947 Taft-Hartley Act required that union officials annually sign a non-Communist affidavit. The same year, the House Committee on Un-American Activities went after Hollywood producers whose films were not sufficiently anticommunist, or whose screenwriters' affiliations were suspect. Some of these producers may have been affiliated with Paramount or Warner Brothers studios, which sent representatives to the Hollywood Committee in Aid of the CIC during the war.[83] Such was the domestic atmosphere of worry and suspicion in which Ida worked while struggling to respond to the growing crisis in China.

11

Liberation

C hiang Kai-shek's forces were effectively destroyed in the battle for Huaihai on January 10, 1949, even before Communist Party troops defeated them in Tianjin and Beiping peacefully surrendered on January 22.[1] In late September, representatives from labor, the peasantry, business, industry, as well as the Democratic League and the Communist met in Beiping to form the People's Political Consultative Conference. The capital was moved back to Beiping and renamed Beijing (lit. "northern capital"). On October 1, Mao Zedong announced the founding of the People's Republic of China.

On the day Shanghai changed hands, USC field director in China, Dwight W. Edwards, reported that influential people in the Communist government were open to dialogue with Western interest groups.[2]

An internal USC debate ensued. All views agreed on the importance of continuing USC services for as long as the Communist government allowed its programs to remain.[3] However, the drastic reduction of American donations as Communist forces gained control in China soon forced the closing of most USC programs.[4] The American public, not the Chinese Communist government, severed the decades-long ties of service and friendship. Ironically, USC's role in shaping the American public's anti-Communist views ultimately worked against their own programs.

Not all Americans jumped on the bandwagon of anti-Communism. Many of these supported Indusco as the best way to maintain ties with China during a period of American political reaction. Some Indusco supporters were former missionaries who simply agreed with the Gung Ho principle of economic self-help. Others maintained their support out of personal friendship with Ida. One remembered Ida's kindness to her.[5] Another reminisced about Ida's mother at a missionary summer camp. "It was a joy to see ... several little girls ... go by and kiss Granny Poo good night."[6]

The American presidential election in November 1948 occurred in the midst of the decisive military campaigns of September 1948 to January 1949. In stark contrast to Republican and Democratic support for Chiang Kai-shek's Nationalists, candidate Henry A. Wallace of the Progressive Party called for immediate withdrawal of American troops and abandonment of bases in China, "cessation of financial and military aid" to Chiang Kai-shek, and large-scale economic aid to a coalition government.[7]

After Harry Truman's victory, Wallace's supporters turned their attention to events in China. Donations to Indusco in 1949 exceeded those of 1948.[8] Indusco sought to capitalize on the progressive public's renewed interest in China by emphasizing their industrial cooperatives and women's programs in Communist strongholds. On the advice of a fundraising consultant, the Indusco board considered abandoning its non-partisan stand.[9] But while Ida advocated for the Bailie School, she did so from a nonsectarian position:

> The Chinese are still the Chinese and the back country villages are still the same poverty-ridden back country villages.... The most important thing is that we are—for good or ill—one world and have to live together on this little planet and the political patterns under which we live are also constantly changing. It is very important [to] ... help the Bailie School, a really international center and non-political.[10]

The Bailie School in Shandan, although well out of the main lines of fire between the Chinese Communist Party (CCP) and the Nationalist Party (Guomindang, GMD), believed it was threatened by Ma Bufang, a brutal Moslem military strongman who ruled Gansu and other nearby provinces. Rewi received word that Ma's forces had scheduled sixty students, teachers, and himself for execution and planned to raze the school.[11] He wrote Ida about the unsettled, confused atmosphere at the school throughout the winter of 1949. By early April, "we are down to two ... corny ... potatoes and the same old pickle beet." However, the movie projector, presumably sent by Indusco, diverted everyone's attention; the film on erosion "brought the house down."[12] Between the Moslem and Nationalist armies, Rewi felt they might not survive.[13]

On September 19, Nationalist soldiers retreated through Shandan after surrendering to Communist forces in nearby Zhangye. In typical fashion, troops looted food, destroyed houses for firewood, and conscripted the townspeople to carry their provisions to the surrounding hills. The next day, a couple of People's Liberation Army (PLA) officers arrived without fanfare, announcing the area had been liberated. The Bailie School's only losses were a donkey and a jeep.[14]

Only a month later did Ida receive word of Shandan's safe liberation. When Rewi's personal letter finally arrived, it was filled with optimism about the fate of the school under the new government.[15] No record has survived of Ida's own feelings as she waited to hear the fate of the school and the man to whom she had devoted so much of herself.

Other cooperative leaders also reported that the cooperatives were in good hands. Even before the official founding of the People's Republic, the provisional government of North China provided loans to farming cooperatives and sought foreign technicians, provided they were not spying for their governments.[16] For the moment, the government put emphasis on consumers' and supply and marketing cooperatives, while studying advanced producers' cooperatives.[17]

After the official founding of the People's Republic of China on October 1, 1949, the American government's scrutiny of Indusco intensified. In late November 1949, a six-page, unsigned, confidential report accused Indusco of being a Communist-front organization. The report set in motion an ongoing investigation by the Federal Bureau of Investigation (FBI), which followed Ida until 1970.

An October Indusco fundraising appeal apparently triggered the anonymous report. Among the signatories of the appeal were members of other "Communist front organizations," which all patronized the same printing company. These were cited by the FBI as evidence of Indusco's Communist politics. "Indusco is deeply interlocked with at least three other organizations which have been concerned with Chinese matters and which have been clearly pro-Communist, namely *Amerasia*, Committee for a Democratic Far Eastern Policy, and the China Welfare Appeal." Ida Pruitt's name as an "editorial adviser" to the *Protestant* magazine was cited as evidence "of unusual force" of her pro-Communist sympathies. That few members of the Indusco advisory board had "Communist connections" was seen only as further proof that Indusco, like other "Communist front" organizations, depended on a small, controlling group to maintain the Communist Party line.

Ironically, the Chinese Communist government was equally suspicious of Indusco. Through the Chinese leftist press in the United

States, Communist officials sharply attacked overseas aid as "philanthropic imperialism" for its political and material support for Chiang Kai-shek, as well as its determination to control Chinese affairs through its charity. Ida cautioned the Indusco board that Indusco's continual membership in USC might very well render ineffective its aid to Shandan.[18] She recognized that the Chinese sought to control and administer their own aid programs. She understood their resentment of outside aid, and viewed the Chinese sensitivity as an "inevitable stage" of nationalism that China had every right to pass through.[19]

Ida was much less patient with American attitudes toward China. In late September, as the People's Political Consultative Conference in Beijing prepared the Common Program for the People's Republic of China, a young, well-informed American journalist aroused Ida's ire with her statement, "But I thought that China was all warlords and confusion. And everyone half starving as in Pearl Buck's *The Good Earth*." This was a simplistic stereotype even for the warlord period between 1915 and 1927. But to so dismiss a nation of over four hundred million people with over three thousand years of recorded history was intolerable to Ida. She often wondered if Americans, more than other nationalities, "sinned most in their over-simplification of every issue."[20] At other times, Americans' rough, angry speech and public rudeness "jangled" Ida's nerves.

There was no doubt that during the summer and fall of 1949, as China's long revolutionary war reached its climax, and both the political left and right attacked Indusco, Ida struggled with anger. For ten years she had fought for Indusco's autonomy within USC in order to receive a portion of the American public's China contributions, donations that supported Chinese working men and women in both Communist and Nationalist controlled territory. In the end, at least 90% of Indusco's money was channeled to Nationalist areas, where high GMD officials undermined the cooperative enterprises and absconded with the American funds. Knowing full well this was happening, Indusco tolerated USC's politics in order to send small sums to Rewi's school and to cooperatives in Communist regions. And now, as events drew to their dramatic conclusion, Indusco was damned by both sides; the American government labeled Indusco a "Communist front" and the Chinese government suspected Indusco's imperialistic ambitions. Ida was caught in the ideological struggles between her "motherland" and "fatherland."

On December 23, 1948, as victory came within reach of the CCP, Ida turned sixty years old. She had spent most of her first fifty years in China and longed to return. Indusco's association with UCR/USC threatened permanently to exile Ida from the land of her birth. As Communists took Tianjin on January 14, 1949, she dreamed of her future:

> ... I must have a long ladder to climb up to a cave ledge high on a vertical cliff ... out of the noise and rush of things and ... read and write in peace.... I started up—Two thirds of the way up, I suddenly realized how silly I was to be afraid of old age and death. I put my watch in my pocket (time and age did not matter any more), and holding tight to my little wooden fisherman in my right hand and my book under my left arm, I went back down the stairs—Father, shrunken and feeble, sat bowed in a chair with a rug over his knees—"Yes that is the way I'll grow old" and I didn't mind any more. "I'll take my Chinese philosophy with me" (the fisherman) and sat down in another chair with my book —[21]

Denied re-entry to her motherland, Ida was drawing China into herself. She taught a semester's course on "Chinese Village, Rural and Family Life" at the Asia Institute, in which she described the character and folkways of the Chinese country people of her childhood, their agricultural tradition and their historical and geographical setting.[22] Her many Chinese friends and guests also brought China closer to Ida. One of the most notable was Delawar Gegan, the Tibetan Buddhist monk with whom she had shared New Year's Eve in 1938.[23]

As 1950 dawned, Ida dreamed of a Chinese doctor, Chinese boys in need, and a trap door. She puzzled how to best help the boys without causing them further trouble, and whether or not to trust the trap door. Unsure how to proceed or whom to trust, Ida buried her face in her husband's chest.[24] Upon waking however, no companion lay beside Ida to comfort her.

As the Gung Ho cooperatives were embraced by the new Chinese government, Ida sought to refocus Indusco's mission. She and other activists in Indusco, as well as in USC, were convinced that the primary importance of their work was to maintain people-to-people goodwill in the face of deteriorating governmental relations. Indusco fund-raising dinners and appeals were surprisingly successful, as some supporters congratulated Indusco for continuing its China program in the climate of Chinese-American hostility.[25]

Ida defined Indusco's greatest service as keeping open the informal communication channels between the American and Chinese people. She especially wanted Americans to understand that their own government, not the Chinese, was restricting the flow of aid to China.[26] Most

Americans remained unaware of the politics of material aid to China. The USC board's communications to its members blurred the source of aid restrictions.[27] The Bailie School still depended on overseas contributions. However, U.S. government restrictions on travel and first-class mail to China, as well as the changing interests of the general American public, severely limited the effectiveness of both Indusco and USC.

In the spring of 1950, the profound uncertainties that lay ahead for Indusco and her own life swept over Ida. She felt as if she were "casting loose from security for the next four years at least." And yet, one of her dreams promised eventual resolution.

> A great blue ocean stretched out wide and limitless before me. Then suddenly, as though I was in a swift boat and it began to come in sight, or as if it came out of the air, a blue blue island, a low range of hills appeared, and I knew I was going to it, to a new life.[28]

Unbeknownst to Ida, on the same day of her dream, an FBI memo instructed agents to closely follow Indusco and its executive secretary.[29] She would not be alone on the hilly, blue island.

Ida was eager for news from China. Correspondents expressed genuinely positive attitudes toward the new government. Chinese students who had returned home wrote to their fellow students still abroad, noting how different the CCP was from GMD propaganda about it. They told tales of efficiency and good order in banks and train stations and of an incorrupt government that brought great improvement in people's lives. Reminding their friends of China's need for technically trained people, the students urged their friends to return home.[30]

The Korean War definitively changed the course of both governmental and nongovernmental U.S.-Chinese relations for a generation. On June 25, after long provocations from both sides, North Korea troops crossed the border at the 38th parallel into South Korea. The U.S. government assumed that the North Korean invasion was led by an international Communist bloc and sent in ground troops in early July. In fact, domestic conflict between North and South Korea as well as the interaction between Stalin, Mao, Kim, and Truman, played a major role in the war's origin.[31]

President Truman immediately sent the Seventh Fleet to the Taiwan Straits, fearing the Chinese Communists would take advantage of the crisis to regain its renegade province. By August, the U.S. ambassador to the United Nations, the U.S. State Department, and President Truman all called for U.S. military action to reunify the two Koreas. General Douglas MacArthur and President Truman both spoke of using atomic weapons along the Korean-Chinese border. As the United States established bases or intervened in Korea, Taiwan, the Philippines, and Indochina, China was "on the way to being encircled."[32]

In early October, China reacted to American encirclement by warning the United States, through the Indian ambassador, that Chinese troops would intervene if U.S. troops moved north of the 38th parallel. On October 17, General MacArthur ordered U.S. troops into Korean provinces bordering Chinese and Soviet territory. Large-scale Chinese troops movements crossed the Yalu River into Korea two days later.[33]

The civil conflict had become a "substitute for World War III." Over three years' time, 300,000 U.S. ground troops and more than a million Chinese soldiers were deployed. Some ten percent of Koreans were killed, wounded, or missing. The bombing of Korea, which was responsible for an estimated 3 million deaths, including a large percentage of civilians, was used by both Chinese and Soviet governments to stoke anti-American fires.[34] An armistice was finally reached on July 27, 1953 that solidified the divide between capitalist and socialist blocs.[35]

Ida experienced periods of despondency about the Korean War. She was alarmed by charges that the U.S. army was using germ warfare techniques in Korea.[36] She compared American leaders to emotionally-disturbed children who "state their fears as facts and then take aggressive action against them.... We have let the dry rot of comfort and the mirage of security sap at our vitals and our strength has turned back on us and eats us up." But her feelings were not limited to Americans. In comments to Rewi, she evoked both biblical and literary references to express her discouragement with the human race's folly.[37]

Desperately, she sought to keep the Bailie School alive as a distant outpost of internationalism.[38] In early 1951, Ida and chairman of the Indusco board, Alfred Sidwell, wrote supporters of their continuing conviction that U.S.-China relations could be restored. In a foreshadowing of nongovernmental organizations a generation later, they explained the critical role of "nonpolitical channels for friendship" such as the Bailie School to maintain some goodwill between the warring countries. Through long, patient, information-filled letters to individual Indusco members, Ida expressed ideas she yearned, in vain, to share with the general American public.

Several Indusco members were distraught about China's "hate

America" campaign. Ida firmly responded that all Chinese people felt strongly about the American bombing of their northern territory on the Manchurian border.[39] Ida reassured other members that nothing in the Bailie School would be used against American soldiers in Korea. The Bailie School's workshops trained students in agricultural and pastoral techniques, manufacturing consumer goods and coal mining.[40]

The question of religious freedom particularly concerned a number of members.[41] With great conviction, Ida affirmed the Christian spirit of the Gung Ho cooperatives, drawing on her own observations and feelings as well as the testimony of others.[42] She referred her Christian supporters to an April 16, 1951 *New York Times* interview of Rev. J. Gilbert H. Baker. Baker, a former China missionary, traced the new Chinese ideal of social equality to Christian missionaries. The clergy in China, formerly "treated as a privileged class, now have to stand at the end of the line."[43] One Indusco member recognized the Bailie School's "excellent work" but would not support the school unless religious training was included in the curriculum. Ida responded that students built the campus church and many faculty members were Christians.[44] Ida concluded by asserting that the values preached by her Southern Baptist father—"the fatherhood of God and the brotherhood of man"—were nowhere clearer than at the Bailie School.[45]

Other members expressed suspicions about China and Indusco's relationship to the Communists. She assured her correspondents that Indusco continued to be nonpolitical under Communist rule, as it had been under the Nationalists. The Bailie School, itself, remained independent until the Ministry of Industry took over its administration in November 1951.[46] In her letters to Indusco supporters , Ida reiterated her basic philosophy:

> I am convinced that people are very much the same all over the world and that most of them care most for living quietly at their own homes and doing their own work. The more we can maintain friendship, therefore, between the ordinary people in different parts of the world, the sooner we will have a world we can all live in without these terrible upheavals ... the school is a small piece of a possible pattern of international good will ... raising the standard of living for villages in the technically backward parts of the world....[47]

Rewi felt strongly enough about the war to speak out, gambling that Shandan's main funding source, New Zealand's Council of Organisations for Relief Services Overseas (CORSO), would not withdraw its support.[48]

In July 1951, as the armistice talks began, he compared his working and writing for the peace movement with that of American abolitionist William Lloyd Garrison. He begged Ida, "Urge me not to use moderation in a cause like the present. I am in earnest.... I will not retreat a single inch, and I will be heard."[49]

Ida supported Rewi's decision to speak out publicly on the radio, knowing Indusco's funding might well suffer by association. "Those things do have to be said.... Fear makes it difficult for people to hear what we have to say...."[50]

Rewi tried to persuade Ida to turn Indusco into an antiwar organization. He suggested the letterhead be changed to "Indusco—An American Committee for Peaceful Relations with China."[51] However, the Indusco board eventually opted for closing down, instead.

Foreign residents' praise for new China continued into the Korean War. Letters from Ida's friends in China supplied her with material for her speeches, informal discussions, and written responses to Indusco members' questions. Talitha Gerlach, a YWCA social worker in Shanghai during the 1930s and a member of both the Indusco board and the International Committee, returned to Shanghai after Liberation.[52] Even more than the new government projects and services, Talitha was impressed with the changed attitudes of ordinary people.

> Certainly a new dignity, respect, purpose for living and concern for the welfare of the masses of the people permeates every aspect of life and work.... Recently I saw a corps of coolies straining and pulling to get their carts, heavily laden with iron rails, across the street car tracks. Immediately the traffic cop left his post and put his shoulder to the wheel to help get the carts across the tracks. Did you ever before see anyone on the street including the policeman give a helping hand?

She wrote of a "new sense of responsibility toward one's fellow human beings and toward the work of rebuilding the nation," greater availability of food, clothing, and health care. Lack of inflation, a stable currency, and well-stocked markets gave the population a sense of confidence in the future, according to Gerlach.[53]

Another of Ida's sources of information about China was Walter Illesley, an engineer for UNRRA Agricultural Industries Services who stayed on with the Bailie School as a top technician-teacher. Even in China's far northwest, the Shandan Bailie School received the *Manchester Guardian, National Guardian, New York Daily Compass,* a full range of short wave bands, and other books and periodicals. Illesley became concerned about the misperceptions about China in the Western press. He believed the East-West struggle between capitalist and Communist ideologies had too greatly influenced the perceptions of Western journalists. Even sympathetic reporters stressed economic reforms and material construction, whereas he perceived the most important change to be in the human spirit.

Illesley, like Talitha Gerlach, based his opinions on his own observations. He reported seeing all sizes of ventilators being transported to factories, "the same factories that in the old days [Rewi] could not persuade to install even the most elementary safety equipment let alone anything for the comfort of the workers."

Illesley's strongest example concerned the drivers for Northwest Petroleum Administration, some of whom he knew personally. The drivers were notorious for carrying illicit cargo and passengers, and for selling gasoline, oil, and truck parts on the black market. They were organized into a powerful secret society that controlled through ruthless tactics such as kidnapping and murder. After being reorganized and participating in study groups, the black market and squeeze activities disappeared completely.

Explaining away the exceptions to these generalities as the result of inexperienced personnel, Illesley confidently concluded, "the tremendous currents that are stirring here will not be reversed or even contained [and] … will have a profound influence on the future of humanity."[54]

Shirley Barton, the China representative of New Zealand's foreign aid organization, CORSO, raved about "breathtaking" works: schools, clinics, nurseries, farms, mutual-aid teams, clean modern factories, huge irrigation projects, housing projects, parks, rest-homes…. But more than the works, she was impressed by "smiling, friendly faces everywhere, spontaneous, enthusiastic welcome given to the 'Friends for Peace.'"[55]

Desperate for news from China, Ida subscribed to *China Monthly Review, China Pictorial, China Reconstructs* and *People's China*. She clipped and saved Lao She's 1952 article "Living in Peking," which reassured readers that the historic sites and quiet, tree-lined streets remained after Liberation. He described in glowing detail the improvements in public health, education, neighborhood organizations, and future plans for urban renewal. More than most Western observers, Ida knew the full significance of sanitation and literacy campaigns for people's well-being and quality of life.[56]

Aside from Lao She's article, Ida found first-hand, detailed reports of

China such as Illesley and Barton's letters to be most valuable. She used these as resources for her lectures to the American Labor Party Club, schools, churches and women's groups.[57] She mailed out numerous copies of friends' letters from China to interested supporters. But Ida realized that most Americans had difficulty accepting information that contradicted the Western press reports of China, comparing the public's cognitive dissonance to her own conflicting values when she joined the cooperatives.[58]

Ida's desire to return to China was reinforced by her friends' enthusiastic letters. Listening to reports by delegates to a Chinese-sponsored Korean Peace Conference, "my eyes ... are never dry.... A great culture shows through all the stories."[59] Periodically, Ida hinted to Rewi of her yearning for China. She hoped that Rewi might pull some strings for his long-time friend. Rewi agreed how good it would be to have Ida back in Beijing translating the new literature, but he denied having any special clout with the authorities.[60]

And so Ida continued to support her mother country in the best way she knew—through Indusco and the Gung Ho movement. Throughout 1951 and into 1952 she raised money, collected books for Shandan, and wrote newsletters for Shandan's loyal supporters. Indusco members, in turn, asked many questions about the school—questions about students and staff, government policies and restrictions—which Ida methodically tried to answer.

In September 1951, Ida underscored to Rewi Indusco's important role disseminating information to the dwindling number of Americans who still supported China. Her letter revealed how little recent information was coming out of Shandan. A new tension between Ida's loyalty to Rewi and her personal standards also surfaced. Ida attempted to ground Indusco's newsletters on factual evidence, not on her ideals or ideological commitments.[61]

During the first half of 1952, as the Indusco board absorbed Rewi's reports, Indusco's landlord refused to renew the office's lease and increasing numbers of advisory board members resigned.[62] Extensive correspondence between Ida and one board member, Evans Clark of the 20th Century Fund, strongly suggests that some members' resignations were triggered by an anonymous "confidential report" naming Indusco as a "Communist front" group. The ongoing military conflict between China and the United States in Korea opened Indusco to further U.S. government scrutiny.[63]

The most immediate cause of Evans Clark's concern was the Cox Committee, a congressional inquiry into tax-exempt charitable foundations led by House of Representatives member, Eugene Cox. A conservative from Georgia, Cox charged that "these creatures of the capitalist system" brought the system "into disrepute" by addressing race relations, education, peace, and the arts, as well as by studying the Soviet Union and the blacklisting program, itself.[64] Liberal members of the Indusco advisory board, such as Evans Clark, were justifiably worried.

Three to four hundred Indusco members continued to support the Shandan Bailie School as an expression of their friendship for China and probably their opposition to U.S. policy in Korea.[65] By June 1952, the Indusco board tried "in all humility and thoughtfulness" to consider the best way forward, acknowledging "all the divergent views even among men of good will".[66] At the June 13 meeting, the Indusco board agreed to dissolve. Individual board members vowed to continue working for Chinese-American understanding through organizations such as the China Welfare Appeal.[67]

In Ida's letter to Rewi about the decision, she wrote, "I can understand the Chinese desire to have their home to themselves while they are putting their new house in order and I can understand their conviction that each of us should be working in our own homelands with our own peoples for this brotherhood of man and the peace it will bring."[68] The great historic force of Chinese nationalism had once again pushed Ida from her job, as it had ousted her from the PUMC Hospital, and her father from missionary work in the 1930s. C.W. Pruitt's heart was broken by the apparent ingratitude of those he had loved. But Ida had been wounded and healed before, and vowed not to take China's new, antiforeign stage personally.

She explained to Rewi that the board decided not to turn Indusco into a peace organization, but some members would work through the China Welfare Appeal.[69] Rewi responded by expressing his profound appreciation for Indusco's work for the cooperatives since 1939. "... He who has been for us, has a true place in our affection. It has been a collective endeavor.... Please do give the Board our heartfelt thanks.... It may be that we shall meet up at some place meet or other.... Love to you."[70]

From 1939 until 1952, Ida Pruitt was the unifying force in the organization she founded. She held various titles through the years: Representative from China, Field Representative, International Field

Secretary, and Executive Secretary. She traveled widely through the United States, Canada, China and Hong Kong, raised money and public consciousness, organized local support groups and built coalitions. She found ways to transport funds, machinery, and personnel through Chinese war zones to the cooperatives. Ida lobbied the Congress and several Presidents, and she struggled tirelessly within the UCR and with her own staff to uphold the vision she shared with Rewi: productive, self-sufficient, self-governing village industry throughout rural China.

The Gung Ho cooperatives, as Rewi and the Snows originally conceived the movement, were an answer to China's wartime refugee crisis and a strategy for enlisting worldwide popular support for China against Japan. However, to Ida, the cooperatives symbolized much more. They embodied aspects of China that few Westerners appreciated. The cooperative philosophy of economic self-reliance countered the alarming economic colonization and consequent image of China as an inferior dependent of Western powers. Grassroots cooperative leadership offered a model of capable Chinese in charge of their lives and country. The cooperative workshops' village settings and decentralized organization promised to preserve the best of the traditional Chinese social structure. And, on a personal level, the Gung Ho movement provided Ida with a new mission in life just when her old one at the PUMC terminated.

As the dominant figure in the American Indusco office, as well as the other half of the "Rewi-Ida Axis," Ida's leadership in Indusco was no less controversial than at the PUMC. From the first year of operation, Ida tried to be open and democratic. Despite its relative inefficiency, she believed in group leadership.[71] She sought advice and suggestions from a wide range of sources, and invited board members' participation in policy development and report writing.[72] The executive board went on record as receiving her initial report "with special enthusiasm and appreciation." Near her tenure's end, the board was equally praiseworthy.[73] Despite the contentious relationship between Indusco and the UCR, UCR board member Lennig Sweet pointedly remarked that it had been a pleasure working with her.[74]

Others noted that her excitement for the cooperatives was "contagious."[75] Staff members in China looked forward to her regular morale-boosting letters.[76] UCR volunteers were inspired by her stories. Numerous Indusco members highly valued Ida's long, personal letters. Close friends compared Ida's leadership style favorably with other American women working for China.[77]

Among others, Ida developed a reputation as a difficult, even hysterical woman.[78] Some board members were embarrassed by her personal attacks or obstructionism at meetings.[79] Her loyalty to Rewi in the name of cooperative principles blind-sighted her on some key issues. She relentlessly struggled to protect Rewi when he seemed to be under attack. She at times lost her temper, for which she later apologized.[80] With Peg Snow, Ida privately strategized to maximize their influence over the Indusco board.[81] The two successfully lobbied to replace Henry Luce/Chiang Kai-shek sympathizers on the board with others more compatible with Rewi's philosophy of decentralization and genuine non-partisanship in China's civil war. Despite her protestations that she wasn't "hard-boiled enough for this game," Ida became a pro at faction fighting.[82] When Peg criticized her judgment, Ida defended her decisions as appropriate:

> I am careful. I am staying within my position.... Someone has to act.... I know I am learning. But I must do things according to my pattern. We all have to follow our own patterns and keep our own integrity. I cannot act a part. I see a job to be done and that is the job to do. I must trust my own judgment after consultation of course.... Peg, someone has to take responsibility. It's on me.[83]

Peg Snow worried that Ida's "false sense of security" would lead to her ouster from the organization.[84] But Ida insisted her sense of inner security was genuine. Quoting both Christianity and Chinese teachings, she again emphasized the importance of a pattern or destiny behind human actions.[85] Although she suffered stomach problems and sometimes lost sleep over internal Indusco disputes, Ida tried not to waste her emotions on worry, preferring to channel her energy into problem solving. "No matter what happens I know that I am working in the right way for the right thing. If we fail, then we will do something else. But I do not think we will fail in the end...."[86]

12

China's American Daughter: Missionary and Pilgrim

The concrete and metal of New York must have felt more oppressive than usual to Ida during the summer of 1952, as she packed boxes and broke up the Indusco office. Ida claimed she felt no sadness closing the office. With "true consecration" she had dedicated herself to the industrial cooperative movement since 1939.[1] The movement's underlying principles of decentralized, economic democracy and empowerment of ordinary people provided Ida with the sense that she was helping to preserve traditional Chinese communities. By mid 1952, the cooperative cause seemed to be in good hands as the Chinese Communist Party installed the Gung Ho leadership in key positions and initiated agricultural producer's cooperatives on a national scale.

Although Ida was pleased that the Chinese government adopted the cooperative model, "something gave way" inside herself. As she visited her brother, cooked for her Chinese daughter's family, and vacationed with Peg Snow in Connecticut, Ida realized she missed the constant crisis mode and intense activity of the Indusco years. "It is a bit dashing to find oneself with no problems at all ... with no work, in fact."[2]

Shortly after the closing of the Indusco office, Ida accepted the chairmanship of China Welfare Appeal (CWA), the only remaining organization working for people-to-people relations with China. Calling herself "the only foot loose person around who knows China," Ida took on the part-time position as a duty. After a brief vacation in France, she planned events for the CWA and gave occasional lectures on China.[3]

However, the void left by Indusco's demise was not filled by the CWA. With the termination of Indusco, Ida's mission in life, as well as her deep bond with Rewi Alley, both required redefinition. For thirteen years, Ida and Rewi had corresponded several times weekly about the cooperatives and other "burning" Chinese issues. After the severance of U.S.-Chinese relations, she and other "friends of China," dependent on the letters of Rewi and other Westerners residents for their information and interpretation of events in China, urged Rewi to continue writing regular letters. But Ida hesitated before reviving her own longstanding correspondence with Rewi, realizing, "How to write … what to write … that will interest you and be of any use to you, means thinking out … the problems that face all of us … how best to use our energies…."[4]

To be useful was an important value to Protestant missionaries. Ida retained and shared this value with Rewi. The New Zealand farm boy and American "mishkid" (missionary kid) both inherited their parents' commitment to living their ideals to the fullest. The two felt a tremendous respect for country people, a respect born of their own rural childhoods. For many years before joining the Gung Ho movement, each had worked with Chinese victims of poverty and dislocation. Independently, Rewi and Ida had each concluded that the key to individual human dignity and material well-being was productive work. The Chinese Industrial Cooperatives provided them with a practical means through which to generate socially useful jobs on a large scale.

The Gung Ho cooperatives offered its leaders like Rewi and Ida something else—an actively nonpartisan stance in China's political struggles. Unlike most middle-of-the-road Chinese and foreigners, whose ambivalence became "fence-sitting inaction," Ida and Rewi chose to actively support Chinese civilians on both sides of the political divide. Increasingly they preferred the Communist Party to the Nationalist, but this preference did not change their actions on behalf of all Chinese civilians, especially the most powerless. Both Rewi and Ida believed that such genuine nonpartisan action was the only responsible position for foreigners to take in China's internal affairs.

After the Chinese Communist victory, the question of nonpartisan action became a mute one. Within a few years, the new government integrated the cooperatives into their national economic program. The two old activists' joint project disappeared, but their mutual commitment to live useful, active lives remained. No longer did they share adventures riding weapons carriers, sleeping in vermin-infested inns or under the stars. Instead, they redefined their usefulness as mediators between Chinese and Western civilization. In Rewi's typically blunt words, "If we can do nothing else, we can at least work so that there be better understanding of cultural values." They mailed each other books on

Chinese poetry, painting, archeology, and other materials for art exhibits and speaking tours. Rewi strongly urged Ida to write her autobiography and to continue translating Chinese literature; Ida, in turn, encouraged his translations of ancient Chinese pacifist poetry, edited his manuscripts, and became his literary agent in the United States.[5]

The friendship between Rewi and Ida contained a strong nurturing quality as well as shared intellectual and political interests. Rewi suffered from a number of ongoing health problems related to his rugged life in the Chinese hinterland. Ida often consulted American doctors on Rewi's behalf and frequently mailed him packages of medicine, vitamins, and other amenities. An American bank account had been established for such expenses, which Ida could access. More important than monetary repayment, however, was Rewi's heartfelt appreciation for Ida's political principles, unflagging support and personal integrity through the years.[6]

The special quality of Rewi and Ida's friendship was obvious to other Gung Ho activists. Ida realized they gossiped: "I was not really a person of any judgment, how could I poor dear, when I was in love with Rewi."[7] But she would have cringed to hear her friend, Peg Snow's characterization of her as Rewi's devoted "girl Friday," or David Crook's description of her feelings as "hero worship."[8] Peg Snow's assessment may have been based on Ida's candid remark to Rewi in 1939: "All my life I have hoped to find a man big enough to follow or a cause big enough to work for wholly. To find both in one is marvelous." Ida assumed Peg and other supporters of the "Rewi-Ida Axis" understood "there is such a thing as loving a person, as we all love Rewi, and being able to see the movement also."[9]

Chinese observers also concerned themselves with the romances of their "Western friends." The television documentary of Rewi's life, filmed during the early 1980s by both Gansu and Beijing television stations, originally included Ida as Rewi's "love interest," but Rewi insisted that the fabricated romance be removed.[10]

Ida eventually understood that Rewi's romantic disinterest in her or any other woman was due to his "war injury," a euphemism for homosexuality.[11] She left behind no record acknowledging Rewi's probable homosexual activities at the Shandan Bailie School. Rewi's homosexuality was probably not known to his left-wing friends in Shanghai during the early 1930s, but was common knowledge among both Westerners and Chinese at the Bailie School. Gung Ho activists discretely accepted homosexual activity by many of the older boys, who later married. None suggested that Rewi took advantage of young boys or in any way compromised his genuine, lifelong commitment to the students.[12]

Ida's original attraction to Rewi may well have had sexual overtones, but her lifelong devotion to him is better understood as a common response by both men and women to this charismatic figure. Brigadier General Evans F. Carlson spoke of Rewi's spiritual quality.[13] Gung Ho activist Israel Epstein concurred that Rewi was the "kind of guy" to inspire devotion.[14] Rumors flew of Rewi's involvement with another of his female confidantes of many years, CORSO representative Shirley Barton. She, like Ida, insisted that her passion was directed to the "cause of China and the world," not to Rewi, despite his considerable charms.[15]

After the Indusco years, as both Ida and Rewi constructed new purposes for their lives, each turned to writing, translation, and researching Chinese archeology. The two continued to mutually support each other in these endeavors and maintained regular correspondence for the rest of their lives. Rewi's birthday letter to Ida in 1968 praised her as "a very wonderful person, steadfast, loyal and true to what you have worked out to be the best." He wished he could bring to her an armful of flowers, especially a flowering plum blossom, or otherwise send something "to give weight to my love which you know you always have."[16] In 1976, Rewi wrote the following poem for Ida, in which he alludes to her birthplace as well as to her well-known book about Ning Lao Taitai.

Ida, daughter of Han
and of the Isles of the Immortals
of Penglai, now herself
the gracious Lao Tai tai
yet ever as young as she feels
in the spirit that is immortal.

Ida,
good comrade through
the tough years of struggle;
deep and sincere in her love
for the common folk of China
to whom she has given her best
for so long.

Ida,
the good American, the quiet

determined worker for deeper
more lasting friendship
with the land in which she
was born, and still loves.

Ida, this salute from old Peking
that a March wind I hope
will take to you, bringing
with it the fragrance
of spring blossom in all
its glory, that is your
glory too.[17]

Ida's correspondence with Rewi and other friends in China, as well as her chairmanship of the China Welfare Appeal, were considered suspect in America of the early 1950s. Frequent communications between private citizens in the United States and Communist countries during the postwar years were subject to close government scrutiny even before Wisconsin Senator Joseph R. McCarthy in February, 1950 led a nation-wide witch-hunt against all suspected Communists. The FBI reviewed Ida's passport history and noted her activities in Indusco as early as 1941.[18] Copies of telegrams between various cooperative leaders were included in Indusco's FBI record throughout World War II. Many names in the files were blackened. This served two purposes: first, to protect the identity of FBI informants within Indusco, and second, to cover up the names of others under investigation. The extent of the blackened material indicates Indusco activists were routinely observed, sometimes by each other.[19]

On at least one occasion, a conscientious private citizen took the initiative to contact the FBI about Indusco's dealings with Communist China. In 1946, Ida had written to the Beauty and Barber Supply Institute of New York, inviting the institute to donate six pairs of shears and four hair clippers to the Bailie School. The institute's director explained, "If ... there is any chance that it would come into the hands of Communistic elements in China, we would hardly care to contribute."[20]

Apparently, the FBI felt no great alarm at the prospect of American scissors cutting "Communistic" hair. Agents did not begin closely following Indusco until the organization was highlighted in right-wing journalist George E. Sokolsky's December 6, 1949 column, "These Days."[21] Sokolsky explained he opposed Indusco because material assistance to the Bailie School inevitably would fall into Communist hands. Further, in Sokolsky's view, aid to the Chinese people could not be distinguished from aid to the government since Communist governments "take and own everything anyhow."[22]

Long-time Indusco supporters clearly were influenced by Sokolsky's column, as well as the Korean conflict that soon followed. A number wrote to Ida, requesting proof that their contributions were not falling into Communist hands. Ida responded patiently, by distinguishing between three meanings of "Communist" and emphatically denied that any American contributions were going to the government. "It is strictly a school for technical training in the making of consumer goods and in agriculture and in pastoral activities and mining of coal. Furthermore it is in West China and far from the scenes of battle."[23] She was equally insistent that no products made at the Bailie School were used in the Korean War. She ended by underscoring her faith that people-to-people friendship such as promoted by Indusco would help to end the conflict in Korea.

A 1950 internal security report on Indusco identified numerous Indusco's incorporators whose connections in other organizations caused suspicion.[24] The name Owen Lattimore was enough to brand Indusco "Communist" in the hysterical climate of public opinion created by Senator McCarthy just a month before. Although McCarthy's speech to the full Senate fell short of calling Lattimore a Soviet spy, his charge that Lattimore had "tremendous power" in the State Department led to five years of hearings by the Senate Foreign Relations Committee, the Senate Internal Security Committee, and the U.S. Justice Department. But before Lattimore was exonerated in 1955, his association with Indusco and his friendship with Ida Pruitt "proved" their own Communist connections.[25]

A single FBI informant reported Indusco as a Communist front organization. Two other informants "of known reliability" denied any knowledge of Indusco's Communist tendencies. Other evidence came from the FBI's interpretation of an article by Peg Snow (under the pen name "Nym Wales") and a list of Communist front groups in the *New Leader*. The bureau concluded from this flimsy evidence that Indusco must be closely watched.[26]

Ida's personal file was activated after the Chinese entered the Korean War. In November 1951, she was the subject of a twenty-one-page FBI report that named her as one of the authors honored by a party held by the Committee for a Democratic Far Eastern Policy. The report went on to describe other suspicious affiliations of Ida's friends and associates, and noted the arrival of CWA's "friendship cargo" to a children's hospital in China.[27] Based on this report, the FBI assumed Ida's "guilt by association" and placed her name on a Security Index card as a Communist.

In subsequent years, the FBI informants found no concrete evidence of Ida's membership in the Communist Party, but retained her name on the Security Index list. With heightening Sino-American tensions over the Taiwan Straits during 1954–1955, she was one of eleven Caucasian Americans designated "potentially dangerous" and subject to detention in the event of war with China.[28]

It is doubtful that Ida was aware of her possible arrest, but she knew of FBI interest in her as an informant. On September 2, 1954, several blocks from Ida's New York apartment, two agents identified Ida as a sixty-five-year old, 5'1½" tall woman of slight build with a prominent nose and eyebrows and full lips. They approached her. After introducing themselves and showing their credentials, the agents offered her an "opportunity to have a confidential talk … and to cooperate with her Government." Ida retorted, "I have nothing to say to you and do not care to engage in conversation at all."[29] Three years later, when approached again, she "only smiled and shook her head."[30]

Ida kept the bureau busy by taking active leadership in a support committee for Eugene Moy, managing editor of *China Daily News*, a Chinese language newspaper in New York Chinatown. In 1954, Moy was convicted of violating the Trading with the Enemy Act. The newspaper had accepted advertisements from Chinese banks that encouraged Chinese in the United States to invest their money at home.[31] "Every time I think of Eugene Moy in prison for no crime it hurts and hurts. He is there because of the lies told [by the U.S. government] about people in China."[32]

The bureau continued to observe Ida through the years, carefully recording the Chinese magazines she ordered, the English-languages materials she mailed to China, her friendships with other suspects, and her trips to Europe. Clearly, one of Ida's friends in New York, who had access to Ida's papers, was an informant. Someone kept the FBI appraised of the contents of Ida's letters from China and her speeches, as well as her vacation plans.[33] In November 1959, an extremely confidential source in San Francisco, whose anonymity the bureau took great care to protect, advised the office that Ida was traveling in China in defiance of the State Department's travel ban.[34]

Only in January 1968, at age seventy-nine, was Ida's name removed from the Security Index. Yet into her eighties, she continued to confound the FBI by ordering magazines with subversive names such as *Progressive Labor*, *Spark*, *Challenge*, and the organ of the Revolutionary Union.[35]

Ida subscribed to revolutionary publications for their information and analysis of China. Judging from letters she received from friends in China, she believed the China coverage in the *New York Times* and other mainstream periodicals to be distorted if not totally false. In addition to the Western press, Ida read numerous Chinese magazines and books, which the U.S. postal service regularly delivered after a favorable U.S. Supreme Court ruling.[36] Second-hand information remained emotionally unsatisfactory to Ida, however. While listening to reports of China by European friends, tears glistened Ida's eyes.[37]

Rewi never forgot Ida's fervent desire to live in China. The two not only shared a common mission to live useful lives promoting Chinese-Western understanding. Each was a pilgrim, of sorts, someone who "journeys long distances to some sacred place as an act of devotion."[38] China's spirit infused both their lives with meaning. Their steadfast work to save China went beyond a secular mission to an act of love and devotion.

Starting in 1956, Rewi urged Ida to visit Beijing to help edit his manuscripts, knowing full well that the American government prohibited U.S. citizens' travel to Communist countries.[39] She joined a lawsuit challenging the government's right to retain the passport of any citizen returning from a Communist country.[40]

Without waiting for a ruling, Ida wrote her old friend, Song Qingling (Madame Sun Yat-sen), of her desire to see her homeland again. To mislead American censors, she sent the letter through friends in Europe.[41] She thought long and hard before defying the American government. Finally, she justified her act of civil disobedience as a form of public pressure on appointed State Department officials, who had instigated the restrictions without a popular mandate.[42]

In early 1959, the Chinese People's Association for Cultural Relations with Foreign Countries issued Ida a formal invitation to visit China for three months. In gratitude for her efforts to promote Chinese-American friendship and understanding, the Association paid for Ida's international travel as well as her in-country expenses.[43]

For the first six weeks, Ida visited friends and familiar places in

Beijing, while assisting Rewi with his writing. Driving through Beijing on the first day, she was immediately struck by the wide streets and tall, modern buildings. In the interest of growth and traffic flow, the historic city walls had been torn down.

Although she tried to sympathize with the city planners' reasons for razing the walls, Ida grieved the loss.[44] The harmonious balance of her beloved city was gone. The huge, Western-style apartment and office buildings, which spread mile after mile, were too "yang," a Chinese philosophical term meaning too masculine and aggressive.

With relief, Ida noticed that many traditional, courtyard-style homes remained. To her, "this gracious form of domestic architecture where the main rooms faced south, where one had an outdoor living room where the family could sit under their own tree ... with some degree of privacy" reflected the "genius" of the Chinese people. She made no mention of visiting her own cherished courtyard home on Xiao Yang Yibin Hutong.

Other surprising impressions were the number of people leisurely strolling or shopping, and the amount of Western-style hand shaking. She also remarked on the unprecedented rainfall in Beijing and equally unusual drought in the Yangtse River valley; people speculated that the atomic experiments were responsible.

By rail, Ida traveled to her home province of Shandong, then to Nanjing and Shanghai. Another journey took Ida across north China to Xi'an, then to Chongqing, where she sailed by boat down the Yangtse River, through the famous Three Gorges. Wherever she toured, her greatest surprise was the expansive urban, industrial growth. The mix of regional accents among factory workers and managers struck her as a positive sign that provincial identification was making way for national loyalty. However, everyone's pride in the large size of their bridge, dam or factory appeared to Ida as unnecessarily defensive, a sad legacy of the inferiority complex bequeathed by the colonial powers.[45]

Tours of the local factories and communes were *de rigueur* wherever Ida traveled. By her own admission, Ida was ignorant of factories and machinery, so she focused her attention on the workers' health and well-being, as well as the human interactions. Everyone looked well fed and energetic. (She noticed only one truly malnourished man in all of her travels.) In meetings of all-women workers, she was "amused" to notice that a man always led the discussions.

Having spent eighteen years making home visits to Beijing's working poor, Ida took special interest in postrevolutionary communal housing and eating accommodations. Shortly before she left the United States, Western newspapers had been reporting the Communist destruction of Chinese families and marriages.[46] Yet everywhere Ida traveled, she saw intact families, sleeping and eating in their own small apartments. The communal dining rooms served mainly as "take-out" restaurants.

Ida duly recorded the figures recited in the obligatory "brief introductions" and calculated that the workers' material needs were well met. Her notebooks filled with descriptions of factory recreational facilities, reading rooms, health clinics, laughing young people, and contented families. She was gratified to observe that many grandparents still participated in the household chores and childcare. Residents in the home for the aged, most of whom had been too poor to afford a wife in the old society, tended vegetable and flower gardens. "The set of their heads on their shoulders was vital. They were useful members of the community and knew it."

The ordinary details of daily life caught Ida's attention: white rice, a sign of preferential treatment served in the home for the aged, the proud demeanor of four-generational families, women's higher status as reflected in the designation of rooms in family homes. Even pigs ate better in New China.

The comparison of ordinary people's lives in 1959 with the abject poverty before 1949 was implicit but strong. Even before the anti-Japanese and civil wars, when the social fabric completely unraveled, vast numbers of Chinese were underemployed, malnourished, poorly clothed, and devoid of hope. As a social worker, Ida could do little for her clients. Productive work, sturdy housing, a secure food supply, and a place in the community were only wistful dreams. By 1959, the new government had fulfilled the dreams of many of China's long-suffering masses. Ida clearly approved. Neither outsiders like Ida nor urban Chinese were aware that an unprecedented famine had already begun, largely caused by Mao and high-level Party officials eager to outdo the Soviets and disdainful of local conditions and popular wisdom.

In 1959, Beijing's food situation had not yet become critical, but by the following year newspapermen, refugees, and United Nations officials all reported severe hunger among China's population.[47] Only decades later was the full extent of the famine confirmed. During the late 1950s and early 1960s, between 25 and 40 million Chinese died of hunger, the largest famine in world history. Although not the most devastating in terms of the percentage of the population killed, China's 1958–1962 famine was the worst completely man-made one.[48]

Along the way, Ida's hosts arranged for her to meet long-time friends. A young anti-Japanese fighter who, in 1938, had hidden in Ida's home, was a member of the provincial judiciary in 1959. A young teacher had become a middle class intellectual and secretary of a small, minority political party. A professor of architecture bubbled over with satisfaction about his life as an educator.

Dining with Bishop and Mrs. Ding, leaders in China's Christian Church, Ida bombarded the bishop with questions about religious freedom under communism, questions that many Indusco members had put to her. Head of the Nanjing Theology School, the bishop also represented the Christian community in the provincial assembly, and participated in city administration and international conferences. He claimed these secular activities never required him to go against his own conscience.

Ida's former Chinese friends most likely had suffered during the "Hundred Flowers Movement," and "Anti-Rightist Movement" of 1957 that persecuted 500,000 intellectuals for speaking out honestly about the revolution's weaknesses. If they shared any concerns about these campaigns or their victimization with Ida, she declined to comment in writing.

With great regret, Ida returned to England, and eventually the United States, after three months in China. The warmth and graciousness of commune members in north China evoked great nostalgia in Ida. She would have liked to stay awhile with these simple country people, who looked and acted like her childhood neighbors in Huangxian. Likewise, she hated to leave Beijing. But her hosts counseled her, as they had done twenty years earlier, that she could better further the cause of Chinese-American friendship from the United States.[49] Conditioned by wartime priorities, gender expectations, and the self-sacrificial ethos of both Chinese and missionary cultures, Ida once more put the greater good before her personal preferences. She consoled herself with visions of returning to live in Beijing someday after U.S. policy toward China changed.[50]

Another twelve years passed before the U.S. government finally began to explore normalizing relations with China. In the interim, Ida continued to give lectures and informal talks about China, supporting her own observations with the latest publications, both Western and Chinese.

By way of introduction, Ida emphasized China's geography, history, and social structure that together shaped the "mental and emotional attitude of the Chinese" during the last hundred years. During the Indochina War, President Nixon began private communications with Beijing. By the spring of 1971, both an American table tennis team and presidential envoy Henry Kissinger were invited to China.[51]

Ida applied for a tourist visa in October 1971, as soon as the "bamboo curtain" parted a bit.[52] However, China was in the throes of its ten-year Great Proletarian Cultural Revolution (1966–1976). All foreign tourists had been barred from 1966 until 1969; in 1971 a few gained permission to visit. Madame Song Qingling smoothed the way for Ida's entry.[53] After seven months' delay, the Chinese People's Association for Friendship with Foreign Countries mailed her an official invitation to visit. This time she would have to pay her own international travel, but her domestic costs were covered.[54]

At age eighty-three, she realized that she would never again live in her motherland. From late October until December 1, 1972, accompanied by a Canadian teenager and her friend Talitha Gerlach, Ida visited with old friends, including Madame Song Qingling. She toured Beijing and Yantai where she had lived as a young missionary teacher, and visited Penglai, where she was born.[55] The cities of Wuxi, Suzhou, and Hangzhou, as well as important sites in China's revolutionary history were also on her itinerary. As before, Ida most enjoyed visiting workers' homes.[56]

However, by this stage in her life Ida approached her travels differently. She reveled in the few remaining old architectural structures of Beijing—the Drum Tower, Bell Tower, and Ming dynasty section of the city wall. In Penglai, the monuments of China's past drew her attention. The lakes, gardens, flowers, and trees gave joy to Ida in ways that the new industrial plants simply failed to do. The copious, statistic-filled notebooks of her 1959 visit were reduced to a single book of obligatory summaries of official "brief introductions." This time, she wrote no narrative of her trip, nor typed an index of her notes.[57]

It is likely that Ida's abbreviated note taking reflected not only her age but also her apprehension about the highly charged atmosphere of the Cultural Revolution. After returning to the United States, Ida's letter of thanks to the Chinese People's Association for Friendship with Foreign Countries ended diplomatically, concealing as much as it revealed: "I am pondering, and will be pondering long, over the spirit of the people I felt as I went from place to place. I have not yet formulated it into words."[58]

Ida had first read Rewi's views of the Cultural Revolution in August 1966 as a passing comment.[59] Several times during the following year, he criticized the coverage by U.S. newspapers and radio broadcasts.[60] Rewi's tours of the countryside and reading of the "big character posters" of Beijing were proof enough for himself that the situation remained "solid and down-to-earth." Borrowing from the rhetoric of the day, Rewi called Mao Zedong Thought "the rock around which the waves of revolution swirl" and enthusiastically mailed Ida several copies of Mao's Little Red Book.[61] The only indication in Rewi's letters that the Cultural Revolution had spun out of control came after the fact—cryptic notes such as: "GCR [Great proletarian Cultural Revolution] is still going, and it will be some time before results can be tabulated."[62] Or: "Things in China are bettering swiftly as provincial Party organizations are formed, and the wheels turn faster."[63]

Ida questioned Rewi about newspaper reports of the Cultural Revolution. Specifically, she wanted his view of the Red Guards, bands of high school or college students who marched around the countryside "making revolution" by destroying anything and anybody they judged to be "feudal."

Rewi answered her questions very perfunctorily.[64] She must have pressed him about the death of writer Lao She, who, in August 1966, drowned in the Taiping Lake under suspicious circumstances.[65] Rewi admitted some of the "scamps" pretending to be Red Guards had committed mistakes in 1966, implying that they may have been responsible for Lao She's so-called suicide.[66] Apparently, Ida also worried that the Cultural Revolution was destroying the Chinese culture, for Rewi responded defensively, "Mao Zedong Thought is very Chinese."[67]

Rewi's letters fail to mention the Cultural Revolution's heavy criticism of the PUMC hospital. In 1966 an exposition of photographs accused PUMC doctors of using patients for medical experimentation.[68] The Red Guards, who were responsible for tremendous brutality and devastation, were harnessed in 1968, and the Cultural Revolution officially ended in 1969. However, atrocities and repression continued until Chairman Mao's death and the arrest of the Gang of Four in 1976, only three years before the opening and reform period began under Deng Xiaoping. Mao's heir apparent, Lin Biao, mysteriously disappeared in

September 1971, just weeks before Ida requested permission to visit China.[69] The political climate apparently remained unsettled.

Ida saw evidence of the Cultural Revolution everywhere she looked. Larger-than-life posters and statues of Chairman Mao reminded her that the cult of Mao continued. Red Guards had wrecked havoc with much of the ancient art and architecture—Buddhist temples, Confucian arches, invaluable ceramics and sculpture. Ida's heart must have been broken, but she wrote nothing in her notes.

As she visited communes, hospitals, schools, and other organizations, Ida's acute powers of observation must have warned her that something was amiss. However, nowhere in her notes did she "sort things out" for herself, as she so often had done during the Indusco days.

Whatever reservation Ida may have felt about her motherland, all in all her homecoming was a joyous occasion to see Rewi and other old friends. Her guides and doctors pampered Ida. At every stop her blood pressure was taken, she was constantly advised to rest, and generally she was treated as if she were made of eggshells, despite her overall good health. Had she been invited, she would have loved to live in the apartment above Rewi's and to collaborate on his biography. She wished to be ten years younger.[70] To Rewi, Ida was "young, poised, and charmingly philosophical" but he was unable or unwilling to obtain an invitation for Ida to stay beyond her visa's expiration.[71]

Upon returning to Philadelphia, where she had moved in 1960, Ida focused her energy on editing her manuscripts. The publication of her essays about Old China took on greater urgency. *A China Childhood* was published in 1978; *Old Madam Yin: A Memoir of Peking Life, 1926–1938* followed in 1979. Ida's primary goal was to preserve some of the best of China's past, qualities she feared would be ignored or destroyed by the "youngsters" now in control of the nation's leadership.[72]

Ida continued to give speeches about China. She remained enthusiastic about New China, utilizing the information and statistics from her latest trip to illustrate the dramatic improvements in daily life. But the Cultural Revolution per se occupied little space in her comments. In fact, her favorite themes contradicted the iconoclastic values of the Cultural Revolution. Whereas Mao preached unending revolution, her lectures invariably described the traditional consensual leadership style of village elders. Mao abhorred stability and order, but Ida defended the Chinese yearning for order. And finally, en route to a Communist classless society, the CCP claimed to represent the leadership of the proletariat. In contrast, Ida praised the traditional Chinese understanding of privilege, which carried with it solemn responsibilities and duties. American society had its privileged class, too, she added, but it had forgotten its responsibilities toward those whose work supported them.

One imagines that Ida's equivocal support for the Chinese government further pushed her to focus on the past. But her own explanation was simpler: "The only way I can write about a place or people is to be there ... for some time. There is no depth to the bird's eye view I have had several times in New China." Somewhat defensively, for she imagined Rewi urging her to write about the present, Ida asserted the value of writing about Old China. "New China is built on the solid strength of the people of Old China.... Old Madam Yin ... shows some of the weaknesses of Old China and some of the strengths of the people....[73] Rewi quickly reassured her of the importance of her books and translations.[74]

No doubt, Ida's focus on traditional Chinese culture instead of current events was partly a function of her age. The turn away from political commentary and toward memoir is common as writers enter their mature years. Seeking to hold onto the past, they apply their best-honed skill to the task. Ida had begun her preservation efforts even before leaving Beijing in 1939 by interviewing her elderly Chinese women friends. *A Daughter of Han* was first published in 1945 before its reissue in 1967.[75]

Many of the traditional Chinese qualities which Ida prized resemble the "Asian values" touted a generation later by conservative politicians in countries such as Singapore, Japan, and Malaysia, as well as in China.[76] Hong Kong's former chief executive Tung Chee-hwa itemized these as: "trust, love, and respect for our family and our elders; integrity, honesty and loyalty to all; commitment to education; a belief in order and stability; a preference for consultation rather than confrontation; ... a preference for obligation rather than individual rights." Tung contrasted these with North American values: "freedom of expression, personal freedom, self-reliance, individual rights, hard work, personal achievement, thinking for one's self."[77]

China's leaders, always resentful of the United States' tendency to force American values onto other countries, are quick to charge the United States with arrogantly intervening in China's national sovereignty. Ida agreed with this criticism of her fatherland. Often, in private correspondence, she lambasted the U.S. government for its air of superiority and attempts to influence Chinese domestic policy. Always sensitive to the crippling effects of Western colonialism on the Chinese psyche, Ida was a staunch defender of national sovereignty.

The radical difference between the traditional values Ida preserved in her writing and the traditionalism of 1990s politicians lies in the motives behind their views. Modern day political leaders evoke Asian values as a defense against their own citizens' initiatives such as the human rights and democracy movements. No similar self-interest motivated Ida. She wrote primarily for Westerners who, ignorant of Chinese culture, try to impose their own way of life on China. Clearly, Ida supported Chinese citizens' empowerment, as evidenced by her longstanding commitment to the Gung Ho cooperatives. However, she fervently believed social change would be most effective if initiated by Chinese, not foreigners, and if built on a firm foundation of Chinese cultural tradition.

How could Ida justify her support of a Chinese government that had presided over one of the worst famines in Chinese history, that grew increasingly unresponsive to citizens' initiatives during the Hundred Flowers Movement, and that terrorized and humiliated a million of its people during the Cultural Revolution? Did she really think that the CCP would accept grassroots social change?

From the vantage point of the early twenty-first century—after the revelation of China's famine, the terror imposed by the Gang of Four, and the severe repression of the 1989 democracy movement—it would be easy to paint Ida as a naive, sentimental old woman who relied too heavily on her friend, Rewi's, political judgments. Such is the advantage of hindsight. However, this portrait of Ida, and of Rewi, assumes two things: first, that the actions and errors of the Chinese Communist Party were inevitable and, second, that early sympathizers of the Communist government should have predicted future Communist behavior.

Viewing the young CCP during its first decade of power, as did Ida, Rewi, and other Westerners living in China, the obvious comparison was with the past, not the future. Scrupulously honest, respectful of civilians, and sincerely patriotic during the war against Japan, the Communists were universally welcomed by both the Chinese people and Western friends because of their exemplary behavior compared to the Nationalist Party.[78] During its first decade of power, the CCP brought social order and economic stability to China for the first time since the fall of the last dynasty in 1911. Under the Communists, the Chinese nation regained its pride and dignity as a strong power worthy of respect by the world community. Supporters saw a bright future for China.

The Western press reported disturbing signs from the beginning of Communist rule. In 1952, for example, the British Legation reported tales of "Red Terror"—people dragged off in chains and tortured in the Beijing prison—and issued a "grave warning" to Australian visitors to China not to fall for Communist propaganda. In response, a delegation of Westerners requested permission to visit the prison. They found unguarded production shops, drama performances, newspaper reading rooms, and an "atmosphere of craftsmen absorbed in their work."[79] A Potemkin village, perhaps, except for the first-hand reports of Western prisoners, who confirmed the rehabilitative function of their incarceration.[80]

So many eyewitness reports contradicted Western press accounts of Communist China that Ida and others soon discredited the capitalist-controlled news media as a source of reliable information. Instead, they relied on their own perspectives and the writings of other friends of China such as Edgar Snow, Han Suyin, and Anna Louise Strong. But these sources were problematic, as well.[81] Perhaps the most infamous example of the shortcomings of eyewitness accounts is Edgar Snow's assertion that China suffered no famine in the early 1960s. Of course, today we know that, even as Snow wrote, China was in the midst of its worst famine in history.

Some critics accuse Snow and other such China experts of becoming a "Special Propaganda Department" to the Communists, helping the Party to "carry on their activities beyond the reach of world opinion and exempt from effective scrutiny."[82] Others note that almost all American visitors, from liberal columnist James Reston to conservative columnist Joseph Alsop, idealized Chinese reality from their personal observations and failed to understand the function of propaganda in Chinese society.[83]

A fair enough criticism of tourists and journalists, these explanations remain unconvincing when applied to Westerners living permanently in China. Certainly, they were treated as guests and given preferential treatment to an extent.[84] However, as they went about daily life, participating in the work force and in schools, making Chinese friends, sometimes marrying into Chinese families, they couldn't be completely "tricked" by propaganda. While acknowledging the CCP's shortcomings, Western residents generally supported the Party as China's best government since the height of the Qing dynasty. These people, primarily

Rewi Alley, but also Talitha Gerlach, Anna Louise Strong, and others, were Ida's friends and most reliable sources. Her Chinese friends may have told her what she wanted to hear, or what was politically safe, or what their national pride required of them, but Ida had no reason to think that her Western friends hid known atrocities and abuses from her.

Ida's failure to detect the great famine during her 1959 journey, or the atrocities of the Cultural Revolution during her 1972 trip cannot be satisfactorily explained in terms of her political naiveté, or a conspiracy among all Western residents to hide the dark side of Communism from her. Ida may well have suspected that all was not well in her motherland. She freely admitted that China was no more perfect than any other country. "It is neither heaven on earth nor a man-made hell."[85] However, Ida was adamant that, whatever its shortcomings, the People's Republic had the right to be recognized and treated as a sovereign, equal state in the community of nations.

Ida's support for New China can best be understood as a reaction against European and American colonialism in Asia, which she had witnessed first-hand prior to the World War II. Ida felt the weight of her government's abuse of power and of white Europeans' sense of superiority—including the missionaries who self-righteously professed to be helping the poor Chinese. She saw her responsibility as reforming her own government and society, not another. Any public disagreement with the Chinese government would have constituted interference in China's internal affairs, the very act she opposed.

Ida was acutely sensitive to the missionary impulse in the American people and government—the expansive, self-confident movement to recreate the world in their own image. Self-identified with the Chinese culture, Ida resented America's efforts to change a great, old civilization. She cringed at missionaries' warped images of "her" people and devoted herself to correcting their misperceptions.

If Ida avoided common American misconceptions of China, she was not without her own biases. No one can observe a different culture in a completely neutral way. As human beings, we define the world and ourselves by distinguishing ourselves from others.[86] But Ida was less a missionary than a pilgrim. If missionaries are convinced of their own religion/culture's correctness and superiority, they are predisposed to view other religions/cultures as incorrect and inferior. On the other hand, pilgrims travel abroad to reinforce their own religious or cultural belief system. Both missionary and pilgrim view the "Other" through a distorted lens, but the nature of the distortions differs. The missionaries' purpose was to convert, so their images were excessively negative. The pilgrims' purpose was to buttress their own beliefs, so they unconsciously selected the aspects of the other culture that reinforced their worldviews.[87]

American pilgrims of the political left and right, missionary children, and others raised in China, traveled to the People's Republic in order to reinforce their values or ideology, be it social equality, socialism, Communism, honest government, the importance of hard work, loyalty, respect for the family, or whatever they imagined China possessed. Ida's pilgrimages were made to reinforce the values of her childhood in China. Raised among the children of Huangxian, nurtured by Dada, home-schooled, and self-identified with Chinese culture her entire life, she made pilgrimages back to her motherland to fill an emotional void left empty in America. Half a century after she first compared her life's journey to the pilgrims' path up Shang Fang Shan, the metaphor still fit.

Epilogue

In 1960, after returning from her China trip, Ida moved from New York to Philadelphia, where her brothers and their families lived and near Swarthmore, where Tania taught Russian literature starting in 1973.[1] Her friendship with China scholars Adele and Allyn Rickett drew her to Powelton Village, a neighborhood of tree-lined streets near the University of Pennsylvania. For the last twenty-five years of her life, Ida actively participated in American politics and community life as a member of Women's International League of Peace and Freedom and the Gray Panthers. She participated in vigils and demonstrations against the nuclear bomb and the Indochina War and in favor of civil rights. She served as the secretary/treasurer of the Powelton Village Neighborhood Association and tutored kindergarten students in the adjacent neighborhood of Mantua.[2]

As one of the oldest of the "old friends of China," Ida continued her role as a cultural bridge-builder. She was an honorary National Board member and frequent speaker at the United States–China People's Friendship Association. She spent hours sharing her love of China with students in the Oriental Studies Department at the University of Pennsylvania. Among the many individuals and groups who sought her help to contact Chinese authorities during the years before normalization of diplomatic relations were British writer Felix Greene, the Quaker organization American Friends Service Committee, and a group of Northeastern University women professors and students.[3] Chinese dignitaries to New York often made side trips to Philadelphia in order to pay their respects to Ida.[4] During the 1960s and 1970s, her small apartment in Powelton Village welcomed the same wide range of guests as her beloved Chinese home on Xiao Yang Yibin Hutong had done in the 1930s.

The bridge that Ida built between her "motherland" and "fatherland" stretched in two directions. While most of her writing and speaking was directed toward explaining China to American audiences, she also responded to the opportunity to aid Chinese understanding of the United States. During the years of nonrecognition between her two countries, she managed an American bank account for Talitha Gerlach, who was working with Madame Song Qingling to establish the Children's Palaces throughout Shanghai. With the funds, Ida systematically purchased and mailed to Talitha several hundred books of American literature and non-fiction, as well as magazine subscriptions and newspaper clippings. These helped to support the libraries of Shanghai's Children's Palaces.[5]

The categories of books included, but were not limited to: U.S. politics, Asian politics, child health and psychology, African-American issues, education, religion, and literature. The last was by far the largest category. Among the 250 clippings and magazines were *The Nation, Parents Magazine, Child Development, Monthly Review, American Dialog, The Churchman, The Bulletin of Atomic Scientists,* and *Church and State.* These materials, as well as a hundred letters and documents, represent liberal and radical perspectives of American society and international relations during the days of the Civil Rights Movement and the Indochina conflict. Certainly, the Chinese authorities welcomed the material that criticized the United States, but one wonders how comfortable the Party officials were in exposing their youth to the underlying messages of democracy, human rights, and popular sovereignty.

During her later years, Ida's passion for life and urge to preserve Chinese culture continued to express itself through literary writing and translation of Chinese literature. Most mornings Ida spent polishing *A China Childhood, Old Madam Yin,* and short stories, including "The Bride of Teh Shan," a sexually provocative story of a village boy's affair with a widow and his arranged marriage.[6] She translated *The Child Bride,* by Wang Ying.[7] In lengthy letters to the editors of English-language magazines in China, she analyzed Chinese expressions and their English equivalents. She frequently corresponded with American literary agents in an ongoing effort to publish Rewi's many manuscripts, as well as those of Chinese friends.[8]

Ida's passionate nature also found expression in several relationships with men. Even in New York, during the intense political fighting of the war years, Ida had continued to view herself as a sexual being and enjoyed being attractive to men.[9] During her twilight years in Philadelphia, she enjoyed a close friendship with John Russell of New York. From 1974 to 1977, when she was in her mid-eighties, Ida carried on a long distance romantic relationship with Richard Hartshorne, a geographer in Madison, Wisconsin. Her daily correspondence expressed joy and longing, which he discretely reciprocated.[10]

Notwithstanding Ida's active involvement in her community and politics, as well as her connections with family, friends, Chinese visitors, and lovers, Ida felt exiled and poorly adjusted to the United States. She wrote Rewi in 1978 that she remained homesick for her "motherland." She cast herself as fundamentally a Chinese but lacking a solid core identity that enabled Chinese immigrants and students living abroad to adjust to a foreign culture.[11]

Yet Ida's recorded dreams reveal her to be more Western than Chinese. Through her conversations with Old Madam Ning and her collection of Chinese folk tales and customs, she was acquainted with traditional Chinese theories of dream interpretation.[12] However, to access her own unconscious, she chose an American psychiatrist trained in Freudian psychology. Her dream images of railroad tracks, a watch, and colonial-style house are all references to Western objects.

At times Ida's dreams were easily traced to her daily concerns. During a time when she feared for the future of Rewi's school in Shandan, Ida dreamed of a Chinese doctor and Chinese boys. By and large, however, her dreams were peopled with Western friends, family and acquaintances.

According to Western dream interpretation, her dream vision of hills is an archetypical signal of expanded awareness or a clear view of one's situation. Ida also made reference to the biblical quote, "I will lift up mine eyes to the hills, from whence cometh my help...." as a source of solace in her youth. However, Chinese dream interpreters do not mention hills.

Ida interpreted her dream of riding across the ocean in a swift boat as a hopeful sign of a new life, whereas a typical Chinese might interpret an ocean dream as a grave omen.[13] To a Chinese, riding in a boat signifies success, whereas to an American interpreter the boat ride symbolizes the journey, itself.[14]

Beyond any formulaic interpretation of dream symbolism lies the personal meaning given to the objects by the dreamer. In Ida's symbology, a small fisherman statue symbolized Chinese philosophy. She carried Chinese philosophy up a ladder and into a cave ... two Western symbolic dream objects that she interpreted as fear of death. Her Chinese philosophy comforted her in times of insecurity and fear. But she was not Chinese.

Perhaps the Chinese spiritual concept of the red cord binding two souls together, a concept that she used to describe her relationship with Jack, provides an apt metaphor for Ida's own complex cultural identity. She was an American bound to China by a strong, red spiritual cord through which flowed China's cultural energy. Without a regular pilgrimage to China, she felt depleted and isolated. When Ida was connected, however, China's great spirit reinvigorated her and, through her life, flowed onward to other Americans.

Ida died in Philadelphia on July 24, 1985 at the age of ninety-six. Tania, whom Ida had rescued from the life of a refugee and cabaret dancer, was at her side near the end. In tribute, Tania later wrote, "She encouraged me to fight for whatever I wanted to achieve and gave me more than I deserved in life."[15] Guijing, whom Ida "kidnapped" from a Chinese madam, remembered her "Gugu" as a wonderful person who protected and defended the little girl.[16]

Friends, neighbors, and former colleagues who attended her memorial service spoke of her "unforgettable personality," a "wonderful presence," her "power clearly beyond ... a modest, little, gentle ... exterior." They felt Ida's "incredible determination and strength to live and live well in face of adversity."[17] Others were struck by her sense of humor, her spirit of service and her profound interest in other people.[18] "Ida was *there* for us." "She acted as if I were enriching her life." "She always made you feel you were a dear, close friend."[19] China scholars Derk Bodde, Adele Rickett, and Allyn Rickett all were struck by Ida's "great joy in living." Allyn Rickett remembered that University of Pennsylvania students talked with Ida more freely than with the faculty members or their parents.[20] Young people saw her as a surrogate grandmother and yet young at heart.[21] A single parent and social activist who had broken with her own parents felt great support from Ida.[22] "We loved her; we admired her, we depended upon her."[23] "Ida's life has given us courage, hope and joy. May her spirit be a comforting guide in the continuing quest for world peace." (sic)[24]

The kindergarten student whom Ida had tutored never forgot the warmth and kindness of the seventy-two-year-old lady who invited her sisters and her to lunch and the movies, and who hosted fifteen of her friends in her home! She so admired Ida that she brought her own young daughter to Ida's memorial service a quarter century later.[25]

From China, telegrams expressed fond memories of Ida as well as "horror and great sorrow" at Ida's passing.[26] Rewi wrote "with her passing China has lost one of her best friends."[27] Louise She (She Hui-chen), one of Ida's students at the PUMC, wrote that Ida was the "catalytic agent" of her own pioneering social work in Hong Kong and Shanghai.[28]

Herein lies Ida Pruitt's legacy. Not only was she a pilgrim seeking her life's meaning in China and a secular missionary who sought to preserve China's spirit through her writings.[29] She was also a catalyst for Chinese-initiated social change. Her social service work at the PUMC during the 1920s and 1930s played a leadership role in establishing Hong Kong's social service agencies. By the late twentieth century, Mainland Chinese schools began to see the need for social workers to help society deal with problems related to economic reform. They turned to the leaders of Hong Kong's social work profession for assistance with their training programs, professionals who in turn had been trained by Ida's students.[30]

Likewise, the Gung Ho cooperatives, in which Ida played a critical leadership role during the 1940s, became a catalyst for cooperatives in India under Nehru and in Spain during the 1950s.[31] By the late twentieth century, worker-owned enterprises spread internationally as the International Labor Organization, the United Nations Development Program, and other nongovernmental organizations became aware of their potential to solve urgent employment problems.[32]

In China, the Gung Ho cooperatives were revived in the 1980s in response to economic reforms of state-owned enterprises.[33] Some of the original organizers returned to leadership positions in the International Committee for the Promotion of the Chinese Industrial Cooperatives (earlier known as "International Committee for Chinese Industrial Cooperatives," ICCIC).[34] The Canadian Cooperative Association has begun a partnership with the ICCIC, whose mission is now capacity building and promotion.[35] As the new generation of coops struggles to create opportunities for some of the millions of workers laid off from state-owned enterprises, the founders of the Gung Ho movement provide an inspiring model. Before her death, new and old leaders recognized Ida's key role in their movement by establishing several coops in Ida's cherished home village, Huangxian, and in Penglai, where Ida's mother traveled to give birth to her first child.

The Shandan Bailie School was revived in 1987 with the support of the Gansu government and international donations. By 2004, enrollment reached 1800, including middle school, high school and adult distance education. Training courses include agronomy, animal husbandry, internet and information technology, enterprise management, and education, among other fields of study. Practical vocational courses, especially in the agricultural sciences, allow students to remain in their home communities and contribute to the support of their families, instead of joining the millions of migrants to large cities.

Ida fought her entire life for the principles on which the school is based—self-reliance, personal dignity, and preservation of the family and community through productive work. In her memory, the Ida Pruitt Memorial Scholarship Project Fund for disadvantaged girl students was established in 2005 to honor the woman who devoted many years to the school and her entire life to China.[36]

Chronology of Modern Chinese History

221 B.C.– 1911 A.D.	China ruled by imperial dynasties
1842	The Unequal Treaty System began after the Opium War
1858	Treaty of Tianjin allowed Western missionaries into interior of China
1894–1895	First Sino-Japanese War. Japan began encroaching in China.
1895–1898	Reform Movement
1900	Boxer Uprising
1905	Revolutionary Alliance formed under Sun Yat-sen. Became the Nationalist Party (Guomindang)
1911	Wuhan rebellion sparked Republican Revolution
1912	Sun Yat-sen briefly became provisional president of Chinese Republic, the last Qing dynasty emperor abdicated, Sun resigned, and Yuan Shikai became provisional president, then dictator of the Republic.
1915	Japan presented Twenty-One Demands, provoked Chinese nationalism. New Culture Movement began.
1916	Yuan died, warlordism ensued.
1919	May Fourth Movement
1921	Communist Party founded
1928–1937	Nationalist Party wrested control from warlords and ruled China from Nanjing under Chiang Kai-shek
1931	Japan seized Manchuria and governed it as Manchukuo
1937–1945	China's War of Resistance against Japan
1945–1949	Chinese Civil War. Nationalists retreated to Taiwan after Communist victory.
1950–1953	Korean War. United States and China cut off diplomatic relations.
1958–1960	Great Leap Forward
1966–1976	Great Proletarian Cultural Revolution

1972	U.S. president Richard M. Nixon visited China
1976	Chairman Mao Zedong and Premier Zhou Enlai died
1979	Normalization of diplomatic relations between China and the United States
1979	Reform and Opening to the world initiated by Deng Xiaoping

Notes

This work depends to a great extent on the personal and professional papers of Ida Pruitt and her parents, C.W. and Anna Seward Pruitt. Unless otherwise indicated, all unpublished documents by Ida Pruitt and her parents, C.W. and Anna Seward Pruitt are located in the Pruitt Collection in the Arthur and Elizabeth Schlesinger Library on the History of Women in America at Radcliffe Institute of Harvard University. All quoted materials with no specific indication of location are also located in the same collection.

The author of this biography had the privilege of using the Pruitt family papers before their donation. Because the research was completed before the papers were catalogued, the designations of the Schlesinger Library's finding aid were not used. The citations listed here are descriptive in nature. Two filing systems of Anna Seward Pruitt's letters are used. Many of Ida Pruitt's own writings, as well as those of scholars and other correspondents, are in typescript or manuscript form. Not all documents were given titles, dates, or page numbers.

Preface

1. Marjorie King (hereafter cited as M.K.), "Before Liberation: The Rural Reconstruction Movement in Kuomintang China" (Master's thesis, The Ohio State University, 1974). Ida Pruitt's books will be discussed in Chapter 7.

2. Papers of Anna and Ida Pruitt are listed in Archie R. Crouch, ed., *Christianity in China: A Scholar's Guide to Resources in the Libraries and Archives of the United States* (Armonk, NY: M.E. Sharpe, 1988). They are deposited in the Arthur and Elizabeth Schlesinger Library on the History of Women in America at Radcliffe Institute.

3. Elizabeth Kamarck Minnich comments, "In defiance of a tradition that has radically divided (not just made distinctions between) subject and author, self and object, feelings and mind, collective and individual identity, an explored subjectivity can become not a pitfall or a threat to the shaky psyche or a slippery slope to solipsism, but a transitional moment essential to understanding." In her "Friendship between Women: The Act of Feminist Biography," *Feminist Studies*, 11.2 (Summer 1985): 303.

Introduction

1. Ida lived with John and Wilma Fairbank for several months in their Beijing house in 1932. They considered Ida as one of their good friends. See John King Fairbank, *Chinabound: A Fifty-Year Memoir* (New York: Harper & Row, 1982), p. 48. See also John and Wilma's interview with M.K., Franklin, New Hampshire, 16 August 1988.

2. Norma M. McCaig, "Raised in the Margin of the Mosaic: Global Nomads Balance Worlds Within," *International Educator* (Spring 2002): 10–17; Elizabeth Murakami-Ramalho, "Globally Mobile," *International Educator* (Spring 2002): 24–34; Edward W. Said, *Culture and Imperialism* (New York: Alfred A. Knopf, 1993), pp. xxvi–xxvii.

3. Noted American writer Pearl S. Buck also grew up among the Chinese people. The comparison of Pearl and Ida's lives and writings is instructive in many ways, most of which are beyond the scope of this biography. A few major points are mentioned in the introduction by way of suggesting the degree of Ida's immersion in Chinese culture. See Peter Conn, *Pearl S. Buck: A Cultural Biography* (Cambridge: Cambridge University Press, 1996), p. 131. Conn asserts that Pearl was more personally acquainted with Chinese "imagebanks" than "almost any Western writer before or since." This biography argues that Ida Pruitt was even more intimately acquainted with the Chinese country people than was Pearl.

4. Conn emphasizes the unusual degree of loneliness, alienation, disorientation, and displacement that Pearl experienced. "Unlike almost every other American of her generation, Pearl grew up knowing China as her actual world, while America was the dreamworld, the place of fantasy and imagination." Ida, too, was lonely and lived much of her childhood in a fantasy world. Whereas Pearl had a warm relationship with her mother and a sister, Ida's mother was cool and intellectual and her only sister died in infancy. Pearl attended a mission girl's school in the city of Zhenjiang (Chinkiang) where she lived, whereas Ida was primarily home schooled in Huang county (Huangxian). To an even greater extent than Pearl's, Ida's childhood was spent among the Chinese country people. See Peter Conn, *Pearl S. Buck*, pp. 24, 26.

5. Alison Donnell and Pauline Polkey, introduction to *Representing Lives: Women and Auto/biography* (New York: St. Martin's Press, 2000), p. xxiv.

6. See Jonathan D. Spence, *To Change China: Western Advisors in China, 1620–1960* (Boston: Little, Brown, & Co., 1969), pp. 289–92. A. Tomasz Grunfeld has examined Americans who shared Ida's point of view. He says, "These ten arrived in China without any preconceived models of their own; but rather came with a willingness to trust and support the Chinese in finding their own answers to their own difficulties." He also points out that where Ida differs from the other Americans is her understanding of and

identification with the Chinese culture and people. See A. Tomasz Grunfeld, "Friends of the Revolution: American Supporters of China's Communists, 1926–1939" (Ph.D. dissertation, Columbia University, 1985), pp. 281–82.

7. Ida Pruitt (hereafter cited as I.P.), "The Story of Little Tiger," and "A Child is Sold," in *China: Yesterday and Today*, ed. Molly Joel Coye and Jon Livingston (New York: Bantam, 1975), pp. 87–97, 162–66; "Ning Lao t'ai-t'ai," in *The Norton Book of Women's Lives*, ed. Phyllis Rose (New York: W.W. Norton, 1993), pp. 630–35.

8. Lois Rudnick, "The Male-Identified Woman and Other Anxieties: The Life of Mabel Dodge Luhan," in *The Challenge of Feminist Biography: Writing the Lives of Modern American Women*, ed. Sara Alpern, Joyce Antler, Elisabeth Israels Perry, and Ingrid Winther Scobie (Urbana: University of Illinois, 1992), pp. 116–17, 125–28; Patricia Spack, *The Female Imagination* (New York: Alfred A. Knopf, 1975), pp. 225–26.

9. In contrast, Conn attributes Pearl's nascent feminism to her volunteer work at a shelter for Chinese slave girls and prostitutes during her late adolescence. Ida experienced no similar encounter with the extreme abuse of women. Perhaps an even more fundamental difference in worldview arose from their fathers' treatment of their mothers. Absalom Sydenstricker, Pearl's father, was "relentlessly patriarchal" to the point of misogyny, whereas C.W. Pruitt played a supportive, passive role in the family. Pearl Buck became an advocate for women's rights. See Peter Conn, *Pearl S. Buck*, pp. 20, 26, 42–43.

10. Joyce Antler, "Having It All, Almost; Confronting the Legacy of Lucy Sprague Mitchell," in *The Challenge of Feminist Biography*, ed. Sara Alpern and others, p. 110; Ida Pruitt suggests that she was repulsed by the only avowed feminist she ever met—her mother's teacher at a village school in Ohio. See I.P., [untitled autobiographical draft], (circa 1932), typescript (TS), p. 5, Ida Pruitt Papers, Arthur and Elizabeth Schlesinger Library on the History of Women in America, Radcliffe Institute, Cambridge, MA.

11. Mike Ashley, *British Kings and Queens: British Royal History from Alfred the Great to the Present* (New York: Carroll and Graf, 2002), p. 297; I.P. interview with M.K. in Philadelphia, 3 December 1983.

12. I.P., "My Home," [autobiographical draft], (n.d.), TS, no. 181–83.

13. For the idea of a constructed identity, rather than a developing identity, this book is indebted to the essays in *The Challenge of Feminist Biography*, ed. Sara Alpern and others, p. 110. See especially reference to Teresa de Lauretis in Alice Wexler, "Emma Goldman and the Anxiety of Biography," p. 50. The mediator role was Ida's "real self," the "constant" mentioned by Joyce Antler in "Having It All, Almost," in *The Challenge of Feminist Biography*, ed. Sara Alpern and others, p. 111.

Prologue

1. Urania Durand Ashley Seward, "The Flitting of the Fenns," (n.d.), TS, [Tallmadge, Ohio]; Myra Pitkin, "The Grandmother's Window," TS, [Tallmadge, Ohio], pp. 1–25; Anna Seward Pruitt (hereafter cited as A.S.P.), "The Grandmother's Window: Added Notes," (n.d.), TS, pp. 1–4.

2. Joan Jacobs Brumberg, *Mission for Life: The Story of the Family of Adoniram Judson, The Dramatic Events of the First American Foreign Mission, and the Course of Evangelical Religion in the Nineteenth Century* (New York: Free Press, 1980), pp. 28, 46–47; Martin Marty, *Righteous Empire: The Protestant Experience in America* (New York: Dial Press, 1970), pp. 47–48.

3. Joan Jacobs Brumberg, *Mission for Life*, p. 41; Barbara Welter, "She Hath Done What She Could: Protestant Women's Missionary Careers in Nineteenth Century America," *American Quarterly*, 30 (1978): 631.

4. Women's Foreign Mission Societies, Presbyterian Church, "Our Mission Field" (New York: Women's Foreign Mission Societies, Presbyterian Church in the USA, 1880), p. 7.

5. A.S.P., "California in the Eighties: As Pictured in the Letters of Anna Seward," *California Historical Society Quarterly*, 16.4 (1937): 291–303; 17.1 (1938): 28–40.

6. A.S.P., "California in the Eighties," *California Historical Society Quarterly*, 17.1 (1938): 37.

7. T.M. Morris, *A Winter in North China* (London: Religious Tract Society, 1892), pp. 46–50.

8. I.P., *A China Childhood* (San Francisco: Chinese Materials Center, Inc., 1978), p. 3; Dean Pruitt (Anna's grandson) interview with M.K. in Philadelphia, 24 December 1983.

9. C.W. Pruitt (hereafter cited as C.W.P.), "Life of Cicero Washington Pruitt, Composed by Himself," (n.d.), TS, part I, p. 3.

10. C.W.P., "Life of Cicero Washington Pruitt," part I, p. 5; Martin Marty, *Righteous Empire*, pp. 61–62.

11. Joan Jacobs Brumberg, *Mission for Life*, p. 44.

12. C.W.P., "Life of Cicero Washington Pruitt," part I, p. 6; part II, p. 1.

13. A.S.P., "Sketch of the Life of Dr. Cicero Washington Pruitt," (n.d.), TS, p. 5.

Chapter 1

1. I.P., *A China Childhood*, p. 38.
2. I.P., *A China Childhood*, p. 1.
3. I.P., *A China Childhood*, p. 2.
4. I.P., *A China Childhood*, p. 5.
5. John King Fairbank, *China: A New History* (Cambridge, MA: Harvard University Press, 1992), p. 222.

6. A.S.P., letters to her family in Ohio in 1894: 49, 96–98, 103. The Pruitt's yearly expenditures amounted to US$1,000 in those days.

7. I.P., *A China Childhood*, pp. 19–20.

8. I.P., *A China Childhood*, pp. 29–30, 41–42, 44.

9. I.P., *A China Childhood*, pp. 37–38.

10. I.P., [random notes], (n.d.), TS.

11. I.P., "New Year's Eve in Peking," *Atlantic Monthly*, 149 (Jan.–Jun. 1932): 47–53; I.P., *A China Childhood*, p. 189.

12. John D. Pruitt, "The Life of Anna Seward Pruitt," TS [St. Davids, PA, 1951], pp. 7–8. A.S.P. to her family in Ohio, 8 January 1899, (1895): 18, 3 and 18 May 1897, 4 December 1898.

13. C.W.P. in A.S.P. 4 December 1898.

14. Mary Schauffler Platt, *The Home with the Open Door: An Agency in Missionary Service* (New York: Student Volunteer Movement, 1920), p. 53; Women's Foreign Mission Societies, Presbyterian Church, "Our Mission Field," p. 22; R. Pierce Beaver, *American Protestant Women in World Mission: A History of the First Feminist Movement in North America* (Grand Rapids, MI: Wm. B. Eerdmans, 1980), p. 50.

15. I.P., [untitled autobiographical draft], (n.d.), TS, chap. 6.

16. A.S.P. to her family in Ohio, (1895): 18, 3 and 18 May 1897, 4 December 1898.

17. Ida remembered feeling this attitude from her mother rather than hearing it directly. "It's nonsense. The Chinese are more civilized than Americans." I.P. interview with M.K., 29 November 1983. See also I.P., *A China Childhood*, chap. 6.

18. A.S.P. to her family in Ohio, 22 March 1891, 31 January 1897, 22 April 1900.

19. A.S.P. to her family in Ohio, 1 January 1900.

20. C.W.P., "Life of Cicero Washington Pruitt, Composed by Himself," (n.d.), TS, part II, p. 1.

21. I.P., [untitled autobiographical draft], (n.d.), TS, chap. 6.

22. A.S.P. to her family in Ohio, (1891): 14, 43; (1893): 190; (1894) vol. 2: 40; (1895): 75; 15 March 1897, November 1897; C.W.P. to A.S.P. family in Ohio, 24 November 1895 and 3 July 1898.

23. A.S.P. to her family in Ohio, (1896): 172; 23 December 1895, 27 December 1897, 1 January 1899.

24. I.P., *A China Childhood*, p. 132; I. P. conversations with M.K. in Philadelphia, 1979–1984.

25. I.P. interview with M.K. in Philadelphia, 15 June 1982 and many other conversations.

26. A.S.P. to her family in Ohio, January 1897, 13 December 1897.

27. A.S.P. to her family in Ohio, 23 September 1897; C.W.P., "Life of Cicero Washington Pruitt," TS, part II, p. 2.

28. A.S.P. to her family in Ohio, 13 November 1898.
29. I.P., [untitled autobiographical draft], (n.d.), TS, chap. 6.
30. Mrs. Roys, *The Missionary Wife* (n.p.: Committee of Missionary Preparation, 1923), p. 16.
31. A.S.P. to her family in Ohio, (1893): 191, (1894) vol. 2: 108–10; (1893) vol. 2: 3; I.P., *A China Childhood*, pp. 34, 39.
32. I.P., *A China Childhood*, pp. 69, 83; A.S.P. to her family in Ohio, (1895): 14.
33. I.P., [untitled autobiographical draft], (n.d.), TS, chap. 8.
34. A.S.P. to her family in Ohio, 10 March 1896, 7 December 1897; I.P., [random notes], (n.d.), TS.
35. I.P., *A China Childhood*, p. 168.
36. A.S.P. to her family in Ohio, (1895–1897): 140; I.P., *A China Childhood*, p. 168.
37. A.S.P. to her family in Ohio, 1 July 1897; I.P., *A China Childhood*, p. 118.
38. A.S.P. to her family in Ohio, 5 June 1898, 17 April 1899, 1 January 1899, 12 February 1899.
39. Sarah R. Mason, "Missionary Conscience and the Comprehension of Imperialism: A Study of the Children of American Missionaries to China, 1900–1949" (Ph.D. dissertation, Northern Illinois University, 1978), pp. 2–4. This dissertation has discussed the literature on missionary children.
40. A.S.P. to her family in Ohio, (1893) vol. 2: 17, (1895–1897): 21, 20 January 1895.
41. A.S.P. to her family in Ohio, 5 April 1897.
42. I.P., [untitled autobiographical draft], (n.d.), TS, chap. 6; I.P. interview with M.K., 1 July 1982; A.S.P. to her family in Ohio, 1 January 1900.
43. C.W.P., "Life of Cicero Washington Pruitt," TS, p. 3.
44. I.P., [untitled autobiographical draft], (n.d.), TS, chap. 12, pp. 1–2.
45. I.P., [untitled autobiographical draft], (n.d.), TS, chap. 23, p. 4.
46. I.P., *A China Childhood*, p. 43; I.P., [random notes], (n.d.), TS.
47. I.P., *A China Childhood*, p. 180.
48. I.P., *A China Childhood*, p. 43.
49. A.S.P. to her family in Ohio, (1894): 116, 6 January 1899, 25 March 1900, 13 June 1898; I.P., *A China Childhood*, p. 46.
50. A.S.P. to her family in Ohio, 24 January 1898; I.P., *A China Childhood*, p. 54.
51. A.S.P. to her family in Ohio, 13 October 1898; I.P., *A China Childhood*, p. 117; I.P., [random notes], (n.d.), TS; M.K. conversations with I.P., 1976–1984.
52. I.P., [untitled autobiographical draft], (n.d.), TS, chap. 6; I.P., *A China Childhood*, pp. 106, 129; I.P. interview with M.K., 15 June 1982; A.S.P. to her family in Ohio, 12 September 1897, 8 January 1899.
53. I.P., *A China Childhood*, pp. 2, 61, 101, 103, 109–10; I.P. interview with M.K., July 1982.

Chapter 2

1. For more on Anna Seward Pruitt's role in the women's missionary movement, see M.K., "Exporting Femininity, Not Feminism: Nineteenth Century U.S. Missionary Women's Efforts to Emancipate Chinese Women," in *Women's Work for Women: Missionaries and Social Change in Asia*, ed. Leslie A. Flemming (Boulder, CO: Westview Press, 1989), pp. 117–36; M.K., "American Women's Open Door to Chinese Women: Which Way Does It Open?" *Women's Studies International Forum*, 13.4 (1990): 369–80. The definitive study of the women's missionary movement is Jane Hunter, *The Gospel of Gentility: American Women Missionaries in Turn of the Century China* (New Haven, CT: Yale University Press, 1984). The body of scholarly literature on missionaries in China informed this study but is too vast for inclusion here. The best analysis of the literature on missionaries as part of the "open door constituency" of American interests in China is Michael Hunt, *The Making of a Special Relationship: The United States and China to 1914* (New York: Columbia University Press, 1983).

2. A.S.P. to her family in Ohio, (1891): 17, 24–25; A.S.P.'s articles in *Our Missionary Helper*, 21 August 1893 and 13 October 1898;

3. A.S.P. to her family in Ohio, (1891): 1, 2, 16, 31, 32.

4. A.S.P. to her family in Ohio, 12 February 1899.

5. I.P., *A China Childhood*, pp. 124, 126

6. A.S.P. to her family in Ohio, 23 April 1899.

7. A.S.P. to her family in Ohio, (1891): 20, 54, 22 March 1897.

8. Julia Mateer in Irwin Hyatt, *Our Ordered Lives Confess: Three Nineteenth Century American Missionaries in East Shantung* (Cambridge, MA: Harvard University Press, 1976), pp. 70–72, 80.

9. I.P., *A China Childhood*, pp. 105–15. In I.P. interview with M.K. on 9 April 1983, Ida referred to her mother's friends as simply "those women."

10. I.P., *A China Childhood*, pp. 61, 123–24, 128–31, 173–74, 184–85.

11. I.P., *A China Childhood*, pp. 130–31.

12. I.P., *A China Childhood*, pp. 131–133.

13. A.S.P. to her family in Ohio, (1893): 21, 44, 119; I.P., *A China Childhood*, pp. 46–47, 49.

14. A.S.P. to her family in Ohio, (1893): 7–8; A.S.P., *The Day of Small Things* (Richmond, VA: Foreign Mission Board of Southern Baptist Convention, 1929), pp. 7–8, 26–27, 80. Dengzhou was established as "Dengzhou Fu" (prefecture) during the Tang dynasty and retained this status through the end of the Qing dynasty. Dengzhou Fu governed nine "xian" (counties) of which Penglai was one. The government of Dengzhou Fu was located in the walled harbor city known as Penglai. After coming to power in 1912, the Republican government abolished all "Fu." Dengzhou Fu was divided into nine "xian" including Penglaixian, Huangxian and so forth. The walled

harbor city where the prefectural government of Dengzhou Fu had been located is still called "Penglai." When the western missions came to Shandong in the 19th century, they erroneously referred to Penglai city as "Dengzhou." See *Shandong tongzhi* (The General History of Shandong) (1915; reprint, Shanghai: Shangwu yinshuguan, 1934), vol. 1, pp. 869–70. I am grateful to Professor Yamaguchi Mamori for drawing my attention to this reference.

15. I.P., *A China Childhood,* p. 62; A.S.P. to her family in Ohio, (1895): 141–42, (1896): 10, 152. The reason for the establishment of a boys' school instead of a girls' school in Huangxian remains obscure but clearly *was not* because Anna Hartwell, another Southern Baptist missionary, had already established one, as Ida believed.

16. A.S.P. to her family in Ohio, 1 and 8 March 1897.

17. A.S.P. to her family in Ohio, (1894): 46, 62, (1895): 141–42, (1896): 134, 190, (1898): 66.

18. A.S.P. to her family in Ohio, (1894): 18, (1895): 72, 149.

19. A.S.P. to her family in Ohio, (1891): 1, (1895): 149, 191. A.S.P. to her family in Ohio, (1893): 13, (1895): 150, 6 January 1899.

20. William Gordon Lennox (1933) in Sarah R. Mason, "Missionary Conscience and the Comprehension of Imperialism," p. 5.

21. A.S.P. to her family in Ohio, 9 March 1897, 20 March 1898, 17 April 1898, 1 May 1898.

22. A.S.P. to her family in Ohio, (1894): 41, 43, (1895): 153.

23. A.S.P. to her family in Ohio, (1896): 84.

24. A.S.P. to her family in Ohio, 6, 13 and 25 February 1898, 8 and 28 March 1898, 24 April 1898.

25. A.S.P. to her family in Ohio, 8 and 19 June 1898.

26. A.S.P. to her family in Ohio, 6 January 1899.

27. A.S.P. to her family in Ohio, 3 July 1898, 6 January 1899, 20 March 1899, (1891): 35, (1895): 148, 16 January 1899, 11 September 1899, 5 February 1900, 10 August 1901.

28. A.S.P. to her family in Ohio, 1 May 1893; Alexander Saxton, *The Indispensable Enemy: Labor and the Anti-Chinese Movement in California* (Berkeley: University of California Press, 1971), p. 230; Ronald Takaki, *Strangers from a Different Shore: A History of Asian Americans* (New York: Penguin, 1989), pp. 110–12.

29. A.S.P. to her family in Ohio, (1893): 181.

30. A.S.P. to her family in Ohio, 8 January 1899, 3 September 1899.

31. A.S.P. to her family in Ohio, 12 September 1897, 8 January 1899, 11 September 1899, 13 May 1900.

32. A.S.P. to her family in Ohio, (1893): 32, (1894): 45. For a full treatment of C.W. Pruitt's life as a missionary in China, see M.K., "A Georgia Evangelist in the Celestial Empire," in *Georgia's East Asian Connection: Into the*

Twenty-First Century, ed. Jonathan Goldstein (Carrollton, GA: West Georgia College, 1989), pp. 112–28.

33. A.S.P. to her family in Ohio, (1893): 9, 12; C.W.P., "Life of Cicero Washington Pruitt, Composed by Himself," TS, part II, p. 3; I.P., *A China Childhood*, p. 185.

34. A.S.P. to her family in Ohio, (1894): 22; I.P. conversations with M.K. about her father from 1980 to 1984.

35. A.S.P. to her family in Ohio, 21 May 1900.

36. A.S.P. to her family in Ohio, (1894): 31, 55, 57.

37. A.S.P. to her family in Ohio, 9 and 31 January 1898, 28 March 1898.

38. John M. MacKenzie describes the rise of music, postcards, cigarette cards, all forms of ephemera, lantern slides and film during the period 1870–1914 as materials used by imperial agencies to influence and manipulate popular opinion. See his *Propaganda and Empire: The Manipulation of British Public Opinion, 1880–1960* (Manchester, England: Manchester University Press, 1984).

39. A.S.P. to her family in Ohio, 23 January 1900, 2 October 1898, 16 and 25 January 1899.

40. Harold R. Isaacs, *Scratches on Our Minds: American Views of China and India* (1958; repr., Armonk, NY: M.E. Sharpe, 1980), pp. 139–40; Joseph W. Esherick, *The Origins of the Boxer Uprising* (Berkeley: University of California Press, 1987), pp. 7, 261–66; Paul A. Cohen portrays the personal experiences behind the carnage in great detail in his *History in Three Keys: The Boxers as Event, Experience, and Myth* (New York: Columbia University Press, 1997), pp. 173–208.

41. A.S.P. to her family in Ohio, 16 January 1899, 5 March 1900. The Boxer Uprising is more commonly known as the Boxer Rebellion in English, but "uprising" is closer to the Chinese term, *qiyi*.

42. A.S.P. to her family in Ohio, 16 January 1899, 18 and 22 June 1900.

43. A.S.P. to her family in Ohio, 22 June 1900; I.P., *A China Childhood*, p. 199; I.P., "China Inland Mission School," (n.d.), TS.

44. A.S.P. to her family in Ohio, 3 and 4 July 1900.

45. A.S.P. to her family in Ohio, 4 July 1900; C.W.P., "Life of Cicero Washington Pruitt," part II, p. 2; I.P. conversations with M.K., Philadelphia, 1976–1984.

46. Dean G. Pruitt (one of A.S.P.'s grandsons) 19 August 1968 addendum to A.S.P. letter to her family in Ohio, 6 July 1900.

Chapter 3

1. I.P., "1900," TS, 13, pp. 236, 238–39.

2. I.P., [untitled autobiographical draft], (circa 1932), TS, p. 2.

3. For a discussion on the heyday of the foreign missions in China, see James C. Thomson, Jr., *While China Faced West: American Reformers in Nationalist*

China, 1928–1937 (Cambridge, MA: Harvard University Press, 1969), pp. 4–5, 35–37; James Reed, *The Missionary Mind and American East Asian Policy, 1911–1915* (Cambridge, MA: Harvard University Press, 1983), p. 13; Kenneth Scott Latourette, *A History of Christian Missions in China* (New York: Macmillan, 1929), p. 496; Paul A. Varg, *Missionaries, Chinese and Diplomats: The American Protestant Missionary Movement in China, 1890–1952* (Princeton, NJ: Princeton University Press, 1958), pp. 7, 50–52.

4. I.P., [untitled autobiographical draft], (n.d.), TS, chap. 14, p. 247.

5. A.S.P. to her family in Ohio, 29 August 1898.

6. A.S.P., "Sketch of the Life of Dr. Cicero Washington Pruitt," (1946), TS, pp. 6–7.

7. I.P., "Another City," (n.d.), TS, chap. 20, p. 1; I.P., [untitled autobiographical draft], (circa 1932), TS, p. 17.

8. I.P., "Another City," chap. 20, pp. 5, 8, 13; I.P. [untitled autobiographical draft], (circa 1932), TS, p. 10; I.P. "Twelve to Fourteen," (n.d.), TS, pp. 9–10.

9. Liu Shaobai, "Yantai: Mirages, Myths and Flourishing Reality," *China Reconstructs* (January 1983): 64–66; Gao Xinxian, "Echoes of Immortality at Penglai," *China Daily* (November 1982): 27.

10. I.P., "Twelve to Fourteen," pp. 10–11; I.P., "Another City," pp. 2, 9, 15–16, 18–19.

11. I.P., [untitled autobiographical draft], (n.d.), TS, chap. 6, pp. 283–84; I.P. "Another City," p. 8.

12. I.P., [untitled commentary in *The Den* literary magazine, inserted in *The Arcade* school yearbook] (College Park, GA), pp. 11–14; I.P. [untitled], *The Arcade* (College Park, GA, 1908), pp. 2, 3, 31.

13. Edward W. Said, *Culture and Imperialism*, p. xiv.

14. I.P., [untitled], *The Den* in *The Arcade*, p. 12.

15. I.P., [untitled autobiographical draft], (n.d.), TS, book II, chap. 3, p. 23; I.P., [untitled], (n.d.), TS, book II, chap. 7, p. 57.

16. I.P., [untitled autobiographical draft], (n.d.), TS, book II, chap. 3, pp. 16, 19, 22, 24; I.P., [untitled autobiographical draft], (n.d.), TS, book II, chap. 6, p. 52.

17. I.P., [untitled autobiographical draft], (n.d.), TS, book II, chap. 1, pp. 3–4, 10, 12.

18. I.P., [untitled autobiographical draft], (n.d.), TS, book II, chap. 4, pp. 25, 37–38, 40.

19. I.P., [untitled autobiographical draft], (n.d.), TS, book II, chap. 7, pp. 55–56; I.P. interview with M.K., 9 April 1984.

20. I.P., [untitled autobiographical draft], (n.d.), TS, book II, chap. 7, pp. 57–58; I.P., [untitled autobiographical draft], (n.d.), TS, book II, chap. 8, pp. 59, 61, 62, 64.

21. Rudyard Kipling, *Kim* (London: Penguin, 1987), pp. 50–51.

22. Said, *Culture and Imperialism*, p. 140.
23. I.P., [random notes], (n.d.), TS.
24. I.P., [untitled autobiographical draft], (n.d.), TS, chap. 8, p. 65.
25. I.P., [untitled autobiographical draft], (n.d.), TS, book II, chap. 7, p. 55; chap. 9, p. 68.
26. In an undated typescript named *Sketch* (p. 6) A.S.P. states that the Pruitts lived in Huangxian, Penglai (in Dengzhou district at that time) and Yantai (Chefoo) three stations of the North China Mission of the Southern Baptists. Huangxian was their place of longest residence.
27. Liu Shaobai, "Yantai: Mirages, Myths and Flourishing Reality," : pp. 64–65.
28. I.P., [untitled autobiographical draft], (n.d.), TS, book III, chap. 13, pp. 478–82, 485.
29. I.P., [untitled autobiographical draft], (n.d.), TS, book III, chap. 13, pp. 481–82, 485.
30. I.P., [C.I.M. School], TS, pp. 1–4; I.P. [untitled autobiographical draft], (n.d.), TS, book II, chap. 13, p. 217; Louise She (She Huichen) to M.K., correspondence, 25 October 1983.
31. I.P., [untitled autobiographical draft], (n.d.), TS, book II, chap. 13, p. 217.
32. I.P., [untitled autobiographical draft], (n.d.), TS, book II, chap. 3, p. 17; I.P., [untitled autobiographical draft], (n.d.), TS, book II, chap. 5, pp. 41–48.
33. Kueiching (Guijing) Ho to M.K., correspondence, during the Memorial Service of Ida Pruitt conducted in Philadelphia on 5 October 1985.
34. I.P., [untitled autobiographical draft], (n.d.), TS, book II, chap. 12, pp. 86–88; I.P., [untitled autobiographical draft], (circa 1932), TS, p. 21.
35. I.P., [Chefoo 1912–1918], TS.
36. I.P., [untitled autobiographical draft], (n.d.), TS, book II, chap. 13, pp. 219–21.
37. I.P., [untitled autobiographical draft], (n.d.), TS, chap. 18, p. 552. Gabriel Lasker, one of Ida's houseguests during the 1930s, commented on Ida's preference for black Nicaraguan cigarettes. See Gabriel Lasker to M.K., correspondence, 18 September 1985.
38. I.P., "USA," (n.d.), TS, chap. 17; I.P., [untitled autobiographical draft], (n.d.), TS, book III, chap. 18.

Chapter 4

1. I.P., "Days in Old Peking," (n.d.), TS.
2. Roger S. Greene, marginal comment on Edith Shatto King letter to him, 3 May 1919, box 143, folder 1034, China Medical Board, Inc., Ida Pruitt files (1919–1939), Rockefeller Archive Center (RAC), North Tarrytown, New York (hereafter cited as I.P. files, RAC).
3. Edith Shatto King to Roger S. Greene, May 1919, box 143, folder 1034, I.P. files, RAC.

4. Betsey Libby to Ida Cannon, 12 February 1920, box 143, folder 1034, I.P. files, RAC.
5. Dr. Franklin C. McLean, director of PUMC, to Edwin R. Embree, secretary of China Medical Board and PUMC Trustees, 6 February 1920, box 143, folder 1034, I.P. files, RAC.
6. McLean to Dr. Henry S. Houghton, acting director of PUMC, 22 February 1920, box 143, folder 1034, I.P. files, RAC.
7. Michael H. Hunt, *The Making of a Special Relationship: The United States and China to 1914* (New York: Columbia University Press, 1993), pp. 301–2, addresses the pivotal roles and functions of such mediators or "cultural intermediaries," among whom he cites voluntary associations in American Chinatowns, Chinese interpreters and informers, the American foreign service, missionaries, and their native assistants.
8. John King Fairbank interview with M.K., 16 August 1988 identified Ida Cannon as the aunt of his wife, Wilma. According to his understanding, Cannon was interested and supportive of Ida Pruitt but was not her teacher or immediate supervisor.
9. I.P., [lecture on Hospital social service], (Chefoo, China, n.d.), pp. 1–2.
10. Ida Cannon to McLean, 21 October 1920, box 143, folder 1034, I.P. files, RAC; Cannon to Embree, 1 February 1921, box 143, folder 1034, I.P. files, RAC.
11. Robert H. Wiebe, *The Search for Order, 1877–1920* (New York: Hill and Wong, 1967), p. 122.
12. I.P., [untitled, autobiographical draft], (n.d.), TS, chap. 18, p. 1; Helen Foster Snow to M.K., 16 May 1983, p. 2. Snow remembered Ida discussing her Dada's influence on her as encouraging passivity and fatalism. Snow asserted that social work training made Ida confrontational and opened her mind to reason and understanding. The analysis in this essay suggests that the Chinese woman was neither passive nor irrational, but modeled an indirect strategy of influence, which did not serve Ida well in the American hospital setting.
13. I.P., [untitled autobiographical draft], (n.d.), TS, chap. 18, pp. 10–11.
14. Porter R. Lee in Clarke Chambers, *Seedtime of Reforms: American Social Service and Social Action, 1918–1933* (Minneapolis: University of Minnesota Press, 1963), p. 93.
15. Robert H. Wiebe, *The Search for Order*, pp. 113, 115, 123, 145, 149.
16. I.P., [untitled autobiographical draft], (n.d.), TS, chap. 18, p. 3.
17. I.P., [untitled autobiographical draft], (n.d.), TS, chap. 18, pp. 1, 4.
18. I.P., [untitled autobiographical draft], (n.d.), TS, chap. 18, p. 67.
19. I.P., [untitled autobiographical draft], (n.d.), TS, chap. 18, pp. 10–11.
20. David Strand, *Rickshaw Beijing: City People and Politics in the 1920s* (Berkeley: University of California Press, 1989), pp. 7–9.
21. David Strand, *Rickshaw Beijing*, p. 7.
22. I.P., [lecture on Hospital social service], p. 3.

23. I.P., "Education for Medical Social Work," (n.d.), TS, p. 4.

24. I.P., "Social Service Department of the PUMC," (n.d.), TS.

25. Daniel B. Ramsdell, "Asia Askew; U.S. Bestsellers on Asia, 1931–1980," *Bulletin of Concerned Asian Scholars*, 15.4 (1983): 2. For a fuller analysis see Harold R. Isaacs, *Scratches on Our Minds: American Views of China and India* (New York: John Day, 1958). Edward Said critiques the representation of the Muslim Orient by European scholars, writers, and educational institutions in *Orientalism* (New York: Vintage, 1979). See also Steven W. Mosher, *China Misperceived: American Illusions and Chinese Reality* (New York: Basic Books, 1990) and Richard Madsen, *China and the American Dream: A Moral Inquiry* (Berkeley: University of California Press, 1995).

26. Frank Ninkovich, "The Rockefeller Foundation, China, and Cultural Change," *Journal of American History*, 70.4 (1983–84): 799–820, has an excellent discussion of the liberal, scientific reform goals of the founders of the PUMC.

27. I.P., *Chinese Medical Journal* (hereafter cited as *Ch. Med. J.*), 49 (1935): 914; I.P., "Education for Medical Social Work," (n.d.), TS, pp. 2–3; I.P., "The Family in Chinese Society," *American Orthopsychiatric Association Conference* (n.p., 1967): 8.

28. I.P., [lecture on Hospital social service], p. 4. This was possible when the Social Service Department had twenty-five workers and student workers for a hospital with more than 300 beds.

29. I.P., *Ch. Med. J.*, 49 (1935): 914. Unmarried mothers are listed apart from obstetrics-gynecology.

30. Social workers submitted reports to Ida in 1934–1935 from these clinics.

31. I.P., "Medical Social Service at the Peking Union Medical College" [unpublished report for the Rockefeller Foundation, 1928], p. 3.

32. Karl A. Wittfogel, in his "Memorandum to the Rockefeller Foundation" (28 March 1939), considered the records to be invaluable to sociological research on China and urged the Rockefeller Foundation take quick steps to protect said materials from loss as the political situation in China deteriorated. W.L. Holland, Research Secretary of the Institute of Pacific Relations, underscored Wittfogel's appeal. No acknowledgement of this appeal is on record in the Rockefeller Foundation files. The fate of the material remained unknown until 1993. At that time, with the invaluable assistance of Dr. Li Weiye of the PUMC and Dr. Liu Xinru, this author found the collection intact and integrated into PUMC patient medical records. This confirms the assertion of Mary Ferguson, *China Medical Board and Peking Union Medical College: A Chronicle of Fruitful Collaboration, 1914–1951* (New York: China Medical Board of New York, Inc.), p. 180. M.K., "The Social Service Department Archives: Peking Union Medical College, 1928–1951," *American Archivist*, 59.3 (Summer, 1996): 218–27.

33. George E. Vincent, chairman of China Medical Board, to Ida Cannon, 6 December 1921, (143-1034). Anonymous staff note to I.P. I.P., *Ch. Med. J.*, 49 (1935): 914.

34. I.P., "Social Service Department of the PUMC," TS, p. 6.

35. "Report of the Employees' Social Service Work," (n.p.) 29 June 1935, p. 2.

36. Ida's own descriptions are confirmed by a former employee, Zhu Xuance, and a former student, Lin Qiwu in an interview with M.K., Beijing, December 1995.

37. David Strand, *Rickshaw Beijing*, pp. 28–29.

38. I.P., *Ch. Med. J.*, 28 (1928): 4, 10.

39. I.P., "Social Service Department of the PUMC," TS, p. 5.

40. David Strand, *Rickshaw Beijing*, p. 23.

41. I.P., [lecture on Hospital social service], 4–5.

42. I.P., *Stories of the People*, (n.d.), TS, chap. 2, p. 1.

43. I.P., *Stories of the People*, chap. 2, pp. 7–8.

44. *Ch. Med. J.*, 49 (1935): 912–13; I.P., [lecture on Hospital social service], p. 9.

45. I.P., *Ch. Med. J.*, 28 (1928): 5–7, 12, *Ch. Med. J.*, 49 (1935): 912. Kao Chun Che, "Annual Report of the Social Service Work at the First Health Station, Peiping, July 1, 1934–June 30, 1935," p. 4, cites the figure of 23 supplemental infant feedings out of 200 cases.

46. I.P., "Social Service Department of the PUMC," (n.d.), TS, p. 7; I.P., *Stories of the People*, chap. 2, p. 2; Walter I. Trattner, *From Poor Law to Welfare State: A History of Social Welfare in America* (New York: Free Press, 1974), p. 124.

47. David Strand, *Rickshaw Beijing*, pp. 203, 210.

48. David Strand, *Rickshaw Beijing*, p. 199.

49. I.P., "Medical Social Service at the Peking Union Medical College" [unpublished report for the Rockefeller Foundation, 1928], p. 3.

50. I.P., "Social Service Department of the PUMC."

51. I.P., *Stories of the People*. Mary Brown Bullock, *An American Transplant: The Rockefeller Foundation and the Peking Union Medical College* (Berkeley: University of California Press, 1980), pp. 81–83, claimed that PUMC service to victims of the civil wars and natural disasters was inefficient and insignificant for a research institute of its quality. Ida corroborates, saying that only one PUMC doctor, Dr. Chu Fu-t'ang (Zhu Futang), responded to the Salvation Army's call to volunteer at its clinic after the Japanese occupation in 1937.

52. I.P., [untitled autobiographical draft], (n.d.), TS, chap. 18, pp. 10–11.

53. I.P., [untitled autobiographical draft], (n.d.), TS, chap. 18, pp. 1, 4, 67.

54. Ramsdell, Isaacs, Mosher, Madsen, and others have addressed the impact of missionary literature on American images of China.

Chapter 5

1. I.P., "The Social Service Department of the PUMC Hospital," TS, p. 2.
2. I.P., "Medical Social Workers: Their Work and Training," *Ch. Med. J.*, 49 (1935): 914.
3. For a breakdown in her staff development by year and by task, consult Ida Pruitt's unpublished writings on the Social Service Department; her 1927–1929 Two Year Report, pp. 61–65; her "Social Service Department of the PUMC," p. 14; the *Ch. Med. J.*, 49 (1935); and staff photo of 1938.
4. Students were selected from Yenching University, Shanghai College, Jinling College, Tsinghua College, and Cheeloo (Qilu) University. See *Ch. Med. J.*, 49 (1935): 915 ff. Ida Cannon urged training in both sociology and medicine. See her *Social Work in Hospitals: A Contribution toward Progressive Medicine* (New York: 1923), p. 192.
5. I.P., "The Social Service Department of the PUMC Hospital," p. 6.
6. I.P., "The Social Service Department of the PUMC Hospital," p. 6.
7. I.P., *Ch. Med. J.*, 49 (1935): 916; I.P. to Dr. C.E. Lim, 1 October 1937; W.C. Chang, chairman of Department of Sociology and Social Work, Yenching University, to I.P., 9 September 1936; I.P., *Stories of the People*. "Social Service Dept.," p. 5; I.P., "Education for Medical Social Work," TS, p. 8.
8. She Huichen (Louise She) to M.K., 18 October 1983.
9. Mary E. Ferguson, *China Medical Board and Peking Union Medical College: A Chronicle of Fruitful Collaboration, 1914–1951* (New York: China Medical Board of New York, Inc., 1970), p. 91; George Tsou, "A Brief Talk on the Family Welfare Agency," 20 April 1935; Dr. Smyly, excerpts from section on Social Service Department, box 142, folder 1032, China Medical Board, Inc., Social Science files (1919–1939), Rockefeller Archive Center (RAC), North Tarrytown, New York (hereafter cited as Social Science files, RAC).
10. Ferguson, *China Medical Board and Peking Union Medical College*, Appendix B, p. 244. I.P. interview with M.K., 25 February 1984.
11. Liu Jinghe, nursing instructor at the PUMC, 1936–1942, interview with M.K. in Beijing, 2 July 1999.
12. Ida M. Cannon, *Social Work in Hospitals: A Contribution Toward Progressive Medicine* (New York: n.p., 1923), pp. 190–91.
13. E. Cockerill, "Can a Hospital Afford Not to Have a Department of Social Service?" *Transactions of the American Hospital Association*, 37 (1937): 734–45, and a reply in the same issue by a hospital administrator, Dr. Michael M. Davis, in L.N. Clark's comments, p. 749.
14. Roger S. Greene to Henry S. Houghton, "Medical Social Service at PUMC," 27 January 1923; I.P. to Dr. T. Dwight Sloan, 20 March 1923, p. 2, box 142, folder 1032, Social Science files, RAC; I.P. conversations with M.K., 1976–1984.

15. Responses to the questionnaire sent to all medical department heads by Roger S. Greene, summarized in inter-office memo from Greene to E.R. Embree, 15 May 1923, box 142, folder 1032, Social Science files, RAC; Andrew Woods to Sloan, 7 March 1923, box 142, folder 1032, Social Science files, RAC.

16. I.P., [untitled autobiographical draft], (circa 1932), TS, p. 32. Ida Cannon took great pains to minimize the threat that the hospital social worker represented to the physicians.

17. Anonymous staff member, personal memo to I.P., (n.d.), pp. 3, 8.

18. I.P. interview with M.K., winter, 1983, in which she chose the term "Chinese grandmother" to describe her relationship with her staff at the PUMC.

19. Anonymous staff member, personal memo to I.P, pp. 21–22, 25–27, 32–33.

20. Una K. Li phone interview with M.K., 12 November 1983.

21. Wilma Fairbank interview with M.K., 16 August 1988 called Ida "too personal, warm, loving, and involved" with her clients to be an effective administrator.

22. She Huichen to M.K., 18 October 1983, p. 1.

23. David Strand, *Rickshaw Beijing*, pp. 182–88.

24. Due to their common educational background, relations between Chinese doctors and Western doctors were more collegial that that between Chinese people and Western missionaries, diplomats, and businessmen. See Bullock, *An American Transplant*, pp. 79–81. Bullock and Ferguson concur with Jessie Lutz, *China and the Christian Colleges, 1850–1950* (Ithaca: Cornell University Press), that almost all students were from missionary schools. See Bullock, *An American Transplant*, p. 99; Ferguson, *China Medical Board and Peking Union Medical College*, p. 56. Lutz suggests this may have *heightened* the student antiforeign feelings. Lin Qiwu, former Yenching University student of Ida Pruitt's, in interview with M.K., Beijing, 1995, asserted that missionary school graduates were on very good terms with their foreign teachers.

25. The official reason for the English-language policy was that the technical medical vocabulary was not yet adapted to Chinese. All of the records in the Social Service Department were in English but Ida realized "there were days when I had spoken no word of English in my work or in my play." I.P., [random notes], (n.d.).

26. I.P., "Days in Old Peking," TS, pp. 51–52.

27. Cockerill, "Can a Hospital Afford Not to Have a Department of Social Service?" p. 749.

28. I.P., "The Family in Chinese Society," (American Orthopsychiatric Association Conference, 1967), TS, pp. 2–3. This is far different from the use of "mediator" as Schintz did in her study of Maryknoll sisters' "mediating role" in China. The latter, more representative of Western attitudes toward Chinese-Western mediation, was a technique for

undermining traditional religious beliefs and life patterns in reformist efforts. See Mary Ann Schintz, "An Investigation of the Modernizing Role of the Maryknoll Sisters in China" (doctoral dissertation, University of Wisconsin, 1978), p. 516.

29. Greg Guldin and Laurel Kendall, "Two Short Reviews of *Old Madam Yin: A Memoir of Peking Life* by Ida Pruitt," *Bulletin of Concerned Asian Scholars (BCAS)*, 12.4 (1981): 67–70.

30. Jim Bertram to M.K., 15 February 1983; Helen Foster "Peg" Snow (hereafter cited as H.F.S.) to M.K., 16 May 1983, p. 2. Both Bertram and Snow discuss Ida's role as a bridge between Chinese and Americans, missionaries and reformers, the nineteenth and twentieth centuries. Kendall *BCAS*, pp. 67–70, discusses Ida as an interpreter of nuances as well as words in her translation of *The Flight of an Empress* by Wu Yong (New Haven, CT: Yale University Press, 1936).

31. I.P., "Thoughts on Religion," (circa 1966), TS, p. 8. See also I.P., *Stories of the People.*

32. Joshua S. Horn, *Away with All Pests: An English Surgeon in People's China: 1954–1969* (New York: Monthly Review, 1969), p. 53.

33. I.P., *Stories of the People.*

34. For a discussion of the career choices of missionary children, see Sarah R. Mason, "Missionary Conscience and the Comprehension of Imperialism," pp. 2–4.

35. Zhu Xuance and Lin Qiwu interview with M.K., Beijing, December 1995.

36. I.P., "Days in Old Peking," p. 51.

37. Wu Yong, *The Flight of an Empress*, transcribed by Liu Kun, trans. and ed. Ida Pruitt (New Haven, CT: Yale University Press, 1936).

38. R.S. Greene to E.R. Embree, 22 December 1922, box 143, folder 1034, I.P. files, RAC. Each department head's evaluation is attached to Greene's summary of 15 May 1923 to Henry S. Houghton. See also R.S. Greene to H.S. Houghton, 23 June 1923, box 142, folder 1032, Social Science files, RAC.

39. T. Dwight Sloan confidential to H.S. Houghton, 4 April 1923, box 142, folder 1032, Social Science files, RAC; Margery Eggleston to I. Burchet, 14 December 1925, box, 143, folder 1034, I.P. files, RAC.

40. I.P. interview with M.K., 14 November 1983; I.P., "Local Patriots," *Stories of the People*, p. 455.

41. Burchet confidential to M. Eggleston, 13 November 1925, box 143, folder 1034, I.P. files, RAC; M. Eggleston confidential to H.S. Houghton, 9 December 1925, box 143, folder 1034, I.P. files, RAC. I.P. interview with M.K., 24 February 1984 suggests she was unaware of or had forgotten Liu's antipathy toward her. Lack of initiative and a tendency not to complete projects were other charges leveled against Pruitt. See M. Eggleston to W.S. Carter, 15 December, box 143, folder 1034, I.P. files, RAC.

42. I.P. memo to Katharine Lyman, 4 May 1936.
43. W.S. Carter confidential to M. Eggleston, 21 January 1926; Dr. A.M. Dunlap to M. Eggleston, 17 July 1926, box 143, folder 1034, I.P. files, RAC; M. Eggleston to W.S. Carter, 15 December 1925. See also R.S. Greene's marginal comment on memo from M. Eggleston to H.S. Houghton, 16 December 1926, box 142, folder 1032, Social Science files, RAC.
44. I.P. to M. Eggleston, 15 July 1926, box 143, folder 1034, I.P. files, RAC.
45. M. Eggleston interview with Janet Thornton, 17 February 1927, box 143, folder 1034, I.P. files, RAC.
46. R.S. Greene to M. Eggleston, 11 March 1927, box 143, folder 1034, I.P. files, RAC; Greene to Rockefeller Foundation, 1 November 1927, box 143, folder 1034, I.P. files, RAC; I.P., "Education for Medical Social Work," p. 5.
47. Janet Thornton to M. Eggleston, 31 January 1927, box 143, folder 1034, I.P. files, RAC; M. Eggleston interview with J. Thornton, 17 February 1927, box 143, folder 1034, I.P. files, RAC; M. Eggleston confidential to H.S. Houghton, 16 March 1927, box 143, folder 1034, I.P. files, RAC.
48. R.S. Greene to I.P., 4 November 1930, box 143, folder 1034, I.P. files, RAC; S.T. Wang to I.P., 4 May 1931, box 143, folder 1034, I.P. files, RAC.
49. The anonymous critique of Ida's temperament and administrative policies was written in 1936.
50. Ida M. Cannon, *Social Work in Hospitals: A Contribution toward Progressive Medicine* (New York: n.p., 1923), pp. 190–91.
51. Liu Jinghe interview with M.K., Beijing, 2 July 1999 described the sense of the nursing students toward I.P.
52. I.P. to "Mac," 8 December 1932; Lois Rudnick, "The Male-Identified Woman and Other Anxieties: The Life of Mabel Dodge Luhan," in *The Challenge of Feminist Biography: Writing the Lives of Modern American Women*, ed. Sara Alpern, Joyce Antler, Elisabeth Israels Perry, and Ingrid Winther Scobie (Urbana: University of Illinois Press, 1992), pp. 116–38.
53. Mary E. Ferguson, *China Medical Board and Peking Union Medical College: A Chronicle of Fruitful Collaboration, 1914–1951* (New York: China Medical Board of N.Y., Inc., 1970), Appendix B, Members of Faculty and Staff, p. 237.
54. Jack McIntosh (J.M.) to I.P., 9 and 13 December 1932.
55. I.P. to J.M., 31 October 1932.
56. The third essay, "Faith," was published in the "Contributors' Club" section, *Atlantic Monthly*, 150 (July–Dec. 1932): 782–83.
57. Wu Yong, *The Flight of an Empress*.
58. J.M. to I.P., 11 and 14 August 1932, 22 September 1932, 12 December 1932.
59. I.P., [handwritten ms], n.d.
60. See for example I.P. to J.M., [handwritten ms], 23 and 27 October 1929. See I.P. penciled note, n.d.
61. I.P. to J.M., circa 1932, 17 December 1932.

62. I.P. to J.M., 15 December 1932.
63. J.M. to I.P., 29 December 1932; I.P. to J.M., 31 December 1932.
64. I.P. to J.M., 19 December 1932.
65. I.P. to J.M., 29 December 1932, 5 January 1933. Sara Everts, a social worker at Massachusetts General Hospital, referred Ida to Taylor.
66. I.P. to J.M., 21 December 1932.
67. I.P. to J.M., 29 December 1932, 2 February 1933.
68. I.P. to J.M., 24 December 1932.
69. I.P. to J.M., 21 December 1932.
70. I.P. to J.M., 29 December 1932.
71. I.P. to J.M., 31 December 1932.
72. I.P. to J.M., 31 December 1932.
73. I.P. to J.M., 16 February 1933.
74. I.P. to J.M., 16 February 1933.
75. I.P. to J.M., 22 February 1933.

Chapter 6

1. I.P., [random handwritten notes and photographs of Shang Fang Shan, which she translates as "Great Square Mountain"].
2. I.P., *A China Childhood*, p. 5. "A House is an Outer Self" is taken directly from the title of chap. 2.
3. I.P., "Beijing time table" [random notes]; John King Fairbank, *Chinabound*, pp. 48–49.
4. James M. Bertram, "Capes of China Slide Away: A Memoir of Peace and War in New Zealand and the Pacific," (n.d.), TS, pp. 190–91.
5. Yamaguchi Mamoru and Michael Crook supplied the translation and location of I.P.'s address in correspondence with M.K., 25 February 2002.
6. I.P., "My Home," pp. 172–73, 176–78, 233–34.
7. I.P. interview with M.K., 18 March 1984.
8. John King Fairbank believed Ida can be understood as a Confucian reformer in the broad sense of Confucianism. Fairbank interview with M.K., Franklin, NH, 16 August 1988.
9. I.P., "My Home," pp. 179, 190, 192.
10. Chi Tang (pseud.) praised the "special blueness" of Beijing's sky in "Beijing haohuai," *Beijing yigu* (A glance at Beijing) (Shanghai: Yuzhou Feng She, 1938), p. 2.
11. I.P., "My Home," pp. 181–83.
12. I.P., "My Home," pp. 188–89.
13. I.P., [random notes], (n.d.).
14. I.P., "The Years Between," (n.d.), TS, p. 18.
15. I.P., [untitled, undated autobiographical draft], chap. 24, for this and much of the material on "Mei Yun."
16. I.P., [untitled, undated autobiographical draft], chap. 27, p. 312. The story of

Jing Feng largely went unrecorded. Whether she was officially adopted or not remains vague.

17. Directory of *Yu Wang Fu* Association of PUMC, Beijing, China, 1917–1950 (privately published in April, 1981), Appendix B, p. 55.

18. I.P., *A Daughter of Han: The Autobiography of a Chinese Working Woman* (1945; Stanford, CA: Stanford University Press, 1967), p. 249.

19. I.P., *A Daughter of Han*, p. 239.

20. I.P., *A Daughter of Han*, p. 248. I.P., [dream record], 5 January 1937, TS. I.P. conversations with M.K., 1984.

21. She Huichen (Louise She) to M.K., 18 October 1983, p. 1.

22. I.P., [untitled essay on Italians in Philadelphia], TS, p. 9.

23. I.P., [untitled, undated autobiographical draft], TS, chap. 7.

24. Tania Manooiloff Cosman, *My Heritage with Morning Glories: A White Russian Growing Up in China* (Washington, DC: Creative Communication Services, 1995); I.P. to Lincoln Reynolds, American Consulate General, about official adoption of a Russian daughter, 4 August 1936. The official status of Guijing is unclear.

25. I.P., *Stories of the People*, TS, pp. 160–69. Ida hired Yang before she moved to Xiao Yang Yibin Hutong. When she went to the United States in 1932, Yang worked for John and Wilma Fairbank, but no record exists of his life after Ida's final departure from Beijing in 1939. Fairbank, *Chinabound*, p. 48.

26. I.P., "My Home," p. 207.

27. Bertram, "Capes of China Slide Away," p. 191.

28. I.P., "My Home," pp. 202, 209.

29. H.F.S. to M.K., 16 May 1983; James Bertram (hereafter cited as J.B.) to M.K., 15 February 1983. Gabriel Lasker to M.K., 18 September 1985, wrote, "In general, her friends were more marginal types ... who needed a safe haven in Peking...." Ruth Bacon described her husband, Philadelphia architect Edmund N. Bacon's experience living in Ida's home in 1932, 5 October 1985.

30. I.P., "My Home," p. 247.

31. Ida's interviews with Old Madam Ning began while Ida was living in the courtyard home with John and Wilma. He remembers Ida and Ning had a marvelous time together. Fairbank interview with M.K., Franklin, NH, 16 August 1988.

32. I.P., chap. 21, pp. 242–43.

33. I.P., "My Home," pp. 184, 217–18; Michael Crook to M.K., 17 September 2003, clarified the description of "gate cave."

34. I.P., "My Home," p. 242.

35. I.P., "My Home," pp. 172–73, 176–78, 233–34.

Chapter 7

1. Wu Yong, *The Flight of an Empress.*
2. Wu, p. 2.
3. Wu, pp. 18, 107.
4. Wu, p. xxii.
5. Wu, p. 50.
6. *Democracy: A Far Eastern Half-monthly of Fact and Opinion*, Peiping. The first five issues were published on 1 May, 15 May, 3 June, 22 June and 8 July 1937, respectively. A sixth issue was published but confiscated by the Japanese police. See I.P., "Committee Meeting for the Magazine democracy," TS.
7. I.P., "Husbands and Wives," *Democracy* (22 June 1937): 123, 125.
8. I.P., [random notes], TS.
9. I.P., [random notes], TS.
10. I.P., [random notes], TS.
11. I.P., "Days in Old Peking," pp. 32–36; L.C. Arlington and William Lewisohn, with an introduction by Geremie Barme, *In Search of Old Peking* (1935; Hong Kong: Oxford University Press, 1987), pp. 28, 175, 338. Appendix B of the book lists each site and its corresponding part of No Cha's body.
12. I.P., "Hospital Social Service in Diagnosis and Treatment," *Ch. Med. J.*, 28 (June, 1928): 1–12; "A Study of Sixty-Nine Adopted Children," *Hospital Social Service* (Sept. 1931): 157–83; "Day by Day in Peking," *Atlantic Monthly*, 147 (Jan.–June, 1931): 611–19; "New Year's Eve in Peking," *Atlantic Monthly*, 149 (Jan.–June, 1932): 47–53; "Faith," *Atlantic Monthly*, 150 (July–Dec. 1932): 782–83.
13. I.P., "Days in Old Peking," pp. 613, 615.
14. I.P., "New Year's Eve in Peking," p. 49.
15. I.P., "New Year's Eve in Peking," pp. 52–53.
16. I.P., "Thoughts on Religion," (circa 1966), TS, p. 1.
17. I.P., "Thoughts on Religion," p. 2.
18. I.P., *A Daughter of Han*, p. 2.
19. I.P., *A Daughter of Han*, pp. 23, 27–28.
20. I.P., *A Daughter of Han*, p. 22.
21. Twentieth century secular American best-sellers about China perpetuate these stereotypes and embellish the view of Asian women as sexually available and subservient. See Daniel B. Ramsdell, "Asia Askew: U.S. Best-Sellers on Asia, 1931–1980," *Bulletin of Concerned Asian Scholars*, 15 (Oct.–Dec. 1983): 2–25.
22. A.S.P. to I.P., 4 December 1945.
23. I.P., *A Daughter of Han*, pp. 68–70.
24. I.P., "New Year's Eve in Peking," pp. 52–53.

25. Stephanie A. Demetrakopoulos approaches the mystical quality of Ida Pruitt's descriptions in her use of archetypes of womanhood in the Eleusinian Mysteries to analyze the bond between women writers and subjects. See Stephanie A. Demetrakopoulos, "The Metaphysics of Matrilinearism in Women's Autobiography: Studies of Mead's *Blackberry Winter*, Hellman's *Pentimento*, Angelou's *I Know Why a Caged Bird Sings*, and Kingston's *The Woman Warrior*," in *Women's Autobiography: Essays in Criticism*, ed. Estelle C. Jelinek (Bloomington: Indiana University Press, 1980), pp. 180–205.

26. I.P., *A China Childhood*, pp. 17, 69, 76.

27. Bell Gale Chevigny, "Daughters Writing: Toward a Theory of Women's Biography," *Feminist Studies*, 9 (Spring 1983): 80–81.

28. Chevigny, "Daughters Writing," pp. 80, 89.

29. Myra Pitkin, "The Grandmother's Window," TS, (Tallmadge, Ohio), pp. 1–25; A.S.P., "The Grandmother's Window: Added Notes," TS, pp. 1–4.

30. I.P., [untitled autobiographical draft], (circa 1932), p. 27; I.P. to M.K., 14 November 1983, Philadelphia, Pennsylvania: "I made the only 'family' structure I knew—a pretty good structure. I was the grandmother figure in the family."

31. Chevigny, "Daughters Writing," pp. 95–96.

32. In I.P.'s prologue, she warns of the threat facing her dear friend. "Unless they (Ning and her family) and all the others are rescued in time, they will live without freedom of soul, at best dry shells of life ... and at worst, in a slavery and destitution that make Lao Tai-tai's days as a beggar seem paradise." I.P., *A Daughter of Han*, pp. 3–4.

33. Alice Walker, "Saving the Life That Is Your Own: The Importance of Models in the Artist's Life," in her *In Search of Our Mothers' Gardens: Womanist Prose* (San Diego, CA: Harcourt Brace Jovanovich, 1983), p. 14.

34. I.P., *Old Madam Yin: A Memoir of Peking Life, 1926–1938* (Stanford, CA: Stanford University Press, 1979), p. 5.

35. I.P., *Old Madam Yin*, p. 1.

36. I.P., *Old Madam Yin*, p. 15.

37. I.P., *Old Madam Yin*, p. 48.

38. Leon Edel, *Writing Lives: Principia Biographica* (New York: W.W. Norton & Co., 1984), p. 28ff.

39. Margery Wolf, *Old Madam Yin*, pp. vii, 127. Explorations of the relationship between first-world author and third-world subject have been made by Ruth Underhill, *Papago Women* (n.p., 1953) and more recently by James Clifford, Trinh T. Minh-ha, Linda Alcoff, and others as a central theme of postcolonial literature.

40. Edel, *Writing Lives*, p. 161.

41. Yamaguchi Mamoru, professor of Chinese Literature, Nihon University, Tokyo, in conversations with M.K., 1–11 January 1996, Tucson, AZ.

42. I.P., *Old Madam Yin*, p. 4.
43. I.P., *A China Childhood*. Despite the official place of publication, this publisher was actually located in Taiwan.
44. I.P., "Days in Old Peking," TS.
45. I.P. conversations with M.K. and M.K. interview with retired China missionaries, who wish to remain anonymous, confirm this concern.
46. Elizabeth Winston, "The Autobiographer and Her Readers: From Apology to Affirmation," in *Women's Autobiography*, ed. Estelle C. Jelinek, p. 111.
47. Edward W. Said, *Orientalism* (New York: Vintage, 1978), p. 2.
48. Edward W. Said, *Culture and Imperialism*, p. xi.
49. Harold R. Isaacs, *Scratches on Our Minds: American Views of China and India* (Armonk, NY: M.E. Sharpe, 1980), p. 40, quoted in Zhang Longxi, "The Myth of the Other: China in the Eyes of the West," *Critical Inquiry* 15 (Autumn 1988): 108–31.
50. Said, *Culture and Imperialism*, p. xviii.
51. Said, *Culture and Imperialism*, p. xxiv.
52. See Alice Tisdale Hobart's review of *A Daughter of Han*: "China across the Tracks," *Saturday Review of Literature*, 9 February 1946. ("Fu Manchu" was the evil oriental genius in a series of popular novels, radio and television programs, and movies beginning in 1913 and continuing into the twenty-first century as inspiration for musical groups and websites.) For other reviews, see *American Sociological Review*, 11 (1946): 766; *American Journal of Sociology*, 51 (1945–46): 582; *Choice* (April, 1980): 290; *Journal of Asian Studies*, 5 (1945): 342; *Journal of Asian Studies*, 40 (November, 1980): 118; *Pacific Affairs*, 53 (Fall, 1980): 531–32; *Sociology and Social Research*, 30 (1946): 328; *Social Research*, 13 (1946): 396–97; *Yale Review*, 35 (1946): 544–45; *Bulletin of Concerned Asian Scholars*, 12: 4 (1981): 67–70.

Chapter 8

1. J.B. to I.P., 15 April 1938.
2. I.P. to J.B., 23 January 1938.
3. I.P., [untitled autobiographical draft], (n.d.), TS; "The Japanese," (n.d.), TS, chap. 1, p. 5.
4. I.P., "The Japanese," chap. 3, p. 4.
5. I.P., "Notes on Relief," (n.d.), TS.
6. See I.P. "The Japanese"; Jonathan D. Spence, *The Search for Modern China* (New York: W.W. Norton, 1990), p. 448; Joshua A. Fogel, "Introduction: The Nanjing Massacre in History," in *The Nanjing Massacre in History and Historiography*, ed. Joshua A. Fogel, with a forward by Charles S. Maier (Berkeley: University of California Press, 2000), p. 6. Fogel discusses the "numbers game" among those whose political interests are vested in either exaggerating or grossly underestimating the number of victims. All contributors address the comparison of the Rape of Nanjing to the German

Holocaust by Iris Chang, *The Rape of Nanking: The Forgotten Holocaust of World War II* (New York: Basic, 1997).

7. *Captains Courageous* is "one of cinema's greatest classic adventure stories," according to www.greatestfilms.org. First released in 1937, the movie was an adaptation of English novelist Rudyard Kipling's 1897 work of the same name. Kipling was one of Pruitt's favorite authors, so she no doubt was eager to see his film.

8. I.P., "My Guest," TS.

9. I.P., "The Japanese," chap. 6.

10. I.P., "The Japanese."

11. J.B. to M.K., 15 February 1983.

12. I.P., "The Japanese."

13. I.P., [diary], 26 February 1938.

14. I.P., [diary], 9 February 1938.

15. I.P., [diary], 20 and 26 July 1938, 4 August 1938.

16. J.B., *First Act in China* (New York Vintage Press, 1938); Edgar Snow, *Red Star Over China* (New York: Random House, 1938).

17. J.B. to I.P., 15 February 1983; H.F.S. to I.P., 16 May 1983, p. 2; I.P., *Stories of the People*, "Red Spears," tells of her help to the noncommunist resistance, as well.

18. I.P., *Stories of the People*, "The Northeasterners," pp. 469–70.

19. I.P., *Stories of the People*, "The Northeasterners," p. 471.

20. Roger Greene and S.T. Wang to I.P., 19 June 1935; J. Preston Maxwell and S.T. Wang to I.P., 11 May 1937; Maxwell to I.P., 13 May 1937, box 143, folder 1034, I.P. files, RAC.

21. H.H. Loucks, acting director, to Dr. Bernard E. Reed, 27 May 1938; Loucks to P.S. Selwyn-Clarke, 27 May 1938. See also V.F. Bradfield, treasurer of PUMC, letter to American Consulate General in Tianjin, 5 May 1938 and Mary Elizabeth Tennent, Rockefeller Foundation International Health Division, to Mr. Edwin C. Lobenstine of the China Medical Board, 11 August 1938, commending I.P. (box 143, folder 1034, I.P. files, RAC).

22. I.P., [Politics at the PUMC], (n.d.), TS, p. 2: "There seems ... to be a feeling, I cannot call it a thought, among some people that all of women's work can be done by one group of women." See also E. Cockerill, *Transactions of the American Hospital Association*, 39 (1937): 734–45.

23. I.P. to J.B., 30 December 1938.

24. I.P. to Agnes H. Schroeder, Case Western Reserve, 18 July 1938; to Edith Baker, Barnes Hospital, St. Louis, 18 July 1938; to Antoinette Cannon, New York School of Social Work, 19 July 1938 and 30 August 1938; and to Margaret Quinn, Joint Vocational Bureau, New York, 30 August 1938.

25. I.P., [note written in Swatow], 27 December 1938.

26. J.B. to I.P., 28 February 1938.

27. J.B. to I.P., 4 March 1938.

28. I.P. to J.B., 29 April 1938.
29. I.P. to J.B., 31 March 1938.
30. I.P., [diary], (n.d.).
31. Rewi Alley (hereafter cited as R.A.), *At 90: Memoirs of My China Years* (Beijing: New World Press, 1986), pp. 104–5, describes his major role in drafting the pamphlet and choosing the nickname "gung ho" ("gong he").
32. S. Bernard Thomas, *Season of High Adventure: Edgar Snow in China* (Berkeley: University of California Press, 1996), pp. 172, 195, 215. The film *Gung Ho!* (distributed by Alpha Video Distributors, Inc.) is based on the experiences of Captain W.S. LeFrancois who served under Lieutenant Colonel Evans F. Carlson, United States Marine Corps. See Evans F. Carlson, *Twin Stars of China: A Behind-the-Scenes Story of China's Valiant Struggle for Existence by a U.S. Marine Who Lived and Moved with the People* (New York: Dodd & Mead, 1940). See also Jack Gallant, "Marine Corps Raider Battalions," retrieved from Navy and Marine Corps World War II Commemorative Committee website: www.chinfo.navy.mil/navpalib/wwii/facts/mcraider.txt
33. I.P., "Japan," (n.d.), TS, pp. 483–84. John and Irene Vincent interview with M.K., 17 July 1994. John Vincent helped the CIC cooperatives by transporting gold bars from Canton to the CIC workers in Shandan.
34. Theodore H. White and Annalee Jacoby, *Thunder out of China* (New York: Wm. Sloane, 1946), pp. 55–56.
35. Lu Wanru, "The Gung Ho Movement and the International Committee for the Promotion of Chinese Industrial Cooperatives," *Training for Trainers Manual* (Beijing: International Committee for the Promotion of the Chinese Industrial Cooperatives, 2002). Other early supporters included Sha Qianli, Zhang Naiqi, S.J. Chen, and P.N. Chung of the Bank of China, J.M. Tan, treasurer, and chief engineer Frank Lem. The central headquarters of the CIC, later called the Association for the Advancement of the Chinese Industrial Cooperatives, was administered by high officials of the GMD government Hang Liwu, Jiang Tingfu, Jiang Jingguo, and Zhang Zhizhong. The secretary general was Liu Guangpei. Leading members of the Communist Party, Deng Yingchao and Dong Biwu, as well as prominent democrats Shen Junru and Huang Yanpei, were also involved.
36. Peter Townsend correspondence with M.K., 2001–2003, and numerous other conversations between M.K. and Gung Ho activists. Douglas Robertson Reynolds, "The Chinese Industrial Cooperative Movement and the Political Polarization of Wartime China, 1938–1945" (doctoral dissertation, Columbia University, 1975), p. 80, cites a meeting on 3 April 1938 as the date when the leadership and initiative for the cooperatives shifted from a wholly foreign group to a largely Chinese one.
37. Nym Wales (Helen Foster Snow), "An Industrial Defense Line for China" (n.p., n.d.), p. 5.

38. H.F.S., *My China Years* (New York: Wm. Morrow, 1984), pp. 302–5; S. Bernard Thomas, *Season of High Adventure*, pp. 193–99.

39. Paul B. Trescott, "John Bernard Tayler and the Development of Cooperatives in China, 1917–1945," *Annals of Public and Cooperative Economics*, 62.2 (1993): 210–21.

40. I.P., [Early draft of "CIC"]; A.L. Carson, "Christian Institutions and the Rural Reconstruction Movement," *China Christian Year Book (CCYB)*, 1936–1937, p. 250; J.B. Tayler, "Progress of the Cooperative Movement," *CCYB*, 1936–1937, p. 268.

41. I.P., "Chinese Women Unbind Their Feet," (circa 1940), TS, n.p.; I.P., [random notes on the CIC], p. 2.

42. I.P. to J.B., n.d. (summer, 1938).

43. Akira Iriye, *Across the Pacific: An Inner History of American-East Asian Relations*, revised ed. (Chicago: Imprint Pub, 1992), pp. 179, 184–88; Warren I. Cohen, *America's Response to China: A History of Sino-American Relations*, 3rd ed. (New York: Columbia University Press, 1990), pp. 118–19.

44. R.A., "In Memoriam: Ida Pruitt," 19 August 1985, TS.

45. I.P., "CIC," [rough notes], (n.d.).

46. I.P., [random notes on the CIC], (n.d.).

47. Willis Airey, *A Learner in China: A Life of Rewi Alley* (Christchurch, Caxton Press and the Monthly Review Society, 1970), p. 14; "Rewi Alley," *Aotearoa*, circa 1947, in Anne-Marie Brady, *Friend of China: The Myth of Rewi Alley* (London: RoutledgeCurzon, 2003), p. 7.

48. I.P., "I Meet Rewi Alley," (n.d.), TS, p. 7.

49. Geoff Chapple, *Rewi Alley of China* (Auckland: Hodder and Stoughton, 1980), p. 26.

50. Airey, *A Learner in China*, p. 28.

51. Chapple, *Rewi Alley of China*, p. 26.

52. Chapple, *Rewi Alley of China*, pp. 27–33, 39; Airey, *A Learner in China*, p. 43.

53. Airy, *A Learner in China*, p. 65.

54. R.A., *At 90: Memoirs of My China Years*, pp. 46–47.

55. I.P., "I Meet Rewi Alley," pp. 11–14.

56. I.P., "I Meet Rewi Alley," pp. 21–22.

57. I.P., "I Meet Rewi Alley," pp. 23–24.

58. I.P., "Back to Shanghai," TS, pp. 2–3; James Bertram, *Beneath the Shadow: A New Zealander in the Far East, 1939–1946* (New York: John Day, 1947), p. 16.

59. I.P., "Back to Shanghai," p. 3; Douglas R. Reynolds, "The Chinese Industrial Cooperative Movement," pp. 232–33.

60. I.P., "Back to Shanghai," pp. 6–7.

61. Douglas R. Reynolds, "The Chinese Industrial Cooperative Movement," p. 233.

62. James Bertram, *Beneath the Shadow*, p. 56.
63. Warren I. Cohen, *America's Response to China*, pp. 126, 130.
64. Joyce Hoffman, *Theodore H. White and Journalism as Illusion* (Columbia: University of Missouri Press, 1995), pp. 35–56.
65. Ralph and Nancy Lapwood, *Through the Chinese Revolution* (London: Spalding & Levy, 1954), pp. 19–20.
66. Douglas R. Reynolds, "The Chinese Industrial Cooperative Movement," pp. 135–39.
67. The third major clique was the Whampoa clique. See *The Nationalist Era in China: 1927–1949*, ed. Lloyd Eastman, Jerome Ch'en, Suzanne Pepper, and Lyman P. Van Slyke (Cambridge: Cambridge University Press, 1991), pp. 26–27.
68. Douglas R. Reynolds, "The Chinese Industrial Cooperative Movement," p. 144. The infiltrator was sent by the Central Cooperative Control Bureau of the Ministry of Economic Affairs, which was controlled by the C.C. Clique.
69. I.P. to E.C. Carter, Institute of Pacific Relations, (n.d.), TS.
70. I.P., "China's Women Unbind Their Feet," p. 6.
71. R.A. to I.P., 20 and 24 July 1939, box 3, Indusco Collection Rare Book and Manuscript Library, Butler Library, Columbia University.
72. I.P., "China's Women Unbind Their Feet," pp.7–8; I.P., "Meng Shih-chung," TS, (n.d.), pp. 1–6.
73. R.A. to E.C. Carter, Institute of Pacific Relations, 25 July 1939, box 3, Indusco Collection.
74. I.P., [random note], (n.d.).

Chapter 9

1. I.P. to J.B., 25 February 1940.
2. J.B. to I.P., 3 December 1939.
3. Robert and Mac's sons, Dean and John Pruitt, both spoke of their grandmother Anna with great affection in interviews with M.K.
4. C.W.P. to I.P., 15 November 1939.
5. A.S.P. to I.P., 9 August 1939, 5 October 1939.
6. A.S.P. to I.P., 20 November 1930.
7. A.S.P. to I.P., 5 March 1939.
8. A.S.P. to I.P., 5 October 1939.
9. A.S.P. to I.P., n.d.
10. Stephen R. MacKinnon and Oris Friesen, *China Reporting: An Oral History of American Journalism in the 1930s and 1940s* (Berkeley: University of California Press, 1987), p. 184 reveals the lack of consensus about the overall quality of China reporting, but concludes that the coverage of the countryside was woefully inadequate. See also Theodore H. White and Annalee Jacoby, *Thunder out of China*, pp. 61–62.
11. James M. Bertram, *Unconquered: Journal of a Year's Adventures among the*

Fighting Peasants of North China (London: Macmillan, 1939).

12. Theodore H. White in *Thunder out of China*, pp. 62–66, confirms Japan's use of terror as a strategic objective. In one particularly haunting scene, White described Chinese peasants stripped naked, lashed to carts, and driven forward by the imperial army as beasts of burden.

13. C.W.P. to I.P., 15 November 1939, 11 December 1939.

14. A.S.P. to I.P., 3, 9 and 21 October 1939.

15. A.S.P. to I.P., 9 and 21 October 1939, 20 November 1939.

16. I.P. to A.S.P. and C.W.P., 26 September 1939.

17. A Hollywood, California Committee in Aid of the CIC was formed and chaired by noted author Lin Yutang. Its members included several executives of Warner Brothers and Paramount Studios, a representative of the Chinese Consulate, a Chinese restaurant owner and the chief of Immigration and Housing. Ida's contacts in Boston included a number of academics such as Professor Ernest Hocking, China scholars Olga Lang and John King Fairbank, Japan scholar Edwin Reischauer, members of the Eastern Cooperative Wholesale organization and Ida's former social work mentor, Ida Cannon. Philadelphia, Cleveland, Princeton, Rochester, San Francisco-Berkeley, Washington, and, of course, New York were early centers of Ida's organizing, as well.

18. The organization usually was called the "Price Committee" for its founders, Harry and Frank Price, former American missionaries in China. Active members of the Price Committee included other China missionaries such as Roger Greene, former director of the PUMC, Dr. Walter Judd, congressman from Minnesota, and Geraldine and George Fitch, advisors to Chiang Kai-shek. See Warren I. Cohen, *The Chinese Connection: Roger S. Greene, Thomas W. Lamont, George E. Sokolsky and American-East Asian Relations* (New York: Columbia University Press, 1978), pp. 214–15.

19. Pearl S. Buck, "Free China Gets to Work; New Industrial Cooperatives Can Supply an Economic Base," *Asia*, 39.4 (April 1939): 199–202.

20. I.P., "Chinese Industrial Cooperatives," *China Today* (October 1939): 12–13.

21. I.P., "China's Industrial Wall; Small and Bombproof Cooperative Industries," *Survey Graphic: Magazine of Social Interpretation*, 29 (March 1940): 186–90. *The Nation, Time,* and *Asia* also covered the cooperatives during the winter of 1939 and the spring of 1940.

22. *Saturday Evening Post*, 213: 12–13+; *Business Week* (8 February 1941): 56–58; *New Republic*, 99: 185; *Catholic World*, 149: 409–14; *Survey Graphic*, 30: 83–86; *Commonweal*, 35: 118–20; *Monthly Labor Review*, 52: 117–22; *Living Age*, 359: 516–21.

23. *The Nation*, 155: 333; *Monthly Labor Review*, 55: 557–58; *Travel*, 79: 31; *New Republic*, 106: 273; *Rotarian*, 62: 32–33; *Colliers*, 111: 74–75; *Business Week* (6 February 1943): 16; *Travel*, 82: 7–9+; *Asia*, 44: 209–11; *Asia*, 45: 106–7.

24. I.P. to Edgar Snow, 21 June 1940.
25. I.P. to J.B., 3 December 1939.
26. I.P. to J.B., 5 January 1940. (He was later given C-3 status.)
27. I.P. to J.B., 3 December 1939: "I am trying to learn to keep my eyes on the goal and go step by step."
28. R.A. to I.P., 10 December 1939, box 3, Indusco Collection.
29. R.A. to Ted Herman, 18 December 1939, box 3, Indusco Collection.
30. R.A. to I.P., 13 October 1939, box 3, Indusco Collection; *A Nation Rebuilds: The Story of the Chinese Industrial Cooperatives in Pictures* (Hong Kong: Chinese Industrial Cooperatives, Hong Kong Promotion Committee, 1940), p. 11.
31. Maud Russell interview with M.K., 14 March 1989, New York.
32. I.P. to J.B., 18 December 1939.
33. I.P. to J.B., 5 January 1940.
34. R.A. to I.P., 19 February 1940, box 3, Indusco Collection.
35. Mao Zedong to Bishop Hall and Chen Han-seng (Hansheng), 25 September 1939 from Yan'an.
36. R.A. to I.P., 4 February 1940, R.A. file, box 3, Indusco Collection. Graham Peck, who worked for CIC at the time of his 1941 visit to Baoji, concluded that the CIC "was not particularly influential even in Baoji" due to competition from opportunistic merchants who sold smuggled goods from Japanese-held territory. See Peck, *Two Kinds of Time* (Boston: Houghton Mifflin, 1950), pp. 171–76.
37. Pauline Keating, "Cooperative Visions vs. Wartime Realities: Indusco and the Chinese Communists, 1938–1944," *New Zealand Journal of East Asian Studies*, V.1 (June 1997): 3–29.
38. I.P. to J.B., 1 January 1940. Ida and other China hands felt constrained to talk freely about China and many other subjects in the atmosphere of "fantastic witch trials, the Dies committee's works, and … fears of jobs."
39. R.A. to I.P., 10 May 1939, 1 March 1940, 18 May 1940, 20 June 1940, box 3, Indusco Collection.
40. Warren I. Cohen, *The Chinese Connection*, p. 229. Another founder of the "Price Committee," B.A. Garside, later established the United China Relief.
41. Immanuel C.Y. Hsu, *The Rise of Modern China* (New York: Oxford University Press, 1990), p. 600. The U.S.S.R. granted loans totaling US$250 million in 1937–1938 and another US$150 million in 1939 at a three percent interest rate. By 1940, Russia had supplied 1,000 planes, 2,000 pilots and 500 military advisers, among them her "best military talent." In comparison, by the end of the war the West contributed US$263.5 million. Of that, America provided US$120 million for nonmilitary purchases and US$450 million for currency stability.
42. H.F.S. to Richard J. Walsh, 24 June 1940.
43. H.F.S. to Hollington K. Tong, 4 August 1940, p. 2. Twenty prominent

Americans, among them Pearl S. Buck and her publisher husband, Richard J. Walsh, Rear Admiral Harry E. Yarnell, John Dewey, Carrie Chapman Catt, Gifford Pinchot, Carl Crow, Arthur N. Holcomb of Harvard University, writer Nathaniel Peffer, and Dr. J. Henry Carpenter, the chairman of Indusco's board of directors, made the request of Generalissimo Chiang, with copies sent to President Roosevelt and Secretary of the Treasury Morgenthau.

44. Eleanor Roosevelt, "My Day," 24 January 1940.

45. Hugh Deane, *Good Deeds and Gunboats: Two Centuries of American-Chinese Encounters* (San Francisco: China Books & Periodicals, 1990), pp. 114–15.

46. H.F.S. to I.P., 14 July 1940; Edgar Snow to I.P., 14 July 1940.

47. Edgar Snow to I.P., 14 July 1940.

48. I.P., *A China Childhood*, p. 5.

49. Dorothy Thompson, "An American Platform," On the Record, *New York Herald Tribune*, 25 June 1940.

50. Dorothy Thompson, "An American Platform."

51. I.P. to Edgar Snow, 21 June 1940.

52. Box 3, Indusco Collection.

53. United China Relief/United Service to China Collection, box 10, folder 5, USC Archive, Seeley G. Mudd Manuscript Library, Princeton University, Princeton, NJ.

54. I.P. to B.A. Garside, 17 November 1940, box 126, Indusco Collection.

55. H.F.S. to I.P., 17 January 1941, box 31, Indusco Collection.

56. W.A. Swanberg, *Luce and His Empire* (New York: Dell, 1972), p. 262.

57. Patricia Neils, *China Images in the Life and Times of Henry Luce* (Savage, MD: Rowman & Littlefield, 1990), p. 57.

58. I.P. to Carlson, 8 August 1941.

59. For one example of the many conversations and internal Indusco discussions of this issue, see Evans Carlson to R.A., 3 December 1941, box 177, Indusco Collection.

60. I.P., [longhand notes on scrap paper], (Sept.–Dec. 1941), box 42, Indusco Collection.

61. I.P. to Carlson, 8 August 1941.

62. I.P. to Lauchlin Currie, 22 September 1942, box 126, Indusco Collection.

63. "Report of the Indusco Committee of Four on Past and Future Participation in United China Relief," (Confidential) 8 July 1943, box 177, Indusco Collection.

64. Edward C. Carter to Lenning Sweet, 28 April 1943.

65. H.F.S. to I.P., 28 April 1943, referring to George Hogg's manuscript, later published as *I See a New China* (Boston: Little, Brown, 1944), pp. 197–98, and in many letters between the Snows, R.A., and I.P.

66. By the time that the CIC began, Rewi Alley had heard about the Communist

Party's populist policies from his friends Edgar Snow and James Bertram, who both had visited the Border Regions governed by Mao's forces. For this reason, his personal sympathies probably lay with the Communists. However, he did not advocate that the CIC cooperatives ally themselves with the CCP.

67. I.P. notes of telephone conversation with Eleanor Lattimore, 21 December 1942. The term "charity imperialism" was used by Owen Lattimore, who himself was brought before the Senate Internal Security Committee in 1950 on charges of being an instrument of a communist conspiracy. Edward C. Carter defended the UCR priorities in his letter to Lenning Sweet, 28 April 1943: "Aid to students and faculty has been urged by the highest Chinese and American governmental authorities as of paramount importance in winning the war and in subsequent rehabilitation." Gil Gott, "Imperial Humanitarianism: History of an Arrested Dialectic," in *Moral Imperialism: A Critical Anthology*, ed. Berta Esperanza Hernandez-Truyol (New York: New York University Press, 2002), p. 35.

68. Hugh Deane to I.P., 1 June 1942, box 23, Indusco Collection; I.P. to Hugh Deane, 3 June 1942, box 23, Indusco Collection.

69. I.P. to Jack Service, Far Eastern Division, State Department, 20 February 1943, box 143, Indusco Collection.

70. Lloyd E. Eastman, "Nationalist China during the Sino-Japanese War, 1937–1945," in *The Nationalist Era in China*, ed. Lloyd E. Eastman, Jerome Ch'en, Suzanne Pepper, and Lyman P. Van Slyke, pp. 158–59.

71. Theodore H. White and Annalee Jacoby, *Thunder out of China*, pp. 174–75.

72. Edward C. Carter to Lenning Sweet, 28 April 1943.

73. Indusco Board, "Notes on a Special Meeting," (Confidential) 28 February 1944.

74. I.P. to Lenning Sweet, 7 September 1943, box 35, folder 7, USC Collection.

75. I.P. to E.C. Carter, 10 June 1944; I.P. to E.C. Carter, 29 June 1944, box 35, folder 6, USC Collection.

76. Alexander DeConde, *A History of American Foreign Policy*, 2nd ed. (New York: Scribner's, 1971), pp. 626, 635.

77. I.P., "China and the Industrial Revolution," (January 1944), TS.

78. "Notes on Committee to Plan the Conference," 12 October 1944, box 142, Indusco Collection; "Discussion about Conference on the Role of the Chinese Industrial Cooperatives in the Economic Progress of China, 3 Feb. 1945," 9 November 1944.

79. I.P. to H.F.S., 13 February 1945, box 31, Indusco Collection.

80. I.P. to Jim Bertram, 29 August 1945.

Chapter 10

1. Ida Pruitt, interview by Henry Milo, *Henry Milo Program*, WINS, 29 January 1946.

2. I.P. to R.A., 7 May 1946.

3. R.A. to I.P., 17 February 1949; *Gung Ho News*, 1.1 (June 1946).
4. *Far East Spotlight*, 4.1 (June, 1948): 3.
5. I.P. to Evans Carlson, 5 May 1946. "Da Jiao" is translated as "Confucianism" in Matthews Chinese-English dictionary. "Dachengjiao" is a term for Chinese Buddhism. Ida was using the term in a more general sense, literally the "big teaching."
6. I.P. to Carlson, 5 May 1946.
7. I.P. to Dick Pastor, 12 June 1946.
8. I.P., [diary], 3 July 1946.
9. I.P., [diary], 4 July 1946.
10. I.P., [diary], 6 and 8 July 1946.
11. I.P., [diary], 4–5 July 1946.
12. Rewi Alley, *At 90*, pp. 175–205.
13. R.A., *Shantan (Shandan) Bailie School: 1946 General Report* (Hong Kong: International Committee for Chinese Industrial Cooperatives, 1946), p. 3; *Shantan (Shandan) Bailie School: 1947 General Report* (Shanghai: International Committee for Chinese Industrial Cooperatives), p. 13.
14. R.A., *Shantan (Shandan) Bailie School: 1946 General Report*, pp. 4–5.
15. R.A., *At 90*, pp. 200–4; R.A., *Shantan (Shandan) Bailie School: 1947 General Report*, pp. 10–38.
16. Reba Esser to I.P., 18 July 1946.
17. "The Social Significance of CIC in Lanchow," *Indusco News*, 41 (1 April 1941): 1.
18. Reba Esser to I.P., 18 July 1946.
19. Chang Kuan Lien (Zhang Guanlian), "Lanchow CIC Work," *Gung Ho News*, 1.4: 1–2; I.P., [notes], 2 July 1946.
20. I.P. to Melvin J. Fox, 20 August 1946.
21. I.P. to Melvin J. Fox, 20 August 1946.
22. Minutes, 1946 International Committee Annual Meeting (Hong Kong), 11 September.
23. Fei Hsiao-tung, "A Memorandum on Industrial Cooperative Movement in China," attached to minutes of 1946 International Committee Annual Meeting, 19 September 1946.
24. Suzanne Pepper, *Civil War in China: The Political Struggle, 1945–1949* (Berkeley: University of California Press, 1978), pp. 302, 326–27.
25. Suzanne Pepper, *Civil War in China*, p. 302.
26. R.A. to I.P., 9 October 1946.
27. Melvin J. Fox to Lennig Sweet, 3 April 1947, box 35, folder 1, USC Collection.
28. Chou Enlai (Zhou Enlai) to Mr. J. Franklin Ray, director, Far East Division, United Nations Relief and Rehabilitation Association (UNRRA), 15 November 1946, box 1, folder 5, United China Relief Collection (hereafter cited as UCR Collection), New York Public Library.

29. Tung Pi-wu (Dong Biwu), director, China Liberated Areas Relief Association (CLARA), November 1946, box 1, folder 5, UCR Collection.

30. B.A. Garside to Governor Edison, 17 October 1946, box 70, folder 4, USC Collection.

31. Louis Hoskins interview with M.K., 17 July 1994 states that in his capacity as treasurer of the CIC, he helped Ida to direct material aid to Yan'an and other liberated areas. As a worker in the nonpartisan Quaker organizations, Friends Ambulance Unit and American Friends Service Committee, Hoskins was in the position to assert that, to his knowledge, the Friends Ambulance Unit and the CIC were the only U.S. agencies to send aid to Communist areas of China, despite our wartime alliance.

32. Suzanne Pepper, *Civil War in China*, p. 304.

33. Peter Townsend to M.K., 17 August, 2002, states: "From 1942 to the establishment of People's China NO Indusco funds went to the Communist-controlled regions." The first contribution from the International Committee to any Border Region after the war was a mobile machine shop and three trucks obtained by Townsend and delivered by barge to a cooperative federation in the Shandong Border Region.

34. Statistics cited in resolution by Indusco Board of Directors, 17 June 1947.

35. "China Moves to Restore Its Co-operatives: Miss Ida Pruitt Reports on a 10,000 Mile Trip Through the Interior," *New York Herald Tribune*, 22 December 1946.

36. "Kuomintang Shift Seen By Red Chief: Chou Predicts Rightists' Fall and Creation of Democratic Regime Within a Year," *New York Times*, 19 December 1946; I.P. marginal comments on reprint of Francis L.K. Hsu, "A Closer View of China's Problems," *Far Eastern Quarterly*, November 1946.

37. E. Perry Link, Jr., *Mandarin Ducks and Butterflies: Popular Fiction in Early Twentieth-Century Chinese Cities* (Berkeley: University of California Press, 1981), p. 36.

38. I.P. to Gladys Yang, 20 October 1978.

39. Randir Vohra, *Lao She and the Chinese Revolution* (Cambridge, MA: Harvard University Press, 1974), p. 141.

40. David Der-wei Wang, *Fictional Realism in Twentieth-Century China: Mao Dun, Lao She, Shen Congwen* (New York: Columbia University Press, 1992), pp. 194–95.

41. Wu Xiaomei, "A Classic Realistic Novel: About Lao She's *Four Generations Under One Roof*," in *Yellow Storm* (Nanjing: Yilin Press, 1992), pp. 597–614. (*Yellow Storm* was first published in London by Gollancz, Ltd. in 1951.)

42. Vohra, *Lao She and the Chinese Revolution*, p. 146.

43. *Yellow Storm*, pp. 10–11; I.P., [autobiographical draft], (n.d.), TS; "My Home."

44. Lao She to David Lloyd, 22 April 1948, in *Lao She Yingwen shuxin ji*

(Collection of letters written in English by Lao She), trans. and annotated by Shu Yue (Hong Kong: Qin + Yuan Publishing House, 1993), pp. 9–10.

45. I.P. to David Lloyd, 3 January 1951.

46. Lena Waters, [newspaper clipping], August 1957; Vohra, *Lao She and the Chinese Revolution*, p. 141.

47. Wu Xiaomei, "A Classic Realistic Novel," pp. 597–598.

48. David Der-wei Wang, *Fictional Realisim in Twentieth-Century China*, pp. 185–86. This view was expressed also by Gu Jingyu to M.K. at the Southwest Conference of Asian Studies, 28 October 1994, Texas A&M University, College Station, Texas.

49. B.A. Garside to I.P., 27 January 1947, box 35, folder 1, USC Collection.

50. I.P. to Lillian McLeed, box 26, Indusco Collection.

51. T. Christopher Jespersen, *American Images of China, 1931–1949* (Stanford, CA: Stanford University Press, 1996), pp. 153–54.

52. Richard M. Fried, *Nightmare in Red: The McCarthy Era in Perspective* (New York: Oxford University Press, 1990), p. 4.

53. Alexander DeConde, *American Foreign Policy*, 2nd ed. (New York: Charles Scribner's Sons, 1971), pp. 669, 674.

54. Jespersen, *American Images of China*, p. 156.

55. Tsou Tang, *America's Failure in China, 1941–1950* (Chicago: University of Chicago Press, 1963), pp. 349–493.

56. Indusco Board of Directors' Resolution, 17 June 1947.

57. R.A. to Max Bickerton, 10 February 1947, box 176, Indusco Collection.

58. *Gung Ho News*, 2.4 (April 1947): 1.

59. The American Board for Medical Aid to China received 27 percent, Indusco received 11 percent, and the China Aid Council received 7 percent, a total of 45 percent of public donations, compared with the three religious agencies receipt of 59 percent. The American Friends Service Committee received 2 percent, and the American-Chinese Committee of the Mass Education Movement 5 percent. Since these were recent additions to USC, they are not considered in this discussion. See 17 June 1947 Indusco resolution.

60. I.P. to Maxwell Steward, 3 October 1947.

61. B.A. Garside to Brinckerhoff, Hill, Hallenbeck, McKenna and Witherspoon, 30 September 1947, box 10, folder 7, USC Collection.

62. I.P. to H.F.S., 26 August 1947.

63. Bronson P. Clark, [memo], 18 November 1947.

64. B.A. Garside to Kohlberg, 22 September 1947, box 70, folder 4, USC Collection.

65. Maxwell S. Stewart, chairman, Board of Directors, Indusco, to B.A. Garside, 5 November 1947, box 35, folder 1, USC Collection.

66. I.P. to Rt. Rev. Hall and Talitha Gerlach, 24 September 1947, box 27, Indusco Collection.

67. Peter Townsend to M.K., 16 August 2003, suggests that Rewi's life was

often reportedly in "danger." But Townsend "knew of no foreign advisors or supporters of CIC who were in danger or suffered persecution or oppression" due to their continuing privileged status.

68. R.A. to Eleanor Hinder, 15 June 1947, box 176, Indusco Collection; I.P., [notes before the 3 June 3 1947 meeting], p. 3.

69. "On the Future of the Industrial Cooperative Movement," 20 July 1947.

70. Peter Townsend to M.K., 16 August 2003.

71. Peter Townsend underscored this in correspondence and telephone conversations with M.K. during 2002 and 2003.

72. Peter Townsend to Melvin Fox, 14 November 1946, box 27, Indusco Collection.

73. Peter Townsend to R.A., 17 June 1947, box 33, Indusco Collection.

74. Peter Townsend to M.K., 16 August, 2003.

75. C. Martin Wilbur, professor of history at Columbia University and member of Indusco Board of Director, in interview with M.K., 16 March 1995, indicates that many board members, including himself, were suspicious of Ida's moves but were not included in her decision.

76. In June 1949, the American Friends Service Committee and part of the China Aid Council, which reorganized as the China Welfare Appeal, withdrew from the USC over the use of political arguments in USC promotional literature.

77. I.P. to Max Bickerton, 4 March 1948.

78. U.S.C. proposal of 22 November 1948.

79. I.P., [notes about 13 September 1948 discussion with Mr. McMullan of China Christian Colleges], (n.d.), TS.

80. B.A. Garside to Kohlberg, 5 October 1948, box 15, folder 9, USC Collection.

81. Indusco board minutes, 14 October and 16 November 1948.

82. H.F.S. to I.P., 12 October 1947, box 31, Indusco Collection.

83. Richard M. Fried, *Nightmare in Red*, pp. 60–61, 68–76.

Chapter 11

1. Suzanne Pepper, "The KMT-CCP Conflict, 1945–1949," in *The Nationalist Era in China, 1927–1949*, ed. Lloyd E. Eastman, Jerome Ch'en, Suzanne Pepper, and Lyman P. Van Slyke, pp. 345–56.

2. During the battle for Shanghai in 1949, Peter Townsend was a special correspondent for the British Broadcasting Company (BBC). In this capacity he was contacted by Lu Ding, head of the Shanghai anti-Guomindang underground, and Ji Zhaoting of the Beijing headquarters of the Bank of China, who asked Townsend to contact John Keswick, chairman of Jardine Matheson. Their message was to urge all foreign owned businesses to continue operation in Shanghai. See Peter Townsend to M.K., 16 August 2003, p. 28.

3. B.A. Garside, "A Report to the Board of Directors," 28 November 1949, box 6, folder 21, USC Collection.
4. Minutes, USC Executive Committee, 8 November 1949.
5. Elizabeth Hale to I.P., 21 November 1950.
6. Bertha Birdson to I.P., 21 April 1951.
7. Henry A. Wallace, "American Fiasco in China," *New Republic* (5 July 1948): 11.
8. Minutes, Indusco Board of Directors, 21 June 1949, p. 2.
9. Minutes, Indusco Board of Directors, Appendix A, 16 November 1948.
10. I.P. to Colin Morrison, 29 April 1949, box 27, Indusco Collection.
11. R.A., *At 90*, pp. 217–24; R.A. to I.P., 3 January 1949.
12. R.A. to I.P., 14 February 1949, 5 April 1949, 4 February 1949.
13. R.A., *At 90*, p. 219. For another account of this moment in the Shandan Bailie School's history, see Barbara Spencer, *Desert Hospital in China* (London: Jarrolds, 1954).
14. "Report from Shandan," TS. Special general meeting of International Committee for the Promotion of the CIC, Shanghai, 6 December 1949.
15. Peter Townsend to I.P., 17 October 1949; R.A. to I.P., 24 October 1949.
16. M.C. Tang to I.P., 30 May 1949.
17. An Fan-chih to I.P., 30 June 1949.
18. I.P. memo to Indusco Board of Directors, 15 June 1949.
19. I.P. to Colin Morrison, 16 August 1949, box 27, Indusco Collection.
20. I.P., "It is not as Simple as That," 28 September 1949, TS. Ida did not record the name of the journalist.
21. I.P., [dream record], 14 January 1949, TS.
22. Asia Institute, brochure for 23 February–12 June 1948; I.P., [notes], (n.d.), TS, pp. 1–9.
23. I.P., [untitled ms], 1949.
24. I.P., [dream record], 3 January 1950, TS.
25. Minutes, Indusco Board of Directors, 16 May 1950, 15 May 1951.
26. Minutes, Indusco Board of Directors, 17 April 1951; I.P. to Natalie Crouter, 19 June 1951. The U.S. post office periodically refused to send first-class mail to China. Indusco deposited money for Rewi's salary and the wheat in an American bank account, awaiting permission to transmit the funds. Second-class printed materials always got through.
27. In January 1950, the USC-affiliated agencies were the American Board for Medical Aid to China, Church World Service, the American-Chinese Committee of the Mass Education Movement, and United Board for Christian colleges in China. See minutes of Board of Directors, USC Adjourned Annual Meeting, 25 January 1950, box 2, folder 5, USC Collection.
28. I.P., [dream record], 12 April 1950.
29. Federal Bureau of Investigation (FBI) File on Ida Pruitt, #100-378105, 12 April 1950.

30. Committee for a Democratic Far Eastern Policy (CDFEP), [Letters written from China by Chinese students who returned late in 1949 or early in 1950 from studies in England to fellow students still studying abroad], April 1950.

31. William Stueck, *Rethinking the Korean War: A New Diplomatic and Strategic History* (Princeton, NJ: Princeton University Press, 2002), pp. 5, 77; Bruce Cumings, *The Origins of the Korean War II: The Roaring of the Cataract, 1947–1950* (Princeton, NJ: Princeton University Press, 1990), chap. 18: "Who Started the Korean War? Three Mosaics," pp. 568–624.

32. Stueck, *Rethinking the Korean War*, pp. 88, 96, 117.

33. Stueck, *Rethinking the Korean War*, pp. 89–92, 104–8.

34. At the "Fifty-Year Retrospective of the Korean War," a panel sponsored by the American Historical Association in Chicago, January, 2000, William Stueck remarked that of the more than 3 million deaths during the Korean War, most were Korean, and most of those were due to U.S. air power, which was insensitive about civilian casualties and which actually prolonged the conflict. At the same panel, Kathryn Weathersby asserted that the Soviets easily rallied support against the United States because of the bombings' ferocity.

35. Stueck, *Rethinking the Korean War*, pp. 1, 65, 179.

36. Bill and Sylvia Powell interview with M.K., 17 July 1994; Jim Wood, "Germ Warfare Charges: They Called it Sedition," *S.F. Sunday Examiner & Chronicle*, 13 March 1977, Sec. A-9. Ida was a friend of Bill and Sylvia Powell, American publishers of the *China Weekly Review* magazine who accused the United States of employing biological warfare in the Korean War. During the Powell's defense against government prosecution for treason in 1956, Ida helped to raise funds. The government later dropped all thirteen charges against the Powells and admitted widespread testing of germ warfare techniques on U.S. cities, although they denied using such weapons in Korea.

37. I.P. to R.A., 16 February 1951.

38. I.P. to Helen (no last name), 4 May 1951.

39. I.P. to Sophia Voorhees, 16 January 1951.

40. I.P. to anonymous, April or May 1951.

41. Dr. Theodora A. Raab to I.P., 24 April 1951.

42. M.K., "Chinese Christians in the Chinese Industrial Cooperatives, 1939–1952," paper presented at the conference "American Missionaries and Social Change in China: Collision and Confluence," Linfield College, McMinnville, OR, 14–17 July 1994. At that conference, several former missionaries expressed their support of both the CIC cooperatives and the Chinese Communist Party as more helpful to the desperately poor of China than was the Nationalist Party of Chiang Kai-shek, who was a nominal Christian.

43. "Missions in China Seen Nearing End: Returned Worker says Native Church is Now on Its Own, a Goal Long Sought Here," *New York Times*, 16 April

1951. Nancy Bernkopf Tucker, "An Unlikely Peace: American Missionaries and the Chinese Communists, 1948–1950," *Pacific Historical Review*, 45.1 (1976): 97–116, analyzes Chinese Communist policies toward religion and the missionaries during their rise to power. She comes to much the same conclusions as did Ida's correspondents from China, although she carefully distinguishes between the treatment of missionaries in rural and urban areas and between Protestant and Catholic Christians. She also identifies two different missionary concerns: protection of their property and fear for the fate of Chinese Christian converts.

44. Peter Townsend to M.K., 16 August 2003, questions the Christian church's existence.

45. Mrs. Alex H. Richardson to I.P., 19 June 1951 and I.P. response, n.d.

46. I.P. to Sophia Voorhees, 16 January 1951; I.P. to C.A. Ellenberger, c/o B.A. Garside, 5 June 1951.

47. I.P. to anonymous, April or May 1951.

48. Anne-Marie Brady, *Friend of China*, pp. 49–51, 62.

49. R.A. to I.P., July 1951, box 10, Indusco Collection.

50. I.P. to R.A., 4 May 1951.

51. R.A. to I.P., 25 January 1952, box 10, Indusco Collection.

52. Talitha Gerlach interview with Glenn Shive, 17 December 1982 in Shanghai.

53. Minutes, Indusco Board of Directors, 13 June 1952; Talitha Gerlach to I.P., 18 May 1952.

54. Walter Illesley to Indusco Board of Directors, inserted in minutes, 23 September 1952.

55. Shirley Barton to Indusco Board of Directors, inserted in minutes, 23 September 1952. Barton was New Zealand representative in China of Council of Overseas Relief Service Organization (CORSO). She served as secretarial and administrative assistant to R.A. and the Shandan school.

56. Lao Sheh (Lao She), "Living in Peking," *China Reconstructs* (Sept.–Oct. 1952): 25–27.

57. Minutes, Indusco Board of Directors, 28 February 1952, reports Ida's lectures to the Friends Select School in Philadelphia, the Reconciliation Clubs of the Community Church, and to a women's group of the Brooklyn Church of the Transfiguration; I.P. to Shirley Barton, 28 September 1952.

58. I.P. to Walter Illesley, 27 September 1952.

59. I.P. to R.A., 21 December 1952.

60. R.A. to I.P., 25 March 1951, July 1951, box 10, Indusco Collection.

61. I.P. to R.A., 26 September 1951.

62. L.R. Bonneau of Carstens & Linnekin to Indusco Board of Directors, 12 June 1952, box 115, Indusco Collection. Box 115 of Indusco Collection contains sixteen letters between 1950 and 1952 from advisory board members tendering their resignations. Most express no hostility toward China.

63. Correspondence between I.P. and Evans Clark, 1 May–4 June 1952, refers to an anonymous "confidential report" about Indusco, but gives no date or other specifics about the report.
64. Richard M. Fried, *Nightmare in Red*, pp. 158–60.
65. I.P., [notes], 13 June 1952, TS; minutes, Indusco Board of Directors, 13 June 1952.
66. I.P. to R.A., 4 June 1952, box 10, Indusco Collection.
67. Minutes, Indusco Board of Directors, 13 June 1952.
68. I.P. to R.A., 17 June 1952, box 10, Indusco Collection.
69. I.P. to R.A., 25 June 1952, box 10, Indusco Collection.
70. R.A. to I.P., 4 and 16 July 1952, box 10, Indusco Collection.
71. I.P. to Reisner, 14 November 1940.
72. I.P., "Matters for the Executive Board to Consider," [memo], 8 August 1941; I.P. to Evans Carlson, 8 August 1941.
73. Maxwell S. Stewart to Max Bickerton, circa 1948.
74. I.P. to H.F.S, 9 October 1947, box 31, Indusco Collection.
75. Sylvia Powell interview with M.K., 17 July 1994, remembering a story told to her by Rose Yardumian about Ida's visit to the ICCIC house in Shanghai, described Ida jumping out of bed in the morning and brightly asking, "What wonderful things are going to happen in the Cooperatives today?!"
76. George Hogg to Ida, 10 May 1941.
77. A comparative study of politically active American women in China has yet to be undertaken. Kay Wilbur interview with M.K., 16 March 1995, described Ida as "determined, persistent, and persuasive," whereas she characterized Maud Russell as "domineering." This author's reading of Helen Foster Snow, Agnes Smedley and Anna Louise Strong also shows these women's style to be more directly confrontational than Ida's style. Pearl Buck, the only other "mishkid" raised in China, was closest to Ida in personality. Yet the differences between the two women remain remarkable.
78. I.P. to R.A., 22 August 1947, box 125, Indusco Collection.
79. H.F.S. to I.P., 12 October 1947.
80. I.P. to Peter Townsend, 7 April 1947.
81. I.P. to H.F.S., 19 February 1942, box 31, Indusco Collection; I.P. memo to Greenberg, Rose, and Field: "We want to get away from this method of doing business but the issues are too big to risk their being destroyed by the grouchiness of one member of the Board." 11 September 1942, box 126, Indusco Collection.
82. I.P. to Jack Service, Far Eastern Division, State Department, 20 February 1943, box 143, Indusco Collection.
83. I.P. to H.F.S., 9 October 1947, 9 November 1947, box 31, Indusco Collection.
84. H.F.S. to I.P., early November 1947, box 31, Indusco Collection.
85. I.P. to Col. Evans F. Carlson, 5 May 1946.

86. I.P. to H.F.S., 12 November 1947, box 31, Indusco Collection.

Chapter 12

1. I.P. to Dick Pastor, circa 7 May 1946.
2. I.P. to R.A., 13 September 1952, box 10, Indusco Collection.
3. I.P. to R.A., 18 September 1952.
4. I.P. to R.A., 13 September 1952, 8 October 1952, box 10, Indusco Collection.
5. I.P. to R.A., 19 September 1952; R.A. to I.P., 9 July 1952, 27 April 1953, 19 July 1953, 14 September 1953, 14 October 1953, 12 November 1953.
6. R.A. to I.P., 16 December 1953.
7. I.P. to H.F.S., 26 August 1947, box 31, Indusco Collection.
8. "Rewi already had a following among the YWCA secretaries in China, all of whom represented Western social conscience. When Ida Pruitt met Rewi in 1938, she decided to devote the rest of her life to being his girl Friday. Rewi was the only man she or any such Western social worker had ever met who came up to their ideal of what a Western man in China should be." Helen Foster Snow, *My China Years*, p. 301; Anne-Marie Brady, *Friend of China*, pp. 28–29, 114; David Crook interview with M.K., 2 August 1992; Peter Townsend to M.K., 17 August 2003, writes: "She felt she was in love with him [Rewi]. ... He had replaced Jim Bertram."
9. I.P. to H.F.S., 26 August 1947, box 31, Indusco Collection.
10. Brady, *Friend of China*, p. 156.
11. I.P. interview with M.K, 1983; Brady, *Friend of China*, p. 45.
12. Anne-Marie Brady, "West Meets East: Rewi Alley and Changing Attitudes Towards Homosexuality in China," *East Asian History*, 9 (June 1995): 113. Ida's attitude toward homosexuality can be seen only through a few comments in her correspondence with James Bertram and Jack MacIntosh. She seemed to view it as unnatural and assured both men of their own heterosexuality. Ida's discomfort with homosexuality may also explain why she excluded her roommate, China activist and lesbian, Maud Russell, from her social life in their apartment on 93rd Street in New York. Maud Russell interview with M.K., 14 March 1989; Annette Rubinstein interview with M.K., 1 August 1992.
13. S. Bernard Thomas, *Season of High Adventure: Edgar Snow in China* (Berkeley: University of California Press, 1996), p. 215.
14. Israel Epstein to M.K., 17 February 1994.
15. Brady, *Friend of China*, p. 114.
16. R.A. to I.P., 12 December 1968.
17. R.A., "In Memoriam: Ida Pruitt," 19 August 1985, TS.
18. Federal Bureau of Investigation (FBI) files #100-23409 and NY#100-101845.
19. Under the Freedom of Information Act, information is blacked out which

may jeopardize national security or the anonymity of FBI operatives and other subjects under observation.

20. FBI File #100-378105, 11 September 1946.

21. FBI File #100-378105, D.M. Ladd to director of FBI, J. Edgar Hoover, 9 December 1949, Hoover to S.A.C., New York, 14 December 1949.

22. George E. Sokolsky, "These Days," *Washington Times Herald*, 6 December 1949.

23. I.P. to Helen (no last name), 4 May 1951.

24. Among those were Marshall Field, who supported the abolition of the poll tax, Richard J. Walsh, president of John Day Publishing Co. (and Pearl S. Buck's husband) who signed an open letter to end the House Un-American Committee.

25. Robert P. Newman, *Owen Lattimore and the "Loss" of China* (Berkeley: University of California Press, 1992), pp. 207–26; I. P. to Owen and Eleanor Lattimore, 9 May 1950.

26. FBI File #100-378105, 12 April 1950.

27. FBI File #100-378105, 25 November 1951, [report on Ida Pruitt], pp. 1–21.

28. FBI File #100-378105, 11 and 18 February 1955, 16 March 1955, 26 April 1955. She was one of eleven Caucasian Americans so-designated.

29. FBI File #100-378105, New York S.A.C. memo to Hoover, 2 September 1954.

30. FBI File #100-378105, New York S.A.C. to Hoover, 22 November 1957.

31. FBI File #100-378105, New York S.A.C. to Hoover, 16 November 1956.

32. I.P. to R.A., 28 January 1956, Rewi Alley Archive, International Committee for the Promotion of the Chinese Industrial Cooperatives (ICCIC) office, Beijing.

33. FBI File #100-378105, 22 July 1964.

34. FBI case ISC "Passport and Visa matters-Conspiracy" (Bufile 105-19153). July 1958 indicates Ida Pruitt was issued a passport for a two- to three-month trip to Europe as a tourist. San Francisco S.A.C., 10 November 1959, 29 December 1959.

35. FBI File #100-378105, 22 January 1968, 12 June 1970.

36. I.P. to Department for Exchange of Publications and Cultural Materials, Chinese People's Association for Cultural Relations with Foreign Countries, 14 September 1965.

37. I.P. to R.A., 28 January 1956, 18 June 1958, ICCIC Office, Beijing.

38. *Random House College Dictionary* (New York: Alfred A. Knopf, 1984), p. 1006.

39. R.A. to I.P., 12 September 1956, ICCIC Office, Beijing.

40. I.P. to R.A., 15 April 1958, 18 June 1958, ICCIC Office, Beijing; Richard M. Fried, *Nightmare in Red*, p. 187.

41. I.P. to Song Qingling, enclosed in I.P. to R.A., 13 December 1958, ICCIC Office, Beijing.

42. I.P. to Harriet Curtis, 22 March 1960.
43. Chu Tu-nan (Zhu Du'nan), president, Chinese People's Association for Cultural Relations with Foreign Countries, 5 February 1959.
44. Israel Epstein interview with M.K., 9 August 1992.
45. I.P. [untitled ms, 1959 China trip].
46. "The United States, when I left it in May 1959, had been fed on stories of family breakup in China, mass feedings, and sex regulated by government decree. Letters from friends when I reached China in August told of the same stories circulating. Though I knew they were not true, could not be true, I wanted to see the communes first hand." I.P., "Communes" [1959 China trip].
47. Frederick Nossal, *Dateline—Peking* (London: MacDonald, 1962), pp. 48–65; Jasper Becker, *Hungry Ghost: Mao's Secret Famine* (New York: Free Press, 1996), pp. xi–xii, 266–74, discusses the hidden dimensions of the famine that American demographers revealed after examining statistics released in the mid-1980s.
48. Fang Lizhi, "The End of Forgetting History," *Bringing Down the Great Wall: Writings on Science, Culture, and Democracy in China* (New York: Alfred A. Knopf, 1990), p. 273. Some estimates are as high as 80 million famine-related deaths in China. The worst famine in terms of the proportion of the population killed was the Irish potato famine in 1845, which killed 1 million of Ireland's 8.5 million people. India's 1896–1897 famine killed 5 million, and China's famine of 1876–1879 killed between 9 and 13 million. See Becker, *Hungry Ghost*, pp. 273–74.
49. I.P. to R.A., 1 June 1979.
50. I.P. to R.A., 21 November 1959, ICCIC Office, Beijing.
51. Harry Harding, *A Fragile Relationship: The United States and China since 1972* (Washington, DC: Brookings Institute, 1992), pp. 37–41.
52. I.P. to Chinese People's Association for Friendship with Foreign Countries, 4 October 1971.
53. R.A. interview with Chris Gilmartin, 6 July 1982, Beijing.
54. Hu Hung-fan to I.P., 14 April 1972.
55. Ida's young Canadian companion was Robbie Melamed, the son of friends Lanie and Andy Melamud. See Lanie and Andy to I.P., 1 July 1972.
56. I.P. to Chairman, Chinese People's Association for Friendship with Foreign Countries, 12 December 1972.
57. C. Martin Wilbur, professor of history at Columbia University and member of the Indusco Board of Directors, interview with M.K., 23 September 1989, states that I.P. was very reticent to discuss China with him after her 1959 and 1972 trips. From this, Wilbur surmised that she harbored deep concerns about her mother country. She may just as well have been concerned about U.S. government's use of any information she might share.
58. I.P. to Chairman, Chinese People's Association for Friendship with Foreign

Countries, 12 December 1972.

59. R.A. to I.P., 26 August 1966.

60. R.A. to I.P., 6 January 1967, 25 February 1967, 3 May 1967.

61. R.A. to I.P., 25 February 1967.

62. R.A. to I.P., 16 January 1969.

63. R.A. to I.P., 22 January 1971.

64. R.A. to I.P., 11 April 1969.

65. Jonathan D. Spence, *The Gate of Heavenly Peace: The Chinese and Their Revolution, 1895–1980* (New York: Viking Press, 1981), pp. 347–49.

66. R.A. to I.P., 25 April 1968.

67. R.A. to I.P., 23 December 1970.

68. Former PUMC social worker, Zhu Xuance and her husband, a graduate of Yenching University's Sociology Department, Lin Qiwu in an interview with M.K., December 1995, commented that the exhibition's charges are impossible to substantiate. Photographs are not sufficient evidence to prove the ethics of medical treatment. The husband and wife accepted the use of experimental medication on PUMC's poor patients as necessary for the greater good. Mary Brown Bullock, *An American Transplant: The Rockefeller Foundation and Peking Union Medical College* (Berkeley: University of California Press, 1980), pp. 18, 30, 38, 42, 188, 229 substantiates the other accusation against the PUMC—its elitist model of medicine.

69. Lin Biao and other passengers died on 13 September 1971 in an airplane crash while attempting to flee China. Ida wrote to the Chinese People's Association for Friendship with Foreign Countries on 4 October 1971.

70. I.P. to R.A., 13 December 1972.

71. R.A. to I.P., 11 December 1972. Rewi was unwilling or unable to use his inside connections to help his own adopted children's families to leave the country. See Brady, *Friend of China*, p. 122.

72. In M.K. conversations with Ida through the years, Ida never criticized the Communist leadership, but occasionally expressed frustration with the younger generation of government leaders.

73. I.P. to R.A., 1 June 1979.

74. R.A. to I.P., 5 July 1979; R.A., "Ida Pruitt," 25 May 1981.

75. I.P., *A Daughter of Han*; I.P., *Old Madam Yin*.

76. See for example Mahathir Mohamad and Shintaro Ishihara, *The Voice of Asia: Two Leaders Discuss the Coming Century* (Tokyo: Kodansha International, 1995).

77. Tung Chee-hwa's remarks are in Jonathan Mirsky, "What are 'Asian Values'? A Justification for Repression," *International Herald Tribune*, 9 April 1998.

78. Chinese journalist Dai Qing's research into the Yan'an period of Chinese Communist history has recently challenged this positive view of the wartime actions of the Party.

79. [Unsigned mimeographed report to Lewis], 1 December 1952.
80. Allyn Rickett and Adele Rickett, *Prisoners of Liberation: Four Years in a Chinese Communist Prison* (Garden City, NY: Anchor Press, 1973).
81. Among those who have explored the problematic aspects of friendship with China are Paul Hollander, *Political Pilgrims: Travels of Western Intellectuals to the Soviet Union, China, and Cuba 1928–1978* (New York: Oxford University Press, 1981); Felix Greene, "The Dilemmas of Friendship: Some Personal Thoughts about China," *Far East Reporter*, December 1982; David Crook, "Expressions of Concern and Criticism are Compatible with True Friendship," *U.S. China Review*, 15.2 (Spring, 1991): 14–15; Anne-Marie Brady, *Friend of China*.
82. Fang Lizhi, "The End of Forgetting History," p. 274.
83. Ching-chang Hsiao and Meirong Yang, "Seeing is Not Believing: American Media Coverage of the Cultural Revolution," paper presented at Voices of China Conference, University of Minnesota, 1991, p. 24.
84. Sidney Shapiro, *An American in China: Thirty Years in the People's Republic* (Beijing: New World Press, 1979), p. 214.
85. I.P., "Report from China," (n.d., after 1959 trip), TS.
86. Zhang Longxi, "The Myth of the Other: China in the Eyes of the West," *Critical Inquiry* (Autumn 1988): 108–31.
87. I am indebted to Paul Hollander's *Political Pilgrims* for this concept, which I have applied to I.P. somewhat differently than Hollander used the term.

Epilogue

1. Theodore Wahl to M.K., 18 October 2003.
2. Margaret Richardson Johnson phone interview with M.K. after Ida's passing in 1985. The woman so admired her tutor that she brought her young daughter to Ida's memorial service.
3. Professor Susan Ogden to I.P., 8 March 1974; Felix Greene to I.P., 25 June 1958, 19 September 1958; I.P. to Greene, 23 April 1959; Greene to I.P., 5 May 1960; Happy Fernandez to M.K., 5 October 1985, described their study group on Classical China that Ida organized for women in Powelton Village.
4. Professor Allyn Rickett to M.K., 17 November 2004. Chinese artist Chen Qi was a close friend and frequent visitor to Ida's apartment, as well.
5. Stuart Schulte catalogued and analyzed the list of book and magazine subscriptions that Ida sent to Talitha Gerlach.
6. I.P., "The Bride of Teh Shan," *New China*, 5.3 (Fall, 1979): 42–46.
7. Wang Ying, *The Child Bride* (Beijing: Foreign Languages Press, 1989). In the introduction by Su Kaiming, "Wang Ying—Heroine in Troubled Times," p. vi, Ida is identified as helping the author to translate the book into English. Judging from the lengthy correspondence between I.P. and various publishers and friends, as well as the multiple drafts of *The Child Bride* among I.P. papers, Ida was in fact the translator. R.A. to I.P., 25 May 1981,

refers to her work style with Wang Ying in terms similar to her work with Lao She. However, for internal political reasons after 1949, a foreigner could not be credited as translator. Therefore, she was not credited as the translator of *The Child Bride*, as she was for Lao She's *The Yellow Storm*.

8. I.P. especially tried to place Rewi's *A Highway, and an Old Chinese Doctor*, which was finally published in Christchurch, New Zealand, in 1973.
9. I.P., [misc. note], (circa 1941–1945), TS, n.p.
10. Richard Hartshorne-Ida Pruitt correspondence, 1975–1978.
11. I.P. to R.A., 28 May 1978.
12. Tony Crisp, *Dream Dictionary* (New York: Dell, 1990), pp. 200–1; Fang Jing Pei and Zhang Juwen, *The Interpretation of Dreams in Chinese Culture* (Trumbell, CT: Weatherhill, 2000).
13. Fang and Zhang, *The Interpretation of Dreams in Chinese Culture*, p. 148.
14. Crisp, *Dream Dictionary*, p. 67; Fang and Zhang, *The Interpretation of Dreams in Chinese Culture*, p. 53.
15. Tania Manooiloff Cosman, "Acknowledgements," in her *My Heritage with Morning Glories: A White Russian Growing Up in China* (Washington, DC: Creative Communications Services, 1995).
16. Kueiching (Guijing) Ho to M.K., 5 October 1985.
17. Unnamed godson, Mary Agnes Brim Hess, neighbor Happy Fernandez, and Ruth Bacon, 5 October 1985.
18. Gabriel Lasker to M.K., 18 September 1985.
19. Jonathan Mirsky to Adele and Allyn Rickett, 9 August 1985; Jack Pruitt to M.K., 5 October 1985; Galia Bodde to M.K., 5 October 1985; Wilma Fairbank interview with M.K., 16 August 1988.
20. Allyn Rickett to M.K. at I.P. memorial service, Society of Friends Center, Philadelphia, 5 October 1985.
21. Rhona Mirsky to Adele and Allyn Rickett, 9 August 1985.
22. Virginia Pierson, [handwritten notes], p. 1.
23. Ruth Crawford Norrick, "Ida Pruitt: A Remembrance," n.d., speaking for the group of friends who gathered at I.P.'s apartment at 93rd and Columbus Avenue in New York during the 1950s.
24. Lanie, Andy, and Robbie Melamud, Western Union Mailgram, 4 October 1985.
25. Johnson to M.K., 1985.
26. Chen Hansheng, Su Kaiming and family, Ruth Weiss, Hsieh Hokeng, 29 September 1985; Israel Epstein and *China Reconstructs* staff, 4 October 1985.
27. R.A., "In Memoriam: Ida Pruitt," p. 3.
28. She Huichen (Louise She) to M.K., 18 October 1983.
29. *A China Childhood* was translated into Chinese by the Liaoning People's Press in 1998. The Foreign Languages Press, Beijing, included both *A China Childhood* and *A Daughter of Han* in its English-language reprint series, "Light on China."

30. The China Youth College for Political Sciences, under the Chinese Communist Party, began the first Social Work Department during the 1990s. Other universities also have established social work programs. Social work professionals from the United States, as well as Hong Kong, have been invited to train Chinese social work students. Among them are Professor James Jorgensen and Christine Jorgensen, M.S.W. (master of social work) of the Graduate School of Social Work, University of Denver, CO, and Mayling M. Chu, associate professor, Social Work Department, California State University, Stanislaus, CA. Chu works with a group of young social work faculty in Beijing to promote medical social work after the SARS epidemic. With communications scholars, she is incorporating social work information into their training and curriculum. She reports that social work students and faculty are interested in learning about the early social work program at the Peking Union Medical College. Jorgensens to M.K., Spring 1999; Chu to M.K., 14 October 2004.

31. Gary B. Hansen, "A Modern Tragedy: The Failure to Enlist Group Entrepreneurship and Workers' Cooperatives in the Battle against Unemployment and Poverty," unpublished paper (Logan: Utah Center for Productivity and Quality, 1993), p. 19; Gary B. Hansen, "Gung Ho: The Chinese Industrial Cooperatives," paper presented at "Helen Foster Snow: Witness to Revolution—A Symposium," Brigham Young University, Provo, Utah, 27 October 2000.

32. Gary B. Hansen, "Using Group Entrepreneurship to Create New Enterprises Systematically," *Small Enterprise Development: An International Journal* 7.1 (March 1996): 24–25.

33. Marjorie King, "Gung Ho! The Chinese Industrial Cooperatives in China's Socialist Market Economy," in *Weaving a New Tapestry Asia in the Post-Cold War World: Case Studies and General Trends*, ed. William P. Head and Edwin G. Clausen (Westport, CT: Praeger, 1999), pp. 27–52.

34. The founder of the first Gung Ho industrial cooperative in 1939, Lu Guangmian, became the vice-chairman of the revived International Committee for the Promotion of the Chinese Industrial Cooperatives. See *Gung Ho Newsletter* (Beijing: International Committee for the Promotion of Chinese Industrial Cooperatives), 30 (1995): 13–15. Zhu Xuefan, another veteran Gung Ho activist, became honorary chairman with Rewi Alley as chairman. Chen Hansheng and others also supported the revival. See *Gung Ho Newsletter*, 33 (1996): 11. For more information about the cooperatives, see www.iccic.org.cn.

35. The International Cooperative Association standards, which are consistent with the original Gung Ho vision, are recognized worldwide. ICCIC Vice-President Lu Wanru, and Executive Secretary Guo Lina conversation with M.K., June 2002. See also Canada-China Co-operative Promotion and Development Project, Project Progress Report, December 2002, as well as

www.iccic.org.cn and www.gungho.org.cn.

36. Chen Xinlu, headmaster of Shandan Bailie School of Gansu Province and Liu Guozhong, assistant principal and teacher at Shandan Bailie School to M.K. and Yamaguchi Mamoru, 10–11 September 2004. For more information about the Ida Pruitt Memorial Fund, see www.idapruittproject.org.

Works Cited

A wide reading in American women's history and in Sino-American relations, particularly the nineteenth century Protestant missionary movement and early twentieth century reform efforts, provided the background and stimulated the research questions for this work. The author's study of missionary women's published books and articles and unpublished correspondence, available at the Presbyterian Historical Society in Philadelphia, offered a context for the in-depth research about Anna Seward Pruitt and her daughter, Ida Pruitt. These background readings are not mentioned in the chapter notes or works cited excepted where specific reference was made to the material in the work.

The research about Ida Pruitt and her family arose from the author's personal friendship with Ida from 1975 until her death in 1984 in Philadelphia, Pennsylvania, where the Pruitt family papers were made available to the author and where the personal interviews and informal conversations between Ida Pruitt and the author were held. Since the conclusion of this research, the papers have been donated to the Arthur and Elizabeth Schlesinger Library on the History of Women in America at Radcliffe Institute. The library's cataloguing system is not reflected in this list of works cited.

Records from the Seward families include genealogical charts, published materials, and unpublished essays about the New England ancestors of the Sewards. The great majority of the material about Anna Seward Pruitt's life in China came from her unpublished letters to her parents, relatives, and friends. Miscellaneous letters date from 1887. Her weekly letters from 1891 until 1907 were recopied and bound by her father, John Seward. Unbound, carbon copies of her letters to her children and other relatives are available from 1924 until 1948. Anna's published articles for the missionary press were too numerous to itemize and were less useful for this study than was her personal correspondence. However, her three published books were essential and are cited here.

Material on Cicero Washington Pruitt's life depends largely on his own unpublished essays about his life and one letter to his family in Georgia, dated 17 February 1890. His wife and daughter also wrote about his life. The Pruitt family's story is developed in the author's dissertation, "Missionary Mother and Radical Daughter: Anna and Ida Pruitt in China, 1887–1939" (Philadelphia: Temple University, 1984).

Material about Ida Pruitt's life came primarily from her own published and unpublished memoirs, her three books, her published and unpublished professional articles about social work, her published and unpublished short stories about the Chinese and the missionaries, her personal interviews with the author, as well as miscellaneous papers, random notes, and dream records. Other useful records include manuscripts, lists, calendars, diaries, letters, and memorabilia. Ida Pruitt's unpublished writings are often unpaginated and undated; at times they are untitled. The following works cited list and the endnotes identify each untitled document descriptively within [ ] marks.

The author's formal, recorded interviews with Ida Pruitt began on 21 April 1976 and continued through 18 March 1984. Innumerable informal conversations supplemented the formal interviews.

Information about the Social Service Department of the Peking Union Medical College hospital was obtained at the Rockefeller Archive Center in Tarrytown, New York and during the author's year-long residency at the PUMC hospital in 1995–1996, during which time over one thousand social work case files were reviewed. This body of files is described in the author's article, "The Social Service Department Archives: Peking Union Medical College, 1928–1951," *The American Archivist* 59.3 (Summer 1996), 218–27. The files are not cited individually here. The Chinese Industrial Cooperative movement was researched for the author's thesis, "The Rural Reconstruction Movement in Kuomintang China" (Ohio: The Ohio State University, 1974) and for several other articles, which are mentioned here as indicated. The staff of the revived International Committee for the Promotion of the Chinese Industrial Cooperatives in Beijing devoted untold hours over several years discussing the cooperatives with the author. These discussions were helpful to contextualize information obtained from the Indusco Collection and the Institute of Pacific Relations Collection at the Rare Manuscript Archives of Butler Library, Columbia University, the United Service to China Collection at the Princeton University Library, the United China Relief Collection and the Maud Russell Collection at the New York Public Library.

Sources not identified by archive or place of publication are a part of the Ida Pruitt Papers at the Schlesinger Library.

ARCHIVES

Ida Pruitt Collection, Arthur and Elizabeth Schlesinger Library on the History of Women in America, Radcliffe Institute, Cambridge, Massachusetts, USA.

Indusco Collection, Rare Book and Manuscript Library, Columbia University Libraries, New York, USA.

Institute of Pacific Relations, Rare Book and Manuscript Library, Columbia University Libraries, New York, USA.

China Medical Board, Inc. Collection, Rockefeller Archive Center (cited in text as RAC), Tarrytown, New York, USA.

Rewi Alley Collection, International Committee for the Promotion of the Chinese Industrial Cooperatives (cited in text as ICCIC) office, Beijing, China.

Social Service Department Archives, Peking Union Medical College, 1928–1951.United China Relief (cited in text as UCR) Collection, New York Public Library, New York, USA.

United China Relief/United Service to China (cited in text as USC) Collection, Seeley G. Mudd Manuscript Library, Princeton University Library, Princeton, New Jersey, USA.

CORRESPONDENCE

Alley, Rewi (Indusco Collection, box 3, folder 10)
——— to Eleanor Hinder, 15 June 1947.
——— to Max Bickerton, 10 February 1947.
——— to E.C. Carter, n.d.
An, Fan-chih to Ida Pruitt (cited in text as I.P.), 30 June 1949.
Barton, Shirley to Indusco Board of Directors, minutes of meeting, 23 September 1952.
Bertram, James to Marjorie King (cited in text as M.K.), 15 February 1983.
Birdson, Bertha to I.P., 21 April 21 1951.
Bodde, Galia to M.K., 5 October 1985.
Bonneau, L. R. of Carstens, and Linnekin to Indusco Board of Directors, 12 June 1952 (Indusco Collection, box 115).
Carlson to I.P., 5 November 1940 (Indusco Collection, box 131, folder 3).
Cannon, Ida to McLean, 21 October 1920 (RAC, box 143, folder 1034).
Cannon to Embree, 1 February 1921 (RAC, box 143, folder 1034).
Chang, W.C. to I.P., 9 September 1936.
Chen, Hansheng, Su Kaiming and family to Ruth Weiss, Hsieh Hokeng, 29 September 1985.

Chou (Zhou), Enlai to J. Franklin Ray, Director, Far East Division, United Nations Relief and Rehabilitation Association, 15 November 1946 (UCR Collection, box 1, folder 5).

Chu, Tu-nan, President, Chinese People's Association for Cultural Relations with Foreign Countries, to I.P., 5 Februray 1959.

Clark, Bronson P. to I.P., 18 November 1947.

Crook, Michael to M.K., 25 February 2002.

Crook, Michael to M.K., 17–22 September 2003.

Epstein, Israel, and staff of China Reconstructs to Pruitt family, 4 October 1985.

Epstein, Israel to M.K., 17 February 1994.

Esser, Reba to I.P., 18 July 1946.

Fairbank, John King to M.K., 8 December 1982 to 12 May 1988.

Fox, Melvin J. to Lennig Sweet, 3 April 1947 (USC, box 35, folder 1).

Garside, B. A. to Brinckerhoff, Hill, Hallenbeck, McKenna, and Witherspoon, 30 September 1947 (USC, box 10, folder 7).

———— to Governor Edison, 17 October 1946 (USC, box 70, folder 4).

———— to I.P., 27 January 1947 (USC, box 35, folder 1).

———— to Alfred Kohlberg, 22 September 1947 (USC, box 70, folder 4).

———— to Alfred Kohlberg, 5 October 1948 (USC, box 15, folder 9).

Gerlach, Talitha to I.P., 18 May 1952.

Greene, Felix to I.P., n.d. No information

Greene, Roger S. to Henry S. Houghton, "Medical Social Service at PUMC," 27 January 1923.

Hale, Elizabeth to I.P., 21 November 1950.

Hartshorne, Richard to I.P., 1975 to 1978.

Hogg, George to I.P., 10 May 1941.

Hu, Hung-fan to I.P., 14 April 1972.

Illesley, Walter to Indusco Board of Director, minutes of meeting, 23 September 1952.

King, Edith Shatto to Roger S. Greene, 3 May 1919 (RAC, box 143, folder 1034).

Lasker, Gabriel to M.K., 18 September 1985.

Libby, Betsey to Ida Cannon, 12 February 1920 (RAC, box 143, folder 1034).

McLean, Franklin C. to Edwin R. Embree, 6 February 1920 (RAC, box 143, folder 1034).

———— to Henry S. Houghton, 22 February 1920 (RAC, box 143, folder 1034).

Melamud, Lanie, and Andy to I.P., 1 July 1972.

Melamud, Lanie, Andy, and Robbie to Pruitt family, 4 October 1985 (Western Union Mailgram).

Mirsky, Jonathan to Adele and Allyn Rickett, 9 August 1985.

Mirsky, Rhona to Adele and Allyn Rickett, 9 August 1985.

Mao, Tse-tung (Zedong) to Bishop Hall, and Chen Han-seng (Hansheng), 25 September 1939.

Ogden, Susan (Prof.) to I.P., 8 March 1974.

Pierson, Virginia to M.K., n.d.

Pruitt, Anna Seward to her family, 1891–1907, 1908–1947.

Pruitt, Ida to Rewi Alley (Rewi Alley Collection, ICCIC).

——— to Evans Clark, 1 May–4 June 1952.

——— to Helen Foster Snow, (Indusco Collection, box 31).

——— to anonymous, April or May 1951.

——— to Chairman, Chinese People's Association for Friendship with Foreign Countries, 12 December 1972.

——— to Chinese People's Association for Friendship with Foreign Countries, 4 October 1971.

——— to Evans F. Carlson, 5 May 1946.

——— to Colin Morrison, 29 April 1949 (Indusco Collection, box 27).

——— to Colin Morrison, 16 August 1949 (Indusco Collection, box 27).

——— to E.C. Carter, Institute of Pacific Relations (Indusco Collection, box 36).

——— to Department for Exchange of Publications and Cultural Materials, Chinese People's Association for Cultural Relations with Foreign Countries, n.d.

——— to Evans Carlson, 8 August 1941.

——— to Gladys Yang, 20 October 1978.

——— to Harriet Curtis, 22 March 1960.

——— to Helen, 4 May 1951.

——— to Jack Service, Far Eastern Division, State Department, 20 February 1943 (Indusco Collection, box 143, folder 1).

——— to Lillian McLeed, UNRRA, n.d. (Indusco Collection, box 26).

——— to M.K., 14 November 1983.

——— to Max Bickerton, 4 March 1948.

——— to Maxwell Stewart, 3 October 1947.

——— to Natalie Crouter, 19 June 1951.

——— to Owen and Eleanor Lattimore, 9 May 1950.

——— to Peter Townsend, 7 April 1947.

——— to John H. Reisner, 14 November 1940.

——— to Rev. Hall, and Talitha Gerlach, 24 September 1947 (Indusco Collection, box 27).

——— to Mrs. Alex H. Richardson, Alex H., n.d.

——— to Shirley Barton, 28 September 1952.

——— to Sophia Voorhees, 16 January 1951.

——— to C.A. Ellenberger, 5 June 1951.

——— to Sophia Voorhees, 16 January 1951.

——— to Walter Illesley, 27 September 1952.

Pruitt, Jack to M.K., 5 October 1985.

Raab, Theodora A. to I.P., 24 April 1951.

Richardson, Alex H. to I.P., 19 June 1951.

She, Huichen to M.K., 18 October 1983.

Snow, Helen Foster (Peg) to Richard J. Walsh, 24 June 1940.

———— to I.P., n.d. (Indusco Collection, box 31).

———— to M.K., 16 May 1983.

Stewart, Maxwell S. to B.A. Garside, 5 November 1947 (USC Collection, box 35).

———— to Max Bickerton, c. 1948.

Tang, M.C. to I.P., 30 May 1949.

Townsend, Peter

———— to I.P. (Indusco Collection, box 33).

———— to Melvin Fox, 14 November 1946 (Indusco Collection, box 27).

———— to Rewi Alley, 17 June 1947 (Indusco Collection, box 33).

Vincent, George E. to Ida Cannon, 6 December 1921 (RAC, box 143, folder 1034).

Anonymous PUMC staff note to I.P, Beijing, n.d.

Yamaguchi, Mamoru to Marjorie King, 25 February 2002.

INTERVIEWS

Bacon, Ruth with M.K., 5 October 1985, Philadelphia, PA.

Bodde, Derk and Galia with M.K., 5 October 1985, Philadelphia, PA.

Crook, David, and Isabel Crook with M.K., 2 August 1992, New York, NY.

Epstein, Israel with M.K., 9 August 1992, New York, NY.

Fairbank, John King, and Wilma Fairbank with M.K., 16 August 1988, Franklin, NH.

Fernandez, Happy with M.K., 5 October 1985, Philadelphia, PA.

Gerlach, Talitha with Glenn Shive, 17 December 1982, Shanghai.

Gilmartin, Chris with Rewi Alley, 6 July 1982 Beijing.

Gu, Jingyu with M.K., 28 October 1994, Beijing.

Guo, Lina with M.K., June 2002, Beijing.

Hess, Mary Agnes Brim with M.K., 5 October 1985, Philadelphia, PA.

Ho, Guijing (He Kueiching) with M.K., 5 October 1985, Philadelphia, PA.

Hoskins, Louis with M.K., at the conference "American Missionaries and Social Change in China," Linfield College, McMinnville, OR, July 14–17, 1994.

Johnson, Margaret Richardson with M.K., telephone interview, 1985.

Li, Una K. with M.K., telephone interview, 12 November 1983.

Liu, Jinghe with M.K., 2 July 1999, Beijing.

Lu Wanru with M.K., November 1995, Beijing.

Lu Wanru with M.K., June 2002, Beijing.

Powell, Bill and Sylvia with M.K., at the conference "American Missionaries and Social Change in China," Linfield College, McMinnville, OR, July 14–17, 1994.

Pruitt, Ida with Henry Milo, 29 January 1946, New York, NY.

Pruitt, Ida with M.K., interviews and conversations, 1976–1984, Philadelphia, PA: 21 April 1976, 15 June 1982, 1 July 1982, March 1983 (no record of day), 9 April 1983, 14 November 1983, 29 November 1983, 25 February 1984, 18 March 1984, 9 April 1984.

Rickett, Allyn (Prof.) with M.K., 5 October 1985, Philadelphia, PA.

Rubinstein, Annette with M.K., 1 August 1992, New York, NY.

Russell, Maud with M.K., 14 March 1989, New York, NY.

Townsend, Peter with M.K., telephone conversations, 2002–2003.

Vincent, John, and Irene with M.K., at the conference of "American Missionaries and Social Change in China," Linfield College, McMinnville, OR, July 14–17, 1994.

Wahl, Theodore, and Tania Manooiloff Cosman Wahl with M.K., 1980–1985, Philadelphia, PA.Yamaguchi, Mamoru with M.K., 1–11 January 1996, Tucson, AZ; 20–26 February 1999, Tokyo; 23–26 July 2001, Tucson, AZ.Zhu, Xuance and Lin Qiwu with M.K., December 1995, Beijing.

ARTICLES

Alley, Rewi. "Ida Pruitt." TS, 25 May 1981.

———. "In Memoriam: Ida Pruitt." TS, 19 August 1985.

———. "Report from Shandan." International Committee for the Promotion of the ICCIC, Shanghai, TS, 6 December 1949.

———. "Shantan Bailie School General Report, 1947," ICCIC.

Asia Institute. [brochure for classes, 23 February–12 June 1948].

Bertram, James M. "Capes of China Slide Away: A Memoir of Peace and War in New Zealand and the Pacific." Ms., n.d.

Brady, Anne Marie. "West Meets East: Rewi Alley and Changing Attitudes Towards Homosexuality in China." *East Asian History*, 9 (June 1995), 97–120.

Buck, Pearl S. "Free China Gets to Work; New Industrial Cooperatives Can Supply an Economic Base." *Asia*, 39.4 (April 1939).

Carson, A.L. "Christian Institutions and the Rural Reconstruction Movement." *China Christian Year Book*.

Chang, Kuan Lien. "Lanchow CIC Work." *Gung Ho News*, no. 1.4.

Chevigny, Bell Gale. "Daughters Writing: Toward a Theory of Women's Biography." *Feminist Studies*, 9 (Spring 1983).

Chi, Tang [pseud.]. "Beijing di haohuai." *Beijing yigu* (A glance at Beijing). Shanghai: Yuzhou Feng She, 1938.

"China Moves to Restore its Co-operatives: Miss Ida Pruitt Reports on a 10,000 Mile Trip Through the Interior." *New York Herald Tribune*, 22 December 1946.

Cockerill, E. "Can a Hospital Afford Not to Have a Department of Social Service?" *Transactions of the American Hospital Association*, 37 (1937).

Committee for a Democratic Far Eastern Policy (CDFEP). Paper, April 1950, no publication information given.

Crook, David. "Expressions of Concern and Criticism are Compatible with True Friendship." *U.S. China Review*, 15.2 (Spring, 1991): 14–15.

Demetrakopoulos, Stephanie A. "The Metaphysics of Matrilinearism in Women's Autobiography: Studies of Mead's *Blackberry Winter*, Hellman's *Pentimento*, Angelou's *I Know Why a Caged Bird Sings*, and Kingston's *The Woman Warrior*." In *Women's Autobiography: Essays in Criticism*, edited by Estelle C. Jelinek. Bloomington, IN: Indiana University Press, 1980.

democracy: a far eastern half-monthly of fact and opinion, Beijing (Peiping), 1937.

Eastman, Lloyd E. "Nationalist China during the Sino-Japanese War, 1937–1945." In *The Nationalist Era in China: 1927–1949*, edited by Lloyd E. Eastman, Jerome Ch'en, Suzanne Pepper, and Lyman P. Van Slyke. Cambridge: Cambridge University Press, 1991.

Far East Spotlight, 4.1 (June, 1948).

Federal Bureau of Investigation (FBI). Case report, "Passport and Visa matters-Conspiracy." (file no.: #100-378105, #100-23409 and NY#100-101845)

Gallant, Jack. "Navy and Marine Corps World War II Commemorative Committee." Retrieved from www.chinfo.navy.mil/navpalib/wwii/facts/mcraider.txt

Gao, Xinxian. "Echoes of Immortality at Penglai." *China Daily*, 27 November 1982.

Gott, Gil. "Imperial Humanitarianism: History of an Arrested Dialectic." In *Moral Imperialism: A Critical Anthology*, edited by Berta Esperanza Hernandez-Truyol and Christy Gleason. New York: New York University Press, 2002.

Greene, Felix. "The Dilemmas of Friendship: Some Personal Thoughts about China." *Far East Reporter*, December 1982.

Guldin, Greg, and Laurel Kendall. "Two Short Reviews of *Old Madam Yin: A Memoir of Peking Life* by Ida Pruitt." *Bulletin of Concerned Asian Scholars*, 12.4 (1981).

Enright, Ray, Randolph Scott, and Robert Mitchum. "Gung Ho!" *Alpha Video*, 1943. (A video tape)

Gung Ho News, 1.1 (June 1946).

Gung Ho News, 2.4 (April 1947).

Gung Ho Newsletter, 33 (1999).

Gung Ho Newsletter, 29 (1995).

Gung Ho Newsletter, 30 (1996).

Hansen, Gary B. "'Gung Ho': The Chinese Industrial Cooperatives." In *Helen Foster Snow: Witness to Revolution—A Symposium*. Provo, UT: Brigham Young University, 2000.

Hansen, Gary B. "Using Group Entrepreneurship to Create New Enterprises Systematically." *Small Enterprise Development: An International Journal*, 7.1 (March 1996).

Hobart, Alice Tisdale. "China Across the Tracks: Review of *A Daughter of Han*, by Ida Pruitt." *Saturday Review of Literature*, 9 February 1946.

Hsiao, Ching-chang, and Meirong Yang. "Seeing Is Not Believing: American Media Coverage of the Cultural Revolution." Paper presented at Voices of China Conference, University of Minnesota, 1991.Hsu, Francis L.K. "A Closer View of China's Problems." *Far Eastern Quarterly*, November 1946.

Fang, Lizhi. "The End of Forgetting History." In his *Bringing Down the Great Wall: Writings on Science, Culture, and Democracy in China.* New York: Knopf, 1990.

Keating, Pauline. "Cooperative Visions vs. Wartime Realities: Indusco and the Chinese Communists, 1938–1944." *Journal of East Asian Studies*, 1998.

King, Marjorie. "American Women's Open Door to Chinese Women: Which Way Does It Open?" *Women's Studies International Forum*, 13.4 (1990).

———. "Exporting Femininity, Not Feminism: Nineteenth Century U.S. Missionary Women's Efforts to Emancipate Chinese Women." In *Women's Work for Women: Missionaries and Social Change in Asia*, edited by Leslie A. Flemming. Boulder, CO: Westview Press, 1989.

———. "A Georgia Evangelist in the Celestial Empire." In *Georgia's East Asian Connection: Into the Twenty-First Century*, edited by Jonathan Goldstein. Carrollton, TX: West Georgia College, 1989.

———. "The Social Service Department Archives: Peking Union Medical College, 1928–1951." *American Archivist*, 59.3 (Summer 1996).

"Kuomintang Shift Seen by Red Chief: Chou Predicts Rightists' Fall and Creation of Democratic Regime Within a Year." *New York Times*, 19 December 1946.

Lao, Sheh (Lao She). "Living in Peking." *China Reconstructs*, September–October 1952.

Liu, Shaobai. "Yantai: Mirages, Myths and Flourishing Reality." *China Reconstructs*, January 1983.

Lu, Wanru. "The Gung Ho Movement and the International Committee for the Promotion of Chinese Industrial Cooperatives." In *Training for Trainers Manual.* Beijing: International Committee for the Promotion of the Chinese Industrial Cooperatives, 2002.

Mason, Sarah R. "Missionary Conscience and the Comprehension of Imperialism: A Study of American Missionaries to China, 1900–1949." Doctoral dissertation, University of Illinois, 1978.

Mirsky, Jonathan. "What are 'Asian Values'? A Justification for Repression." *International Herald Tribune*, 9 April 1998.

"Missions in China Seen Nearing End: Returned Worker Says Native Church Is Now on Its Own, a Goal Long Sought Here." *New York Times*, 16 April 1951.

Ninkovich, Frank. "The Rockefeller Foundation, China, and Cultural Change." *Journal of American History*, 70.4 (1983–84).

Norrick, Ruth Crawford. "Ida Pruitt: A Remembrance." TS, n.d.

Our Mission Field. New York: Women's Foreign Mission Societies, Presbyterian Church in the USA, 1880.

Our Missionary Helper. c. 1893.

Pepper, Suzanne. "The KMT-CCP Conflict, 1945–1949," in *The Nationalist Era in China, 1927–1949*, edited by Lloyd E. Eastman, Jerome Ch'en, Suzanne Pepper, and Lyman P. Van Slyke. Cambridge: Cambridge University Press, 1991.

Pitkin, Myra. "The Grandmother's Window." TS, [Tallmadge, OH, USA].

"Project Progress Report." In *Canada-China Co-operative Promotion and Development Project.* December, 2002. TS, Canadian Cooperative Association and ICCIC.

Pruitt, Anna Seward. "The Grandmother's Window: Added notes." TS, n.d.

———. "Sketch of the Life of Dr. Cicero Washington Pruitt." TS, n.p., 1946.

Pruitt, Cicero Washington. "Life of Cicero Washington Pruitt, Composed by Himself." TS, n.d., part I & II.

Pruitt, Dean G., addendum to Anna Seward Pruitt, 19 August 1968.

Pruitt, Dean G., letter to Anna Seward Pruitt, 6 July 1970.

Pruitt, Ida. "Another City." TS.

———. "Twelve to Fourteen." TS.

———. [Autobiography]. TS, c. 1929.

———. "Back to Shanghai." TS.

———. "The Bride of Teh Shan." *New China*, 5.3 (Fall 1979).

———. [Untitled]. Chapter 6. TS.

———. [Untitled]. Chapter 18. TS.

———. "Another City." Chapter 20.

———. "China and the Industrial Revolution." TS, January, 1944.

———. "China Inland Mission School." TS.

———. "China's Industrial Wall; Small and Bombproof Cooperative Industries." *Survey Graphic: Magazine of Social Interpretation*, 29.3 (March 1940).

———. "Chinese Industrial Cooperatives." *China Today*, October 1939.

———. "Chinese Women Unbind their Feet." TS, c. 1940.

———. [China Inland Mission School]. TS.

———. [Lecture on Hospital Social Service]. (Chefoo, China), TS.

———. [Politics at the PUMC]. TS.

———. [Random notes on the China Industrial Cooperatives]. TS.

———. *Stories of the People.* TS.

———. "A Study of Sixty-Nine Adopted Children." In *Hospital Social Service*, September 1931.

———. "Thoughts on Religion." TS, c. 1966.

———. [Untitled], TS, chapter 13, Book II.

———. [Untitled]. TS. 1949.

———. [Untitled manuscript about 1959 China trip]. TS.

Pruitt, John D. "The Life of Anna Seward Pruitt." TS. St. Davids, PA, 1951.

Ramsdell, Daniel B. "Asia Askew; U.S. Bestsellers on Asia, 1931–1980." *Bulletin of Concerned Asian Scholars*, 15.4 (1983).

Reynolds, Douglas Robertson. "The Chinese Industrial Cooperative Movement and the Political Polarization of Wartime China, 1938–1945." Doctoral dissertation, University of Columbia, 1975.

Roosevelt, Eleanor. "My Day." 24 January 1940.

Rudnick, Lois. "The Male-Identified Woman and Other Anxieties: The Life of Mabel Dodge Luhan." In *The Challenge of Feminist Biography: Writing the Lives of Modern American Women*, edited by Sara Alpern, Joyce Antler, Elisabeth Israels Perry, and Ingrid Winther Scobie. Urbana, IL: Illinois University Press, 1992.

Schintz, Mary Ann. "An Investigation of the Modernizing Role of the Maryknoll Sisters in China." Doctoral dissertation, University of Wisconsin, 1978.

Schulte, Stuart. "List of Books and Magazines according to Category (Subject) received by Talitha Gerlach from Ida Pruitt." TS, August, 1990.

Seward, Anna. "California in the Eighties: As Pictured in the Letters of Anna Seward." *California Historical Society Quarterly*, 16.4 (1937).

Seward, Anna. "California in the Eighties: As Pictured in the Letters of Anna Seward." *California Historical Society Quarterly*, 17.1 (1938).

Seward, Urania Durand Ashley (Uda). "The Flitting of the Fenns." TS.

"The Social Significance of CIC (Chinese Industrial Cooperatives) in Lanchow." *Indusco News*, 41 (1 April 1941).

Sokolsky, George E. "These Days." *Washington Times Herald*, 6 December 1949.

Tayler, J. B. "Progress of the Cooperative Movement." *China Christian Year Book*, 1936–1937.

Thompson, Dorothy. "An American Platform." *New York Herald Tribune*, 25 June 1940.

Trescott, Paul B. "John Bernard Tayler and the Development of Cooperatives in China, 1917–1945." *Annals of Public and Cooperative Economics*, 62 (1993): 2.

Tucker, Nancy Bernkopf. "An Unlikely Peace: American Missionaries and the Chinese Communists, 1948–1950." *Pacific Historical Review*, 45.1 (1976).

Wales, Nym (Helen Foster Snow). "An Industrial Defense Line for China." n.p., n.d.

Walker, Alice. "Saving the Life That Is Your Own: The Importance of Models in the Artist's Life." In *In Search of Our Mothers' Gardens*. San Diego, CA: Harcourt Brace Jovanovich, 1983.

Welter, Barbara. "She Hath Done What She Could: Protestant Women's Missionary Careers in Nineteenth Century America." *American Quarterly*, 30 (1978).

Weathersby, Kathryn. "Fifty Year Retrospective Look at the Korean War." Keynote address, annual conference of the American Historical Association, Chicago, January 2000.

Winston, Elizabeth. "The Autobiographer and Her Readers: From Apology to Affirmation." In *Women's Autobiography: Essays in Criticism*, edited by Estelle C. Jelinek. Bloomington, IN: Indiana University Press, 1980.

Wu, Xiaomei. "A Classic Realistic Novel: About Lao She's *Four Generations Under One Roof*." In *Yellow Storm*. Nanjing, China: Yilin Press, 1992.

Zhang, Longxi. "The Myth of the Other: China in the Eyes of the West." *Critical Inquiry*, 15 (Autumn 1988).

Minutes and Unpublished Reports

Dong, Biwu (Tung Pi-wu). "Statement." November, 1946. USC Collection, box 1, folder 5.

Indusco Board of Directors. "Notes on a Special Meeting." (Confidential) 28 February 1944.

Indusco Board of Directors. Memo. 17 June 1947.

Indusco Board of Directors. Resolution. 17 June 1947.

Indusco Board of Directors. Minutes. 14 October 1948.

Indusco Board of Directors. Minutes. 16 November 1948.

International Committee for the Promotion of the Chinese Industrial Cooperatives. Minutes, annual meeting, 11 September 1946.

Fei, Hsiao-tung. "A Memorandum on Industrial Cooperative Movement in China." Attachment to the minutes of ICCIC meeting. Hong Kong, 19 September 1946.

Garside, B. A. "A Report to the Board of Directors." 28 November 1949. USC Collection, box 6, folder 21.

Kao, Chun Che. "Annual Report of the Social Service Work at the First Health Station." Peiping (Beijing), 1 July 1934–30 June 1935.

"Notes on Committee to Plan the Conference." 12 October 1944. Indusco Collection, box 142.

"On the Future of the Industrial Cooperative Movement." 20 July 1947.

Pruitt, Ida. "Report of the Employees' Social Service Work." TS, 29 June 1935.

———. "Social Service Department of the PUMC." TS.

"Report of the Indusco Committee of Four on Past and Future Participation in United China Relief." (Confidential). 8 July 1943. Indusco Collection, box 177.

Tsou, George. "A Brief Talk on the Family Welfare Agency." TS, 20 April 1935.

United Service to China. [Proposal]. 22 November 1948.

United Service to China. Minutes of the executive committee, 8 November 1949.

United Service to China. Minutes of the adjourned annual meeting of the Board of Directors, 25 January 1950. USC Collection, box 2.

Wittfogel, Karl A. "Memorandum to the Rockefeller Foundation." 28 March 1939.

Books

Airey, Willis. *A Learner in China: A Life of Rewi Alley.* Christchurch, New Zealand: Caxton Press, 1970.

Alley, Rewi. *At 90: Memoirs of My China Years.* Beijing: New World Press, 1986.

Arlington, L.C., and William Lewisohn. *In Search of Old Peking.* 2nd ed. Hong Kong: Oxford University Press, 1987.

Beaver, R. Pierce. *American Protestant Women in World Mission: A History of the First Feminist Movement in North America.* Grand Rapids, MI: Wm. B. Eerdmans, 1980.

Becker, Jasper. *Hungry Ghosts: Mao's Secret Famine.* New York: Free Press, 1996.

Bertram, James M. *Beneath the Shadow: A New Zealander in the Far East, 1939–1946.* New York: John Day, 1947.

———. *First Act in China: The Story of the Sian Mutiny.* New York: Viking Press, 1938.

———. *Report of Crisis in China.* London: Macmillan, 1937.

———. *Unconquered: Journal of a Year's Adventures among the Fighting Peasants of North China.* London: Macmillan, 1939.

Brady, Anne-Marie. *Friend of China: The Myth of Rewi Alley.* London: Routledge, 2003.

Brumberg, Joan Jacobs. *Mission for Life: The Story of the Family of Adoniram Judson, The Dramatic Events of the First American Foreign Mission, and the Course of Evangelical Religion in the Nineteenth Century.* New York: Free Press, 1980.

Bullock, Mary Brown. *An American Transplant: The Rockefeller Foundation and the Peking Union Medical College.* Berkeley, CA: University of California Press, 1980.

Cannon, Ida. *Social Work in Hospitals: A Contribution toward Progressive Medicine.* New York: n.p., 1923.

Carlson, Evans F. *Twin Stars of China: A Behind-the-Scenes Story of China's Valiant Struggle for Existence by a U.S. Marine Who Lived and Moved with the People.* New York: Dodd & Mead, 1940.

Chambers, Clarke. *Seedtime of Reforms: American Social Service and Social Action, 1918–1933.* Minneapolis, MN: University of Minnesota Press, 1963.

Chang, Iris. *The Rape of Nanking: The Forgotten Holocaust of World War II.* New York: Basic Books, 1997.

Chapple, Geoff. *Rewi Alley of China*. Auckland, New Zealand: Hodder and Stoughton, 1980.

Cohen, Paul A. *History in Three Keys: The Boxers as Event, Experience, and Myth*. New York: Columbia University Press, 1997.

Cohen, Warren I. *America's Response to China: A History of Sino-American Relations*. 3rd ed. New York: Columbia University Press, 1990.

———. *The Chinese Connection: Roger S. Greene, Thomas W. Lamont, George E. Sokolsky and American-East Asian Relations*. New York: Columbia University Press, 1978.

Cosman, Tania Manooiloff. *My Heritage with Morning Glories: A White Russian Growing Up in China*. Washington, DC: Creative Communication Services, 1995.

Crisp, Tony. *Dream Dictionary*. New York: Dell, 1990.

Cumings, Bruce. *The Origins of the Korean War II: The Roaring of the Cataract: 1947–1950*. Princeton, NJ: Princeton University Press, 1990.

Deane, Hugh. *Good Deeds and Gunboats: Two Centuries of American-Chinese Encounters*. San Francisco: China Books & Periodicals, 1990.

DeConde, Alexander. *A History of American Foreign Policy*. 2nd ed. New York: Scribner's, 1971.

Edel, Leon. *Writing Lives: Principia Biographica*. New York: W.W. Norton & Company, 1984.

Esherick, Joseph W. *The Origins of the Boxer Uprising*. Berkeley, CA: University of California Press, 1987.

Fairbank, John King. *China: A New History*. Cambridge, MA: Harvard University Press, 1992.

———. *Chinabound: A Fifty-Year Memoir*. New York: Harper & Row, 1982.

Fang, Jing Pei and Zhang Juwen. *The Interpretation of Dreams in Chinese Culture*. Trumbell, CT: Weatherhill, 2000.

Ferguson, Mary E. *China Medical Board and Peking Union Medical College: A Chronicle of Fruitful Collaboration, 1914–1951*. New York: China Medical Board of New York, Inc., 1970.

Fogel, Joshua A., ed. *The Nanjing Massacre in History and Historiography*. Berkeley, CA: University of California Press, 2000.

Fried, Richard M. *Nightmare in Red: The McCarthy Era in Perspective*. New York: Oxford University Press, 1990.

Hunter, Jane. *The Gospel of Gentility: American Women Missionaries in Turn of the Century China*. New Haven, CT: Yale University Press, 1984.

Hansen, Gary B. "A Modern Tragedy: The Failure to Enlist Group Entrepreneurship and Workers' Cooperatives in the Battle Against Unemployment and Poverty." Logan, UT: Utah Center for Productivity and Quality, 1993.

Harding, Harry. *A Fragile Relationship: The United States and China since 1972*. Washington, DC: Brookings Institution, 1992.

Hoffman, Joyce. *Theodore H. White and Journalism as Illusion.* Columbia, MO: University of Missouri Press, 1995.

Hogg, George. *I See a New China.* Boston: Little, Brown, 1944.

Hollander, Paul. *Political Pilgrims: Travels of Western Intellectuals to the Soviet Union, China and Cuba, 1928–1978.* New York: Oxford University Press, 1981.

Horn, Joshua S. *Away with All Pests: An English Surgeon in People's China, 1954–1969.* New York: Monthly Review Press, 1969.

Hsu, Immanuel C.Y. *The Rise of Modern China.* New York: Oxford University Press, 1990.

Hunt, Michael H. *The Making of a Special Relationship: The United States and China to 1914.* New York: Columbia University Press, 1993.

Hunter, Jane. *The Gospel of Gentility: American Women Missionaries in Turn of the Century China.* New Haven, CT: Yale University Press, 1984.

Hyatt, Irwin. *Our Ordered Lives Confess: Three Nineteenth Century American Missionaries in East Shantung.* Cambridge, MA: Harvard University Press, 1976.

Iriye, Akira. *Across the Pacific: An Inner History of American-East Asian Relations.* Rev. ed. Chicago: Imprint Publications, 1992.

Isaacs, Harold R. *Scratches on Our Minds: American Views of China and India.* Armonke, NY: M.E. Sharpe, Inc., 1980. First published in 1958.

Jespersen, T. Christopher. *American Images of China, 1931–1949.* Palo Alto, CA: Stanford University Press, 1996.

Kipling, Rudyard. *Kim.* London: Penguin, 1987.

Lao She. *Yellow Storm.* Translated by Ida Pruitt. In *Lao She II: Modern Chinese Literature Library.* Nanjing, China: Yilin Press, 1992. First published in New York in 1952.

Lao She Yingwen shuxin ji (Collection of letters written in English by Lao She), trans. and annotated by Shu Yue. Hong Kong: Qin + Yuan Publishing House, 1993.

Lapwood, Ralph and Nancy. *Through the Chinese Revolution.* London: Spalding & Levy, 1954.

Latourette, Kenneth Scott. *A History of Christian Missions in China.* New York: Macmillan Co., 1929.

Link, E. Perry Jr. *Mandarin Ducks and Butterflies: Popular Fiction in Early Twentieth-Century Chinese Cities.* Berkeley, CA: University of California Press, 1981.

Lutz, Jessie. *China and the Christian Colleges, 1850–1950.* Ithaca, NY: Cornell University Press.

MacKenzie, John M. *Propaganda and Empire: The Manipulation of British Public Opinion, 1880–1960.* Manchester: Manchester University Press, 1984.

MacKinnon, Stephen R., and Oris Friesen. *China Reporting: An Oral History of American Journalism in the 1930s and 1940s.* Berkeley, CA: University of California Press, 1987.

Madsen, Richard. *China and the American Dream: A Moral Inquiry.* Berkeley, CA: University of California Press, 1995.

Marty, Martin. *Righteous Empire: The Protestant Experience in America.* New York: Dial Press, 1970.

Mohamad, Mahathir, and Shintaro Ishihara. *The Voice of Asia: Two Leaders Discuss the Coming Century.* Tokyo: Kodansha International, 1995.

Morris, T.M. *A Winter in North China.* London: Religious Tract Society, 1892.

Mosher, Steven W. *China Misperceived: American Illusions and Chinese Reality.* New York: Basic Books, 1990.

A Nation Rebuilds: The Story of the Chinese Industrial Cooperatives in Pictures. Hong Kong: Chinese Industrial Cooperatives, Hong Kong Promotion Committee, 1940.

Neils, Patricia. *China Images in the Life and Times of Henry Luce.* Savage, MD: Rowman & Littlefield, 1990.

Newman, Robert P. *Owen Lattimore and the "Loss" of China.* Berkeley, CA: University of California Press, 1992.

Platt, Mary Schauffler. *The Home with the Open Door: An Agency in Missionary Service.* New York: Student Volunteer Movement, 1920.

Pruitt, Anna Seward. *The Day of Small Things.* Richmond, CA: Foreign Mission Board of Southern Baptist Convention, 1929.

Pruitt, Ida. *A China Childhood.* San Francisco: Chinese Materials Center, Inc., 1978.

———. *A Daughter of Han: The Autobiography of a Chinese Working Woman from the Story Told Her by Ning Lao Tai-t'ai.* Palo Alto, CA: Stanford University Press, 1967. First published by Yale University Press in 1945.

———. *Old Madam Yin: A Memoir of Peking Life.* Palo Alto, CA: Stanford University Press, 1979.

Reed, James. *The Missionary Mind and American East Asian Policy, 1911–1915.* Cambridge, MA: Harvard University Press, 1983.

Rickett, Allyn and Adele. *Prisoners of Liberation: Four Years in a Chinese Communist Prison.* Garden City, NY: Anchor, 1973. First published by Cameron Associates in 1957.

Roys. *The Missionary Wife.* n.p.: Committee of Missionary Preparation, 1923.

Said, Edward W. *Culture and Imperialism.* New York: Knopf, 1993.

———. *Orientalism.* New York: Vintage, 1979.

Saxton, Alexander. *The Indispensable Enemy: Labor and the Anti-Chinese Movement in California.* Berkeley, CA: University of California Press, 1971.

Shapiro, Sidney. *An American in China: Thirty Years in the People's Republic.* Beijing: New World Press, 1979.

Snow, Edgar. *Red Star Over China.* New York: Random House, 1938.

Snow, Helen Foster. *My China Years.* New York: Wm. Morrow, 1984.

Spence, Jonathan D. *The Search for Modern China.* New York: W.W. Norton, 1990.

Spencer, Barbara. *Desert Hospital in China.* London: Jarrolds, 1954.

Strand, David. *Rickshaw Beijing: City People and Politics in the 1920s.* Berkeley, CA: University of California Press, 1989.

Stueck, William W. *Rethinking the Korean War: A New Diplomatic and Strategic History.* Princeton, NJ: Princeton University Press, 2002.

Swanberg, W.A. *Luce and His Empire.* New York: Dell, 1972.

Takaki, Ronald. *Strangers from a Different Shore: A History of Asian Americans.* New York: Penguin, 1989.

Thomas, S. Bernard. *Season of High Adventure: Edgar Snow in China.* Berkeley, CA: University of California Press, 1996.

Thomson, James C. Jr. *While China Faced West: American Reformers in Nationalist China, 1928–1937.* Cambridge, MA: Harvard University Press, 1969.

Trattner, Walter I. *From Poor Law to Welfare State: A History of Social Welfare in America.* New York: Free Press, 1974.

Tsou, Tang. *America's Failure in China, 1941–1950.* Chicago: University of Chicago Press, 1963.

Varg, Paul A. *Missionaries, Chinese and Diplomats: The American Protestant Missionary Movement in China, 1890–1952.* Princeton, NJ: Princeton University Press, 1958.

Vohra, Randir. *Lao She and the Chinese Revolution.* Cambridge, MA: Harvard University Press, 1974.

Wang, David Der-wei. *Fictional Realism in Twentieth-Century China: Mao Dun, Lao She, Shen Congwen.* New York: Columbia University Press, 1992.

Wang, Ying. *The Child Bride.* English text edited by Monica Faulkner. With introduction, "Wang Ying—Heroine in Troubled Times," by Su Kaiming. Beijing: Foreign Languages Press, 1989.

White, Theodore H., and Annalee Jacoby. *Thunder out of China.* New York: Wm. Sloane, 1946.

Wiebe, Robert H. *The Search for Order, 1877–1920.* New York: Hill & Wong, 1967.

Wu, Yong. *The Flight of an Empress.* Transcribed by Liu K'un. Translated and Edited by Ida Pruitt. With an introduction by Kenneth Scott Latourette. New Haven, CT: Yale University Press, 1936.

Yu Wang Fu Association. *Directory of PUMC, Beijing, China, 1917–1950.* n.p., 1981.

Index